D1125167

INSIGHT GUIDES

THE PACIFIC NORTHWEST

Discovery CHANNEL

APA PUBLICATIONS
Part of the Langenscheidt Publishing Group

✷ INSIGHT GUIDE
THE PACIFIC NORTHWEST

Editorial
Project Editor
Martha Ellen Zenfell
Updater
Pat Kramer
Editorial Director
Brian Bell

Distribution

United States
Langenscheidt Publishers, Inc.
46–35 54th Road, Maspeth, NY 11378
Fax: (718) 784 0640

Canada
Thomas Allen & Son Ltd
390 Steelcase Road East
Markham, Ontario L3R 1G2
Fax: (1) 905 475 6747

UK & Ireland
GeoCenter International Ltd
The Viables Centre, Harrow Way
Basingstoke, Hants RG22 4BJ
Fax: (44) 1256 817988

Australia
Universal Press
1 Waterloo Road
Macquarie Park, NSW 2113
Fax: (61) 2 9888 9074

New Zealand
Hema Maps New Zealand Ltd (HNZ)
Unit D, 24 Ra ORA Drive
East Tamaki, Auckland
Fax: (64) 9 273 6479

Worldwide
Apa Publications GmbH & Co.
Verlag KG (Singapore branch)
38 Joo Koon Road, Singapore 628990
Tel: (65) 6865 1600. Fax: (65) 6861 6438

Printing

Insight Print Services (Pte) Ltd
38 Joo Koon Road, Singapore 628990
Tel: (65) 6865 1600. Fax: (65) 6861 6438

©2002 **Apa Publications GmbH & Co.**
Verlag KG (Singapore branch)
All Rights Reserved
First Edition 1987
Fourth Edition 2002

ABOUT THIS BOOK

This guidebook combines the interests and enthusiasms of two of the world's best-known information providers: Insight Guides, whose titles have set the standard for visual travel guides since 1970, and Discovery Channel, the world's premier source of nonfiction television programming.

The editors of Insight Guides provide both practical advice and general understanding about a destination's history, culture, and people. Discovery Channel and its website, www.discovery.com, help millions of viewers explore their world from the comfort of their own homes and encourage them to explore it firsthand.

Insight Guide: Pacific Northwest is carefully structured to convey an understanding of the region and its culture as well as to guide readers through its vast variety of sights and activities:

◆ The **Features** section, indicated by a yellow bar at the top of each page, covers the natural and cultural history of the region in a series of essays.

◆ The main **Places** section, indicated by a blue bar, is a complete guide to all the sights and cities worth visiting. Places of special interest are coordinated by number with the maps.

◆ The **Travel Tips** listings section, with an orange bar, is packed with information on travel, hotels, shops, restaurants and more. The section begins with general tips, followed by a state-by-state breakdown, and an index on the back-cover flap helps you find what you need quickly.

Map Legend

—– ·–	International Boundary
——	State Boundary
– – –	County Boundary
–·–	National Park/Reserve
– – –	Ferry Route
✈ ✈	Airport: International/ Regional
🚌	Bus Station
ⓘ	Tourist Information
✉	Post Office
✝ † ✝	Church/Ruins
†	Monastery
☪	Mosque
✡	Synagogue
🏰	Castle/Ruins
🏠	Mansion/Stately home
∴	Archeological Site
∩	Cave
𝟙	Statue/Monument
★	Place of Interest

The main places of interest in the Places section are coordinated by number with a full-color map (e.g. ❶), and a symbol at the top of every right-hand page tells you where to find the map.

The contributors

This book was project edited by **Martha Ellen Zenfell**, who has managed many books for Insight Guides, including titles on California, US National Parks, and *USA: On the Road*, a large coast-to-coast guide to America. A Southerner by birth and a Londoner by choice, Zenfell had been responsible for getting the original *Insight Guide: Pacific Northwest* updated each year, before embarking on this ambitious new edition with practically all new text and all new pictures.

In this she was aided by the extremely capable **Pat Kramer**, a Northwest native who writes and takes pictures. This last skill was particularly useful when covering such a large area as Washington and Oregon, as Kramer went to places and shot images of topics that were beyond the brief of most of our regular photographers – Washington's Walla Walla Sweet Onions, for example, and a Danish farmer's obsession with rocks in Petersen, Oregon.

This book is based in spirit – if only a little in practice – on the first edition of the guide. That was written in the 1980s when Microsoft had yet to revolutionize the corporate world, and a "chip" was little more than something off the old block. Few territories have changed as much in the past few years as the Pacific Northwest, which this edition aims to reflect.

Hats off to the original team, however, some of whom still remain in the Northwest. **Janie Freeburg** and **Diana Ackland** were the project editors who assembled **J. Kingston Pierce**, **Helen Abbott**, **Richard M. Pintarich**, **Elizabeth DeFato**, **Lee Foster**, **Charles Ackley**, **David Gordon** plus others too numerous to name. That book was updated by **Giselle Smith**, formerly of *Seattle Magazine*, with contributions from **John Wilcock** and **Susan Dumett**.

Also too numerous to name are the many photographers who contributed both to this volume and to the original. Contributing to both was **Ed Cooper**, who has documented the region for decades. For this edition, special thanks must go to **Randy Wells** and especially to **Jerry Dennis**, who flew in at our request from London to cast his foreigner's eye over the territory. **David Whelan** and **Sylvia Suddes** helped with text editing. Proofreading and indexing were undertaken by **Penny Phenix**.

The PACIFIC NORTHWEST

INSIGHT GUIDE

CONTENTS

Seattle's Space Needle: a symbol of the 21st century built in 1962

Travel Tips

Places

THE SPIRIT OF THE NORTHWEST

This is a region of water and ancient traditions. The landscape is dramatic – and so, often, are the people

Water – the spirit of life – is the major factor affecting the Pacific Northwest. Water in the form of rain (either too much or too little), snow, lakes, rivers, sounds, inlets and, of course, the ocean. This varied region is surrounded by water, or the evidence of water's action on the landscape. The effect is extraordinary. Looking at the states of Washington and Oregon from an imaginary vantage point high above the Cascade Mountains, one cannot help but notice the differences in the countryside and the lifestyles that these craggy barriers to water create.

The western portion is green and fertile, ripe with vegetation year-round. It is heavily populated in comparison to the east and, in the summertime, it is a gorgeous playground for the sports-minded, with sailing, fishing, hiking, backpacking and all manner of outdoor activities. To the east, the arid stretches of land that lie in the rain shadow of the mountains are patchworked with irrigated agricultural riches. The east has lakes, rivers and miles of golden, waving wheatfields – as well as recreational wonders of its own.

Evidence of the Cascade Mountains's volcanic origins is everywhere. In Oregon, the caldera of Mount Mazama, a dormant volcano that last erupted 7,700 years ago, cups the enchanting blue waters of Crater Lake, the deepest in the country. To the north, the great mass of Washington's Mount Rainier rises like a titan.

To the west, the snow-dusted peaks of the Olympic Mountains seem to float above the wild, wave-battered Pacific Coast, where bald eagles soar over waters populated by seals, sea otters and migrating whales. Temperate rainforest cloaks Olympic's western slope, where annual rainfall in excess of 120 inches (300 cm) nourishes an emerald cathedral of Douglas fir, Sitka spruce, western red cedar, and thick growths of mosses and ferns.

In among all this, of course, are the Pacific Northwesterners themselves. Around 35 tribes or bands of Native Americans live in the region, many of them conversant with the traditions passed on by their elders, like canoeing and carving. As for the rest, although those on the east side of the Cascades can be as different from those on the west as their contrasting landscapes imply, certain characteristics unite them: an unwillingness to suffer fools, a rugged and individual outlook. The spirit of the Northwest, you might say. ❏

PRECEDING PAGES: Diablo Lake from the North Cascades Highway, Washington; Painted Hills, John Day Fossil Beds National Monument, central Oregon; Olympic National Park, northwest Washington; the coast near Bandon, South Oregon.
LEFT: a Lummi native in traditional dress.

OLD OREGON
TERRITORY
1848

CANADA

WASHINGTON

Columbia River

Until the Barlow road
was opened in 1846,
emigrants rafted
wagons down the
Columbia from
The Dalles.

SAND
POINT

SPOKANE
HOUSE 1810
SPOKANE

KULLUSPELL
HOUSE 1809
by David
Thompson
Idaho's first
building

Flathead
Lake

SALISH
HOUSE 1809

GREAT FALLS

FORT BENTON
built in 1850, head
of steamboat
navigation

The Pronghorn
good meat bu
trappers pre
buffa

NACHES PASS

1836
WHITMAN MISSION
OLD FORT
WALLA WALLA
PENDLETON

Columbia R.

THE
DALLES

John Day R.

LA GRANDE

BAKER

MISSOULA
1860

HELENA
1864

BUTTE

VIRGINIA
CITY

MONTANA

Yellowstone
Lisa's Fort, 1807,
Montana's first
trading post.

MILE
1877

Salmon River

IDAHO

SHERIDAN

Yellowstone
Lake

CODY

On the
last stretch of the
trail, the milk cow
and the saddle horse
haul the remnants
of a covered wagon

Malheur
Crossing

VALE

OLD FORT
BOISE 1834
Boise R. BOISE

CALDWELL

CLENNS
FERRY

Island
Crossing

FORT
HALL
1834

Jackson
Lake

FORT
HENRY 1810

Gray's
Lake

SODA
SPRINGS

FORT
BONNEVILLE
1832

AFTON

BIG
PINEY

CASPER

Independence
Rock

First cabin
in Wyoming
Robert Stuart
party 1812

Lake Abert

Owyhee R.

Pig Route

TWIN
FALLS

City of Rocks

Records
Bluff

Snake River

POCATELLO

Bear
River

Emigrant
Springs

South Pass

Sweetwater River

WYOMING

FORT
Wyo
peri

Harr
Lake

Black
Rock
Desert

NEVADA

Humboldt River

ELKO

WELLS

Thousand
Springs

Great
Salt
Lake

OGDEN

OLD FORT
BRIDGER
1842

Bridger's
Pass

BARREL
SPRINGS

He
JO

Winnemucca
Lake

HUMBOLDT

Humboldt
Sink

Along the Humboldt River
Digger Indians shot poisoned
arrows from ambush and stole
cattle at night.

SALT LAKE CITY

Green River

COLORA

Pyramid L.
RENO

CARSON CITY

Prior to 1830 all western
trails were known
to the ever-daring,
all-enduring trapper

UTAH

MOAB

DOVE
CREEK

Rio Grande

Colorado River

NIA

LAS
VEGAS

PAROWAN

CEDAR CITY

SA NA

SANTA FE

TA

Old Oregon Trail

LEGEND OF TRAILS

OLD OREGON TRAIL	1843
THE APPLEGATE TRAIL	1846
THE BARLOW ROAD	1846
OTHER DEVIATIONS FROM THE MAIN TRAIL	
THE OLD SPANISH TRAIL	1785
LEWIS AND CLARK	1804-1806
THE SANTA FE TRAIL	1822-1880
FREMONT'S TRAIL	1843
THE MORMON TRAIL	1846-47+
NACHES PASS TRAIL	1853
OVERLAND STAGE ROUTE	1859-1869
THE PONY EXPRESS	1860-1861
THE BOZEMAN TRAIL	1866
BUTTERFIELDS DENVER STAGE	1866

NORTH DAKOTA

Lewis & Clark winter headquarters 1804 - 1805

Pushed westward by settlers the lordly Sioux finally went to war. For ten years he and his Cheyenne brother made travel unsafe on the Oregon Trail.

SOUTH DAKOTA

Migration swelled from 875 souls in 1843 to 15,000 in 1852. The patient ox pulled the wagons. He was an easy keeper, did not fight the mud or quicksands, at river crossings and required no expensive harness.

NEBRASKA

Every mile of the Oregon Trail had its graves. Some, the wolves or Indians found and violated.

Bent's Fort in 1826 was the only post between Council Grove and Santa Fe

KANSAS

Sign where the Oregon Trail branched from the Santa Fe Trail - 2000 miles to Oregon - History's longest wagon road.

Road to OREGON

IOWA

In the 1820's steamboat over the work of keel b the lower Missouri. Fr to Independence by w off over 300 miles of r winding road for the

MISSOURI

Independence became the "jumping off point" for all overland caravans, bound West, about 1832

Scene in Independence.

"A multitude of shops had spr to furnish the emigrants and Fe traders ... for their journ was an incessant hammer ... blacksmith sheds, where ... were repaired, and horses a oxen shod." Parkn

FORT LARAMIE

First built of logs at the mouth of Laramie River, named Fort William 1834. Location changed 1842 - built of adobe bricks - named John. Made a government post in 1849

Decisive Dates

10,000 years ago, migrants from Asia settle throughout the Pacific Northwest, the forefathers of today's Native Americans.

1527 Spain's galleons establish limited presence in North Pacific along West Coast.

1579 Sir Francis Drake spends summer at Whale Cove, Oregon, falsifying map to thwart Spaniards.

1720–40 Russian explorations and trade motivate Spain to mount expeditions.

1775 Spain claims part of the territory that is now Washington state.

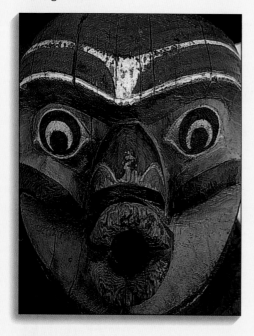

1778 Captain Cook's third expedition lands and subsequently discovers the value of sea otter pelts.

1785–94 Twenty five British coastal expeditions open fur trade with the Native people; 15 American vessels arrive to trade furs.

1789 Spain's Esteban José Martinez fortifies Spanish claim to Nootka Sound.

1792 Britain's George Vancouver and Spain's Bodega y Quadra map the coastline.

1792 American Robert Gray discovers the Columbia River, names it after his ship, the *Columbia*.

1795–1804 Fifty American vessels arrive to trade fur; epidemics begin among Native tribes.

1804–06 Lewis and Clark's expedition to the Pacific Ocean arrives and lays claim to the area.

1805–14 Forty American vessels arrive to trade furs, compared to three British ships.

1807–12 David Thompson explores region overland from the north seeking the mouth of the Columbia River.

1811 John Jacob Astor's Pacific Fur Company establishes a post at Astoria.

1812–41 Russia covets land and trade, but has inadequate supplies and distribution.

1813 British naval vessel occupies Astoria [War of 1812]; North West (Fur) Company buys the post.

1818 British and American joint occupancy of the region is declared.

1825 Sea otter population nearly extinct.

1828–29 George Simpson initiates Hudson's Bay Co (HBC) and exports lumber and salmon.

1830–1840s American missionaries, mountain men and a few settlers begin to arrive.

1830–33 Malaria kills Indians living along the lower Columbia and Willamette rivers.

1840–48 Via the Oregon Trail, 11,512 migrants arrive in Oregon to farm; others head for California to settle and pan for gold.

1843 American settlers and French "Canadian" fur traders organize a government for Oregon.

1844 President James K. Polk defines "Manifest Destiny," declaring USA to be entitled to the entire region from California to Alaska (including present-day British Columbia in Canada).

1846 Final decline in European desire for beaver pelts. The Oregon Treaty defines 49th parallel as the boundary between the US and Canada.

1847 After outbreak of measles kills half the Cayuse tribe, missionaries at Whitman Mission in southern Washington are murdered.

1850s Newcomers bring quantities of plants and animals to region including cattle and horses, wheat and potatoes.

1851 Seattle is founded.

1859–60 Oregonians vote on a new state constitution; United States controls territory; Portland becomes leading city of the Pacific Northwest.

1860s–1900 Fishing, mining, logging and corporate agriculture established; docks and sawmills appear near Seattle.

1880s Railroads arrive; population increases.

1885–1915 Utopian communities are established throughout region; in politics a cycle of radicalism, then reaction to radicalism, leads to conservative politics in the 1920s.

1887 Washington Indians launch their first suit to defend treaty fishing rights.

1889 Constitution of Washington state is written.

1891 Oregon Legislature funds the dredging of a shipping channel extending from Portland approximately 70 miles (115 km) to the Pacific Ocean.
1893–98 Gold is found in Yukon and Alaska; Seattle provides supplies to the miners and surpasses Portland in popularity.
1894 University of Washington established.
1901 Wallin and Nordstrom open Seattle shoe store, forerunner of the retail giant Nordstrom.
1903 Oregon enacts progressive legislation giving 10-hour day to women workers.
1905 Portland hosts Lewis and Clark Centennial Exposition celebrating its emergence from a frontier town; citizens plant thousands of roses.
1909 City of Seattle celebrates prodigious growth and civic refinements by hosting a world's fair: the Alaska-Yukon-Pacific Exposition.
1910 Near Seattle, William Edward Boeing founds what is to become one of the great corporations of commercial aviation.
1916 Seattle, assisted by the US Army Corps of Engineers, completes locks permitting ships to travel from Puget Sound to Lake Washington.
1917 Organization called the "Wobblies" spearheads large-scale strike in the lumber industry for an 8-hour day; War Department ends it.
1920s Seattle's ratio of men to women is 14 to 1, Portland's 1.05 to 1; Washington and Oregon pass laws in 1921 and 1923 to forbid Japanese immigrants from owning land.
1930s Mining and farming hit by economic downturn; Grand Coulee Dam and Columbia Basin irrigation project completed on Columbia River; Civilian Conservation Corps begins programs in forests and wildlife protection.
1938 Bonneville Dam completed.
1940s During World War II, aluminum factories in Spokane and Portland area, plutonium plants at Hanford (providing material for atomic bombs), and aircraft manufacturing at Seattle draw on power from the Columbia Basin.
1943–46 World War II internment of Japanese and Japanese Americans.
1952–1960s Exclusionary immigration policies reformed; Korean War and later Cold War galvanize politicians to look at Washington state.
1950s–1990s Boeing becomes leading private employer for Seattle area; Puget Sound becomes harbor for nuclear submarines.

PRECEDING PAGES: route of the Oregon Trail, 1843.
LEFT: figure from Northwest totem pole.
RIGHT: Bill Gates, billionaire and Washington native.

1962 Seattle hosts World's Fair; city brands itself "space age," savvy and futuristic.
1970s Hundreds of thousands of Asian immigrants arrive; environmental movements begin in earnest.
1971 First Starbucks opens in Seattle.
1974 City of Spokane hosts World's Fair.
1980s Spiral migration as relatives of 1970s immigrants arrive.
1980s Severe decline in salmon populations and degradation of forests; environmental activism increases. These trends are still continuing.
1980 Mount St Helens erupts, kills 57 people, and spreads ash over much of the Northwest.
1990s Seattle, through Bill Gates's Microsoft, plus

Portland with anchor Intel, become important centers for world technological, software and communications innovation.
1996 The discovery of a 9,300-year-old skeleton in Kennewick, Washington, throws into question the origins of the first inhabitants of the Americas.
1999 Man caught importing bomb materials from Canada through Washington; Federal government nixes removal of river dams to restore salmon runs. Riots disrupt World Trade Organization in Seattle.
2001 Earthquake 6.8 on the Richter Scale shakes Seattle; Boeing decides to relocate corporate headquarters to Chicago, citing "traffic" as a cause.
2002 A time capsule with items dating from 1889 is unveiled in Seattle Center. ❑

ROCKY BEGININGS

Glaciers on a march to the sea and the Pacific Rim of Fire were just
part of the dramatic collision that created the Northwest

The geology of the Pacific Northwest is the product of eons of plate tectonics, volcanism and glaciation. Unfortunately, there were no tourists around to record the Pacific Northwest's Paleozoic shoreline in snapshots, but we can read evidence in the rocks. Some 300 million years ago, Pacific Ocean waves lapped at beaches that today lie high and dry, not far west of the Idaho border. Stretching from northern California to Canada was a sweeping bay. The Pacific Northwest was yet to form.

The majestic Cascades

The Cascade mountain range divides the Pacific Northwest north to south, from the Canadian border to the knot of peaks and precipices in southern Oregon. Two of the majestic, snow-capped mountains – Mount Rainier and Mount Hood – give dramatic backdrops to the region's largest metropolitan areas: Seattle and Portland respectively. The Cascades also divide the Northwest into wet and dry halves. The west is wet. To the east, land is caught in the semi-arid rain shadow of the mountains. Huge, green Douglas fir and ponderosa pine trees, as well as magnificent scenery of towering peaks, are so common as to be almost visual clichés of the region, but in fact, much of eastern Washington and Oregon is dry, ocher-colored land. National volcanic monuments preserve some of the best sites and show examples of the effects of the volcanic events through the ages. Evidence of massive lava flows are everywhere, providing both educational and tourist opportunities.

When the continents were young and restless, the Americas were parting from Europe and Africa, and butting against the Pacific Ocean floor. The two plates collided and the heavier ocean bottom dove beneath North America. As the North American continent

LEFT: more than 200 million years ago, a shallow sea covered the Northwest's interior; now it is a plateau.
RIGHT: Captain's Rock overlooks the Columbia River near Wallula Gap.

skidded over the hard bedrock sea floor, it scraped off the soft coastal plain and continental shelf, pushing the lighter materials ahead of it. The debris grew until it formed a new range of coastal mountains along what was then the western edge of North America. These mountains are the Wallowas and the

Blues. The Klamath Mountains in southern Oregon and California's sierras were also a part of this new coastal range, but in the course of 100 million years they went their separate ways, with the Klamaths most likely standing for a time as a huge island in the blue Pacific. Also about 100 million years ago, a small continental landmass joined the Washington coast forming the Okanogan Highlands. About 50 million years later, another continental shelf impacted with North America to create the North Cascade Mountains.

When a descending basalt ocean floor slides 60 miles (95 km) into the the earth, as the Pacific floor did beneath the encroaching North

American landmass, it melts and begins a slow return to the surface in fiery, liquid form. Volcanism, in its various forms, is the next player in our story. Washington is located along one of the most celebrated zones of volcanism, the Pacific Rim of Fire. The convergence of tectonic plates drives an internal fury that creates mountain ranges and island arcs. The eruption of Mount St Helens in 1980 is a recent example of this power. A chain of ash- and lava-spewing volcanoes thus emerged along the western edge of the continent.

The sun rose and set millions of times on this corner of the world before anything close to the

present Northwest coastline was established. It was only 35 million years ago that the bed of the Pacific Ocean cracked and began sinking parallel to the coastline. Behind it emerged a north–south line of volcanoes in the bay, the predecessors of today's Cascade Range. The volcanoes stretched across the mouth of the old bay, creating an inland sea. Over the next 10 million years this sea filled with sediments. Some slid from the shore, and some were deposited by volcanic activity that tossed more than 1,000 ft (300 meters) of ash and molten rock into the captured body of water. The coast ranges of the Olympic Mountains and the Willapa Hills are newcomers to the landscape,

being comprised of tilted and folded sea floor, embedded formations of basalt and other debris. Continuous erosion created sheets of sediment on the ocean floor that are still being pitched upward.

The *coup de grâce* for this huge inland waterway came when the western Cascades abruptly ceased their volcanic belching. Fissures opened up just east of the sea, spewing huge quantities of molten basalt, and raising hundreds of square miles of the sea bed by an average of 500 ft (150 meters).

The Columbia Plateau

There is general agreement that the eruptions which formed the flood basalts of the Columbia Plateau were among the greatest outpourings of magma known on earth. Approximately 15 million years ago, a series of eruptions poured highly fluid magma from open vents and covered a huge region. This occurred repeatedly over thousands of years, building formations over 10,000 ft (3,000 meters) thick. Remnants are found today in the layered, many-sided basalt columns seen all over central eastern Washington and northern Oregon. Today the Columbia Plateau covers about 225,000 sq. miles (520,000 sq. km) in eastern Oregon, eastern Washington and Idaho, and is the world's second-largest known basalt flow.

Fifteen million years ago, at about the same time that basalt flows were covering the land in this area, the northern half of the Coast Range began to emerge. These mountains weren't built up from the debris piled against the continental plate by the descending Pacific Ocean floor. Instead, sediments that had accumulated beneath the part of the sunken floor nearest today's Oregon and Washington coastlines lifted the stranded floor, bending it high to form the Coast Range and to expose the fossils of the former seabed.

Snake in hell

Rivers were cut through this geological turmoil. The Snake River, at the eastern edge of Oregon, fought a course over the new land, digging a path deeper and deeper, creating what we know today as Hell's Canyon. At more than a mile down from rim to river, this is the deepest canyon in North America. Then there is the mighty Columbia River. For eons this river pushed relentlessly through the Coast Range and etched its way into the strata of what we recognize today as the Columbia Gorge, exposing thick layers of basalt along the gorge's walls, revealing millions of years of formation.

Next, glaciers on a march to the sea chewed much of Washington and Oregon's landmass. During countless ice ages, the most recent ending about 10,000 years ago, the land surface was gouged and redistributed to form the modern landscape. Perhaps the most astonishing remnant of the many ice ages is the broad region in the Columbia Basin known as the Channeled Scablands, created during several continental glacial events. Ice dams created vast

as evidence of its southern rampage Grand Coulee, a huge chasm at the head of which is Dry Falls, a ghost falls that, at 3 miles (5 km) across and 400 ft (120 meters) high, is a stunning geological wonder. Today we can also see the greatest influence of glaciers in the valleys of Western Washington as the Puget Sound basin and Grays Harbor.

More eruptions

About 8,000 years ago, Native Americans were here to witness the explosive eruption of Mount Mazama – the large crater now holds Oregon's picturesque Crater Lake. More recently, in May

lakes in the interior basins of the Rocky Mountains. Warming conditions caused failure of the dams and the largest release of floodwaters known from earth history. The westward-flowing Columbia backed up behind this ice dam until it overflowed its banks to the south. A huge channel 35 miles (56 km) long was gouged in southern Oregon. The liberated river splashed over a basalt ledge to create a prehistoric cataract 40 times mightier than Niagara Falls. When the iceflow retreated, the Columbia returned to its old westward channel, leaving

1980, Washington's Mount St Helens gave Northwest residents an all-too-powerful demonstration of the forces that created this region. The blast destroyed hundreds of acres of forest, and killed 57 people. Fortunately, prevailing winds blew most of the ash eastward, sparing the cities from the worst of the hot powder.

This was not the first time that Mount St Helens had demonstrated its power and it probably won't be the last. Native American cultures in the Pacific Northwest, such as the Salish and Klickitat Indians, refered to Mount St Helens as *Loo-Wit Lat-kla* or *Louwala-Clough*, fire mountain or smoking mountain. We may live to see that very image. ❏

LEFT: a fossilized leaf from Lava Lands, Oregon.
ABOVE: petroglyphs speak of earlier inhabitants.

COMPLEX SOCIETIES

The legendary "niceness" of Pacific Northwest inhabitants
started with Native Americans. But it has been known to slip

It is generally agreed that the Native Americans of the Pacific Northwest were among the richest Native populations in North America, their wealth supplied by nature. Their chief resources were the abundant and reliable annual salmon run, plentiful wild game, seafood from the ocean, and territories fertile with roots and berries.

Ample and easily available food was only one part of the equation, as they also had many mouths to feed. The second key was their industrious and inventive technological nature. They built massive salmon traps, smokehouses, storage cellars and construction facilities. The people here had also developed the most complex social structures in North America – social structures that governed them and gave them leisure time in which to develop distinctive arts as well as a rich cultural life.

Extended families

Northwest Coastal Nations had scant understanding of the word "tribe." They tended to live in stable villages of extended families, groups that never adopted tribal names but simply spoke of each other as "of our people." And they lived well, residing in huge cedar-plank lodges up to 110 ft (35 meters) long. Canadian artist Paul Kane described what he saw as "the largest buildings of any description among Indians, divided in the interior into compartments to accommodate eight or ten families."

Coastal Natives were fiercely independent. Promotion to leadership positions within a village was more often than not based upon a man's capabilities, rather than upon his familial heritage or material wealth. It was expected that a leader would set a fine example to others. Historian Gordon B. Dodds explains further that "leaders would be followed, not obeyed, as each individual participated in warfare or the

LEFT: Northwest Natives included "the Duke of York."
RIGHT: drawing of a Flathead Indian taken from an account of an exploration of Washington Territory.

hunt on an individual basis, and if a man decided to return home he suffered no stigma for deserting the cause." Societies were typically divided into three broad social groupings. The upper class were accorded privileges of honor and rank while the slave class had no rights and could be murdered at will with no

consequence. A middle class of skilled artisans and clever workers could use their abilities to ascend to the upper classes.

Many languages

Most warfare consisted of raiding other villages to procure slaves. Some were then ransomed back for large amounts of goods, while those kidnapees without status performed any and all menial tasks for their enslavers.

Early white travelers, weaned on tales of rampaging red men of the Midwestern plains, were perplexed by this different breed of Natives, and befuddled by the many languages and dialects spoken along the coast. "The

Northwest contained many mutually unintelligible language groupings," wrote the historian Dorothy Johansen. In western Washington, the predominant tongue was Coast Salish. In Oregon from the mouth of the Columbia to Tillamook Bay and east to the Cascades, Chinookan languages were spoken. The Tillamooks belonged to the Coast Salish language group. The Klatskanie on the Columbia, a band on the Willapa River, and another on the Rogue River, were enclaves of Athapascan-speaking peoples.

SPEAKING IN TONGUES

Many dialects were spoken by Northwest tribes. In order to communicate, something called "Chinook jargon" was developed – an amalgam of Native tongues.

reached the region, he found Northwest Natives familiar with a surprising vocabulary of words such as "musquets, powder, shot, knife, file, damned rascal, (and) son of a bitch" – words that were apparently used frequently in trading.

Natives of northwest Washington shared many of the customs familiar to tribes as far north as southern Alaska. Leisure afforded by the abundance of nature allowed them to become great sculptors of wood, a skill most apparent in the representation of family heraldic crests or

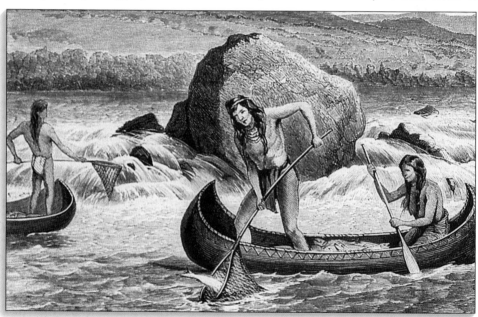

"Within the major language groups so many different dialects were spoken that neighbors could not easily communicate verbally with one another." To communicate in light of this linguistic jigsaw puzzle, the Natives had developed something known as "Chinook jargon," a curious amalgam of many Native tongues.

Native polyglots

With the incursion of European sea traders into the area, many French, English and Russian words were also absorbed into the *lingua franca* of the Northwest coast. When explorer William Clark arrived in this area in the early 19th century, long after maritime trade had

totems carved on poles or painted on boards. Large cedar trees, plentiful along the coast, were made not only into excellent canoes and huge longhouses, but also into storage chests and watertight containers for cooking. The water temperature was controlled by hot rocks pulled from the fire and dumped into the containers. Woven cedar strips were fashioned into rainproof hats and women wore skirts made from strands of white cedar bark, "the whole being of sufficient thickness when the female stands erect to conceal those parts usually covered from familiar view, but when she stoops or places herself in any other attitude their battery of Venus is not altogether impervious to the penetrating eye of the amorite." It's little wonder that, in winter winds, these Native women preferred to be wrapped in furs.

Accumulation of wealth in materialistic Northwest Indian society gave rise to the *potlatch*. This was a complex ritual, involving the paying of witnesses who arrived for the three-week ceremony during which all the tribes' legal matters such as marriages, divorces, berry-patch allotments, widow's settlements, trials and retributions were decided, witnessed and remembered. Initiations, adoptions and honors were also bestowed. Engagements were announced, birthrights and fishing territories were defined.

The whole event culminated with spectacular rituals performed by secret societies. The celebrations also served to reinforce the leadership of the strongest and wealthiest patrons through the copious giving of gifts to those who were then charged to "remember" what had transpired. This "remembering," of course, substituted for a written language to document a complex set of civil transactions. If there was ever a dispute over a benefit such as a promotion or allotment granted during one of the ceremonies, the witness, who had been gifted, could be called upon to provide verbal testimony on behalf of the person from whom they had received the gift.

Life on the dry side

While the coastal Natives lived among a preponderance of natural riches, peoples east of the Cascade Mountains often suffered shortages of supplies. Their population was scattered, only concentrating where mighty runs of salmon, steelhead and eel coursed up the Columbia and its tributaries. Most fortunate of these people, perhaps, were those around Celilo Falls in the Columbia Gorge. Falls were among the greatest obstacles for spawning fish that had to leap high into the air while hurdling this surging barrier. Fishers perched on fragile platforms above the falls could harvest up to 500 fish a day. On the eastern plateaus of what are now Washington and Oregon, the diet of salmon had to be supplemented by mammal meat, particularly deer, with fruit, roots and

assorted nuts. Native Americans in the extreme southeast of the region struggled for food over what meagre pickings there were. In this arid environment, the Paiutes, for instance, often had to subsist on reptiles, rodents, grasshoppers and assorted common bugs. Ever the western wit Mark Twain once remarked that these Natives would eat "anything they can bite." The Klamaths and Modocs of southern Oregon were rather more prosperous, enhancing their diets with waterfowl from local lakes.

One trait shared among Northwest Indians, from whatever part of the land, was their rich oral tradition. They often shared ribald fireside

tales of larger-than-life creatures – Coyote, Blue Jay, Beaver, Raven and Wolf. Antics of characters in Northwest Native mythology at first seem slapstick, but these lively tales describe how the world evolved, and point out the importance of natural resources.

As in the era of the maritime fur trade, epidemic diseases unknown to Native Americans prior to contact with Europeans had a devastating impact upon their populations in the era before the mid-19th century. These were illnesses against which Natives had no immunities and little resistance. Epidemics such as smallpox, measles and influenza did not strike once; rather they recurred over the decades, so

---

LEFT: netting salmon from a canoe made of cedar.
RIGHT: British explorers called this Puget Sound Native "Queen Victoria."

that groups of Indians who were recovering from one epidemic would then be hit by another. A group who had experienced small-pox and acquired some immunity, for example, might be struck next by measles or typhoid. The impact was not spread evenly across the region, however; groups on the Columbia Plateau suffered less than those along the coast.

Ghost dancing

Natives were also struck by illnesses that became endemic, including venereal disease and tuber-culosis. Afflictions weakened Indians and their societies, at the same time as colonizers

has access to the ocean. Government-sponsored attempts to get the Makah to farm were unsuc-cessul, and between the founding of the reser-vation in 1855 and the Great Depression of the 1930s, the Makah Indians continued the whal-ing, sealing and fishing that had sustained them for centuries. The Makah incorporated new technologies and learned how to speak English, but they also kept traditional occupations alive and maintained a measure of prosperity – some-thing most Washington tribes could not claim.

The third form of Native American resistance was litigation. Natives pressured the US to live up to the terms of the treaties it had signed in

approached the Pacific Northwest, and dimin-ished Natives' ability to resist colonization.

Native American cultures were influenced by contact with the pioneers in many ways, but some First Nations found ways to retain aspects of their culture and resist assimilation. But tra-ditional religion had to be practiced in secret. In 1850 the Wanapum prophet Smohalla experi-enced a visionary dream encouraging Indians to live according to their old customs. During the late 1800s, Ghost Dancing became a way for so-called Dreamers to resist acculturation to white ways. Unfortunately this practice was met with several punitive raids by Whites. The Makah reservation in northwest Washington

the mid-19th century. For example, Yakama peoples launched the first cases to enforce Indian fishing rights on the Columbia River in 1887 and 1905. Native groups kept these issues alive in the courts throughout the 20th century, until the US government finally began to accept the Indian position during the 1970s.

The right to fish

The Boldt decision of 1974, upheld by the US Supreme Court in 1979 and further expanded with regard to shellfish during the 1990s, cemented the rights to fish that Indians had claimed, based on the original treaties. Specif-ically, the Boldt decision guaranteed Indians the right to catch one-half of the commercial salmon harvest every year, as the treaties originally guaranteed. With the precipitous decline of runs of salmon, this decision has placed pressure on both Indians and non-Indians to cooperate with one another to protect the remaining salmon fisheries.

Termination

Between 1933 and 1941, construction of the Grand Coulee Dam on the Columbia River eliminated upstream runs of salmon on the Columbia, and wiped out the fishery at Kettle Falls. Later, the fishery at Celilo Falls was destroyed in order to create the John Day Fossil Beds National Monument, and this loss is still mourned.

The mobilization for World War II and the Cold War recruited Native Americans into the armed services or defense-related jobs, and many did not return. In 1953, Congress officially adopted a policy known as "termination," by which it aimed to subject the Indians to the same laws and entitle them to the privileges and responsibilities of other US citizens.

Across the United States, only 3 percent of all Indians were terminated, but among these were the Klamath Nations of southern Oregon, and the 61 tribes and bands of western Oregon. Termination was supposed to provide an economic benefit, as tribal resources would be sold and the proceeds distributed to members of the tribe. The Klamath, for example, anticipating receiving $43,700 apiece, were "terminated" in 1961. This produced a temporary bonanza, but over time the Klamaths went from prosperity to relative poverty. Western Oregon groups similarly experienced unanticipated adversity from this termination policy, and by the 1970s and 1980s were taking steps to reverse the process and restore the formal relationship with the Federal government.

By the 1960s and 1970s, Indian policy changed again. The Federal government generally sided with tribes and bands in court disputes over treaty matters. Of course, many Indians and non-Indians were still dissatisfied, and the matter of Indians' dependency on the government and its social and welfare services

remains contentious. Nonetheless, there soon emerged a general consensus that Native Americans, with Federal support, ought to have more self-determination.

Casinos and cash

The restoration of fishing rights in the 1970s, and the legalization of Indian casinos in the 1980s and 1990s (both of which were contested by non-Indians as well as by some Indians), offered considerable opportunities for tribal economic development. However, these opportunities were uneven. Some tribes, like the Lummi on northern Puget Sound, tended to do

better in the new fishing regime than others. In the matter of gambling, some tribes were able to finance and successfully open casinos, but others were not. Of the tribes that operated casinos, those that did so in urban areas prospered more than those whose casinos were isolated.

Finally, the matter of dependency continues to loom large. Northwest Indians aspire to self-determination, but many of their efforts remain wedded to Federal recognition and Federal benefits. Non-Indians continue to challenge those benefits, and Natives spend much time wondering how they can achieve autonomy and whether they can rely on the US government and its ever-changing policies. ❏

LEFT: frontiersmen introduced Natives to worldly evils such as "firewater."
RIGHT: modern Yakima boy at a rodeo in Washington.

A NEW FRONTIER

*Every country wanted a piece of the remarkable Northwest territory,
from Spain to Britain, from Russia to America*

For almost a century, the Spanish viewed the Pacific Ocean as their private lake. But smugness turned into consternation in 1579, when British sea dog Francis Drake appeared off the west coast of South America. His arrival on the *Golden Hind* caused alarm, not least because of his ever-growing chest of Spanish gold, silver and other bounty. Of almost equal concern was that Drake turned his ship north, rather than sail around the toe of South America. To the Spanish, Drake's route home was as mysterious as his arrival in the Pacific. Had the rival British fleet finally discovered the fabled Strait of Anian, that legendary western gate of the sought-after Northwest Passage that linked the east coast of North America with the west? If so, the Spanish days of maritime supremacy were definitely numbered.

Lucre, legends and liars

In fact, Drake hadn't discovered the Northwest Passage. Escaping from the Spanish, he had headed north to the Pacific Northwest, where he found the rain "an unnatural congealed and frozen substance," and an atmosphere of the "most vile, thicke and stinking fogges." Recent evidence points convincingly to the idea that he spent the winter of 1589 farther north than once believed, specifically, at Whale Cove in present-day Oregon. He falsified his records lest they fall into Spanish hands. Finally he turned the *Golden Hind* south to cross the Pacific, stopping along the way in northern California, which, together with most of the West Coast, he dubbed "New Albion" in defiance of Spanish claims.

Tales of the mythic Northwest Passage lived on. It would take 150 years before lucre, legends and liars would prompt thorough investigations and, as a result, the beginning of the end of a romantic notion. In the meantime, tales continued as an alluring prospect to those

pioneers who would open up the land that became known as the Pacific Northwest.

Russians had begun searching for the Northwest Passage decades before Drake arrived. They knew the value of furs in the markets of China, and their fur hunters, the *promyshlenniks*, pushed relentlessly eastward across the

frozen wastes of Siberia in search of sable and sea otter pelts. From there these hunters moved through Alaska and south into the Pacific Northwest. For many years, the Russians traded with the Natives and had a free hand in the exploitation of the Northwest sea otter.

Then, between 1740 and 1840, several nations arrived on the scene to compete with one another – and with the Native Peoples – to take control over the area. Spain "showed little interest in a region so pitifully lacking in either economic resources or good harbors," and had to be roused from "her imperial lethargy" by Russian advances toward Alaska. Spanish ships traveled far up the North American coast to

LEFT: pioneer wagons on the grueling Oregon Trail, painted by N.C. Wyeth.
RIGHT: British captain James Cook cruised the waters in 1778 looking for the elusive Northwest Passage.

investigate the Russian invasion. Their captains were relieved to find no permanent eastern European settlements. Spanish officials intended to secure the region – or at least its coastline – as a buffer zone between Russian colonies to the north and Spain's center of imperial activity down south in Mexico.

Exploring the "New World"

The British arrived in search of the reputed Northwest Passage. In 1776, Captain James Cook undertook his third voyage around the world for the British Royal Navy. The English government offered a £20,000 prize for the dis-

vessels came to claim, defend, Christianize and explore the territory, but never to do business. Typically, the Spanish mapped an area, constructed a wooden cross high on a hill and departed. In some cases, Natives set the crosses ablaze before the Spanish passed out of view.

The British, by contrast, sent 25 vessels in the decade 1785–94. All but a few of them participated in the maritime fur trade. Ever practical, the British fleet scouted the territory for economic resources and good harbors.

Americans were entering the picture, too. In the spring of 1792, two ships sailing off the coasts of present-day Oregon and Washington

covery of the passage, though Cook saw not the "least probability that ever such a thing existed." Because of bad weather Cook cruised the Northwest coast during 1778, but missed the mouth of the Columbia River as he headed north. He and his crew traded metal in exchange for furs, which his seamen used for bedding and clothes. Following Cook's murder in the Hawaiian islands in 1779, his crew continued to China, where they discovered their furs fetched a pretty penny. As word spread, the British hustled back to the Northwest coast for more fur trading.

Compare this with the Spanish approach. Between 1774 and 1795, the Spanish sent a handful of expeditions from Mexico. These

were both intent on probing the craggy coastline. One was the British sloop *Discovery*, commanded by Captain George Vancouver who, as a midshipman, had accompanied Captain Cook on his West Coast expedition.

The other ship was the *Columbia*, flying the colors of the United States and captained by Yankee fur trader Robert Gray. Vancouver was interested in exploration; Gray had his eyes on lucrative furs. Gray and Vancouver met at sea and exchanged news – though both withheld key information about their respective voyages from each other. Vancouver was happy to hear that Captain Gray had found little profit in the waters around what is today Washington's

Olympic Peninsula. Vancouver went on to explore the Straits of Juan de Fuca and the Gulf of Georgia, and was the first to circumnavigate what is now known as Vancouver Island, giving Great Britain a strong claim to the entire area.

Vancouver and Puget

Vancouver and Second Lieutenant Peter Puget directed two separate explorations of today's Puget Sound. Vancouver's surveys proved that an easily navigable Northwest Passage did not exist, but in the process, he discovered and named innumerable Pacific Northwest landmarks, many of them after himself.

his eastern employers. They was far more interested in furs. Vancouver and Gray had amicably divided their interests in the Pacific Northwest, but their respective countries – Britain and America – would prove less willing to do so.

Between 1795 and 1804, 50 American vessels arrived to trade fur, compared to nine British ships. After Spanish claims were pushed below 42° latitude in the 1819 treaty, and after the vague claims of the Russians had been resolved north of 54°, 40 minutes in 1828, the US and Great Britain would fight fiercely for control of Oregon Country. Both countries shored up their claims with overland explorations.

Gray continued south to where his fellow captain had reported that the sea changed "from its natural to river coloured water." He sailed the *Columbia* through a treacherous bar, discovering a spacious harbor at the mouth of a mighty river, second only to the Mississippi in North America. This great waterway was named Columbia after Gray's vessel. Yet the thrill of geographical discovery and the fact that it afforded the United States claim to the entire valley of the Columbia meant little to Gray or

The Hudson's Bay Company (HBC) was the agent for the British, and the dominant force in the Northwest. Taking advantage of the fur resources and the new overland exploration abilities, David Thompson traveled far west in 1797–98, establishing trading posts across what became Idaho, Oregon and Washington.

Lewis & Clark

In 1804 President Thomas Jefferson sent captains Meriwether Lewis and William Clark to explore the practically unknown Louisiana Purchase, which the United States had bought from Napoleon for $15 million, and which included all of what is now the Midwest. Jefferson didn't

LEFT: trading fur for goods and guns.
ABOVE: Fort Astoria, Oregon, was established as a fur trading center in 1811.

exactly believe the remote Pacific Northwest would ever become part of his United States. He viewed the Rocky Mountains as a natural western boundary for the country, but worried that the British had taken "control" of the Northwest. Following an arduous 4,000-mile (6,000-km) trek, the explorers finally glimpsed the Pacific Ocean on November 15, 1805, and wintered near the mouth of the Columbia River at Fort Clatsop. Disappointed to find no ship on the river to sail them back to civilization, the group returned overland in 1806, bringing back meticulously plotted maps, observations of animal life and valuable scientific collections.

In 1807, the London-born explorer David Thompson crossed the Howse Pass to the source of the Columbia River and traveled its length. He then explored the Kootenai, Pend Oreille and Clark Fork river basins. In 1810, prevented by the Piegan Blackfeet from using Howse Pass, he went north to the head of the Athabasca River and across the mountains, mapping all of the Columbia River system. American fur traders began to move in and saw so many Hudson's Bay Company flags, they joked that the initials HBC stood for "Here Before Christ." Thompson was responsible for establishing British sovereignty down to the lower Columbia River, so in 1811 he was only

a little concerned when he found that Yankee fur trader John Jacob Astor, on behalf of the Pacific Fur Company, had established Fort Astoria at the mouth of the Columbia. It was considered proper that during the War of 1812, for instance, the crew from a British sloop-of-war "captured" the quickly abandoned Fort Astoria, unaware that through Thompson it had already been sold. It wasn't until 1818 that they agreed upon a formula for joint occupation.

US and British power struggle

Between 1805 and 1814, 40 American vessels were operating in the fur trade, compared with only three British ships. Then, by land, Dr John McLoughlin, the HBC "facteur" (all-powerful boss) was positioned to make matters as rough as possible for American beaver-trappers pouring into "his" Oregon Country. McLoughlin's duties were to monopolize the fur trade, impose peace upon the numerous Indian tribes, and prevent agricultural settlement. The Hudson's Bay Company district under his management became the most profitable of all the company's enterprises in North America.

When it became apparent that the fur trade was declining, he sent trapper Peter Skene Ogden to the Northwest's eastern reaches to trap every fur-bearing rodent before Yankee trappers came prowling. Ogden and his men spent six years in the wilds, exterminating every beaver they could find, all to no avail; nothing would stem the westward movement of Americans. Ever since Lewis and Clark published their journals of the Northwest, the imagination of the nascent United States was caught. Oregon Country belonged to them.

Before Europeans migrated to North America, Native societies underwent changes and adaptation as cultures evolved, climates changed, and as contact with one another introduced new cultural elements. Once Europeans began colonizing North America in 1492, Native societies were affected by an unfamiliar, accelerated wind of change. Even tribes in the Pacific Northwest, isolated from sites of European colonization, were affected. When European (including Russian) and American fur traders arrived from afar, Native Americans were the only ones who could provide the desired pelts. They monopolized the supply of furs by hunting the pelts themselves. Natives acquired pelts from each other by purchase or by theft. Those with the most furs then monopolized a new supply of exchange goods. Metal, in the form of pots and tools, was particularly coveted. Natives were not necessarily passive victims of European and American capitalism. Some saw in these maritime traders an opportunity to improve their lives.

The Oregon Trail

The overland migration of Americans to Oregon along the famous "Oregon Trail" began in earnest in 1843. That year, there were about 150 Americans residing in Oregon Country; by 1845 there were 5,000 or more – mainly clustered in the Willamette Valley. Most arrived by way of an overland wagon trail, bringing a new and epic means of cross-country travel. The sudden arrival of a resident US population, of settlers rather than fur traders, soon shifted the balance of power. Meanwhile, back east around late April or early May the grass was long enough for the arduous four to six month journey to begin.

The Oregon Trail (more correctly, the Oregon-California Trail) generally followed the Platte River to its headwaters, then crossed the mountains. In southern Idaho, the California Trail split off. The Oregon Trail then followed the Snake River to the Columbia River – which flows into the Pacific Ocean. Prior to 1846, pioneers reaching The Dalles on the Columbia River had to float their wagons and their worldly belongings through a set of treacherous rapids on a hired raft or boat. The exorbitant fee was $50 per wagon and $10 a person.

Pioneer diaries are replete with accounts of capsizings and drownings in the icy rapids. Jesse Applegate succinctly described the last leg of their dust-eating, wearisome trek west in 1847: "A scene of human misery ensued which scarcely has a parallel in history…the loss of life and property was enormous…"

Another pioneer, Sam Barlow, upon reaching The Dalles in 1845, decided that after six months of bumping across the mountains and plains, his battered wagon wasn't worth the $50 to float it down the Columbia. Hearing rumors of a Native American trail that crossed the Cascade Mountain barrier just south of the snow-covered flank of Mount Hood, he decided to try a mountain crossing instead. "God never made a mountain but that he provided a place for man to go over or around it, he said."

In 1846 Barlow opened this land route into the Willamette Valley, the steep, dangerous Barlow Road, considered the most grueling part of the entire Oregon Trail. Oxen and horses perished, wagons were abandoned or their contents discarded, Pioneer E.W. Conyers lamented that, by the time members of his party had reached the valley, they were completely out of food. He prayed, "We live in the hope that there will be plenty for all when we arrive at our destina-

TALES FROM THE TRAIL

A family of four settlers traveling West from Missouri needed over 1,000 lbs (454 kg) of food to sustain them on the 2,000-mile (3,200-km), extremely hazardous journey. The only practical way to haul that much food was by mule- or oxen-drawn wagon. The wagon box measured only 4 ft by 10 ft (1.2 by 3-meters). Most emigrants loaded them to the brim with food, farm implements and furniture – often over a ton of cargo. All this was supported by massive axles. If an axle broke, the travelers were in serious trouble. Without a spare, they were forced to abandon the wagon or reconfigure it as a two-wheeled cart, reducing their chances of survival.

LEFT: William Clark, half of the 1804 expedition from the East that ended at the Pacific Ocean.
RIGHT: Meriwether Lewis; he and William Clark traveled the length of the Columbia River.

tion. My! Oh, my! What a hungry crowd the people of Oregon will have to feed during the coming winter, and the great majority of them have no money to buy with." But arrive they did.

In gold we trust

Beginning in 1843 and over the next 25 years, between 300,000 and half a million people went West on the Oregon Trail. About one in ten died along the way. Most went to California in search of gold. Some forked north to Oregon's Willamette Valley looking for farmland. One small group founded Alki-New York, which was the beginning of Seattle. The glory

Oregon farmers-turned-goldminers found the pickings easy, gathering surface deposits called placer gold. But as the claims were picked over, they soon returned to Oregon, bringing $2 million worth of nuggets with them. Oregon finally had a currency beyond wheat, potatoes and rocks. In 1849, the legislature minted standardized coins – so-called "Beaver Money," gold coins stamped in $5 and $10 denominations.

Shrewd Oregon prospectors returned from unsuccessful forays secure in the knowledge that 100,000 California miners would pay handsomely for Oregon products. The value of produce and lumber went up in proportion. In

years of the Oregon Trail finally ended in 1869, when the transcontinental railroad was completed. Late in the 1840s, a surprise awaited newcomers to the Willamette Valley. In spite of good weather, crops rotted in unattended fields and once-productive farms surrendered to weeds. Two newspapers folded as the valley's population appeared to consist of "only a few women and children and some Indians." In all, by 1849 only 8,779 people were found living in what is now the state of Oregon. Blame it on California. Gold had been found there. It seemed the sudden exodus of two-thirds of Oregon's male population for gold-laden California spelled doom for the territory's hopes. Some

crazy gold-fevered California, Oregon eggs sold for a dollar apiece. After 40 years of poverty, Oregon Territory was booming.

Ever in search of untapped deposits, California prospectors eventually ventured north to the hills of southern Oregon. There, in 1851, nuggets were found. Thousands of shovels began turning up rich pockets of gold dust, and millions of dollars worth were extracted from places with names such as Rich Gulch and Sailors Diggings. Gold was found in ancient stream beds and on ledges high up in the hills. Miners even struck it rich along the Oregon coast south of Coos Bay.

The timing was propitious. The 1850 Donation Land Act had stimulated settlement, giving each Oregon settler 320 acres (130 hectares) and, as a bonus, an additional 320 acres (130 hectares) in his wife's name. With most of the rich Willamette Valley lands rapidly being claimed, the Gold Rush in southern Oregon opened previously remote yet fertile valleys to a ravenous market.

The wilderness soon sprouted bustling towns, with Jacksonville as the metropolis and Scottsburg as its transportation nexus. Mule trains shared trails with stagecoaches running between San Francisco and Portland, opening a route that would later become part of the Oregon & California Railroad land grant. The Hudson's Bay Company and the British watched helplessly as upstart Americans poured into the verdant valleys and, worse, began moving north of the Columbia River. Native Americans had ceased to be contenders on the scene. Between 1774 and 1874 the population of Natives along the Northwest coast declined by 80 percent, from roughly 200,000 people to around 40,000.

In 1844 US President Polk began clamoring for "Manifest Destiny," interpreted as the United States' sacred right to possession of all the territories between the Atlantic and Pacific oceans – including Canada. He declared himself willing to go to war for it. In response, Britain and the United States signed the Oregon Treaty. This extended the international border between the US and what would become Canada along the 49th parallel, effectively dividing the region between the Americans and the British.

The HBC remained influential in British Columbia to the north, and Americans continued to populate Oregon Country, which now gained official US territorial status. Abraham Lincoln, an Illinois lawyer and later 16th president of the United States, was selected as the territory's first governor. However, he refused the offer because his wife, Mary Todd Lincoln, objected to moving to such a remote outpost.

Isn't somewhere else called that?

In December 1852, a petition was submitted to Congress to recognize yet another new territorial division. Kentucky Representative Richard Stanton objected to the proposed name "Columbia" as it could be confused with the

District of Columbia in the East. Stanton suggested the territory be renamed "Washington" after the first president, George Washington. Congressmen complained that this would confuse it with the city of Washington, DC. However, on March 2, 1853, President Millard Fillmore signed a bill creating a "Territory of Washington." As predicted, the name has caused confusion ever since.

To be or not to be

Oregon, at this time, was mulling over US statehood. In 1854, and twice thereafter, residents of the Oregon Territory rejected the idea of creat-

ing a state. Many wanted to follow the lead of Texas, which had formed the Lone Star Republic. But statehood finally came on the heels of an 1857 US Supreme Court case, Dred Scott v. Sandford. The decision made it illegal for a territorial legislature or the US Congress to prohibit slavery in any Federal territory – only a sovereign state was allowed to do that.

If Oregon were a state, residents reasoned, it would allow them to legislate against slavery. So, when offered the option of Oregon statehood again in 1857, residents voted seven to one for the idea. On February 14, 1859, President James Buchanan laid his quill to the proclamation admitting Oregon as the 33rd state. ❑

LEFT: the California Gold Rush of 1849 had a profound effect on the Oregon Territory.
RIGHT: Oregon becomes the 33rd state, 1859.

SPECIAL SEATTLE NUMBER

THE COAST

ALASKA AND GREATER NORTHWEST

VOL. 18   NO. 3

SEPT. 1909.

LOIS STO CO.

SEATTLE
The METROPOLIS

The Coast Publishing Company
14th and Main St., SEATTLE, U.S.A.

Copyright, 1909, by Honor L. Wilhelm.

PRICE FIFTEEN CENTS

BOOM TIME TO MODERN TIMES

From the wagon train to the World's Fair to the World Wide Web,

the Pacific Northwest has catered to the dreams of pioneers

Oregon, followed closely on its wagon wheels by Washington, attracted new-comers with the promise of a better life. For many this meant farmland, particularly the fertile Willamette Valley. Those who came relied on family and community networks for support, and once settled, tended to concern themselves first with their own subsistence; selling their surplus crops came second. They developed politics that saw virtue in "small freeholders" – family men who owned a limited amount of property – rather than the wealthy, mercantile or working classes. In general, they also distrusted big business – and in particular the railroads.

Newcomers from everywhere

Situated at the confluence of the Columbia and Willamette rivers, and a port for ocean-going vessels, Portland quickly became the leading city of the Northwest. Farm produce from the Willamette Valley, minerals from Idaho, and wheat from eastern Washington's Walla Walla all shipped to market through Portland. San Francisco capitalists quietly discovered the vast forests a little farther north on Puget Sound, and sawmills slowly appeared. At Seattle, Port Gamble and Port Ludlow, the deep waters and forested shorelines offered docks for shipping lumber and wooden products to San Francisco.

After the 1850s, throughout the Pacific Northwest, the urban and industrial economy began to overtake agriculture. Still, so long as water remained the cheapest method of trans-portation, the most important port would dom-inate the Northwest and that was Portland, commanding the Columbia River watershed.

Beginning in the 1880s, the railroads arrived in the region, and threatened Portland's influ-ence. In 1887 the Northern Pacific completed its Cascade Division through the Yakima Valley and

Stampede Pass to Tacoma. James J. Hill's Great Northern Railroad reached Seattle in 1892 and boosterism lured immigrants to northwestern Washington. More railway lines in the 1880s and 1890s brought growth to Vancouver (Canada), and further eroded Portland's leadership. Spo-kane, Washington, emerged as the metropolis for

the "Inland Empire." The arrival of railroads stimulated an enormous population boom throughout the region. In the 1880s, Pacific Northwest population grew by almost half a mil-lion, Washington by 275,000. Governor Miles C. Moore proudly reported an influx of more than 95,000 newcomers between 1887 and 1889 alone, a figure greater than the entire population of the Washington Territory seven years earlier.

Logging and lumbering

The Northwest, densely forested with evergreen trees, was a natural center for logging, but a more powerful draw for many migrants was the quest for gold. Many men, though, saw the

---

LEFT: around the turn of the 20th century, Seattle made a bid for Portland's wealth and popularity.
RIGHT: miners came to Seattle to outfit themselves for the Alaskan Gold Rush in the Klondike.

advantages of a paycheck after a few grueling seasons prospecting in the outback, and the forest industry was there to oblige. By 1884, sawmills around Puget Sound consumed 1 million board feet of wood a day. Rafts of logs from around the Hood Canal and the western shore of Puget Sound floated to mills at Port Gamble and Port Ludlow. Seattle and Tacoma profited and grew.

The first mill in Seattle was Henry Yesler's steam-powered sawmill at the center of an area known as "Skid Road," where a log slide sent

UPSTART CITY

Seattle had always been something of an upstart city. The fact that the first town-site was named "Alki-New York" gives an indication of its aspiration.

timber from the hill to the sawmill at the waterfront. Later, in the 1930s, the name "Skid Row" – meaning a run-down area of destitution – came, both literally and metaphorically, from Skid Road.

Shipping trees to the world

In 1880, 160 million board feet of timber was felled and more than 1 billion board feet in 1890. Reports claimed that only half of the native timber in what is now Washington's Thurston County was left standing by 1890.

Though most of the lumber was carried by sea going vessels, railroads helped the market expand. Oregon offered more favorable rates for freight than Washington, and California imported some 200 million board feet in 1883 and 1884, plus 323 million in 1889. Puget Sound was crowded with vessels shipping to foreign markets, too. Wood was shipped to Australia, Chile, Argentina and China. Single cargoes might be as large as 1 million board feet, and valued as high as $20,000.

All this exporting of timber brought enormous prosperity to the loggers and merchants of Seattle and Portland.

Klondike fever

Seattle has always been something of an upstart city. The fact that the first town-site was named "Alki-New York," meaning "New York by-and-by," (*alki* is Chinook jargon) illustrates the aspiration. Seattle is the Northwest's largest metropolis today, through industriousness and ingenuity, and also good fortune. The city was settled in 1851, and named after the Duwamish chief Sealth, who was befriended by some of the town's earliest pioneers. Residents of Seattle had big dreams for their town, but never quite enough capital to lend them reality.

Suddenly, magic. Gold was discovered in Alaska and the Yukon in Canada. A telegram on July 17, 1897, announced that "the steamship *Portland* has just arrived in Seattle with a ton of gold on board," and the next Gold Rush was on. Hopeful prospectors came in droves from California, Oregon and Colorado. Women too, packed their bags and set off in hopes of a husband or just a pretty penny. The *Portland's* return voyage to Alaska was with a full complement of passengers.

Although the initial finds were on Canadian soil, local towns Vancouver and Victoria were ill-prepared to service the rush. American cities, on the other hand, competed to provide supplies and transportation for would-be miners. Erastus Brainerd was Seattle's publicity man. In magazines all over the world, he advertised Seattle's virtues and its links to Alaska.

Besting its rivals Tacoma, Portland and San Francisco, Seattle became the main loading point for Klondike prospectors or "sourdoughs." Ships of every size crossed Puget Sound to Elliott Bay, where eager men and their supplies waited for a passage north. There were always more men than there were berths to carry them.

In 1898, a government assay office was established in Seattle. In its first four years of business, more than $174 million in gold passed over its scales. The little city on Elliott Bay grew rich on what the sourdoughs spent in its stores and houses of entertainment. By the time the Alaska and Yukon Gold Rushes had dwindled in the early 1900s, Seattle challenged Portland as the great Northwest metropolis.

In the 1880s, over-expansion and economic recession fermented trouble in paradise. In November 1885, sinophobes in Tacoma marched through the rain, rousted Chinese residents from their homes and loaded them onto a train

"escorted" to the city's waterfront, scheduled to be shipped off to San Francisco until a writ of *habeas corpus* stopped the expulsions. But it didn't calm the town. Anti-Chinese groups were formed, and militiamen were called in to keep the peace. In February of 1886, the majority of Seattle's Chinese population, believing that persecution was inevitable, left for California aboard the steamer *George W. Edler*.

Black plight

Oregon, on the other hand, was notorious for its racist behavior toward blacks. Though its citizens passed the 13th Amendment to the US

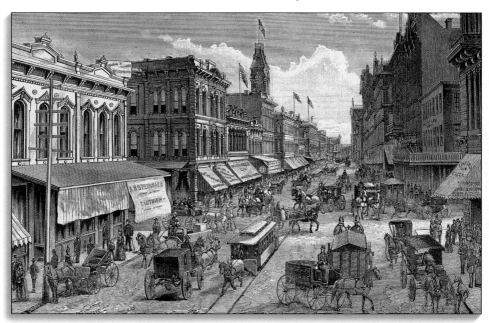

bound for Portland. A year later, Washington passed a law forbidding Chinese from owning property in the state. Both Oregon and Washington pushed for the riddance of the Chinese from their shores. Many had come as construction workers on the railroads, others arrived for the Gold Rushes. In early 1886, men in Seattle knocked on the doors of Chinese homes, told the occupants that their buildings were condemned and suggested they leave town immediately. Three hundred and fifty Chinese were

Constitution to abolish slavery, the 14th Amendment, guaranteeing citizenship to blacks, barely passed the Oregon Legislature. Then the governing body voted to rescind the 14th ratification – twice. The governor at the time didn't even bother to call a legislative session to vote on black suffrage – the 15th Amendment. Oregon didn't manage approval of this amendment until 1959 – 89 years after the US Secretary of State declared it ratified.

The great Seattle fire

Back in 1889, Seattle's development was due another major turning point. On June 6, a handyman named John Beck noticed a pot of glue

LEFT: the Northwest, forested with huge evergreen trees, became a center for logging.
ABOVE: Portland in 1887.

had caught fire in a downtown paint store. He threw a bucket of water on the flame, which mixed with turpentine and wood shavings and caused a fiery explosion. Beck and his boss fled, and the Great Seattle Fire began. That week had been hot and dry, and Seattle, constructed almost entirely of wood, was a tinderbox. The fire spread extremely quickly, the fire department was unprepared, and by that night virtually the entire downtown business district had burned to the ground. Seattle had long suffered from poor planning, so after the fire, downtown merchants replanned and rebuilt the city with bricks and mortar, effectively raising

Centennial Exposition. The fair and its subsequent publicity paid off handsomely for Portland. In a good-housekeeping project for the exposition, the town planted hundreds of beautiful rose bushes along its streets, a move that in time gave rise to its nickname the "City of Roses." Not only did investors realize a 21 percent return, but in the five years following the fair, the population of the Portland area doubled, reaching 270,000 in 1910.

Intercity rivalry

So it was not surprising when in 1909 the rival city of Seattle celebrated its prodigious growth

it by one level. Some of the original structures were kept, and form a part of Seattle's fascinating "Underground" network *(see page 95).*

In 1903 the Olmsted Brothers, sons of the man who landscaped Central Park in New York, were hired by Seattle to lay out a city park system. Parks were a way of mastering nature while at the same time appreciating it. It was around this time, too, that residents of Seattle and Tacoma began making trips to newly established Mount Rainier National Park.

Portlanders were alarmed by the pesky upstart Seattle draining their business. Something had to be done, but what? In 1905, it was decided Portland would host the Lewis & Clark

and recent civic refinements by hosting a World Exposition, the Alaska-Yukon-Pacific Exposition (A-Y-P). This fair, too, meant many things to the city. It announced Seattle's passing of its "frontier" stage and its arrival as a major American city. In the end, the A-Y-P proved as prosperous as the Lewis & Clark Exposition, drawing 3,740,551 visitors over its 138-day schedule and convincing many people from other parts of the country to return and settle here. In 1910, the population of Seattle for the first time exceeded that of Portland – surpassing it by 30,000. These expositions put Portland and Seattle on the map, and the Pacific Northwest became a saleable item.

In 1916, newly prosperous Seattle, assisted by the US Army Corps of Engineers, completed the Seattle Ship Canal. With the help of a system of locks, ocean-going vessels could easily navigate from Puget Sound through Lake Union into Lake Washington. These projects had good economic – but enormous environmental – consequences, and in particular the region's salmon runs were devastated. These were, however, not seen at the time as high priorities.

CITY OF ROSES

In 1905, Portland's Lewis & Clark Centennial Exposition proved to be wildly successful, not only supplying the city with a nickname, but doubling its population.

opportunities and high wages for defense work encouraged people to migrate to the Northwest, where the shortage of workers was so acute that Portland's Kaiser Company ran trains from the East and South for shipyard recruits. The number of manufacturing companies around Portland doubled between 1940 and 1946. Large war machinery plants around Puget Sound – including Boeing Aircraft and the Puget Sound Navy Yard at Bremerton – were starved for help. Lumber companies, mining concerns and agricultural

Depression and war

Economically, politically and culturally, the Pacific Northwest had played catch-up with the rest of the nation. In 1929, this began to change. National crises – the Great Depression, World War II, then the Cold War – transformed the Pacific Northwest dramatically.

First, the Depression. Levels of employment bottomed out in 1933, rose through 1937, then declined again. Even on the eve of World War II, the Northwest economy was mired in depression. Significant numbers of new jobs came from the launching of the Columbia Basin Project, a massive, Federally funded effort to "tame" the Columbia and Snake rivers. There, between 1933 and 1941 armies of men built the mammoth Grand Coulee and Bonneville dams for hydroelectricity, farm irrigation, and to permit inland navigation by ocean-going vessels. The Civilian Conservation Corps also created make-work programs in parks and forests, wildlife protection, public housing, irrigation projects and Olympic National Park in 1938.

Consequently, by the time America joined World War II in 1941, the Pacific Northwest had an infrastructure that enabled it to mobilize for war to an extent that would have been impossible only a decade earlier. Aluminum factories in Spokane and the Portland area, a plutonium plant at Hanford and aircraft manufacturing at Seattle all drew electrical power from the Columbia Basin. The economy of the Pacific Northwest reached new heights. As America geared up for war, increased job

industries frantically produced goods to meet the demand. The population of the entire Northwest leapt again by about 30 percent during the early 1940s.

No land, no aliens

But the outlook wasn't as rosy for the Japanese and Japanese-Americans who made their homes in Oregon and Washington. Constituting the region's largest minority population in 1941, the Japanese met with discrimination in both states. Washington had passed laws in 1921 and 1923 prohibiting the ownership of land by "aliens." Oregon farmers in particular resented the industrious Japanese, whom they

LEFT: paddle steamer on the Columbia River, 1905.
RIGHT: due to its natural and industrial resources, the Northwest survived both World Wars and prospered.

saw as impinging on a sound American industry. After the bombing of Pearl Harbor in 1941, President Franklin D. Roosevelt instructed military commanders nationwide to remove persons of Japanese ancestry from areas that might be considered militarily significant. The Japanese Internment Act, signed by President Roosevelt, imprisoned over 9,000 Japanese-Americans for the duration of World War II. Japanese in the Seattle area were sent to camps in Wyoming and Idaho, while their homes and businesses were confiscated or fell into ruin. corrected

After World War II, the United States remained geared up to a war footing. It became

engaged in an entirely new level of international relations, not for four or five years – the time between Pearl Harbor and Nagasaki – but for practically 50 years, from 1939 until the fall of the Berlin Wall in 1989.

Trees and fish were still important to the area – they had, after all, helped build the two states – but post-war population and military industrial growth were shaping a new profile for Oregon and Washington. The Northwest shed its backwoods image in favor of one more in keeping with the 20th century. Defense contracts, a strong US military and naval presence, the growth of Boeing, now retooling as a commercial aviation operation, the Cold War need for secret

supplies of refined uranium and plutonium for the arms race, all served to bring high prosperity to the region. Washington state in particular prospered. Its employees received higher wages on average as its economy became more technologically oriented with the importance of science, space, weapons research and engineering to Cold-War mobilization.

The ultimate success of Boeing, the aircraft manufacturing giant, depended on more than government contracts and political connections. Using the profits generated by supplying the US Air Force with planes, the company skillfully diversified its output through the 1950s and 1960s so that it produced airliners for commercial customers as well as fighters, bombers and transporters for the military.

World's Fair

Just as Portland's Lewis & Clark Centennial Exposion and Seattle's Alaska-Yukon-Pacific Exposition ushered in the 20th century, so the Space Needle and Seattle's World's Fair of 1962 introduced the Pacific Northwest to itself and the world as a place of "the future." Standing at the base of Seattle's 605-ft (185-meter) Space Needle, and looking up at its white spidery legs and flying saucer-like top immediately conjures the "jet-age" dreams for which the Space Needle is such an obvious symbol. The structure has become an iconic symbol for Seattle, just as the Eiffel Tower is for Paris. Both it and the Pacific Science Center at its base continue to attest to the high-tech, aerospace-oriented thinking that was and continues to be so much a part of the energy of Puget Sound.

The World's Fairera brought dramatic change. Students in the 1960s and early 1970s demonstrated on campuses decrying US involvement in the Vietnam War. At the same time, the Pacific Northwest developed a pride in itself and acquired a certain cachet. The Northwest came to be seen as a clean, enriching and an environmentally conscious area, just as attractive to disillusioned Americans as its earlier enticements were to the wagon-train pioneers, then the gold miners. Northwesterners enjoyed the bright, romantic picture of their land, and promoted the region as exclusive – a home fit for the enlightned few.

Residents loved it when Oregon Governor Tom McCall in the 1970s invited the world to "visit our state of enchantment – but, for heaven's sake, don't stay." Billboards echoed the sentiment, "This is God's country;" they boasted, "and it's ours."

The numbers and ethnicities of those coming to the United States changed after World War II. America's military involvement in Korea and southeast Asia brought increasing numbers, joining residents of Chinese, Japanese and Filipino descent who had already established substantial communities. Both the Civil Rights Movement and resistance to the Vietnam War accelerated changing attitudes of white Americans to people of Asian descent.

A new breed

Asian immigrants during the 1970s, 1980s and 1990s were different from their predecessors. Previous arrivals had mostly been laborers, but now immigrants brought a range of skills and training. In the late 1980s immigrants from India, the Philippines, China and Korea ranked among the nationalities with the most professional and managerial workers. From the 1960s to the 1980s, some Asian Americans came to be viewed as a "model minority." In 1996 the state of Washington elected as governor Gary Locke, the first Asian American outside of Hawaii to hold such an office.

In the late 1950s, 1960s and 1970s, a new environmental movement began to crest. During the 1970s Governor Tom McCall of Oregon gave voice to the new perceptions of the Northwest by suggesting that measurements of "success" in the Northwest might be redefined. "Unlimited and unregulated growth leads inexorably to a lowered quality of life," he said.

Most Northwesterners were not yet prepared to renounce growth altogether, so they spoke instead of "regulating," "managing" or "limiting" it. The first Oregon efforts were mainly to deter migrating Californians. Oregonians discouraged newcomers with jokes about high annual rainfall, the state bird being the mosquito, and put the word out that the state animal was the earth worm. The Governor promised to erect a "Plywood Curtain" and bumper stickers read

> ### ASIAN AMERICANS
>
> Unlike previous generations, Asian immigrants brought a new range of training and skills. In 1996, the state of Washington elected the first Asian American outside of Hawaii as its governor.

"Don't Californicate Oregon." Whatever the underlying humor, growth was questioned more openly than ever before.

Given the Northwest's ecological sensitivities, it was ironic that the 1980s and 1990s brought two well-publicized environmental crises. Both revolved around endangered species of animals: the Northern Spotted Owl and the threatened runs of salmon. Each were held to be indicator species for the health of broader ecosystems, the old-growth forests and

riverine watersheds. Of course, no solutions for these problems found widespread agreement, though the discussions fueled a general movement toward greater environmental awareness.

Conservation

Tom McCall, Oregon's governor from 1967 to 1975, created "greenways" (long narrow parks). He instituted a state department of environmental quality; passed a law requiring minimum deposits on beverage bottles and cans, protected parts of six streams as "wild and scenic" rivers, expanded the state park system and developed a far-reaching land-use planning system. This created urban-growth boundaries

---

LEFT: the 1962 World's Fair portrayed the Northwest as a place for the 21st century.

RIGHT: the growth of Boeing brought regional wealth.

and mandated complex state land-use guidelines. Initially, Washington was more reluctant, but eventually followed a similar path.

High tech and new businesses

The Pacific Northwest today shows relics from the past amid the symbols of the present. In the dust of eastern Oregon are old stagecoach stops and abandoned mining operations. Seattle has Native American totems by the revitalized docks, where tall ships once loaded lumber. An ever-renewing Pacific Northwest is emerging, born through some of the suffering of the past.

The new Northwest strives to meet a future more complex than any of its richly colored past. The industries that traditionally sustained the Northwest – lumber, agriculture and fishing – have fared poorly. On the cusp of the new millennium, commerce turned confidently to aviation and aerospace, biotech, software and high technology.

The super fast-growing marvel of Microsoft attracted thousands of young, bright professionals from all over the world. In its early days, Bill Gates's wonder of the age of technology produced more employee-millionaires than any other company in history. It still keeps its finger on the pulse, or – as some might say – its grip on

the throat, of the future. Gates talks of a network of private satellites spanning the globe to revolutionize telecommunications. The heady high-tech 1990s also brought a boom in silicon chips, attracting yet more talented migrants to serve Intel, Amazon.com and the other local information technology businesses.

There were high-profile protests at the World Trade Organization summit in 1999, and an earthquake in 2001, but the Pacific Northwest hasn't skipped a beat. In fact, these may be simpy measures of the momentum of change. Other Pacific Rim countries, particularly Japan, are now in financial hiatus. Since roughly half the world's population is said to live in the area defined as the Pacific Rim, Seattle and Portland have their sights firmly fixed on these nations as potential trading partners, as they reconfigure their economies once again.

Topical concerns

Northwest issues of the day include earthquake preparation, declines in the salmon harvest, balancing economic and ecological policies, renovating and enlivening neighborhoods, potential electricity and water shortages, the probable decline of the miracle tech industries during the country's post-millennium slowdown, and reconfiguring America's defense capabilities in light of the "War on Terrorism" following the 2001 attack on the Pentagon and New York's World Trade Center.

But because of the Northwesterners' range of innovative talent and creative capabilities, the high levels of educational achievement and the appetite for change, analysts continue to make overwhelmingly optimistic predictions for the region long term.

Portland has completed an impressive new airport terminal, and Seattle has one at SEATAC scheduled to come on stream in 2005. It shouldn't be long before there's another World Expo-style global gathering to celebrate and stimulate yet more triumphant accomplishments. The next waves of innovation will surely bring more pioneers to the dynamic, fascinating and forward-looking Pacific Northwest. ❑

LEFT: 1990s companies like Microsoft and Starbucks attracted the best and the brightest young people.
RIGHT: anticapitalist protests at the 1999 World Trade Organization summit held in Seattle hint at a more thoughtful, less materialistic 21st century.

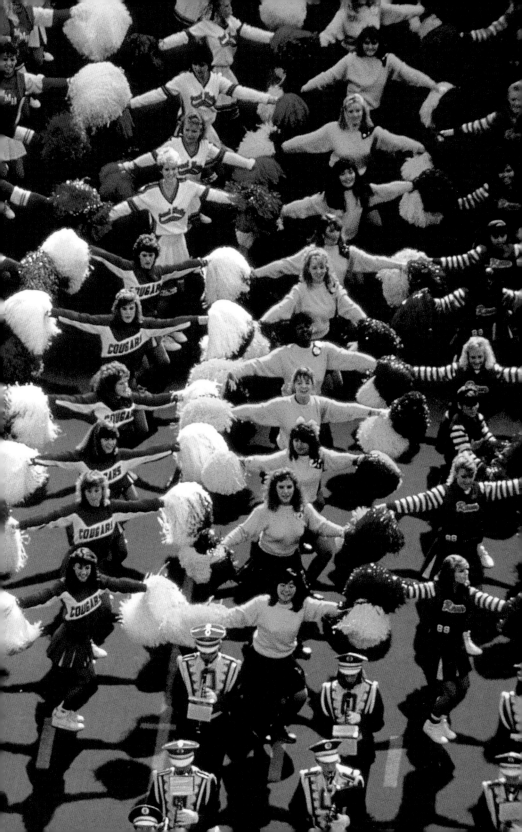

LIFE IN THE NORTHWEST

The Pacific Northwest is made up of singular individuals and maverick movements. No wonder they won't stand in line for service

Northwesterners all agree about one thing: one of the most pressing issues for discussion is the health of the salmon. There the consensus ends. On this, like most issues, they have at least three distinct goals: protecting the fish themselves, in the way that blue whales or giant pandas are protected; maintaining fishery stocks, whose purpose is to allow people to eat fish; and preserving the wild environment in which the fish spawn.

Two hundred years ago, there was no distinction between these goals. Northwest tribes took a heavy, steady but sustainable catch from the salmon runs, in an unspoiled river environment. Today these issues are hotly disputed and of concern to the general population.

The Cascade curtain

That the health of the salmon and the forests are two common preoccupations in Northwestern life may reflect a single shared value: a fierce pride in the land. Everything from cultural institutions to voter habits, from watching television ads to visiting art galleries, illustrates the two dominant variations on this theme. One is a dream of tamed landscapes with irrigated farms and orderly gardens, where nature is manicured and tailored to human specifications. The other is a harking back to the romantic wilderness of free-swimming salmon and untouched stands of tangled old-growth forest – a realm of Native American solitude and grandeur.

Dubbed the "Cascade Curtain," folks east of the Cascade Mountains show an overwhelming preference for the first picture with its promise of work, jobs and money. Along the urban corridor west of the mountains, ambitions start to favor the second view. This outlook is shared by the mass of college-educated voters and reveals an interesting paradox; Seattle and Portland are two of only a handful of

PRECEDING PAGES: University of Washington pom-pom girls; a migration of sandpipers, Grays Harbor.
LEFT: a Hood River apple farmer, Oregon.
RIGHT: dangerous sports are very popular.

urban centers in the world where people flock in order to live closer to nature. Though the wilderness is still clearly visible everywhere, and still untamed throughout most of the region, in the damp cities west of the Cascades a lot of energy is directed at restoring the tangle of maiden-head ferns, Douglas Fir and cedar

trees found in backyards not long ago. Dubbed "dry-siders" and "wet-siders," there are long-standing snobberies among both and the arguments rage on. Each sees the other's view as quite undesirable and wholly unsustainable.

Senator Stephen A. Douglas, for whom Douglas County is named, foresaw the East/West, dry/wet division. When Congress was considering Oregon statehood in the mid-19th century, popular legend has it, he stood before a large map of the proposed state, raised his cane and dragged its foot from the top to the bottom of the Cascade Mountains. "This is your natural boundary!" Douglas thundered. "There is the line marked by nature as the eastern boundary of your state. Oregon should lie wholly west of the Cascade Mountains."

Of course, as the map shows, his advice went unheeded. It is significant, though, that the Northwest remains a land of individuals and maverick movements of many colors. In the late 19th century, more than half a dozen utopian communities sprang up in the area. It is said that, in the mid-1930s, US Postmaster General James A. Farley raised his glass and offered a toast to "the forty-seven states and the

BEST OF BOTH

Seattle and Portland are two of only a few urban centers in the world where people flock in order to live closer to nature. Where else can you ski in the morning and listen to a symphony in the evening?

soning townspeople. Today, pockets of survivalists and militia pepper the backwoods of both states. All continue to predict the collapse of society as we know it, and some have been suspected of giving it a helping hand.

We don't do lineups

Maybe it's a Western thing – a "don't fence me in" thing. Journalists have occasionally detected a peculiarity of Northwestern behavior; visitors usually notice it. Although the politeness of residents is well-

soviet of Washington." Most of these idealistic colonies came and went, their members initially attracted by the concept of sharing goods but discouraged by practical difficulties like insufficient building materials and corrupt leadership.

Oregon's Bhagwan Shree Rajnees was the bearded leader of a group of red-clad disciples who arrived from India in 1981. He famously kept innumerable Rolls Royces, his preferred gift of devotion from acolytes. The Beaver State became their special place of refuge, as they believed the rest of the world was about to lapse into a nuclear holocaust. The Bhagwan was deported in the late 1980s and high-level group members were later convicted of poi-

known, for some mysterious reason they never seem to form tidy line-ups. Instead, patrons waiting for service stand around in clusters, each occupying their own personal space. Each pretends to all the world that they are not really in a line at all.

Periodically, one customer edges up to the counter and the rest shuffle around in a zigzag sort of crabwalk. Whether using a bank automated teller machine or entering a coffee shop, people are scattered around the concourses. Unless there are specific directions such as "take a number" or "line-up here," outsiders need to observe carefully to discern who is waiting purposefully and who is just hanging out. Like feline predators hiding in tall grass, people surreptitiously wait and will pounce mercilessly on those who trespass their invisibly defined turf. There are many theories about why Northwesterners won't line up. The prevailing view is that it confirms the popular self-image of independence.

The mind business

From this same wellspring of individuality, and a prevailing concern for the natural habitat, over the past two decades the

> **INFORMALITY PREVAILS**
>
> The necktie is a rare adornment. To attract bright, young workers, many communities have invested in bike lanes and trails. Who wants to wear a necktie bicycling to work in the rain?

trucks and freighters. Raw materials don't have to be mined or felled, which means less pollution, less consumption of fossil fuels and other exhaustable resources and, so far at least, vastly greater profits for all concerned.

Businesses compete fiercely for talented workers as well as markets, and attractive locations give employers here a leg up. Quality living environments attract the brightest employees, and each year thousands of eager new college graduates roll into the region, looking for, and

Northwest has set a pace for environmental conservation. The Northwest has also been something of a beacon in the new businesses of the mind, rather than of matter – the production of intellectual property instead of solid objects.

The economic benefits are clear, but some argue that there may be an ecological bonus, too. Shipping bits and bytes about the globe can often be achieved using only the electricity needed for a phone line – without the use of

LEFT: the traditional: Natives in a canoe race.
ABOVE: the brash and the beautiful: Seattle's Monorail passes through part of architect Frank Gehry's Experience Music Project building.

mostly finding, employment. Each is eager to make a place for themselves in the great Northwest. When critical mass is reached, pools of skilled labor attract businesses. Employers follow good workers as often as workers follow good jobs.

Silicon Forest

The so-called Silicon Forest companies – Intel in Oregon; Microsoft, Amazon and the long-standing Boeing in Washington – are, in Northwest lingo the "spawners," of related research and development, innovations and technologies to service them. Synergies like these have significantly enhanced the wealth of the area.

Retirement and investment income are large sources of new money. House prices over the past decades have soared, but by picking and choosing, retirees have maximized their investments. Many predicted that a series of bombshell court rulings and legislative actions ratcheting down logging, fishing and mining would cripple the rural population. In fact for a decade or so, small-town growth has actually begun to outpace urban growth. Retirement, recreation, conservation, restoration, tourism and high-tech offer Northwesterners a whole range of ways to get off the stress-inducing boom-bust rollercoaster of urban price spiralling.

Don't Californicate

Small towns are growing, and some concerns follow. "It's not the end of the world, of course," says Dave, a recent retiree to Bend, Oregon, "but overcrowding is our greatest fear." Traffic? No. He's talking about lines at the nearby ski lifts. Today's retirees are often on the go, looking for small towns with good transportation options and great medical facilities, as well as keeping a keen eye on home prices, taxes and cost-of-living indexes. People seem to be searching for the elusive "quality of life" thing. And they find it here.

For the past quarter of a century, the Northwest and its actions have been followed in fits and starts by the rest of the United States. The region has made concerted efforts at revitalizing historic districts in numerous cities and towns, plus invested in inner city and highway beautification programs that have pumped life into the region. The standoff over fish, dams and forests is simply a reflection of the tensions generated by the region's rapid growth and spectacular wealth. Seattle and Portland continue to think of themselves as unspoiled, close to nature, less materialistic and overbuilt than southern California – a local synonym for hell.

One can see the basis for all these views. The natural setting is spectacular and people are always heading out to go kayaking, skiing, camping or mountain climbing. In the Northwest overall, leisure travel and the recreation businesses rival the resource industries in jobs and sales. No wonder informality prevails.

The necktie is a rare adornment. To boost competitiveness, many communities have invested in impressive networks of bike lanes and trails designed to reduce their dependence on the automobile. Who wants to wear a necktie bicycling to work in the rain? Parks, marinas, bicycle trails and lakefront swimming zones are abundant, well maintained and accessible. Poor people in New York might open a fire hydrant to cool down; poor people in Seattle are never more than a stone's throw from a pleasant beach. If the climate were not quite so rainy, everyone might want to live here.

Limitless abundance

While the Endangered Species Act seems to concern itself only with protecting salmon, for most people in the region the ideal is to have their fish and eat them, too. Overall, an important part of the region's self-esteem is linked, not just with eating salmon, but almost as much with the idea that they're swimming fulsomely in every lake and stream just waiting to be eaten. It is truly a land based on an historical view of limitless abundance. Some fear this may eventually be lost. Many are determined to preserve it. In the meantime, for visitors, the Pacific Northwest continues to be a fascinating place to explore – with or without a fishing rod.   ❏

LEFT: Asian people make up a large percentage of the Northwest's recent population.
RIGHT: windsurfing, sailing, jogging, hiking – any pursuit will do as long as it's outdoors.

NORTHWEST NATIVES

The cultures of 35 bands and tribes live on in the beat of a powwow drum,
the fire of a salmon feast, and the beliefs and visions of its people

From the misty rainforests of the Olympic Peninsula to the snowcapped peaks of the Cascade Range, from the frigid, raging waters of the Columbia River to the placid, rippling surface of Flathead Lake, the native Northwest is a remarkable region of vast environmental and cultural diversity. Before the arrival of white people, the Northwest coast was one of the most densely populated and culturally rich areas in the American West. The bounty of natural resources supported a great blossoming of cultures, languages and material wealth among the Northwest tribes of Puget Sound and the Oregon coast.

These included the Makah, Duwamish, Quileute, Suquamish, Chinookians, Tillamook, Alseans, Siuslawans, Athapaskans and other nations northward along the Canadian coast. To the south were the tribes of the Columbia Plateau, who supported themselves on the frenzied salmon runs of the Columbia River, as well as on an abundance of game and wild foods.

To the east, the Okanogan, Yakima, Sanpoil, Wenachi, Colville, Spokane, Kutenais, Umatilla, Cayuse, Klickitat, Tenino, Kalapuya, Klamath, Modoc and Nez Perces peoples ranged across the valleys, mountains and rugged canyon lands of inland Washington, Oregon, Idaho and western Montana. Among the first native people in the West to learn the art of horsemanship, they occasionally rode onto the plains to hunt buffalo, adopting many of the customs and accoutrements of Plains Indian life.

Today, the cultures of the native Northwest live on in the beat of the powwow drum, the smoldering fires of the salmon feast, the hands of artists and craftsmen, and the beliefs and visions of the people. For all their high-tech gloss, Washington and Oregon are still lands of luxuriant natural beauty, rich with the traditions and rhythms of the Native American life.

LEFT: a powwow in Spokane, Washington, home of the Confederated Tribes of the Colville Indian Reservation. **RIGHT:** tribes and individuals in Oregon own around 2,800 businesses; this is a Northwest trend.

Tribes of Puget Sound

In 1854, on the watery frontier of Puget Sound, a group of Indian tribes from Washington Territory gathered with US military officers to sign the Treaty of Medicine Creek. Whites were settling the region and wanted more land. The tide of change was flowing, and one great leader,

recognized by all as a peacekeeper, uttered these words in the Duwamish tongue: "Every part of this earth is sacred to my people. Every shining pine needle, every sandy shore, every mist in the dark woods, every clearing and humming insect is holy in the memory of my people. The sap which courses through the trees carries the memories of the red man."

Chief Sealth, (aka Seattle) for whom the city of Seattle is named, watched as the Indian world succumbed to white settlement. The way of life of his tribe and many others was forever altered, but not extinguished. Over the past 150 years, many tribes in the Puget Sound area have survived the changes, evolving and yet preserving their heritage. Like the environment in which they developed, the cultures of the Northwest coast were rich and diverse. Like the frenzy of a salmon run, they were given to explosive expressions of material wealth. Like the lush growth of Pacific forests, language, beliefs and artistic vision blossomed.

Before white people came, Indians lived on a bounty of roots, berries, seeds, game and, most importantly, salmon. They wove their clothes and baskets from grasses and made houses, tools

STOMMISH FESTIVAL

The best opportunity to meet the Lummi is at the Stommish Festival in early summer at Gooseberry Point. Visitors can watch canoe races and buy coastal Indian art.

and canoes from cedar trees. They shared their fortune at celebrations called *potlatches*, where members of different tribes gathered to celebrate a marriage, a good hunt, a reburial, or the first salmon run of the season. The guests feasted, exchanged gifts and played stick games. The hosts were wealthy families who competed with each other in gift-giving; the more gifts given, the greater the honor.

The spiritual life of the Northwest natives was richly connected with the natural world. Every living thing was believed to have a spirit, and each person had a song to summon the spirit's help. There were ceremonies throughout the year, many to honor the spirits of the animals and fish that provided food. These ceremonies were conducted before hunting, fishing or whaling to ask the animal spirits to be generous, and again afterward, to give thanks.

Today, there is new dialogue and these practices are being revived. Questions have been asked about teaching Native American religion in schools, and tribes can stop major development in an area by declaring that the surrounding land was sacred to them.

Native Americans inhabit the modern world. Although much of their heritage is preserved, they no longer live in longhouses, paddle canoes or wear clothes of woven reeds. What travelers see now is a mixture of old and new. On the dark waters of the Hood Canal, a Skokomish family fishes for salmon in a small powerboat. Casinos run by Native tribes have sprung up and brought a new prosperity. New rights for harvesting timber and benefiting from the fruits of the land have brought prosperity to places where there was previously no more than a tumbledown house with an abandoned car out front. Tribal bureaucrats continue to proliferate, taking care of each day's business. There are court settlements to deal with, and public relations campaigns to monitor.

Participate in a legacy

For an in-depth look at the story of Native Americans, the Burke Museum at the University of Washington and the Daybreak Star Art Gallery are good starting points. If time allows, catch a boat on Seattle's Pier 56 across the harbor to Tillicum Village on Blake Island, where visitors are treated to traditional Northwest dancing, storytelling, wood-carving demonstrations and a salmon feast cooked over an open fire.

At the northwesternmost tip of the continental US in the Olympic Peninsula, lies the wild, lush Makah Reservation. Controversial in recent years for resuming whale hunting, the Makah have a Cultural and Research Center for regional native history. The Lummi are the farthest north of the Puget Sound tribes. Their 13,500-acre (5,500-hectare) reservation is on the shores of Lummi Bay and Puget Sound, where they have fished for centuries.

Traditionally, they used weirs, reef nets and stakes, sophisticated tools that have been adopted by non-Indian fishermen. The best opportunity to meet the Lummi is at the Stommish Festival in early summer at Gooseberry Point. Visitors can watch canoe races, sample smoked salmon and buy coastal Indian art.

Colville and Yakima Nations

One of the largest reservations in the Pacific Northwest, the Colville Indian Reservation is located in north-central Washington, bounded on the east and south by the Columbia River and on the west by the Okanogan River. Within the boundaries of this 1.4-million-acre (560,000-hectare) reservation, lush grasslands sweep to

autonomous ethnic and political units during aboriginal times, except for the Nez Perce and Palouse, who occupied the central area of the Columbia Plateau.

The Nez Perces were among the first Indians in the Northwest to make friendly contact with whites. The Lewis and Clark Expedition spent several weeks with the Nez Perces and its men and horses were treated well. The Nez Perces often boasted that in 70 years, they had never killed a white man. Their friendship was a thin shield against the onslaught of white prospectors. When gold was discovered in Chief Joseph's Wallowa Mountains in the

the edge of dense coniferous forests, while lakes and rushing rivers sparkle against the backdrop of jagged gorges and mountainsides.

This is inland Washington's Indian Country, marked by petroglyphs, native myths and a rich and colorful history. Eleven bands make up the Confederated Tribes of the Colville Indian Reservation. These include the Wenatchee, Moses/Columbia, Okanogan, Entiat/Chelan, Methow, Palouse, Nez Perce, Nespelem, Colville, Sanpoil and Lake bands. All were

LEFT: Chief Seattle (Sealth) of the Duwamish tribe.
ABOVE: a 1910 postcard with the caption "Return of the Whale Hunters: Indians of Puget Sound."

1870s, the cry went out for the removal of the tribe *(see page 63)*. Today, things have changed. As progressive business people, the Confederated Tribes of Colville have invested in tribally owned tourist ventures. One of the most impressive is Roosevelt Recreational Enterprises, operating luxury houseboat rentals on Lake Roosevelt in the heart of Coulee Dam National Recreation Area.

Omak Stampede

Their week-long celebrations attract drum groups from as far away as the Dakotas and Montana. Small community rodeos are held in the area all summer long, including the Omak

Stampede rodeo and Indian encampment. The Omak Stampede is famous for its Suicide Race, in which young riders guide their mounts down an impossibly steep hill, rush headlong into the treacherous currents of the Okanogan River, swim across, and then dash into the rodeo arena *(see page 160)*.

Changing with prosperity

Indian tribes and individual Indians across the country are now poised to share in the benefits of the American economic system. In Oregon, native groups and individuals own around 2,800 businesses and the trend is mirrored

across the Northwest. In many cases, this is due to direct or indirect benefits from casino revenues – these are infusing money into reservation economies and enabling tribal members to invest in business opportunities. Participation in the American economic system requires access to capital, usually in the form of credit, as well as a likely source of repayment for that credit.

Many tribes and tribal members – especially those located in rural areas – now look to local banks for this capital. And while banks are providing the debt capital, bankers are also serving as a resource for tribal communities to take full advantage of the opportunities now open. The structure of the economies, the effects of gam-

ing on economic development, and the emerging private sector in Indian Country is having a profound effect on Native American welfare.

There have been favorable court rulings, the legalization of gaming and a new sense of determination. The Affiliated Tribes of Northwest Indians is dedicated to promoting tribal self-determination and sovereignty. Each tribe continues to hold annual gatherings. Some are called "powwows" and some are called "celebrations." A *potlatch* is by invitation only, but the public is welcome at powwows.

Visitors must research the exact dates and times, which vary from year to year. Don't hesitate to ask if you're not sure what to wear, how to act, what to bring, or if a donation is required. Each tribe also holds community events. If you are planning to be on or near a reservation, call ahead and ask whether any events are scheduled that will be open to the public. Colleges and universities in major Northwest cities often have urban Indian organizations that sponsor powwows and events.

Visiting the Yakima Nations

The Yakima people come from south-central Washington. The place to begin a visit to their reservation is at the Yakima Nation Cultural Center near the tribal headquarters in the town of Toppenish. In addition to a library, theater and restaurant, the complex houses the Yakima Nation Museum, with exhibits on the region's ecology and native cultures.

There are full-size models of a willow earth lodge, *tule* (reed) tepee and sweat house, and special exhibits that feature the work of native artists. The gift shop has a good selection of beadwork, baskets and silver jewelry, all by Yakima or other native artists. Inquire at the Cultural Center about the Toppenish Powwow and Yakima Nation Summer Encampment, the biggest social gatherings of the year.

Both of these events are held over the Fourth of July weekend and feature intertribal dancing, crafts, food and hand games. The Yakima Powwow, in September, is also an important event on the national powwow scene. Here, in the dust and boiling heat, is the most expressive part of Native American life, a true melding of the old and the new. ❏

LEFT: a modern canoe racer from the Lummi, the farthest north of the Puget Sound tribes.

Chief Joseph and the Nez Perce

I n 1871, the ailing Tuekakas counseled his son Chief Joseph: "When I am gone, think of your country. You are the chief of these people. They look to you to guide them. A few more years and the whites will be all around you. They have eyes on this land."

Twice before, government men had tried to relocate the Nez Perce, and twice Tuekakas had successfuly resisted. The Nez Perces had long ranged over the grasslands, canyons and high-country forests west of the Bitterroot Mountains. They had welcomed Lewis & Clark and befriended the white settlers, but friendship was not enough. Americans wanted their land. After Tuekakas' death, government men came again to command the band to a reservation. "If ever we owned the land," Joseph explained, "we own it still, for we have never sold it."

The young chief's logic fell on deaf ears. The government delivered an ultimatum: leave in 30 days or be driven out by force. Warriors cried for blood, but Joseph knew the odds and decided the tribe would not fight. "Better to live at peace," he said, "than to begin a war and lie dead."

Within 30 days, Joseph's people began a grueling journey, losing much of their livestock to raging rivers and predatory whites. Then, one night, a group of hot-headed braves slipped out of camp and murdered 11 whites. "I would have given my own life if I could have undone the killing of the white men," Joseph said later, but before reparations could be made, soldiers were upon them.

Over the next four months Joseph led the band of 650 people over 1,300 miles (2,000 km) of rugged country, evading then engaging troops far superior in number and firepower. In the group were chiefs Toohoolhoolzote, Looking Glass and Ollokot. This was one of the most heroic and strategic retreats ever fought by Indian warriors.

They made for refuge in Canada, possibly joining Sitting Bull's band. But 30 miles (50 km) from the border, they were halted. With his camp bogged down by snow and surrounded, Joseph gave up his rifle. His speech to the soldiers at the Bear Paws is well known in American history: "I am tired of fighting. Our chiefs are killed. Looking Glass is

dead. Toohoolhoolzote is dead. The old men are all dead. It is the young men who say yes and no. He who led the young men (Ollokot) is dead. It is cold and we have no blankets. The little children are freezing to death. My people, some of them, have run away to the hills, and have no blankets, no food; no one knows where they are, perhaps freezing to death. I want to have time to look for my children and see how many I can find. Maybe I shall find them among the dead. Hear me, my chiefs. I am tired. My heart is sick and sad. From where the sun now stands, I will fight no more forever."

Despite promises that were made, Joseph and his people were sent to a punitive internment camp

in Kansas, where nearly 100 died. After exile and a deadly bout of malaria, a few survivors were allowed to return to a reservation in Lapwai, Idaho. But not Joseph. Despite pleas to join his people, Joseph was exiled to the Colville Reservation in Washington, where he died in 1904.

Recalling the Nez Perce war, a military man expressed the opinion of many: "I think that, in his long career, Joseph cannot accuse the Government of the US of one single act of justice."

Today the town of Joseph, Oregon and a mountain peak in the Wallowa Mountains retain his name. Of the Wallowa Valley, he said "I buried my father in that beautiful valley of the winding waters. I love that land more than all the rest of the world." ❏

RIGHT: a town and a mountain peak in Oregon are named for Joseph, the honorable Nez Perce chief.

A TALE OF TWO CITIES

Breathtaking scenery, clean air, good food, low taxes –
can Portland and Seattle really have it all?

Portland and Seattle have their histories, and probably their futures, in pioneering. It started with the pioneers of the Oregon Trail, who had to displace the imperial ambitions of the Hudson's Bay Trading Company in order to establish their settlements. It continues to this day, with the cities home to some of the leading trailblazers in software, information technology and biotechnology. Portland and Seattle are leading-edge towns, but with a relaxed and friendly nature, even among the considerable population of nerds.

Land of larger chance

The railroad companies worked hard in the late 1800s to promote the Pacific Northwest. At one time the Northern Pacific Railroad employed almost 1,000 agents in Europe extolling the joys of farming in the West. A promotion booklet by the Oregon, Washington Railway and Navigation Co. raved about "this place where pleasures abound." Perhaps they were telling it like it was, because Collier Cobb, who claimed to be one of the nation's foremost economists, wrote, "Nature must have ordained that Puget Sound should be the trade center of the Pacific." The turn of the 20th century saw brochures with titles like "Seattle: Seaport of Success." One flyer was headed "The State of Washington Calls You to the Land of Larger Chance Where Life Is Still in the Making, First in Opportunity."

In 1928, the *Seattle Star* insisted that "population is still the big need of Seattle and the Pacific Northwest," although later that year the Chamber of Commerce was able to claim that its boosterism was paying off and that the past seven years had seen an increase in cars from California from 8,000 to 50,000. Visitors to Mount Rainier National Park had increased by almost 400 percent, to 219,000 a year.

LEFT: Portland and Mount Hood seen from the International Rose Test Garden.
RIGHT: this rocket is one of the symbols of Seattle's funky neighborhood, Fremont.

What a difference in attitude today when a popular bumper sticker reads "Have a Good Trip – Back to California." British born, Northwest-based writer Jonathan Raban says locals choose to believe that most of the newcomers are Californians "who bring with them escalating real estate prices and demands for first-class

food and deferential service." Anti-California jokes, Raban wrote in *Hunting Mister Heartbreak: A Discovery of America*, allowed Seatleites and Portlanders to vent their disquiet and anger at the effects of mass immigration without being tagged as racist. "You could happily jeer at a Californian in a way that you would not dream of jeering at a black or an Asian." This being America, of course, soon to spring up was a group called UCLA – United Californians Looking for Acceptance.

The influx has been the Northwest norm, usually fueled by a major breakthrough in transportation. In September 1870, *Harper's Weekly* ran a story extolling Seattle as the

"Mediterranean of the Pacific" and the future "Queen City." Within a few years Seattle's population exceeded 43,000, inflated by rumors that the city would be the terminus for the transcontinental railroad. Tacoma became the western terminus of Henry Villard's Northern Pacific Railroad in 1883, but a decade later James R. Hill, a one-eyed Canadian visionary, brought to town his Great Northern Line.

There is a port in Portland

Portland's current standing as one of the world's busiest ports dates to 1891, when the Oregon Legislature funded the dredging of a

shipping channel extending from the city approximately 70 miles (115 km) to the Pacific Ocean. Today, the port owns and operates five marine terminals, seven business parks and the Portland Ship Yard. Much of the outbound tonnage, including lumber, wheat, livestock and wool, goes to Asia. All those Japanese cars make Japan the port's top import trade partner, followed by Korea, China and Australia. The total value of waterborne trade through the port is more than $9 billion annually. All told, the port's marine-related operations and activities employ more than 60,000 workers.

A logging livelihood spawned Portland, but the "Silicon Forest" has sprouted high-tech and

information technology endeavors. Leading firms, including Intel, Tektronix, Hewlett Packard, Wacker Siltronic and Fujitsu, host large operations in the area. In all, Portland is home to more than 1,200 high-tech companies, and, according to recent figures, electronics accounted for more than 30 percent of all manufacturing-related jobs in the region. Economists were taken by surprise when the growth in these sectors more than made up for the broad-based losses in shipping due to the "Asian downturn" of the late 1990s.

The three leading Portland industries are now high technology, forest products and agriculture. Shipbuilding, chemicals and metallurgy were the first major industries in the city and continue to hold sway, while Portland's other businesses include food processing, meat packing and textile manufacturing. The city is a canning center and packages huge quantities of fruits and vegetables from the Willamette Valley, plus fish from the nearby rivers.

Portland is also home to the headquarters of Nike, the sportswear giant, employing about 5,000 of the company's employees at the "Nike World Campus." Portland also provides the home base of the leading large-truck manufacturer, the Freightliner Corporation, which employs about 4,000 workers. The single mightiest Portland employer is retail shopping mall empire Fred Meyer Stores, where 13,600 people work in retail merchandising.

High tech, high stakes

Washington's two biggest companies remain dominant in their fields. Although the corporate headquarters has relocated to Chicago, Boeing's manufacturing remains here, and a huge aircraft contract with China will keep it busy in the 21st century. Microsoft, the $4.5 billion software giant on a 265-acre (107-hectare) campus in Redmond, has drawn thousands of whizz kids to the area and in its early day created more instant millionaire-employees than any other US company.

The *Washington Post* bought 80 percent of Mammoth Micro Productions, and Meredith Corp (*Better Homes & Gardens*) bought into Multicom Publishing, which is another CD-ROM maker. Microsoft co-founder Paul Allen's Starwave Corporation produces CD-ROMs in collaboration with big names like Clint Eastwood and Peter Gabriel. Sega chose Seattle to host the first of its 150 Interactive Entertainment Centers, featuring virtual reality attractions, motion simulators and high-tech gimmickry.

"Seattle is becoming a hotbed of people who came from film, TV, games, computers and music," says Lucie Fjeldstad, who chairs Seattle film production company Shadowcatcher. Seattle's innovative art scene includes Northwest CyberArtists, whose members combine experimental music, art, dance and technology and avant garde shows, such as a water fountain controlled by music or data gloves that point to a spot to make sound come from it.

million people. The Seattle-area population grew 38 percent between 1970 and 1990, but developed land increased by 87 percent, and the miles each household drives have risen more than three times faster than the population.

Lost land and rural rebound

Washington and Oregon lose 75,000 acres (33,000 hectares) of commercial land each year to development, says Dietrich. This is land permanently lost, as the clear cuts of timber companies are not replaced. At the turn of the 20th century, when paved highways were nonexistent, Seattle had just 50,000 people and rivers

"These things wouldn't happen in the Bay Area or Los Angeles because there's no economic incentive to them," says Marc Lucas, founder of Lone Wolf and a writer of software used in professional audio equipment. "The Northwest has a better ethic for the creation of new media."

The Pulitzer prize-winning author William Dietrich writes about the environment for the *Seattle Times*, and he pulls together some interesting statistics. The Census Bureau forecast that by 2020 Washington would gain 2.7

were still undammed. People in Snohomish County noted that the statistics were predicting the adjoining areas would absorb most of the upcoming influx. In response, the county voted to create "urban growth" areas to accommodate the increased population. This latest example of what is known as "rural rebound" didn't sit well with local environmentalists.

"It's coming down to a battle between the ruralness of Snohomish County and giving in to the forces of sprawl driven by greed," retorted Ellen Gray of the local Audubon Society. The ripple effects of re-zoning 8,000 acres (3,200 hectares) of agricultural land puts pressure on beleaguered farmers to sell out to developers,

LEFT: Portland's Pioneer Courthouse Square.
ABOVE: the Seattle Aquarium.

encroaches on Native American lands and fishing rights, and makes flooding more likely by altering a watershed that absorbs heavy rains.

Two things certain; one is taxes

Seattle is not a cheap city to visit by American standards. Retail sales tax is added to most retail sales and some services at 8.8 percent. An additional 0.5 percent is applied to restaurant food and beverage purchases.

Taxes for residents are much friendlier. King County offers an attractive tax structure for many who live here. Washington State collects no personal income tax, no corporate income

tax, no unitary tax, no inventory tax, no tax on interest, dividends or capital gains, no sales or user tax on machinery and plants. However, almost all property in King County, real and personal, is subject to assessment and taxation. The rates are considered reasonable.

Portland is known for its favorable business-taxation climate, noted by the absence of sales tax, and business inventory and occupation taxes. In addition, the city has famously low travel taxes. The 9 percent total, the lowest among most major US cities, includes state taxes, local occupancy taxes and any other surtaxes business travelers or tourists might be charged. Oregon's constitutionally dedicated

State Highway Fund derives most of its revenue from three major highway user taxes: vehicle registration fees, motor vehicle fuel taxes (primarily the gasoline tax), and motor carrier fees (the weight-mile tax). The real residential trick is to live in Vancouver, Washington. It's across the river from Portland, Oregon. Portland has no sales tax. Live in Washington with no personal income tax and shop in Oregon (no sales tax). Perfection.

What's in a name?

Portland has many nicknames, the best known of which is "The City of Roses." Above the city, visitors can wander through fragrant paths of rose bushes at the International Rose Test Garden, where more than 400 varieties have been cultivated continuously since 1917. Other variations and names include "Rose City," "Puddletown," and "Stumptown," but it is also nicknamed "Bridgetown" for the bridges that unite east and west Portland. In keeping with its kindly nature, occasionally the city closes the downtown bridges to motor traffic and gives free rein to bikers, hikers and runners.

Portland's current name came from a coin toss in 1845. Two men, Asa Lovejoy and William Overton, filed a land claim for an area known as "The Clearing." Overton sold his shares to Francis Pettygrove and the two of them couldn't agree on a name. To resolve the deadlock, they flipped a coin – now known as the Portland Penny. Lovejoy, who was from Massachusetts, picked Boston. But Pettygrove won, and he chose Portland, the city in his native state of Maine.

David Swinson Maynard, popularly known as "Doc" Maynard, gave Seattle its name in the 1840s. Maynard had made a friend in Olympia, a *tyee* (chief) of the tribe living near the mouth of the nearby Duwamish River, Chief Sealth (pronounced *see-alth* and sometimes *see-atl*). Maynard, with a sense of public relations, suggested the settlers abandon the name "Duwamps" and adopt the anglicized "Seattle" in homage to his friend.

Be nice or else

Portland and Seattle vie, politely, of course, for the reputation of the most courteous city. Seattle's claim was strong, but took a beating during the ugly scenes at the 1999 World Trade Organization summit. In Seattle, drivers give way to walkers at crossroads, while in Portland deciding who proceeds at a four-way stop can result in a delay of handwaving and "you-go-first" gestures as each driver yields to all others.

One distinction between the two cities is traffic. Many Portland commuters walk, jog or cycle to work, or take advantage of the Free Fare Zone for bus travel. Outside of the immediate downtown area, Seattle is notorious for its perpetual gridlock. The traffic is so bad that the famed Seattle manners and consideration nosedived in August of 2001, when a group of weary commuters crossing a busy canal bridge encouraged a suicidal woman to "get it over

wonderful settings. Mount Rainier for Seattle and Mount Hood for Portland, give spectacular backdrops and, happily for the terminally fashionble, auspicious feng-shui. The cities share reputations for damp climates, but residents are undeterred; everybody enjoys outdoor sports anyway. After feasting on Dungeness crab cakes, Northwest style is to start working it off.

Inventive cuisine

Outdoor dining remains popular, since both Seattle and Portland offer excellent seafood, fruit and vegetables in an inventive cuisine.

with,": "just do it" and "jump." Despite three hours persistance by paramedics who tried to talk her down, she followed the advice of the impatient motorists. Increasing road congestion was cited as the cause.

Work it off

Both cities are still regularly placed near the top of "Most Livable Towns in the US" lists, helped by beautiful networks of large, contiguous parks, the great outdoor life and the

---

LEFT: outside one of Portland's many microbreweries.
ABOVE: state-of-the art Safeco Field, home of Seattle's baseball team, the Mariners.

Chefs draw on inspiration from the diverse cultural mixes of the Northwest. There are, among many others, Chinese, Japanese, Korean, Cambodian, Italian, German, Irish and English influences in almost every area of city society, and they all go into the pot to inform the characteristic "Northwestern Cuisine." Portland claims to have the largest number of restaurants per capita in the US. "Gourmet" coffee was popularized and is still popular here; likewise the trend of microbreweries. A fun thing to do in either city is to sit down with a coffee or a microbrew, and mull over which trend will be leading the next wave of pioneers to the forward-looking Northwest. ❏

FOOD AND DRINK

Freshly caught salmon chargrilled with herbs from the chef's own garden,
washed down by a local Pinot Noir. Sounds good? Read on

Northwest cuisine is delightful to experience and a pleasure to describe. The starting point is "fresh" – seasonal local produce is the best there is. Chefs develop strong relationships with local farmers and suppliers, while their state-of-the-art kitchens invariably compost food scraps.

Whether enjoying fresh mint tea and exquisite shortcake with fresh strawberries from the flatlands of the Skagit Valley, or treating yourself to a five-hour, nine-course extravaganza replete with herbs from the restaurant garden, the food of the Northwest brings on contented post prandial sighs.

Cuisine themes

On top of the fruit and vegetables comes an overlay of Asian influences – Pan Asian fusion cuisine combining flavors from Japanese to Indonesian. The final ingredient to compete the emerging tradition is, of course, seafood. Superfoodies will already know that the best shellfish is available toward the month of October.

And once these ingredients are put together, what does it all amount to? "Grilled Coho Salmon with Roasted Hazelnut Butter" is a classic example of a Northwest-style dish. Try it one hungry night and see.

Some signature ingredients are proudly prominent in dishes because they are fine examples of the region's produce. These include Oregon pears, fresh or smoked salmon, stone fruits, fresh herbs, Walla Walla onions, oysters, prawns (large shrimps) and Dungeness crab, wild mushrooms, several types of berries, mussels, clams and scallops, fish from local waters (and some from Alaska), local lentils, split peas and chickpeas, Northwest hazelnuts, Tillamook cheeses and ice creams.

It's easy to stay local here. Dinner could start, for instance, with a beer from a local microbrewery, move on to freshly caught salmon

char-grilled with herbs accompanied by a Washington or Oregon Pinot Noir, and finish with a cheesecake dessert topped with local blackberries. All this and a waterside view of Puget Sound, or a snowpeaked Mount Hood. Other than not having to pay the bill afterward, what more could anyone ask for?

Apples and pears galore

Washington apples, it is claimed are "The Best Apples on Earth" Growing extensively east of the Cascades and shipped throughout the United States and Canada, favorite varieties include Jonagold, Fuji, Braeburn Cameo and the famous Pink Lady.

Washington is the best known brand name for apples in the United States. A typical year's apple crop destined for the fresh market is estimated at 77 million boxes. As for pears, of over 3,000 known pear varieties in the world, only a few are grown for commercial production. In the USA these are almost all produced in Oregon and Washington, where growing conditions

LEFT: a chili day at Pike Place Market, Seattle.
RIGHT: Northwest cuisine themes usually include some type of fish.

are ideal. The Hood River and the Medford area in Oregon are particularly notable patches, and pears from these specific regions are worth seeking out.

Many berries

Strawberries, blueberries, gooseberries, blackberries and raspberries are widely available in season. Additionally, there are special local varieties. Marionberries are a cross between the Pacific Coast wild blackberry, loganberry and the raspberry; these are the berry of choice

when it comes to local pies. Boysenberries have a blackberry shape with a raspberry flavor and are much sought-after. Huckleberries – a tart-tasting blueberry – are more common here than in other parts of the States. Some favor the blonde version of the common raspberry – known, appropriately, as a golden raspberry.

There are extensive bog fields of cranberries in western Washington, making Thanksgiving extra special. The exquisite Rainier cherry is an outstanding regional specialty, a creamy yellow-red variety of blushing flavor. It is only produced here because of the local volcanic soils. Rainier cherries are the sweetest and most pampered of cherries, as delicate as they are delicious.

The story of the Walla Walla Onion (also known simply as a "sweet" onion) began nearly a century ago on the island of Corsica, off the coast of Italy. There a French soldier, Pierre Pieri, found a sweet onion seed and brought it to eastern Washington state.

At the time, Pieri's neighbors were Italian immigrant gardeners. Impressed by the onions, they and Pieri harvested seeds and through careful selection over generations, they bred a unique variety. Walla Walla Sweets are so succulent they can be eaten like an apple.

Walla Wallas are an onion without "bite," exceptional and jumbo sized. Best eaten raw or lightly cooked, they are perfect additions to barbecued hamburgers, sandwiches and fresh salads. As with all vegetables in Northwestern cuisine, overcooking is outlawed; steamed vegetables should crunch.

Coffee bons mots

Coffee is more than a lifestyle choice here, it's an industry. According to the *New York Times* Portland, Oregon consumes more gourmet coffee beans per capita than anywhere else on earth, though some Milanese in Italy might take issue. Anyway, coffee is a Northwest must. Coffeehouses, espresso bars and coffee carts pepper the cities.

Chain outlets belong to Starbucks, Tullys and Seattle's Best Coffee. Starbucks began as a single store in Seattle's Pike Place Market in 1971, and now has more than 1,900 locations worldwide. Starbucks attracts boycotts over its cut-throat business tactics, and for this reason many residents prefer the independant coffee shops, which can be found on any street (sometimes several on the same street).

Standard coffee lingo is understood everywhere. The strength – single or double – starts with the number of pure-coffee shots in the cup. Some shops offer triples and a couple even serve quadruple shots for those who want instant hypertension. "Flavors" like amaretto are created by adding Italian syrups. Some like a helping of powdered vanilla, nutmeg, chocolate or cinnamon. For this, locals ask for a drink "with room," lest it be filled "to the rim."

Then there's the milk: "non-fat" is exactly that and tastes watered down. "Percent'" refers to 1- or 2-percent fat milk. "Whole" means straight from the cow. Caffeinated, half-caffeinated ("half-caf") or decaffeinated ("decaf") are important considerations when the heart starts to race.

Practice this phrase: "I would like a double half-caf no foam percent amaretto cap with room." If you want black stuff, ask for an "Americano," if you want to sample what the locals prefer, ask for a "latte." "Frappuccino" is a chilled cappuccino concoction that's perfect on a hot day.

RUN SALMON RUN

Northwesterners have had a close relationship with salmon throughout their entire lives. From Native Americans to Portland yuppies, they are either saving them or savoring them.

Cohos (pronounced co-hose), also known as Silver salmon, are very common here. They are also valued for their tasty red meat. Sockeye is unique among the Pacific salmon in that the young rear for a year or two in local lakes before migrating to salt water. They rank first in commercial value and are also a valuable recreational resource. Though their name is famous (in cannery lingo, at least) and they can be quite desirable, they aren't the very best-tasting fresh fish. Chum and Pink salmon are

Get to know your salmon

Northwesterners have had a close relationship with salmon for their entire history. They are still forever either saving them or savoring them. Asking for "salmon" will get you nowhere — a wider vocabulary is called for, and well rewarded, so here are a few pointers: Chinook salmon, also known as King salmon, *tyee* salmon or sometimes Columbia River salmon are the most highly valued because of their size and firm red and flavorful flesh.

LEFT: coffeehouses are everywhere in the cities, satisfying a craving for mochas and lattes.
ABOVE: the famous jumping salmon.

the most commonly canned species and though increasingly economically important, are not sought-after as a fresh fish. In the past few decades, fish farms have begun to farm smaller salmon. In shops, markets or restaurants, you should find these priced lower than "wild" or freshly caught salmon.

Oysters and crabs

Having so much water around, as coastal Washington and Oregon certainly do, has distinct advantages for lovers of shellfish. Southern Puget Sound oysters are noted for their high nutritional content, with meat that is plump with glycogen, yet firm, and very sweet. Northwest oysters characteristically have a crisp, briny but mild flavor followed by a watermelon rind-like aftertaste. Most are cultivated on oyster farms, a method that provides a presentable fluted shell with a deep cup that is barnacle-free. They grow quickly, reaching market size in a little over a year.

The native Washington oyster, *Ostrea lurida*, also known as the Olympia oyster, was first commercially harvested from Willapa Bay. Indigenous to the West Coast, this tiny oyster is prized for its robust, metallic flavor. The Olympia is a slow-growing mollusk; a century ago it was harvested so widely for the schooner

trade, its population drastically declined. This led certain private interests to cultivate oysters in areas staked out on the basis of specific, private tidelands that continue to exist.

Today the world's largest oyster hatchery is in Quilcene, Washington. It is capable of producing more than 30 billion oysters per year, and is also the largest shellfish seed hatchery in North America. Over 15,000 acres (6,070 hectares) of Pacific coast tidelands are used exclusively as growing beds. A state-of-the-art production facility at South Bend, Washington, can process as many as half a million oysters per working shift, while still maintaining very high quality-control standards.

For lovers of shellfish, the Dungeness crab is well-known and highly desirable. *Cancer magister* got its common name, the Dungeness crab, (pronounced *dun*-jen-us), from the town of Dungeness in the Strait of Juan de Fuca, Washington, where they were first harvested commercially in the mid 1800s. Today, crab farming and harvesting is big business in Alaska, as well as in Washington and Oregon. The Dungeness crab, or so-called "cool crab," is considered the benchmark standard for its quality, texture and taste. Modern crab fishermen harvest only the larger male crabs, usually delivering them live to processing plants where they may be specially prepared for live-air shipment, or cooked and packed ready for the market.

Hand crafted ales

Great beers are part of the fabric of life in the Northwest. With a huge number of breweries per capita, Oregon in particular has become an epicenter in the renaissance of craft brewing; Washington is in hot pursuit. There are hundreds of brew pubs, microbreweries and craft brewers throughout the two states. Regional microbreweries produce limited lines of specialty beers. Brewpubs are the restaurants attached to these breweries, popular for both inventive beers and delicious food. The local industry also supports growers with an exceptional variety of hops and barley and, of course, there is no shortage of fresh water.

If you are new to beer tastings, here is a quick primer. Ales and lagers are produced differently in order to come up with their distinct flavors and aromas. Ales and stouts have terrific fruity, assertive flavors, and are made using top-fermenting yeast and a warm, fast fermentation process. Lager beers like Pilsner, Bock and Oktoberfest are made using bottom-fermenting yeasts producing slightly sulfury, crisp, understated flavors and aromas. Dark beers are made with roasted barley.

Vistors often sample more than one brewpub while trying to decide on their favorite hops taste – bitter, tangy or puckery; best lager from a small range; best black beer from a good range of offerings; and best beer never tasted before. The latter is easily accomplished here, with such a range of choices. There are also brewery festivals and tasting events. In a celebration of cultural diversity and historic brewing traditions, the late-July Portland International Beerfest features the finest beers from around the globe. It is held to increase beer awareness and reward beer lovers with tastes, sights and sounds.

Fruit of the vines

With a little over a quarter of a century of production experience, the Pacific Northwest is enthusiastically endorsing a young, rapidly growing wine industry. With fewer than 10 wineries in 1975, the industry now has over 200 producers and is the nation's second-largest producer of *vitis vinifera* grapes – premium European varieties – including Cabernet Sauvignon, Pinot Noir, Chardonnay and Riesling.

influenced Willamette Valley, which has been likened to a "cooler, wetter Napa Valley." Washington state leads the Northwest region in wine and grape production with around 16,500 acres (6,000 hectares) in premium *vinifera* vineyards.

Eastern Washington's two fertile river valleys, the Yakima and Columbia basins, are situated just north of the 46° latitude, similar to the Bordeaux and Burgundy regions of France. However, grapes travel an average of 200 miles (320 km) from vineyard to winery here. The majority of wineries are located near the metropolitan centers of the west.

Pacific Northwest wineries are mostly small, family-owned operations, tucked away into hillsides. They traverse farmland, lush fir forests and sagebrush-dotted deserts.

Washington grapes are mostly grown on the eastern side of the Cascade Range in an arid environment with long, warm, sunny days and cool nights. Oregon's grapes are grown on the west side of the mountains in the marine-

LEFT: in the Northwest, if you can grow it, buy it or catch it, you can eat it or drink it.
ABOVE: most of Washington's wine grapes are grown on the east side of the Cascades; most of Oregon's are grown on the west side of the Cascades.

Oregon's primary grape-growing regions are in the western part of the state on hillsides overlooking the fertile Willamette, Rogue and Umpqua river valleys. Oregon's premier varieties include Pinot Noir, Chardonnay, White Riesling, Gewurztraminer, Pinot Gris, as well as surprisingly refreshing fruit and berry wines. Sparkling wines, produced using the traditional French champagne method, are an important new addition. But for the moment, most of the production seems to be by German or Swiss methods, which are leading to fresh, clean-tasting wines. There is also an ongoing effort to produce better and better red wines, particularly in the Pinot Noirs. ❏

SAND AND SURF

Rocky shores, sandy beaches and buoyant water make the perfect habitat for sea anemones, plovers, dolphins and whales

Bold shafts of light race across the pinks and purples of the irregular substrate… twisted bullwhips embrace the tangled masses of bladderwrack and laver… highlights of red and orange lifeforms… grinding rocks… groaning timber… A commentary on Picasso's last canvas? A transmission from the *Voyager* space probe? No, just a page from a Northwest tidepooler's notebook. Other entries penciled in this weatherbeaten book describe days spent searching for razor clams on a beach in Puget Sound, watching whales from a windswept overlook on the Pacific Ocean, and launching a kite from a rolling sand dune.

Lovers of the outdoors escape to the unrestricted, unchanged splendor of the thousands of miles of wild aquatic habitats along the beaches, preserves, bays and estuaries that line Puget Sound, the San Juan Islands and the open coasts of both Oregon and Washington. Here, an unrivaled abundance of birds, mammals, fish and invertebrates populate the shore.

Seashore habitats

The shores here are new ones. As the glaciers receded and revealed virgin stretches of land, seawater moved in and gradually sculpted the volcanic rock and cobbled till into notched fjords, buttresses and spires. Rocky shores, placid sandy strips, and mixed beaches of stones, sand and silt developed between the prominent glacial sculptures. Each type of beach has its own wildlife ecology – plants and animals particular to their own eco-niche. Beachwalkers can discover several distinctive habitats and identify hundreds of plants and animals between the tidemarks of Northwest seashore.

Rocky habitats are common along northern shores of Washington's Olympic Peninsula and the Strait of Juan de Fuca. At regular intervals down the Oregon coast are the jagged granite boulders, eroded sandstone pillars, blowholes

and arches; these stunning beach vistas have been the mainstay of countless color calendars. Crashing waves pound the cliffs in a continuous state of war, regaining the very fortresses that once sprung from the ocean during the postglacial epochs. The craggy northern beaches are often lined with forests of evergreen, spruce,

cedar, hemlock and fir. Trees cling perilously to the eroded cliffs, while far below lie casualties of the never-ending struggle – bleached tangles of driftwood heaped at the water's edge.

The interior beaches of southern Puget Sound are peaceful reminders of passive resistance as sand and mud, slowly deposited by a network of rivers and streams, reclaim the bays and inlets through the process of siltification. The characteristic aroma of intertidal life is salty, sandy and a little earthy. Regional aquaculturists have honed the science of shellfish production, yielding the Quilcene oyster and, more recently, a tasty but diminutive Olympic cousin, the Yaquinna. When tidal conditions and the harvest quotas

LEFT: starfish are common near Port Townsend in Washington state.
RIGHT: seagull on the sand, San Juan Island.

permit, these calm bays are the best places to search for clams or mussels. Throughout the year, birdwatchers tally a full roster of gulls, sandpipers, plovers and ducks. The coarse-grained coastal sand beaches of southern Washington and central Oregon may be slim on sealife but are rich in rolling dunes, flowering dune grasses and unparalleled photographic rewards.

Exploring seashore gardens

The Northwest Straits marine ecosystem is naturally interconnected from mountain tops to deep fjord bottoms, from tiny invertebrates to top predators like the killer whale, and from

a variety of invertebrates that draws divers from around the world: sponges, mollusks, crustaceans, sea stars, urchins and sea cucumbers. Especially popular are edible shellfish including mussels and abalone.

Sea anemones are called "flowers of the sea." Strikingly colored relatives of the jellyfish and corals, they use harpoon-like threads on their radial tentacles to ensnare floating prey. Pink and green aggregate anemones resemble faded flowers, like zinnias. They cover the cobbled rocks of mixed beaches and can divide like an amoeba to form countless clones. A favorite of tidepoolers, the green anemone is a true sea

Pacific Ocean tides to fresh waters from rivers and streams. Where the 40–50°F (4–10°C) Japanese current bathes the shore in nutrients from offshore upwelling, the sea has blossomed forth a wealth of strange and beautiful lifeforms. This nurturing environment stacks animal upon animal, color upon texture in a subtle gradient of life in every available niche.

The moving waters of the Straits bathe kelp beds and reefs close to rocky shores. Prolific kelp and other seaweeds provide food, shelter and camouflage for many prey species. Reefs harbor a distinctive fish community including rockfish and lingcod, and the birds and mammals that prey on them. Clinging to the rocks is

farmer. It gets its luminescent body cast from zoochlorelle, a microscopic algae cultivated within the anemone's tissues. The real flowers in this aquatic garden are the red-headed, and red and green anemones, the largest and most brilliantly colored deepwater blossoms, seen only during extremely low tides.

Another pigment from nature's palette is in the purple or ochre sea star, a five-rayed, rough-skinned hunter of shellfish. Other stars contribute equally vibrant hues – the bright-red blood star, dusky rose star, and the safety-orange and blue-streaked sun star are all frequently found by walkers along the beach. A colossus among Pacific sea stars, the twenty-rayed star attains a length of 3 ft (1 meter), and may possess as many as 24 arms. The thorns in this rose garden are red, purple and green sea urchins – bristling pincushions that are related to the sea stars. Urchins thrive in a variety of habitats, from surging surf-swept beaches to the calmer kelp-forested inlets. Huge red urchins prefer deep-water lairs, and congregate in prickly mats at the bottom of tidepools.

Snacktime for shorebirds

As the tide moves out, shorebirds move in for a midday snack from the litter of live and dead beach animals. The tranquility is shattered by the clamor of herring gulls, mew and glaucous winged gulls, squabbling for the leftovers. In the mudflats, dunlins, whimbrels, plovers, sandpipers and killdeers gingerly negotiate the exposed bottom with slender legs and long beaks, in search of shellfish, crabs and worms. Farther from shore, the waterfowl – coots, scaups and buffleheads – tread water, passively feeding on floating plants, or diving to root around in the sediment. A large silvery-backed Arctic loon stops fishing to emit a long, yodeling cry. Many waterfowl arrive from the far north in autumn. Their numbers increase as the handsome canvasbacks, widgeons and harlequin ducks join the offshore flotilla.

Perennial favorites on the remote outer shores, black oystercatchers use their chisel-shaped beaks to pry limpets from rocks or to chip away the shells of mussels. Tufted puffins dive through the waves and fill their brilliantly banded beaks with herring and surf smelt, then alight beside stately rhinoceros auklets in their island rookeries. An elegant great blue heron silently stalks through the grasses that line a salt marsh. Visitors are unlikely to forget sighting their first bald eagle surveying the shoreline panorama from an eyrie high atop a sturdy cedar tree.

Seashore update

About 220 fish species inhabit the waters in and around Washington and Oregon. Many of these are less abundant than they were just a few years ago, in some cases, alarmingly so. Puget Sound is suffering significant losses. Through-

out the shared waters, stocks of long-lived rockfish are low, and lingcod stocks have collapsed. Herring, hake and pollock stocks are at average levels in the Strait of Georgia, but reduced in Puget Sound. Pacific cod are badly depleted here, and at low levels in the Strait of Georgia.

English sole appear to be averagely common in both areas. Only the spiny dogfish is in historically high abundance throughout the waters. The good news is that after the cessation of El Niño (unusually warm ocean temperatures, accompanied by thunderstorms), the sardine schools are back, bringing with them record numbers of salmon and other aquatic life.

Marine mammals

At the top of the food chain are the marine mammals: the cetaceans (whales, dolphins and porpoises); sea otters; and the pinnipeds (seals and sea lions). All of these animals, by evolutionary standards, are recent arrivals to the ocean coast, yet they show a mastery of the aquatic realm. They, like us, enjoy the diversity of sealife along the broad stretches of unoccupied coast that characterize the Northwest.

To spy the sleek black dorsal fin of a speeding orca, to see a barnacle-encrusted gray whale or catch a glimpse of a lone sea lion peering out from between the waves – these are unforgettable high points of a beachwalk or a ferry

LEFT: although numbers are down, 220 fish species can still be found here; these are sockeye salmon.
RIGHT: Dungeness crab are common to Washington's Dungeness Spit, the longest natural sandspit in the US.

ride. While many of these animals were once ruthlessly slaughtered for the short-term economic gains of whaling and the fur trade, they now receive rigorous Federal protection that prevents any additional exploitation. Some, like the Washington sea otter, maintain only token populations, and are being carefully monitored.

Several Northwest species, however, are staging dramatic comebacks. Now both humans and marine mammals have another chance. The marine mammals are in a better position to strengthen in numbers and thrive unmolested in their habitat along Pacific shores. Whale-watching tours enable visitors to appreciate the

that these misconceptions have been shed, orcas have been escalated to near-celebrity status. They are models for plush stuffed toys, T-shirts, mugs and bumper-stickers.

Their voices, a mixture of clicks, whistles and screams, have appeared on several record albums. And the sighting of a 6-ft (2-meter) tall orca dorsal fin cutting through the waters will bring cheers from any observer.

Orcas travel in family groups called pods; three such groups are year-round residents of Puget Sound. Individuals have been identified by subtle differences in fin and body markings, and a whale museum at Friday Harbor on San

thrilling and educational sight of a breaching gray whale, an orca spyhopping, or a teeming seal rookery.

Celebrity dolphins

The largest and most impressive member of the dolphin family is the orca, commonly called the killer whale. These strikingly marked glossy black-and-white predators were once harpooned and shot at by mistrusting fishermen. Their mistrust was unwarranted.

While the 30-ft (9-meter) orcas present competition as unsurpassed hunters of salmon, cod, sharks, seals and even other dolphins, there are no records of them assaulting humans. Now

HOW TO SPOT A WHALE

Pods of gray whales pass the Oregon Coast and the Olympic Peninsula on their 5,500-mile (8,900-km) migration from the Arctic to their breeding grounds in Southern California and Mexico, and again on their return trip north. Southward migration is from December to early February. Immature whales, adult males and females without calves head back "home" first, passing the Northwest in March and April. In May come females with calves. Early-morning hours, prior to the onset of wind-blown whitecaps, are the best time to see them. Scan the horizon for a "blow" – a whale's exhalation into the air – and stay with it. Other whales should follow.

Juan Island has informative exhibits and lots of practical advice on how to see these inspiring Washington residents.

Planning a beachwalk

Beachwalkers should always consult a tide table before setting out. These indispensable charts, available at boating or fishing supply stores, detail the time and magnitude of daily high and low tides. Northwest tides can rise 10 ft (3 meters). Stretches of easy shoreline attractive to hikers and tidepoolers, can, six

WHALE WATCHING

Charter boat operators offer different packages and tours. Some companies are more eco-friendly than others, so you might want to ask around before choosing.

lines have dangerous undertows, and many places are not suitable for swimming. Some conditions are even unsafe for surfwalking.

Buying and studying a good field identification guide to Northwest marine life will add enjoyment of any shorewalk. However, nothing compares to a sighting of the real thing.

With a visit to the Seattle, Tacoma, Newport or Seaside (Oregon) aquariums, or any of the excellent, smaller regional interpretive nature centers along the coast, beachwalkers can get a good

hours later, be under several feet of seawater. Misjudging the time of tidal change can result in being stranded, as tides silently sneak in to fill the route behind an unwary hiker, or even worse, can result in a fatality.

By checking the tides, beachwalkers might also be rewarded by seeing habitats or shorelife that are exposed to daylight only a few times each year. Another important thing to note is that long stretches of both states' Pacific shore-

LEFT: the orca (killer whale) does not harm humans, and is, in fact, a member of the dolphin family.
ABOVE: beachwalkers will be rewarded with wonderful sights, but be sure to check tide tables.

preview of some of the fish they are likely to encounter. The easiest beachwalks are in the summer months, although ocean weather is often very good in September.

Cloud-free days

Coastal weather is mild, and tides are lowest at midday. In winter, hardy beachcombers take advantage of the gaps between maritime squalls. Armed with flashlights and lanterns, the low night-time tides offer exotic midnight rambling. But even on the sunniest, cloud-free days, the coastal climate can change abruptly, so phone the weather service for an extended regional forecast before heading out. ❑

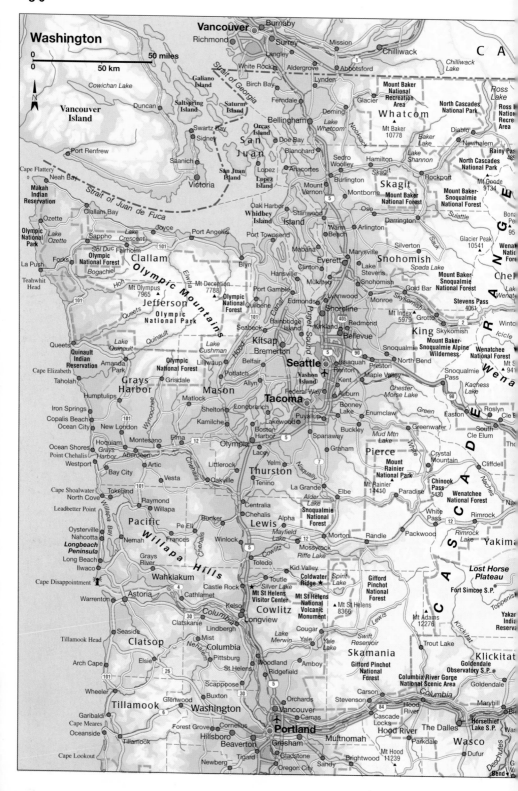

Washington

0 ___ 50 miles
0 ___ 50 km

N

Vancouver Island

Cowichan Lake
Duncan
Saltspring Island
Galiano Island
Saturn Island
Swartz Bay
Sidney
Saanich
Victoria
San Juan Island
Lopez Island
Lopez
Orcas Island
Doe Bay
San Juan
Port Renfrew
Cape Flattery
Neah Bay
Makah Indian Reservation
Ozette
Clallam Bay
Lake Ozette
Olympic National Park
Sappho
Sol Duc
Fairholm
Lake Crescent
Joyce
Port Angeles
Forks
La Push
Teahwhit Head
Bogachiel
Olympic National Forest
Hoh
Mt Olympus 7965
Mt Decention 7788
Jefferson
Olympic National Park
Queets
Quinault
Queets
Quinault Indian Reservation
Amanda Park
Lake Quinault
Olympic National Forest
Cape Elizabeth
Taholah
Humptulips
Grays Harbor
Grisdale
Iron Springs
Copalis Beach
Ocean City
Hoquiam
New London
Montesano
Elma
Ocean Shores
Grays Harbor
Point Chehalis
Aberdeen
Artic
Westport
Bay City
Vesta
Cape Shoalwater
North Cove
Tokeland
Oakville
Leadbetter Point
Raymond
Willapa
Pacific
Bunker
Pe Ell
Oysterville
Nahcotta
Frances
Nemah
Winlock
Longbeach Peninsula
Grays River
Long Beach
Ilwaco
Wahkiakum
Cape Disappointment
Warrenton
Astoria
Cathlamet
Castle Rock
Kelso
Clatskanie
Longview
Cowlitz
Seaside
Lindbergh
Columbia
Mist
Clatsop
Tillamook Head
Nehalem
Pittsburg
Arch Cape
Elsie
St Helens
Woodland
Wheeler
Scappoose
Ridgefield
Glenwood
Buxton
Washington
Garibaldi
Forest Grove
Cornelius
Hillsboro
Beaverton
Tillamook
Cape Meares
Oceanside
Tigard
Newberg
Cape Lookout
Gladstone
Oregon City

Vancouver
Burnaby
Richmond
Surrey
Langley
White Rock
Birch Bay
Aldergrove
Lynden
Ferndale
Bellingham
Lake Whatcom
Blanchard
Anacortes
Burlington
Mount Vernon
Montborne
Oak Harbor
Whidbey Island
Stanwood
Island
Warm Beach
Mabana
Clinton
Hansville
Mukilteo
Port Gamble
Edmonds
Quilcene
Seabeck
Bainbridge Island
Kingston
Poulsbo
Seabeck
Kitsap
Bremerton
Belfair
Nashon Island
Seattle
Tacoma
Federal Way
Bonney Lake
Auburn
Kent
Maple Valley
Bellevue
Redmond
Kirkland
Issaquah
Preston
North Bend
Snoqualmie
Renton
Shoreline
Lynnwood
Monroe
Gold Bar
Everett
Lake Stevens
Snohomish
Marysville
Arlington
Silverton
Darrington
Oso
Sedro Woolley
Hamilton
Rockport
Newhalem
Diablo
Concrete
Mount Baker National Forest
Mount Baker-Snoqualmie National Forest
Skagit
Glacier Peak 10541
Wenatchee National Forest
Chilliwack
Mission
Abbotsford
Chilliwack Lake
Mount Baker National Recreation Area
North Cascades National Park
Ross Lake
Ross National Recreation Area
Whatcom
Mt Baker 10778
Baker Lake
Lake Shannon
Rainy Pass
Mt Goode 9134
Bonanza Pk
North Cascades National Park
Lake Chelan

White
Kamilche
Shelton
Longbranch
Lakewood
Boston Harbor
Olympia
Spanaway
Lacey
Littlerock
Yelm
Tenino
La Grande
Graham
Pierce
Mud Mtn Lake
Mount Rainier National Park
Mt Rainier 14410
Paradise
Chinook Pass 5430
Wenatchee National Forest
Crystal Mountain
Cliffdell
Roslyn
Cle Elum
South Cle Elum
Easton
Greenwater
Buckley
Enumclaw
Puyallup
Kachess Lake
Naches
Rimrock
Rimrock Lake
White Pass
Packwood
Randle
Morton
Mossyrock
Riffe Lake
Cowlitz
Toledo
Winlock
Chehalis
Centralia
Alpha
Mayfield Lake
Lewis
Pe Ell
Thurston
Nisqually
Elbe
Alder Lake
Snoqualmie National Forest
Yakima
Coldwater Ridge
Silver Lake
Mt St Helens Visitor Center
Mt St Helens National Volcanic Monument
Spirit Lake
Mt St Helens 8366
Gifford Pinchot National Forest
Fort Simcoe S.P.
Lost Horse Plateau
Toppenish
Yakama Indian Reservation
Cougar
Yale
Yale Lake
Lake Merwin
Swift Reservoir
Skamania
Mt Adams 12276
Trout Lake
Klickitat
Amboy
Gifford Pinchot National Forest
Columbia River Gorge National Scenic Area
Goldendale Observatory S.P.
Goldendale
Orchards
Stevenson
Carson
Maryhill
Vancouver
Camas
Portland
Gresham
Multnomah
Cascade Locks
Hood River
The Dalles
Wasco
Mt Hood 11239
Brightwood
Parkdale
Dufur
Sandy
Horsethief Lake S.P.
Bend

Seattle
Tacoma
Portland

Strait of Georgia
Strait of Juan de Fuca
Puget Sound
Hood Canal
Lake Washington
Olympic Mountains
Grays Harbor
Willapa Bay
Willapa Hills
Cascade Range
Columbia
Nooksack
Skagit
Sauk
Suiattle
Skykomish
Icicle
Green
Naches
Klickitat
Columbia
Deschutes

King
Snohomish
Skagit
Whatcom
Clallam
Jefferson
Mason
Grays Harbor
Thurston
Pierce
Lewis
Pacific
Wahkiakum
Cowlitz
Skamania
Klickitat
Yakima
Kittitas
Clatsop
Columbia
Tillamook
Washington
Multnomah
Wasco

C A

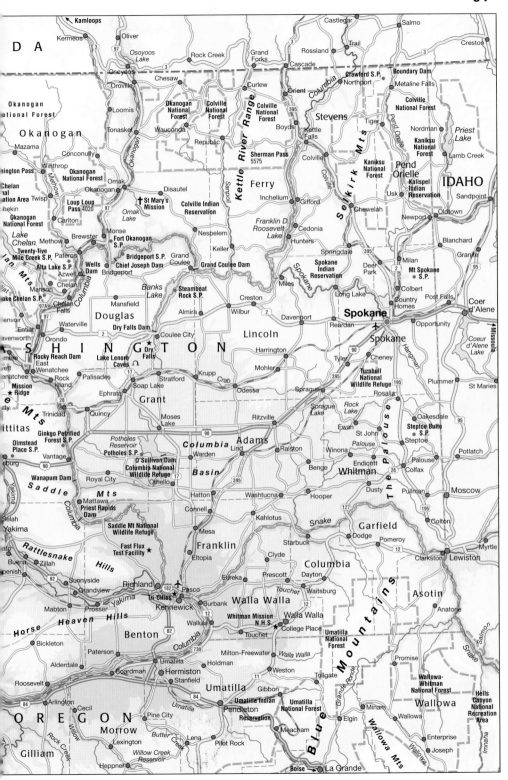

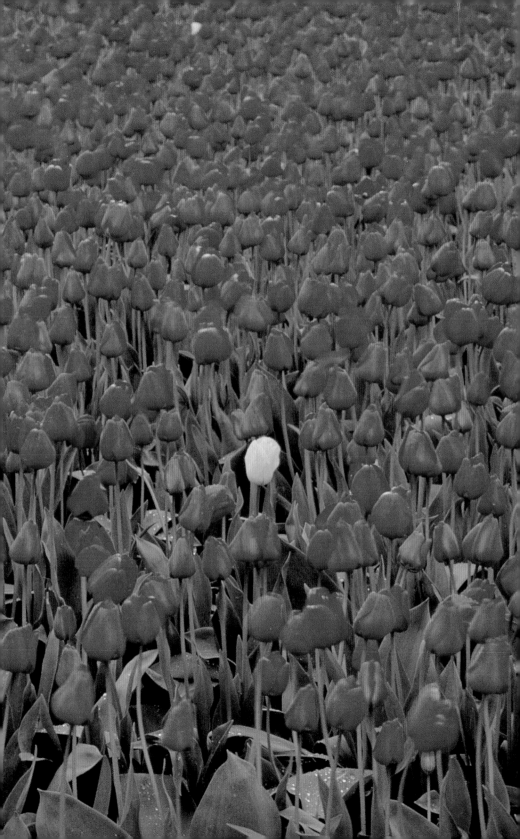

WASHINGTON

*A detailed guide to Washington State, with principal sites
clearly cross-referenced by number to the maps*

After centuries of living on the fringes of the public's consciousness, Washington burst onto the public arena during the last
years of the 20th century. The "Boeing Boom;" the "innovative economy" that spawned Microsoft, Amazon.com and a host of
others; the retail entrepreneurs who started – and ran with – Nordstrom and Starbucks; the fortunes made by foreign trade with Pacific
Rim countries – all of these created tremendous opportunities and
attracted to the state some of the brightest people in the world. But
with a slow-down in the economy and a couple of high-profile riots
in formerly serene Seattle, Washington began to take a long, hard
look at itself. What will emerge from this self-scrutiny may be the
most interesting phase yet in a region that can boast its share of
boom-and- bust cycles.

No matter how innovative or ruffled its urban residents become,
though, some things remain unchanged. Washington's natural beauty,
for instance. The west side beckons with its miles of coastline and
verdant river valleys. The east has a drier landscape, dramatic geologic
wonders dotted with lakes, and the subtle colors of fertile plains.

Washington, in general, is a sporty, heady, active place. Playing
well is serious work here. City dwellers in particular point out that
there are few places in the world where you can wake up to a view
of snowcapped mountains, ski in the morning, sail in the afternoon
and attend a symphony in the evening. You can be a technology engineer during the week and a ski instructor at the weekend; you can
hike to Alpine lakes one day and bike to vineyards the next.

This is only possible when economic resources are on a par with
natural resources – in other words, where whims can be indulged –
and here they can be. When warm months replace gray clouds, thousands head for their favorite fishing hole, campsite, river or lake –
and there are always enough of these to go around. Washington ranks
fourth in the US in the number of visits to state park per person,
which is more than three times the national average.

From sandy coastal beaches and sheltered Puget Sound islands to
sunbaked lakes and lava flows east of the Cascade Mountains, few
states can match the powerful natural beauty of these surroundings.
In the state of Washington, visitors too can travel from magnificent
coastal beaches to dense rainforests, and from spectacular Alpine
peaks to high desert canyons carved by prehistoric floods – all the
way sampling crisp Washington apples, award-winning wines, and
the pleasures of emerging Northwest cuisine. A cycle of boom-and-
bust years? Long may they continue. ❑

PRECEDING PAGES: Mount Shuksan in Washington's North Cascades National Park;
Seattle skyline from the city's Queen Anne Hill.
LEFT: tulip field in Skagit County, Washington.

SEATTLE

*Gorgeous, prosperous, home of Microsoft and Starbucks –
Seattle hitched its fortunes to the Alaska Gold Rush
and has never looked back*

Map
on page
92

Seattle is an oddly shaped city. From the vantage point of a satellite high overhead, it glows in a different way to other metropolises. Seattle is long and skinny and shaped like a cigar; it clings north to south alongside the island-filled body of saltwater known as Puget Sound.

Seattle's spectacular environs, scattered with mountains and freshwater lakes, make it a city that people choose to live in for its geographic characteristics alone. But getting around involves bowling along narrow corridors where the next place of touristic interest can be up to 30 miles (50 km) from where you first started – and there's usually a body of water to cross. This chapter describes attractions that tend to be found in clusters.

Gold Rush town

Seattle dates from 1851 but didn't really blossom until the Alaska Gold Rush of the late 19th century, when the city glittered with racy Wild West "underground" prostitution and illegal drinking dens. Little more than a century and a half old, it has had little time to develop Boston's ostentatious history, or duplicate the frantic enterprise of New York. As a result, its historic attractions, outside of Native American culture, are focused around Pioneer Square and Yesler Way, near the city's lively waterfront.

Seattle's cosmopolitan flavor is centered around the International District, with its well-differentiated Asian restaurants and shops; in this part of town it pays to know the difference between sushi and sashimi, between Cantonese and Szechwan cuisine. The waterfront area features a plethora of maritime attractions and the fresh salty air of Puget Sound – it feels good to breathe deeply when sitting in Waterfront Park or while boarding a Washington State Ferry to a local island.

Once dismissed by Easterners as a forested wilderness where only lumberjacks, cowboys and Indians roamed, Seattle has in the past few decades found itself to be a migration mecca. To no one's surprise, tired Easterners find relaxed, friendly residents, accessible sights and rain-scrubbed greenery in place of big city smog, crime and slums. Anyone wishing to explore Seattle in detail can turn to our companion volume, *Insight Guide: Seattle*, where in more than 300 pages the city and its surroundings are analysed, characterized and illustrated by a series of locally based writers and photographers.

With only 55 guaranteed days of sunshine a year, visitors can expect to see some fog, drizzle, mist or at minimum, cloud; most years it rains an average of

LEFT: a symbol of Seattle.
RIGHT: Pike Place Market.

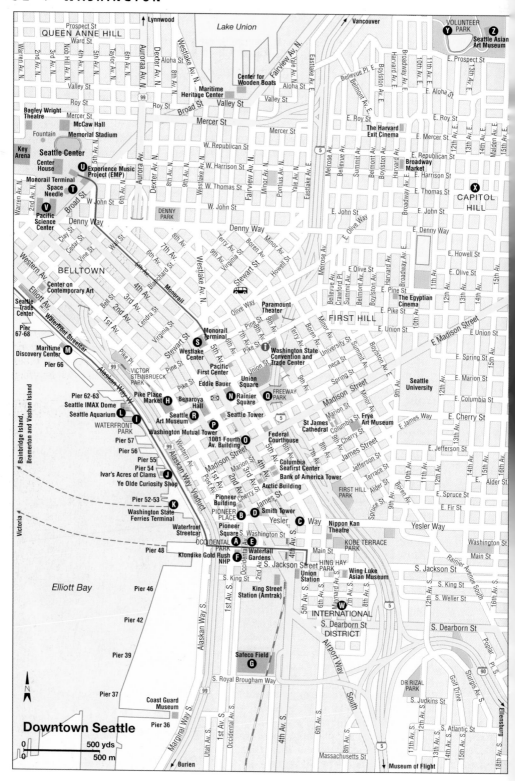

Downtown Seattle

Prospect St
Lynnwood
Lake Union
Vancouver

QUEEN ANNE HILL
Ward St

VOLUNTEER PARK

Y

Z Seattle Asian Art Museum

Center for Wooden Boats

Maritime Heritage Center

Bagley Wright Theatre

McCaw Hall

Memorial Stadium

Fountain

Key Arena

Seattle Center

Center House

U Experience Music Project (EMP)

Monorail Terminal

Space Needle **T**

V Pacific Science Center

Denny Way

DENNY PARK

The Harvard Exit Cinema

Broadway Market

CAPITOL HILL **X**

BELLTOWN

Center on Contemporary Art

Seattle Trade Center

Pier 67-68

Maritime Discovery Center **M**
Pier 66

FIRST HILL

Paramount Theater

The Egyptian Cinema

Monorail Terminal **S**

Westlake Center

i Washington State Convention and Trade Center

Pacific First Center

Pike Place Market **H**

Pier 62-63
Seattle IMAX Dome
Seattle Aquarium **L** **I**

WATERFRONT PARK

Pier 57

Pier 56

Benaroya Hall

Eddie Bauer

Union Square

N Rainier Square

O FREEWAY PARK

Seattle Tower

R Seattle Art Museum

Washington Mutual Tower

Seattle University

St James Cathedral

Frye Art Museum

Pier 55
Pier 54
Ivar's Acres of Clams
Ye Olde Curiosity Shop **J**

1001 Fourth Av. Building **O**

Federal Courthouse

Columbia Seafirst Center

Bank of America Tower

Pier 52-53 **K**

Washington State Ferries Terminal

Waterfront Streetcar

Arctic Building

Pioneer Building

PIONEER PLACE **B** **D** Smith Tower

Pioneer Square **A** **E**

Yesler **C** Way

Nippon Kan Theatre

KOBE TERRACE PARK

FIRST HILL PARK

Pier 48

Klondike Gold Rush NHP **F**

Waterfront Gardens

OCCIDENTAL PARK

HING HAY PARK

S. Jackson Street

Union Station

Wing Luke Asian Museum

Elliott Bay

Pier 46

Pier 42

Pier 39

King Street Station (Amtrak)

W INTERNATIONAL DISTRICT

DR RIZAL PARK

Pier 37

Coast Guard Museum

Pier 36

Safeco Field **G**

0   500 yds
0   500 m

Map
on page
92

38 inches (96 cm). It's not that much really, but it comes in a constant drizzle. Even the humor is pluvial: "a visitor to Seattle arrives on a rainy day. He gets up the next day and it's raining. It rains the day after that, and the day after that. He goes out to lunch and sees a youngster and asks out of despair, 'Hey kid, does it ever stop raining around here?' The kid says, 'How do I know? I'm only six.'"

Weather, weather everywhere

There is an upside to all this precipitation: in winter, snow in the nearby higher-altitude mountains makes for excellent skiing. Seattle's climate is best between June and September, but even then it's a good idea to come expecting rain.

The average maximum temperature in July is 72°F (21°C); the average winter low in January is 36°F (2°C). Some say general cloudiness and light mists make the city seem even wetter than it really is. It snows an average of 11 inches (27 cm) a year, but in the city none of it stays on the ground. If you are one of the lucky visitors who happens to catch a clear-weather glimpse of the snow-covered dome of Mount Rainier looming on the horizon, consider yourself fortunate.

The dampish weather has also nurtured a profusion of bookstores, and according to *Publishers' Weekly,* Washingtonians are the nation's most avid book buyers and borrowers. George Bernard Shaw, who said "thank heavens the sun has gone in, so I don't have to go out and enjoy it," would have loved it here. When it's sunny, Seattle residents quickly pack up their personal sports gear and get cracking. Ever optimistic, it is a fact that Seattle sells more sunglasses per capita than any other major city in the nation. No surprise, then, that "The Happy Face" – that perpetual smiling, yellow sun – is said to have originated in Seattle.

Pioneer Square Ⓐ, south of the downtown area, is a 17-square-block National Historic District and Seattle's oldest neighborhood. Warm red-brick buildings

BELOW:
Seattle sits
on Elliott Bay.

line the streets here. Shops selling wares from antiques to handmade toys, as well as eateries and art galleries, occupy spaces where speakeasies and opium dens once lurked. A great pergola of ornate ironwork shading carved wooden benches is situated in **Pioneer Place** (1st Avenue and Yesler Way), which is at Seattle's heart. The 60-ft (18-meter) **totem pole** and **bronze bust** of **Chief Seattle**, the city's namesake, are reminders that Seattle as "Queen City of the Pacific Northwest" first emerged into world consciousness during the Klondike Gold Rush a century ago. Even earlier, this was the site the founding settlers chose when they left Alki Point in the 1850s for a superior harbor on Elliott Bay.

Pioneer Square also was the place of the original "Skid Road," a term born when huge trees were "skidded" along a steep log-bed road down **Yesler Way** to a mill on the waterfront. By the 1930s, Skid Row – as it became known – was a national term for an area frequented by the homeless (although at the time the mill employed almost half the people in town). Later, it became the place to buy provisions before heading for the goldfields.

Nowadays the neighborhood is the hub for bookstores and internet startups. One venerable establishment is the **Elliott Bay Book Company** (101 South Main Street; tel: 206 624-6600). The books are great, and the food in the large café downstairs is pretty good, too.

In the early 20th century the business center moved uptown, and the original purpose of "Skid Road" as a place to find a day job, declined. However, traces remain. As crowds of young people lounge at coffeehouses, the homeless hang out on the street and on the few patches of grass still remaining; in places upscale art galleries share city blocks with gun dealerships and missions.

Tallest building

The handsome 42-story **Smith Tower** (2nd Avenue and Yesler) was erected in 1914 in an attempt to anchor business in the area. The tower, once the pride of Seattle, was for many years the tallest building west of the Mississippi. A look at the city from its **observation floor** (daily 10am–10pm; tel: 206 682-9393; fee) shows glittering skyscrapers to the north; to the south is Safeco Field. A primary landmark in the Pioneer Square restoration, the **Grand Central Arcade** (214 1st Avenue South) was once a hotel; it now has two levels of bookstores and gift shops surrounding a chandeliered brick courtyard, as well as a bakery offering a likely candidate for the best cinnamon rolls in the city.

In the arcade, visitors can watch artisans – including ivory carvers, glassblowers and silversmiths – perform their meticulous crafts. For soothing the soul, **Waterfall Gardens** (219 2nd Avenue) lies behind slatted wooden walls – an oasis of rushing water, bamboo and sculptured rock. **Occidental Park** (Occidental and 1st avenues) displays four totem poles carved by artist Duane Pasco: 35-ft (10-meter) tall *Sun and Raven*; *Killer Whale*, a huge beast with a man riding on its tail;

LEFT: Smith Tower and Pioneer Square.

Map
on page
92

and two large carvings representing *Tson-qua*, a cannibal figure, and *Bear*.

Poor drainage after Seattle's Great Fire of 1889 necessitated raising the street line one level. As a consequence, the Square can now be explored via a secret subterranean city. **Underground Tours** (610 1st Avenue; 90-minute tours; year-round; tel: 206 682-4646; fee) is a favorite with first-time visitors. Saucy guides entertainingly describe life in old Seattle while negotiating a maze of sunken storefronts.

Nighttime on Pioneer Square

Popular **Klondike Gold Rush National Historic Park ❻** (117 South Main Street; daily 9am–6pm; tel: 206 553-7220; free) is a Federal museum recalling those crazed days when rough-and-ready gold-seekers by the tens of thousands converged on Pioneer Square. Here they purchased millions of dollars-worth of food, clothing, equipment, pack animals and steamship tickets on their way to the Yukon.

The Square comes alive at night, espe-

cially on weekends or after a baseball game at nearby Safeco Field. Historic district becomes entertainment district, with one of the city's liveliest nightspots, from sports bars to hard-rock taverns to romantic eateries: **Doc Maynard's** (610 1st Avenue in Pioneer Square) is a bar from the early 19th century; **Aristocrat's Club Bar & Grill** (220 4th Avenue South and Main Street) is considered one of the best hip-hop clubs; and everyone rushes to **FX McRory's** (419 Occidental Avenue South) after a baseball game.

When the sports fans and the club crowds depart, Pioneer Square reverts to its former leisurely pace. And baseball fan or not, visitors are impressed by the nation's most expensive ballpark. Don't miss the tour of **Safeco Field ❼** (team store on 1st Avenue; tours are event-dependent but usually 12:30pm and 2:30pm; tel: 800 696-6274; fee).

State-of-the-art Safeco Field opened in July 2000 as the $400-million-plus home of the beloved Seattle Mariners. The

BELOW: jazz on a summer's night, Pioneer Square.

field's retractable roof opens to reveal a stunning view of Downtown to the north. Soon, however, that view will be partially blocked by a new professional sports venue being built on the site of the former Kingdome – a stadium for the NFL's Seahawks and soccer matches. Right now at Safeco it's possible to walk on home plate, sit in the press box and peek in the luxury suites.

The best piece of (unsubstantiated) Safeco trivia is that 1.2 million lbs (over 500,000 kg) of peanut shells and burger napkins are hauled out of the stadium after every game. Grab lunch before or after a visit to the **Pyramid Alehouse** across the street. If your energy has come back, check out the samples given during the alehouse's **brewery tour** (45 minutes long, tel: 206 682-3377 for details).

Those flying fish

When the retail price of onions rose from 10¢ to $1 per pound between 1906 and 1907, housewives shrieked and Seattle

City Councilman Thomas Revelle called for an investigation. Farmers told of being cheated by middlemen and receiving bungled commissions. As a solution, Revelle proposed a public street market to sell direct to the consumer.

Built on stilts on the headland overlooking Elliott Bay, **Pike Place Market** (Mon–Sat 9am–6pm, Sun 11am–5pm; tel: 206 682-74553) started simply enough, but its popularity was immediate and the original hillside arcade soon grew into a maze of corridors, stairwells and hidden shops. Today, after several resurrections, the market remains a vital part of the city, visited by more than 9 million people each year, and patronized by almost everyone in town, regardless of social status.

In former times, "Dry Row" along the west wall had no access to running water. Opposite was "Wet Row," where running water was available. Today, the oldest continually operating farmers' market in the country allows craftspeople to sell their wares from the dry tables and local farmers to sell fresh produce from the wet tables. A shallow trough still carries runoff from the farmers' tables.

The market is a decidedly odiferous attraction, a free-form conglomeration of sights, smells, sounds and interesting characters. Salmon periodically fly through the air as market traders throw them to each other over the heads of customers. Nearby, vegetable and flower displays are turned into works of art. Countless eateries serve up tastes of the world and its maze-like corridors are a haven for some 230 small businesses. This is the place to buy antique playing cards, opals from Australia, imported cigarettes, incense, T-shirts and shoes – all within an old-fashioned, cozy complex with some of the best views of the harbor to be found anywhere.

Licensed street musicians play for loose change at several designated spots. **Summer Sundays on Pike Place** (Stewart and Virginia streets; June–Sept, 10am–4pm; free to watch) feature famous chefs giving cooking demonstrations. Visitors who find fresh food particularly fascinating can walk down yet another level to **Pike Place Market Heritage Center** (1531

LEFT: Seattle's streetcar runs along its waterfront.

Map on page 92

Western Avenue; daily 10am–6pm; tel: 206 682-74553; free). The center illustrates the history of the market and periodically presents cooking demonstrations, tastings and children's activities. **Market Heritage Tours** (1-hour tours; Wed–Sat 11am and 2pm, Sun noon and 2pm; 206 682-74553; fee), a project of the Market Foundation, is designed to present Pike Place Market traditions to the public. The **Alibi Room**, 85 Pike Street, is a trendy cocktail bar tucked away in an alley and the **Pink Door**, 1919 **Post Alley**, is also fun; both have a great view of Puget Sound.

Waterfront piers

Centered on **Waterfront Park** ❶ below Pike Place Market, the promenade and piers that line **Elliott Bay** are in constant action, with maritime industries, shops and restaurants jostling for business, ferries and freighters docking and the occasional seaplane flying overhead. Part of what makes Seattle unique is its fine, deep harbor; the large piers that are of interest to visitors are numbered sequentially from 48 to 70. A pedestrian bridge from downtown Seattle and all major bus routes lead to the Waterfront, while the **Waterfront Streetcar** runs from Pioneer Square to Pier 70. Various plans have been proposed for more pedestrian-friendly access, especially since the frighteningly busy Alaskan Way Viaduct highway was severely jolted during the 2001 earthquake, which registered 6.8 on the Richter scale.

Starting from the south end at 101 Alaskan Way is **Pier 48**. Trawlers and tugs use this pier for lay-up moorage and provisioning operations, as do Washington State ferries (but there is no loading here). **Pier 54**, a public boat landing, precedes the landmark **Ye Olde Curiosity Shop** ❷ (Mon–Thur 9:30am–6pm, Fri–Sat 9am–9pm, Sun 9am–6pm; tel: 206 682-5844) at the foot of Spring Street. This dotty oddity shop was created when J.E. Standley arrived in Seattle in the late 1890s during the Yukon Gold Rush – a period that attracted prospectors, traders

BELOW: fish vendor puts on a show at Pike Place Market.

and wide-eyed entrepreneurs bent on fortunes in the northwest. Standley loved curios from a young age and was known to collect an overabundance of tat: ivory trinkets, totem poles, Indian baskets and shrunken human heads.

Today, more than a century later, as the fifth generation prepares to take over the operation, the collecting frenzy remains undiminished. Each year the shop averages a million visitors, who come to gawk at the mummified body in the back, and buy hard-to-find souvenirs in the front.

"It would take a week to see everything in the store," the owners say. Items run from dime-store prices to $20,000 for a totem pole, but most of the culturally significant ones – often dangling from the ceiling – are not for sale.

Acres of clams

Pier 52 Terminal ⓚ is the jumping-off point for **Bainbridge Island**, a 35-minute one-way trip, and **Bremerton**, a 1-hour trip one way. For those who venture much

farther, to the **Olympic Peninsula** *(see page 131)*, Washington State Ferries (tel: 206 464-6400) leave from here. The ferries take vehicles, but for those with cars who choose to walk on, it's important and almost impossible to find a parking space along the waterfront first. It's touted as the least expensive way to take a "cruise" and more than 8 million visitors a year use this cheap ferry service.

Next to the Fireboat Station, you can order a huge helping of seafood from **Ivar's Acres of Clams** (tel: 206 624-6852) and sit undercover – but outside – while watching the boats and seagulls. Ivar's was the first in a chain of restaurants developed by the late Ivar Haglund, long known as Seattle's premier prankster, promoter and restaurateur. From Pier 54 the **Elliott Bay Water Taxi** (May–Nov every 30-minutes, daylight hours, weather permitting; tel: 206 553-3000), a 70-passenger boat that accepts bicycles, sets sail for **Seacrest Marina Park** in West Seattle.

From **Pier 55 and 56** there are a choice of surprisingly informative **harbor tours** (Argosy Cruises; tel: 206 623-1445), or an enchanting adventure only 8 miles (12 km) across the water. Here, on an island, visitors find a Pacific Northwest Indian experience: tribal dances, totem carving, and fresh salmon baked over an open alder-wood fire.

Tillicum Village (4-hour boat tour; May–Sept daily, Oct–Apr Sat–Sun; tel: 206 443-1244; fee) is located on picturesque **Blake Island State Park**.

From 2004, Waterfront Park will overlap with the **Olympic Sculpture Park**, organized by the Seattle Art Museum and dedicated to the exhibition of outdoor sculptures. The name "Olympic" honors the site's remarkable vista of Washington's Olympic Mountains.

On **Pier 59**, the **Seattle Aquarium** ⓛ (open daily: summer 10am–7pm; winter 10am–5pm; tel: 206 386 4320; fee) provides a fish's-eye view of life above and beneath the waves, plus perky sea otters. The aquarium is a fun and friendly place; in autumn it's particularly satisfying to see salmon return up the fish ladder cannily positioned here.

LEFT: Ivar's Acres of Clams on the waterfront was the first in what is now a chain of restaurants.

Map on page 92

Right next door, the **Seattle IMAX Dome** (same hours; tel: 206 622-1869; fee) presents numerous big-screen experiences, the most popular being the ongoing film of the 1980 eruption of Mount St Helens. Nearby, the bare wood deck of **Pier 62–63** becomes a concert venue every summer, where artists perform amid an expansive setting of skyscrapers, boats and sunsets.

Pier 66, home to the **Bell Street Pier Cruise Terminal** (tel: 206 615-3900), is where enormous cruise liners dock on their way to Alaska and Hawaii. Other attractions include a state-of-the-art conference center, restaurants and a marina. The Bell Street Pier also handles the needs of large fishing vessels and workboats; every kind of facility, service and equipment used by the marine industry is accessible here and it's fun to watch.

Also at Pier 66, **Odyssey, the Maritime Discovery Center**  (Tues–Sat 10am–5pm, Sun noon–5pm; tel: 206 374-4000; fee) has hands-on exhibits where visitors can pilot a virtual container ship through Puget Sound or haul in plastic fish on a fake factory trawler.

Piers 65 through 69 house fish packers and Port of Seattle offices, while Pier 70 is a return to average boardwalk fare with live music, seafood and crafts shops in a rustic building. Completing the waterfront tour at the north end is the **Elliott Bay Bicycle Path**, a green promenade leading from **Myrtle Edwards Park** at Pier 70 to a public fishing pier by Magnolia Bridge.

Downtown Seattle

North of Pioneer Square are both the downtown and the financial districts. At 5th and Union streets, architect Minoru Yamasaki's striking **Rainier Tower** – now also known as **Rainier Square** – balances on a narrow base and is graced with three stories of elegant shops around an atrium. A carpeted underground concourse leads to **Eddie Bauer**, a sports-clothing retailer whose enormous success is a sign of Seattle's casual nature.

Opened in 1969, the **1001 Fourth Avenue Building** stands 50 stories high, has a free **observation perch** on the 46th floor, and once ranked as the second-tallest structure in the West. Since it opened shortly after the Space Needle, it's also known as "the box the Space Needle came in." Its courtyard is graced by Henry Moore's bronze, *Three Piece Sculpture: Vertebrae*, as well as a wealth of public art pieces.

Local developer Martin Selig's Darth-Vaderesque **Bank of America Tower** (formerly Columbia Seafirst Center) at 701 5th Avenue is 76 stories high, making it the tallest building west of the Mississippi. With commanding views of Puget Sound, the Olympic Mountains, Mount Rainier and the Cascade Mountains, it is served by 46 elevators, a public observation room on the 73rd floor and the (free) **Bank of America Gallery**.

The 55-floor **Washington Mutual Tower** at 1201 3rd Avenue is allegedly the most strikingly handsome building in the city. Since 1995, "Belle" and "Stewart," two endangered peregrine falcons, have been nesting on top this building and each April welcome several newborns,

called eyasses (Peregrine Hotline, tel: 206 654-4423). The baby birds remain in the nest for about six weeks before their first flight. The public can view the falcon family live via a color television monitor inside the tower.

Breathing spaces in the middle of this high-rise setting are few and welcome. **Freeway Park** ⓠ between Hubble and Spring, built partially over a freeway to reconnect two divided neighborhoods, is an interesting setting for free lunchtime concerts. With a waterfall to mask the din of traffic, plus trees, flowers, pools and a "gorge", city tensions are calmed.

Architect Robert Venturi's postmodern-style downtown branch of the **Seattle Art Museum (SAM)** ⓡ (100 University Street; Tues–Sun 10am–5pm, Thur 10am–9pm, closed: holidays; tel: 206 654-3255; fee) is fronted with a massive sculpture of a manual worker, called *Hammering Man*. It displays an impressive collection of more than 21,000 objects, including Old Master paintings, contemporary Northwest art

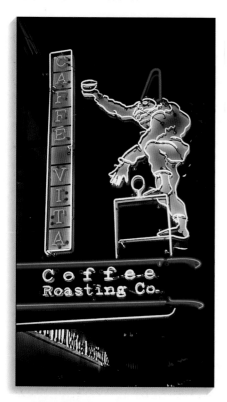

and African masks. Visitors can also enjoy lectures, the **Museum Store** and the **Café**.

Directly across from the Art Museum is compelling **Benaroya Hall**, opened in 1998. The building was designed by Mark Reddington and has soaring windows and stunning chandeliers by Dale Chihuly. The jewel of the interior is **Taper Auditorium**, a 2,500-seat space that is an eloquent home for the Seattle Symphony. Downtown Seattle also has a wealth of low, older buildings with extensive terra-cotta molding and decoration.

The arts scene

Although Seattle's theater scene is considered one of the most active in America, Seattleites tend to prefer home-grown talent, and a look through the city's listings will produce few well-known names. But make no mistake: talent is here. Exceptions to the who's-that?-rule are glass art's Dale Chihuly, rock's Ann and Nancy Wilson from Heart, native Kurt Cobain's widow Courtney Love, the internationally acclaimed Pacific Northwest Ballet (tel: 206 441-9411 for tickets and details), sax player Kenny G, actor Tom Skerritt, and writers Ann Rule and Tom Robbins.

The British travel writer Jonathan Raban makes the Pacific Northwest his home and writes about the quirks of the region; David Guterson's *Snow Falling on Cedars* (1994) was set in the misty San Juan Islands and was made into a film; TV's *Frasier* is set here; and Annie Dillard wrote *The Living* (1992), a romantic tale of the Pacific Northwest set in the late 19th century. The best-known Seattle-based film, *Sleepless in Seattle* (1993) was set on a Lake Union houseboat.

Curiously, the Seattle area has also launched internationally known, offbeat contemporary cartoonists, such as Matt Groening, originator of *The Simpsons*, and lampoonist Gary Larson. Free tabloids such as *The Weekly* and *The Stranger* cover the arts scene.

Pacific Northwest Ticket Service (tel: 206 232-0150; booking fee) sells tickets to all types of events, while **Ticket/ Ticket** (tel: 206 324-2744; booking fee) sells half-price day-of-show tickets to theater,

LEFT: coffeehouses are ubiquitous.

Map on page 92

music, comedy and dance performances.

The **Westlake Center** ❺, at 1601 5th Avenue, might be considered the heart of Seattle's shopping district. Interspersed with Starbucks coffee shops on seemingly every street are a good collection of downtown shops, including the flagship store of **Nordstrom**, the nationwide department store chain known for its politeness, established in Seattle in 1901.

The third level of the Westlake Center is the place to catch the **Seattle Center Monorail** (Mon–Fri 7:30am–11pm, Sat–Sun 9am–11pm; tel: 206 441-6038; fee), which travels every 10 minutes from Downtown to the "campus" of the **Seattle Center** in just 2 minutes.

Designed for the 1962 World's Fair on the back of a napkin, a 74-acre (30-hectare) **urban park** today features a number of facilities including the globally known, futuristic Space Needle, three major museums, two amusement parks, shops and places to eat, as well as a skate park.

The graceful landscaping, fountains, and large open spaces make the park an ideal site for summer festivals, although visitors are warned to be careful when walking around the base of the Space Needle after dark. The **International Fountain**, a favorite lounging area, is a mainstay from the World's Fair, but was completely redone and expanded in a $6.5 million project in 1995.

Most famous landmark

Most notable in the Seattle Center is the **Space Needle** ❼ (219 4th Avenue North; daily 8am–midnight; tel: 206 905-2100), the building with the halo and Seattle's most famous landmark. Inside, the bottom contains a gift shop, **SpaceBase**; near the top is a revolving restaurant called **SkyCity** (tel: 206 905-2100; reservations required; elevator ride free for restaurant patrons). At the very top is a large circular observation area, the **O-Deck**.

A 41-second elevator ride (fee) first takes visitors 500 ft (150 meters) above ground to the restaurant; second stop at 520 ft (158 meters) is Seattle's 360° premier panoramic viewing experience. The restaurant and the viewing-deck operate

separately. For those who keep count, the total structure is 605 ft (184 meters) in height; about the equivalent of a 60-story building. Remarkably, the perfectly balanced restaurant rotates with a one-horse-power electric motor and that piece of equipment reportedly has the highest gear ratio in the world – 360,000 to 1. The Space Needle is fastened to its foundation with 72 bolts, each of which is 30 ft (9 meters) long. Although the Needle was built to withstand a wind velocity of 200 mph (325 kph), severe storms occasionally do force it to close.

The Needle has withstood several tremors, including a 1965 earthquake measuring 6.5 on the Richter scale and a 2001 repeat at a higher 6.8 level. The original designers enabled the structure to withstand even greater jolts, although a $20 million revitalization effort in 2000 reinforced this. A beam of light that shines skyward from the top of the Space Needle, the **Legacy Light**, honors leaders and commemorates special occasions in Seattle. The restaurant

RIGHT: dancin' in the street.

has had mixed reviews ever since it opened. Sometimes the food is overpriced tourist fare, and sometimes (depending on the chef or the management), the food can be pretty good, if still pricey. The view remains superlative, however, whether seen from the restaurant or from the O-Deck, in the middle of the day or at midnight, when the structure closes.

Hendrix woz here

At the base of the Space Needle, referred to as "the Needle's jacket dropped on the ground" is the unmistakable purple, silver and red metallic undulating heap of a building called **Experience Music Project (EMP)** ⓤ (325 5th Avenue North; Sun–Thur 9am–9pm, Fri–Sat 9am–11pm; tel: 206 367-5482; fee). It was opened in true rock-star fashion in June 2000 when the music lover and tech-billionaire Paul Allen lifted a Dale Chihuly glass guitar above his head and hurled it to the ground, signaling the opening of his personal dream-come-true museum. Some say EMP resembles a

guitar smashed by Seattle native Jimi Hendrix; some argue that its shapes are based on the components of the inner ear. Still others say it's an unsightly blob. But no one can ignore the ever-unfolding structure clad in psychedelic shades of aluminum and stainless steel designed by renowned architect Frank Gehry, of Bilbao's Guggenheim Museum fame.

The rock 'n' roll museum cost Paul Allen about $100 million to build and serves as an interactive music museum combining hands-on experiences with interpretive exhibits telling the story of the creative process in American popular music. State-of-the-art technology, a world-class collection of artifacts and exciting multimedia presentations make EMP the first of its kind in the world.

Each visitor is provided with a MEG or Museum Exhibit Guide, wireless headphones that let users hear recordings and the narration of their choice as they move throughout the museum. The entrance fee is expensive, but it's easy to spend hours looking around; concerts are given here, too and are usually covered in the fee. The Turntable Restaurant, Liquid Lounge, and EMP Store are free to enter.

Butterflies and science

The Seattle Center is more than simply needles and spins, rock 'n' roll, however. Under graceful lace-like spires, the **Pacific Science Center** ⓥ (200 2nd Avenue North; daily 10am–6pm; tel: 206 443-2001; fee) features five buildings of interactive science exhibits, a tropical Butterfly House, two IMAX theaters – one with 3D technology – a planetarium and laser light shows. The fee includes more than 6 acres (2.5 hectares) of hands-on exhibits, plus the planetarium shows, but the IMAX theaters cost extra.

The **Children's Museum** (305 Harrison Street; Mon–Fri 10am–5pm, Sat–Sun 10am–6pm; tel: 206 441-1768; fee) at Center House, where the monorail disembarks, has interactive child-size exhibits that invite little visitors to explore world cultures across the globe and through time. **Fun Forest Amusement Park** (305 Harrison Street; summer daily noon–

LEFT: the Space Needle design was originally just a sketch on a napkin.

Map
on page
92

11pm; winter Fri–Sun, noon–8pm; tel: 206 728-1586; fee) includes rides for thrill seekers including an adrenaline rush on the roller coaster or a quick spin around a carousel. The Fun Forest also includes the **Entertainment Pavilion** (same hours), with three rides, laser tag, mini-golf and a video arcade. Seattle Center's **Skate Park** – designed by skateboarders – is an 8,900 sq-ft (826-sq-meter) outdoor park for all skill levels, welcoming in-line skaters and skateboarders from dawn until dusk.

Continuing "on campus" at Seattle Center, **Northwest Craft Center** (305 Harrison Street; tel: 206 728-1555; free) is one of Seattle's oldest galleries, opened in 1963 and continuing to feature the work of local and national ceramicists, sculptors, painters, jewelers, glass-blowers and print-makers. **Seattle Center House** has dozens of fast-food eateries, from Pizza Haven to The Frankfurter, plus stores with crafts and good Northwest souvenirs.

Also of note are a **Berlin Wall Display** and a children's play area.

BELOW:
Experience
Music Project,
designed by
Frank Gehry.

The International District

Seattle's prosperous Asian neighborhood is not known as "Chinatown," but as the **International District (ID)** Ⓦ because so many different Asian nationalities now call this home. Running from 5th Avenue South to 8th Avenue South, the area was originally a refuge for Cantonese forced laborers, who were released after the completion of the railroad.

The ID later survived the depletions of both the 1880s anti-Chinese riots and the World War II internment of Japanese-Americans. The history of Asian-Pacific Americans is told at the **Wing Luke Asian Museum** (407 7th Avenue South; Tues–Fri 11am–4:30pm, Sat–Sun noon–4pm; tel: 206 623-5124; fee), a pan-Asian collection dedicated to Wing Luke, the son of an immigrant laundryman and the first person of Asian ancestry to be elected to office.

While the International District is small, there are about 40 Asian-cuisine restaurants, plus herbalists, massage parlors,

acupuncturists and – unfortunately – exotic pets. **King Street** is the center of Chinese remedy activity, with shark fins, mandrake roots, trussed poultry, pungent herbs and secret ingredients sold with a dollop of advice by shopkeepers. A favorite remedy is to cure male "tiredness."

The House of Dumplings (512 South King Street; tel: 206 340-0774) serves extremely good *dim sum* and Uwajimaya (519 Sixth Avenue) has a cooking school, a bookstore and a sushi bar, as well as being the largest all-Asian supermarket in the West. **Hing Hay Park**'s dragon mural and bright pagoda, donated by the City of Taipei, is the setting for martial- arts exhibitions and Chinese folk dancing.

A giant brass dragon graces the nearby **Children's Park**. The district's other park, named **Kobe Terrace** after Seattle's Japanese sister city, features an 8,000-lb (3,600-kg) stone lantern and a quiet place to contemplate the meeting of East and West. **Nippon Kan Theatre** (628 South Washington Street; Mon–Fri 11am–5pm;

tel: (206) 224-0181; free except for special events), built in 1904, is now designated a historic landmark and offers an eclectic mix of events.

Capitol Hill

Once the residence of Seattle's wealthiest citizens, **Capitol Hill** ⊗ now has the most diverse and youth-oriented population in the city. Seattle's gay community, grunge rockers and a rich ethnic mix of people share the area with long-time residents of elegant old homes and classic apartment houses, as well as with numerous entertainment venues and coffeehouses.

Nearby, the Central Area and South Seattle neighborhoods have long been the heart of the city's African-American community and, in the 1930s, the area began establishing a reputation for jazz and blues musicians. Ray Charles, Quincy Jones, Jimi Hendrix and Ernestine Anderson all lived in this neighborhood at some time.

The connoisseur's eye will be attracted to **Volunteer Park** ⊗, a luxurious 40-acre

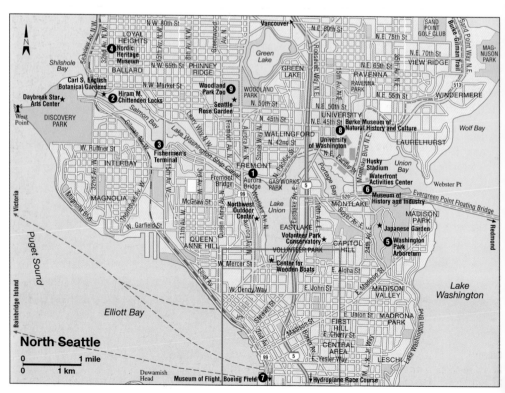

Maps, pages 92 & 104

(16-hectare) space on Capitol Hill's northern crest. Circling drives and manicured lawns lead to a conservatory and an old water tower with a 75-ft (20-meter) vantage point.

The park was home to the Seattle Art Museum for more than 50 years and now hosts the renovated **Seattle Asian Art Museum ❷** (1400 East Prospect Street; Tues–Sun 10am–5pm, Thur 10am–9pm; tel: 206 654-3100; fee), which presents a thousand years of beauty – Asian works of art from ceramics to furniture. A walk through the area adjacent to and just east of Volunteer Park is a good way to see a cross-section of Seattle's older residential architecture, much of it well-preserved.

Lakes Washington and Union

It is said that one out of every five Seattleites owns some kind of boat: Seattle's houseboat population is the largest east of Asia. No surprise, then, that boat-loving visitors seek out the attractions in the lake district. That said, even landlubbers will enjoy the neighborhood of **Fremont ❶**, which lies at the northwest corner of Lake Union. Once a home for hippies, artists and a group of very strange public-art sculptures, the area has been well and truly discovered. But just because you can't afford to buy a house in Fremont anymore doesn't mean you can't enjoy a day wandering around it's shops, galleries and cafés.

The **Hiram M. Chittenden Locks ❷** (daily 7am–9pm), also known locally as the **Ballard Locks**, are a US Army Corp of Engineering feat that provide Seattle with a 25,000-acre (10,000-hectare) inland freshwater harbor connecting **Lake Washington** and **Lake Union** by way of **Salmon Bay** to Puget Sound. The locks are among the busiest in the country.

As well as getting up close to the locks, visitors can do a number of other things: watch – through underwater windows – migrating salmon and steelhead bypass the locks; view the **Carl S. English Botanical Garden** (free), and stop by a **visitor center** (3015 Northwest 54th Street; June–Sept daily 10am–6pm; Oct–May Thur–Mon 11am–5pm; tel: 206

783-7059) to watch an orientation video.

A memorable way of seeing Seattle by land and sea is to take a tour in a restored World War II amphibious landing craft – a DUKW. The enjoyable **Ducks of Seattle tour** (90-minute rides; summer 9:30am–7pm; winter 11:30am–5pm; tel: 206 441-4687; fee), covers Downtown, Pike Place Market, Pioneer Square and then splashes into Lake Union. Buy tickets and board Downtown on the corner of 5th and Broad, across from the Seattle Center.

Seattle is the nation's sea-kayaking capital and the waters all around the city are ideal for leisurely paddling. Kayakers can even pull up at waterfront restaurants for a meal. For a memorable water experience, contact **Northwest Outdoor Center** (2100 Westlake Avenue North; Apr–Sept Mon–Fri 10am–8pm, Sat, Sun and holidays 9am–6pm; tel: 206 281-9694). This is the place for kayak rentals, equipment and advice.

The city's Scandinavian heritage remains

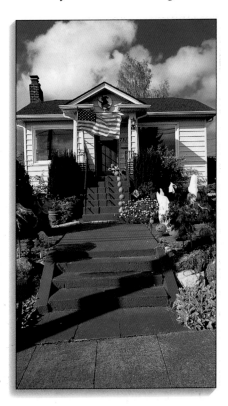

evident in a maritime neighborhood of north Seattle where the Alaskan fishing fleet winters at **Fishermen's Terminal ❸** (3919 18th Avenue West) before re-embarking on its quest for salmon. A working dock, the terminal is not strictly a tourist attraction. However, onsite is a fine **Fishermen's Memorial** dedicated to those who have lost their lives at sea.

Historic downtown **Ballard** has brick streets, numerous galleries and lively taverns full of local music; it is definitely one of the up-and-coming neighborhoods of the area. This popularity is set to explode when the Seattle monorail finally links Ballard to Downtown and West Seattle.

The **Nordic Heritage Museum ❹** 3014 Northwest 67th Street; Tues–Sat 10am–4pm, Sun noon–4pm; tel: 206 789-5707; fee) is here – the only museum in the country to honor immigrants from five Nordic countries – Denmark, Finland, Iceland, Norway and Sweden – in collections of photographs, costumes and century-old fishing and maritime implements.

On the shores of Lake Washington, south of the University District on Union Bay, **Washington Park Arboretum ❺**, (23 Arboretum Drive East; dawn to dusk; tel: 206 543-8800; free) is a 200-acre (80-hectare) park with over 5,500 species of rare trees and other flora, both native and imported. From Downtown, take bus 11 to Madison Street. In 1957 plans for a special garden were drawn up by seven distinguished landscape designers in the Tokyo Metropolitan Park Department and given to the people of Seattle.

Along Lake Washington Boulevard, the **Japanese Garden** (Mar–Nov daily 8am–6pm; fee) has koi carp-filled pools, an Azumaya shelter and a **Tea House** symbolically representing a compressed world; take bus 11 or 84.

At the north end of the arboretum, the **Museum of History and Industry ❻** (daily 10am–5pm; tel: 206 324-1126; fee) has thousands of items dealing with the growth of Seattle and the Puget Sound region, and is more interesting than its dry-sounding name implies. Photographs and artifacts trace the city from its frontier days to its emergence as a logging and shipping center. The collection includes nautical and aviation equipment like a 1920s Boeing mail plane, antique cars and costumes; take bus 25, 43 or 48.

Airplanes and dinosaurs

The balance of Seattle's major attractions are spread out in various corners of this elongated city: south of the lake district is the popular **Museum of Flight ❼** (9404 East Marginal Way; daily 10am–5pm, Thur 10am–9pm; tel: 206 764-5700; fee), located beside the runway at **Boeing**; from downtown Seattle, take bus 174. One of Boeing's original buildings, the **Red Barn**, is part of the museum, its **Great Gallery** home to a collection of aircraft hanging from the glass ceiling. This permanent exhibition is unquestionably a tribute to Seattle's airline industry-giant, Boeing, but nonetheless covers the entire history of flight from Leonardo da Vinci's visionary drawings to the NASA space program.

The **Burke Museum of Natural**

LEFT: North Seattle' Woodland Par Zoo is one of America's finest.

Map
on page
104

History and Culture ❽ (17th Avenue Northeast and Northeast 45th Street; daily 10am–5pm, Thur 10am–8pm; tel: 206 543-5590; fee) focuses on the Pacific Northwest native culture and the Pacific Rim, with exhibits on the geology and biology of Washington State, plus dinosaur skeletons; from Downtown, take bus 7. It is located on the University of Washington campus in the **University District**, itself an interesting area of discoveries.

Top zoo and high tech

The 92-acre (37-hectare) **Woodland Park Zoo** ❾ (5500 Phinney Avenue North; daily: winter 9:30am–4pm; summer 9:30am–5pm; tel: 206 684-4800; fee) in North Seattle is considered among the top ten zoos in America. It is a world leader in freeing animals from cages and letting them roam in natural settings. Among the habitats are a butterfly exhibit, the Trail of Vines, Northern Trail, a tropical rainforest, the African savannah and an elephant habitat reminiscent of Thailand.

Also on the grounds is the estate's formal rose garden. Outside the zoo are wooded picnic areas. The east side of the park has tennis courts and the remains of an old buggy road that heads toward **Green Lake**, a mecca for the summer sun- and fitness-crowd.

In **Renton**, the **Spirit of Washington Dinner Train Experience** (625 South 4th Street; tel: 425 227-7245; reservations) recreates the nostalgia of passenger rail as visitors ride and dine in vintage rail cars. From Renton to Woodinville, the journey meanders along the shores of Lake Washington and over the historic Wilburton Trestle. There is a 45-minute stopover at **Columbia Winery**, founded in 1962 by ten friends, seven of whom were University of Washington professors.

And finally, the answer to one of the most frequently asked questions by visitors: so where is the headquarters of Microsoft? The answer is: not in the city at all, but in the neighboring area east of Seattle called **Redmond** (see page 118).   ❑

BELOW:
Seattle's
Museum
of Flight.

Map on page 110

TACOMA

*Washington's third-largest city has a busy harbor
and lies in the shadow of Mount Rainier,
the peak after which it is named*

Tacoma was named after the local Native American word for Mount Rainier and originally pronounced "tahoma." Located only 30 miles (48 km) south of Seattle, this busy port town is easily accessible by public transportation from its better-known neighbor. It overlooks activity-filled **Commencement Bay**, a well-protected harbor, and is the shipping and warehousing center of the state. *(For more on Mount Rainier, see page 182.)*

Shipping, a subject unlikely to grab the attention of many, is surprisingly interesting in the Pacific Northwest, with a wealth of fascinating detail. Few people realize, for instance, that a huge number of the Japanese games and computer software sold throughout the United States is unloaded at the ports here.

Big money

The merchandise hauled in one of the many container ships that regularly berth here can be worth hundreds of thousands of dollars. It is for this reason that the "pilot" who single-handedly operates the huge red cranes that off-load this merchandise is treated like a king: he is allowed to work only a certain number of hours per week, and is paid handsomely for doing so. With cargo so valuable, this is one guy you don't want arriving for work with a hangover.

For an overview of harbor proceedings, visit the **Port of Tacoma Observation Tower** (1 Sitcum Way; tel: 253 383-5841; free) or the **Commencement Bay Maritime Center** (705 Dock Street; Mon–Fri, noon–5pm; tel: 253 272-2750; free), an old warehouse showcasing the maritime heritage of Tacoma's working waterfront.

The six-block outdoor **Broadway Plaza** mall – good for specialty shopping and its attractive waterfront – is anchored by the popular **Sheraton Tacoma Hotel** (1320 Broadway Plaza; tel: 253 572-

3200), which has spectacular views and is a short walk away from the theater district with its **Broadway Center for the Performing Arts Ⓐ** (tel: 253 591-5890).

Ruston Way has 2 miles (3 km) of walkways snaking along the waterfront, while near 7th Avenue, **Antique Row Ⓑ** is a good place for upscale gifts. Anyone who savors the harbor can opt for a jaunt aboard the *Emerald Queen* Casino (2102 Alexander Avenue; tel: 253 594-7777), a riverboat offering dining, gambling and entertainment. Back on land, a popular eatery promises every table with a view of Puget Sound: **C.I. Shenanigans** (3017 North Ruston Way; tel: 253 752-8811).

Tacoma's museums are within walking distance of Broadway Plaza. These

include the **Tacoma Art Museum** **C** (12th and Pacific Avenue; closed Mon; tel: 253 272-4258; fee) with exhibitions of 19th- and 20th-century art including Degas and Renoir, and pieces by Tacoma's famous resident, Dale Chihuly. In fact, so successful has been Chihuly and the Studio Glass Movement, a **Museum of Glass** **D** (934 Broadway; tel: 253 396-1768; fee) opened in 2002. With a ground level of glass and steel topped by a tilted glass cone encased in stainless-steel mesh, the museum is a celebration of the medium that has come to be associated with the Pacific Northwest.

Another museum is the fine **Washington State History Museum** **E** (1911 Pacific Avenue; daily; tel: 253 272-3500; fee) presenting the soul, spirit and stories of Washington, including "The Life and Legacy of Woody Guthrie." One block from the area's most famous landmark, the blue-roofed **Tacoma Dome** **F**, is **Freighthouse Square** (East 25th Street and East "D" Street; daily; tel: 253 305-

0678) encompassing 70 original shops and popular for its fast-food **International Food Court**. The market's decor preserves the heritage of the old Milwaukee, St Paul and Pacific Railroad with maps, memorabilia and paintings.

Antiques and an aquarium

The city's residential districts contain many original Victorian homes from the turn of the 19th century, with turrets, gables and leaded windows. One to seek out is the elegantly decorated colonial home with bay views, **Commencement Bay B&B** (tel: 253 752-8175; reservations). The "small town" **Proctor shopping district** is at Tacoma's north end. Established more than 100 years ago, it is home to the **Antique Mall** **G** (2701 North Proctor and North 27th) and the **Proctor Farmers' Market** (June–Aug Sat only 9am–2pm).

Nearby, on a prominent point of land that juts into the bay with the broad blue of Puget Sound as a backdrop, is the 500-acre (200-hectare) **Point Defiance Park**,

BELOW: the logging railroad retraces the lumberjack experience.

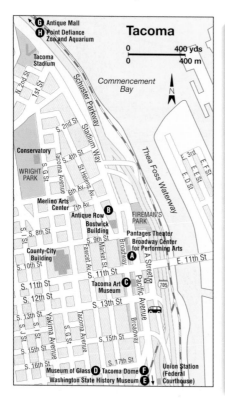

founded in 1888 and home to the **Zoo and Aquarium**  (5400 North Pearl Street; summer 10am–7pm; winter 10am–4pm; tel: 253 591-5337; fee), with sharks, beluga whales, polar bears and pachyderms. The beluga whales in particular are worth a visit; keep in mind that in August 2001, a Federal judge rejected environmentalists' pleas for protection for a dwindling population – around 350 – of these important creatures in Cook Inlet Alaska, so we may be seeing the last of them.

Lumberjack experience

Take a quick walk through **Never Never Land** (June–Aug; tel: 253 591-5845; free), a rag-tag park with figurines depicting children's stories, and the **Fort Nisqually National Historic Site** (June–Sept daily 11am–6pm; Oct–May Wed–Sun 11am–4pm; tel: 253 591-5339; fee), a Hudson's Bay Company outpost built in 1833. Also in the park is the 14-acre (6-hectare) **Camp 6 Logging Exhibit Museum** (Apr–Oct Wed–Sun 10am–4pm; tel: 253 305-1000;

free), which is chock full of old steam-powered logging camp equipment. Here, too, the **Summer Logging Train Ride** (June–Sept weekends only noon–6:30pm; tel: 253 305-1000; fee) completes the lumberjack experience.

Bison, moose and other native Northwest animals roam happily in a comprehensive wildlife park just 35 miles (55 km) from Tacoma at **Northwest Trek Wildlife Park** (Eatonville; daily 9:30am–3pm; tel: 360 832-6117; fee). In addition to nature trails with views of wolves, cougars and wolverines, an enclosed tram takes visitors through free-ranging herds of bison and past habitats teaming with waterfowl.

For railroad enthusiasts, **Mount Rainier Scenic Railroad** (Hwy 7, Elbe; May–June, Sept weekends; July–Aug daily; tel: 360 569-2588; fee) offers excursions that chug across spectacular bridges, clickety-clack through tall forests and let off steam by **Mineral Lake** – all pulled by vintage steam locomotives through Mount Rainier's foothills. Bring a picnic lunch. ❏

BELOW: two famous sights: the Tacoma Dome and Mount Rainier.

Map
on page
114

PUGET SOUND AND THE SAN JUAN ISLANDS

*Here you can find pretty towns, rural tranquility
and a leisurely, maritime-based life – all
within easy reach of Seattle*

Sculpted by the repeated advance and withdrawal of numerous glacial periods, Puget Sound is an ocean inlet and estuary – a vast inland sea – where ocean saltwater mixes with freshwater precipitation draining from the land. More than 10,000 rivers and streams pour into its maze of passageways, convoluted bays and forked inlets. When taken as a whole, these add up to a stunning 2,354 miles (3,800 km) of shoreline.

A whale of a time

The Sound gives western Washington its character as it stretches south some 100 miles (160 km) from Admiralty Inlet and Whidbey Island, beyond which lie the Straits of Georgia and Juan de Fuca. Within these Straits are the clustered island-jewels known as the San Juans. Nearly 100 orcas, in three family pods, reside in the San Juan Islands during the summer months, which makes whale-watching a favorite activity. Many companies offer naturalist-guided tours. A large western extension of the Sound is interesting Hood Canal.

With excellent deepwater harbors, including Seattle, Tacoma, Everett, and Port Townsend serving as outports for farmlands along the river estuaries, Bremerton's naval shipyard adds military shipping to the Sound's noted volume of local and international trade. The average depth is 450 ft (140 meters).

Known as *Whulge*, the region was occupied by Native Americans for about 8,000 years before European Juan Perez encountered it in 1774 – four years before Captain James Cook momentarily thought he'd found the long-sought Northwest Passage. The body of water was eventually named for Peter Puget, a trusted lieutenant of Captain George Vancouver, who commanded several small-boat expeditions, including a week-long tour of Southern Puget Sound. Born in London in 1765, Puget first went to sea at age 12, served on British naval ships in the West Indies. At age 26, he signed up for Vancouver's voyage. Eventually, he was promoted to captain of the *Chatham*, the small tender that sailed with Vancouver's *Discovery*. His obscurity is only one of the indignities endured by most of those whose names are attached to its landmarks – Puget, Rainier, Whidbey, even the skipper himself, George Vancouver.

By the time they returned from their four-year voyage in 1795, the British had

LEFT: ferry approaching Friday Harbor, San Juan Island.
RIGHT: Whidbey Island woman.

lost interest in exploration. They faced more urgent matters, such as Napoleon: Puget's distinguished naval career included action against Napoleon's navy. He died in 1822. His memorial in Woolsey remained in obscurity until it was tracked down by a local researcher as recently as the 1970s.

While much of the Sound is healthy, the rapid growth of industry, urban development and recreational usage have placed serious environmental pressures on certain sections. But for the first-time visitor the rewards are numerous. From the deck of a ferryboat it is easy to downshift from a bustling cosmopolitan atmosphere to timeless rural tranquility and experience soft sea-winds moving through pine trees in the space of an hour. With the aid of a bicycle or a vehicle, explorers can travel to quaint seaside villages, through verdant farms, windswept beaches or wildlife sanctuaries.

For Puget Sound in general, summer maximum temperatures average around 72°F (22°C) and average winter lows run about 30°F (–1°C). Rainfall is 55 inches (140 cm) annually – higher than in Seattle. For the purposes of this chapter, the town of Seattle serves as the center point, because we assume most visitors will come from the bigger town. Puget Sound places are then described to Seattle's west, east, north, then south. (*For more on ferries, see page 116.*)

Bainbridge Island

Bainbridge Island ❶ (Chamber of Commerce, tel: 206 842-3700), located west of Seattle on the **Kitsap Peninsula**, is easily accessible from downtown Seattle via the Washington State Ferry or by car across the **Agate Passage Bridge**. Predominantly a bedroom community, this semi-rural island is peppered with trim farmhouses, beach-with-a-view mansions and half-way-finished renovations. **Winslow Way** is lined with small shops and restaurants.

The **Bainbridge Island Vineyards and Winery** (682 Hwy; Wed–Sun noon–5pm, closed: holidays; tel: 206 842-9463; tasting fee) is just a short

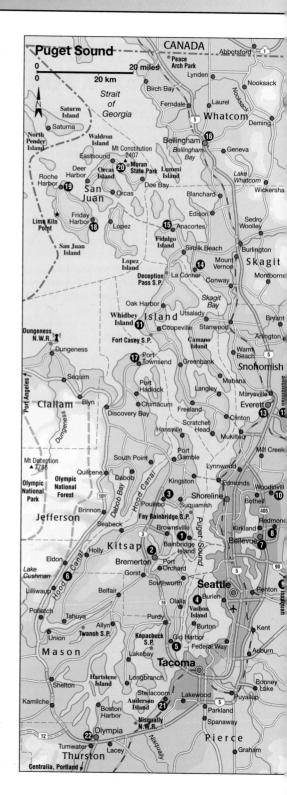

Map
on page
114

walk from the ferry up Rt 305. There is a vineyard tour with a winegrower or winemaker every Sunday afternoon. **Fay Bainbridge State Park** (north on Rt 305 and right on Day Road; tel: 206 842-3931) features views of downtown Seattle. Garden lovers rave about the 150-acre (60-hectare) **Bloedel Reserve** (north on Rt 305; Wed–Sun, closed: holidays; tel: 206 842-7631; fee), a former estate with fine formal gardens, nature trails and an attractive manor house.

Deep purple sky

On the opposite end of Bainbridge Island is **Fort Ward**, established during World War I to protect the Bremerton Navy Yard. There are no campsites here, but the rocky beach at sunset shows off the island's highlights: the **Olympic Mountains** casting their silhouettes against a deep purple sky and the lights of reflected ships across the darkened waters.

After the short ferry ride from Seattle to **Bremerton ❷**, there is no doubt that the **Puget Sound Naval Shipyard** is the county's largest employer. Mothballed and to-be-overhauled Navy vessels loom along the shore of **Sinclair Inlet**. Downtown Bremerton's waterfront park includes the Vietnam-era naval destroyer **USS Turner Joy** (tours May–Sept; tel: 360 792-2457; fee). From here **Naval Shipyard/Mothball Fleet Tours**, which are narrated 45-minute tours (May Sat–Sun; June–Aug daily; tel: 360 377-8924) leave for the shipyard and **Kitsap Harbor**.

In the ferry terminal itself, the free **Bremerton Naval Museum** (summer only; tel: 360 479-7447) illustrates US naval history with models of ships, naval weapons, photographs and memorabilia. The **Naval Undersea Museum** is 10 miles (16 km) north of Bremerton and houses the country's largest collection of submarines, torpedos and undersea mines.

For a scenic loop, you can travel Washington State Ferries to Poulsbo via the Edmonds–Kingston ferry and return via the Bainbridge Island ferry. In order to do

BELOW:
Bainbridge
Island from
the ferry.

this, from Kingston, take state Rt 104, veer left as it becomes Bond Road at Streibles Corner, then follow it to Front Street by the water. **Poulsbo** ❸ (pronounced *pauls*-bow) is dubbed "little Norway" due to its reputed resemblance to the famed fjords. A white-spired Lutheran church peers over the bay, and a wooden breakwater shelters the fishing fleet. Colorful murals in rosemaling technique depict Norwegian lifestyles. The very interesting **Paulsbo Marine Science Center** (daily 11am–5pm; tel: 360 779-5549; fee) encourages visitors to get up close to more than 100 species of marine life typical of the Puget Sound region.

On the way back, consider taking Lemolo Drive, which curves around **Liberty Bay** and has great mountain views.

Chief Sealth's grave

Fjord Street is a block up the hill from Front Street. The road hooks up with Rt 305 shortly before the Agate Passage Bridge. Detour north off the highway to

visit the **Suquamish Museum** (15838 Sandy Hook Road; May–Sept daily 10am–5pm; Oct–Apr Fri–Sun 11am–4pm; tel: 360 598-3311 ext. 422; fee) and nearby **Chief Sealth's grave**. This is the place to reflect on Chief Sealth, more commonly known as Chief Seattle, the man who smoothed relations between Indians and non-Indians, and gave the town its name. "The Earth does not belong to us, we belong to the Earth," he said.

Of note is Poulsbo's recent neighbor. **Bangor** is home to about 20 Trident submarines and a number of naval operations.

Just south of Bainbridge Island, the mainly residential **Vashon Island** ❹ is completely dependent on the ferry system. It offers some pleasant walks along beaches including **Inspiration Point** with, on a clear day, a powerful view of Mount Rainier. Ferries head in three directions from here: west to Southworth, east to Fauntleroy and south to Tacoma. Just west of the **Tacoma Narrows Bridge** (replacement for the infamous earlier bridge that

BELOW: everyone travels by ferry

TRAVELING BY FERRY

For Washington residents, ferries are a vital means of commuting; for visitors, they are a delightful way to travel. Comely to watch as they power across Puget Sound and cruise among the San Juan Islands, ferries are relatively inexpensive, and fun to ride as they ply waters shared by orcas and seals, freighters and kayakers. For all Washington State Ferries (schedule information, tel: 206 464-6400), tickets are sold on-the-spot or by reservation and the ferry system accepts both walk-on passengers or vehicles with passengers.

During the summer, Clipper Navigation (tel: 206 448-5000; reservations necessary) offers three daily departures from Seattle aboard its passenger-only, high-speed catamarans, arriving in the beautiful harbor town of Victoria in British Columbia, Canada, two to three hours later. This makes a delightful weekend trip, which can be coupled with shopping – particularly rewarding when the exchange rate favors the American dollar – or taking a whale-watching tour. Aim to return at sunset, a breathtaking experience as the boat winds in among the smaller islands. Also available is a five-hour trip traveling through the San Juan Islands with a stop in Friday Harbor. Seating is limited on the catamarans, so book ahead.

Map
on page
114

collapsed in the wind in November, 1940) is **Gig Harbor ❺**, a charming fishing community, lying an easy one-hour drive from Seattle. While Gig Harbor does have a wealth of galleries, shops and restaurants, it has avoided the saccharin cuteness of other tourist towns. Local sailors consider it one of the most beautiful harbors in the world. Clams, crabs and oysters abound in **Kopachuck State Park** Scuttle about during low tides, seeing what you can scoop up.

Hood Canal

Part of the North Kitsap Peninsula, **Hood Canal ❻** offers another escape from the urban scene. Stop and swim, then take a boat or picnic at **Twanoh State Park** near the south end. Along this 100-mile (160-km) canal route, waterfront residences, small towns, little restaurants and public sites for digging clams and harvesting oysters pass by in constant succession. Motorists follow a circular route traveling by ferry from Seattle to Bremerton,

driving southwest to **Belfair** (the site of a state park) and following Rt 106 to **Union** near the canal's south tip. From here, the route heads north on Rt 101 for about 50 miles (80 km) along the west side of the fjord. To complete the loop, return to Seattle via the Hood Canal Bridge and a Kingston–Edmonds or Bainbridge–Seattle ferry. For an update on road conditions, tel: 800 695-7623. The **Hood Canal Bridge** floats on the water to the north – one of the three longest floating *(pontoon)* bridges in the world. Two other pontoons cross Seattle's Lake Washington.

Hamma Hamma Oyster Farm (tel: 360 877-5811) is on Hwy 101 between Lilliwaup and Eldon, and offers a 20-minute weekday tour to see the processing plant and shellfish beds. Additionally, the **Kimberly T. Gallery and Sculpture Garden** and the **Bronze Foundry** (Tues and Thur; tel: 360 427-3857), a fine-art casting foundry, located off Hwy 101 near **Shelton**, are open during business hours, and for pre-scheduled group tours.

BELOW:
Bremerton
Naval Museum.

East of Seattle

Moving into the vicinity immediately east of Seattle, **Bellevue ⑦** is noted for its **Museum of Doll Art** (1116 108th Avenue Northeast; Mon–Sat 10am–5pm, Sun 1–5pm; tel: 425 455-1116; fee), an award-winning private collection of more than 1,200 rare and collectible dolls, teddy bears, doll houses and other childhood memorabilia. You don't have to be under-age to appreciate this collection.

A few miles northeast is **Redmond ⑧** and the headquarters of Microsoft. Tall fir trees, forested trails, snow-capped mountain vistas, architecturally pleasing buildings, basketball courts, soccer fields, Lake "Bill," a store, a museum, food pavilions and shuttle buses are here, but nothing on the Microsoft campus is open to the public.

In **Issaquah ⑨**, animals and fish are the theme. Of interest is **Cougar Mountain Zoological Park** (19525 Southeast 54th; May–Oct Fri–Sun only; tel: 425 392-6278; fee), a small teaching zoo specializing in threatened or endangered animals, including cougars, reindeer and birds. From early September through November, the grand spectacle and local pastime is watching mature chinook and coho salmon return home from the Pacific Ocean. Visitors to the free, well-developed **Issaquah Salmon Hatchery** (25 West Sunset Way; daily 8am–4:30pm; tel: 425 391-9094) can view fish all year round, as well as see exhibits on the salmon's life cycle and habits.

Nearby **Hedges Cellars** (195 Northeast Gilman; Mon–Sat 11am–5pm; tel: 425 391-6056; tasting fee) has won gold medals for its Cabernet Sauvignon and Merlots; for microbrew fans the **Issaquah Brew House** (35 Sunset Way; tel: 425 557-1911) features a brewery and a 21-tap brewpub. The ale to ask for is Bull Frog.

The earth's 46° north parallel runs through the wine-growing regions of France's Bordeaux-Burgundy country and Eastern Washington too, drawing many comparisons between Washington wines and French ones. Additionally, the diverse climate of the region, ranging from long, warm summer days to cooler nights, allows Washington wineries to produce a variety of good wines. It's particularly strong on fruit wines, like strawberry and pear.

Wineries

Wine lovers head for **Woodinville ⑩**. The most popular is **Chateau Ste Michelle Winery** (14111 Northeast 145th Street; 40-minute tours daily, closed: holidays; tel: 425 415-3300; tasting fee), which welcomes more than 250,000 visitors a year for a tour of the chateau and historic 87-acre (35-hectare) grounds – once home to Seattle lumber baron Frederick Stimson. Also offered are classes and concerts, while the premises contain a glass-art gallery.

Other Eastside wineries include **Columbia Winery** (14030 Northeast 145th Street; daily; tel: 425 488-2776; tasting fee; *see page 107);* **Facelli Winery** (16120 Woodinville-Redmond Road Northeast; weekends only; tel: 425 488-1020; tasting fee); and **Silver Lake Sparkling Cellars** (17721 132nd Avenue Northeast; daily; tel: 425 486-1900; tasting fee).

For a change of pace, tour **Spectrum**

LEFT: Microsoft campus at Redmond.

Map
on page
114

Glass, the country's largest strained-glass manufacturer (Mon–Fri; 1-hour tours; tel: 425 483-6699; free), which merges old-world methods with modern technology. The tour can be dangerous (flying glass), so children must be at least 10 years old, and everyone should wear long pants.

As well as wine, the Eastside also has its share of breweries. Among them is the **Redhook Ale Brewery** (14300 Northeast 145th Street; brewery tours Mon–Fri 1pm–5pm, Sat–Sun noon–5pm; tel: 425 483-3232; small fee), producers of well-built beers, with a brewpub and live entertainment weeknight evenings.

The town of Woodinville is also the home of the **Herbfarm**, (14590 Northeast 145th Street; tel: 206 784-2222; reservations required) a well-known restaurant cultivating the good life that serves nine-course dinners. Although extremely pricy, meals are often booked months in advance. Near the town of Carnation, **Remlinger Farms** holds a large farmer's market, along with a **Country Kitchen** restaurant and bakery. Also on site is a petting farm, a train, pony rides and a hay maze.

North of Seattle

Two ferry terminals transport commuters to **Whidbey Island** ⓫, the longest island in the lower 48 American states, and onward to **Port Townsend**. Named for Joseph Whidbey, master of the *Discovery*, Whidbey was Captain Vancouver's right-hand man for the voyage, and commanded many of the small-boat expeditions that charted the Puget Sound shoreline. Historians have not been able to trace his life after his return to England.

Today, visitors' first stop of interest on Whidbey is **Langley**, a waterfront community known for its small galleries and pleasant inns. Once part of a triangle of forts established in 1890 to protect the Sound, **Fort Casey** is now a state park with a museum in the former lighthouse. A state ferry departs from nearby **Keystone** for Port Townsend (for information, tel: 360 678-5434). **Coupeville**, established in 1892, belongs to the National Historic District and is known for its antique shops, bed-and-breakfast inns and

the **Island County Historical Museum**. Its Victorian homes are full of fascinating maritime lore dating from the days of sea captains and rum runners.

The bulk of Whidbey Island's population resides toward the north end at shabby **Oak Harbor**, a naval-base town, which should be treated with caution. **Deception Pass State Park**, 9 miles (14 km) north of Oak Harbor, is one of Washington's busiest state parks. An impressive bridge spanning the rocks of Deception Pass connects Whidbey to **Fidalgo Island** near Anacortes. Rugged cliffs drop to meet the turbulent waters, while the park is notable for its views of Puget Sound, old-growth forests and abundant wildlife. The **Maiden of Deception Pass**, the story pole of the Samish Indian Nation, is located on **Rosario Beach** in the north part of the park.

At least a dozen inns are scattered through the center and south end of Whidbey, offering a choice of charming old farmhouses, glass-and-cedar mansions by the sea or restored Victorian homes. The

Whitbey Inn Bed-and-Breakfast (106 First Street, Langley; tel: 360 221-7115), **Home by the Sea** (2388 East Sunlight Beach Road, Clinton; tel: 360 221-2964), **Cliff House and Cottage** (727 Windmill Drive, Freeland; tel: 360 331-1566) and the **Victorian House** (602 North Main Street, Coupeville; tel: 360 678-5305) are only a few of these wonderful establishments, most of which offer excellent food and a quietly relaxing atmosphere.

Everett and vicinity

Back on the mainland, the community of **Snohomish** ⓬ is the place to look for antiques, as the town has more than 450 antiques dealers, including stores specializing in old toys and fine furniture. Snohomish's restaurants and parks are also worthwhile. Other attractions include the turn-of-the-19th-century Victorian home that's been converted into the **Blackman Museum**, and the **Pioneer Village**, with its restored houses, general store, weaver's cottage and blacksmith shop.

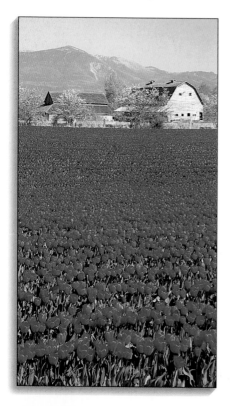

Situated on the mainland between Whidbey Island and the sharp Cascade peaks, **Everett** ⓭ has a concentration of wood-processing mills, miles of smokestacks and floating logs, but is most notable as the home of the colossal **Boeing Company** (guided tours Mon–Fri 9am–3pm; tel: 206 544-1264; fee; no cameras. Tickets must be picked up the morning of the tour around 9 am, and children must be at least 4 ft 2 inches/127 cm in height). Though the company has now moved its headquarters to Chicago, Boeing continues to be an economic engine for the state, generating billions of dollars in revenue, and working out of one of the largest buildings (in volume) in the US; they say the world. Visitors to the factory get to view lots of airplanes, notably, Boeing 747s, 767s, and 777s, in various stages of construction.

The Boeing Company operates in three principal segments: Commercial Airlines Operations; Military Aircraft and Missiles, and Space and Communications. Commercial Airplanes develops, produces and markets commercial jet aircraft as well as providing support services to the airline industry worldwide. Military Aircraft and Missiles researches, develops, produces, modifies and supports military aircraft, including fighter, transport and attack aircraft, plus helicopters and missiles.

Space and Communications researches, develops, produces, modifies and supports space systems, missile-defense systems, satellites and satellite-launching vehicles, rocket engines, and information and battle management systems.

For a change of pace, you can go see a working lumber mill and experience the industry that first put the Northwest on the map. **Buse Timber and Sales** (tel: 425 258-2577; ask for tour appointment; free) produces 50 million board feet of lumber and timber cuttings each year. The company sells cut lumber, wood chips for paper, sawdust, beauty bark for landscaping and dry shavings. It also smells absolutely wonderful (if you like wood).

Visitors can also arrange to climb aboard nuclear-powered aircraft carrier USS *Abraham Lincoln* and six other vessels at the **Everett Naval Station** (seasonal tours,

LEFT: Skagit County is known for its tulips.

Map on page 114

tel: 425 304-5665 or 425 304-3201; free) Tours of the *Lincoln* last about one hour; frigate and destroyer tours are a little shorter, lasting about 45 minutes.

Skagit County

The area around pretty **La Conner** ⓮, a little town on Swinomish Channel with shops, Victorian homes and lovely aquatic views, is primarily famous for its bulb farms bursting into color each spring. Yellow daffodils bloom March and April, while tulips are best in mid- to late April.

A popular stop for tourists, it is also home to the **Skagit County Historical Museum** and the much more substantial **Museum of Northwest Art** (121 South 1st Street; closed: Mon; tel: 360 466-4778; fee). Inspired during the 1930s and 1940s, this museum owes it beginnings to four Northwest artists who spent time in this valley: Guy Anderson, Kenneth Callahan, Morris Graves and Mark Tobey. They drew artistic sustenance from nature and Asian influences, creating a fresh style and a regional identity.

From January to April, thousands of snow geese from Siberia spend the winter in the **Skagit Wildlife Recreation Area** (near Ross Lake; tel: 360 902-2402; free). At the first signs of spring, they all leave – an awesome sight as 24,000 or more geese fly off within a timespan of 24 hours. Take-off is no earlier than April 17 and no later than May 5. Bald eagles also gather here during the cold winter months.

Nearby **Anacortes** ⓯ (visitor info, tel: 360 293-7911) is the place from which Washington State Ferries depart for the San Juan Islands and **Vancouver Island** in **British Columbia**. Poke around town, visit the fishing fleet and spin around **Washington Park** with its loop road. Historic attractions include the *W.T. Preston*, a steamboat restored as a museum, and a train depot where events are held. The downtown area has been revived with a few interesting shops and restaurants.

Canada calling

Bordering Canada's province of British Columbia, the spine of the Cascades is dominated by 10,775-ft (3,284-meter)

Mount Baker (Glacier Public Service Center, tel: 360 599-2714), which is 56 miles (90 km) east of Bellingham on Hwy 542. Mount Baker is a volcanic peak that is popular as a skiing resort in the winter, and as a hiking destination in the summer *(see page 191).*

Bellingham ⓰ (tel: 800 487-2032 for visitor information) is the home of scenic **Western Washington University**, a campus known for its outdoor sculpture garden. A refurbished warehouse with plank floors, **Boundary Bay Brewery and Bistro** (tel: 360 647-5593 for a tour) features unfiltered and handcrafted ales and lagers. Rated one of the top 25 breweries in the country by *America's Best Brews*, the company also received medals at the 17th Annual Great American Beer Festival in 1998. Three microbreweries in the state won a total of four medals, and Boundary Bay received two of those.

North of Bellingham is **Ferndale** with its **Historic Pioneer Park** (May–Sept Tues–Sun) and **Peace Arch Park**, the

RIGHT: a tulip farmer near La Conner, Skagit County.

garden that extends across the border between the United States and Canada.

A lovely stretch of accessible coastline is along **Chuckanut Drive**, which offers gratifying views of the San Juan Islands and **Chuckanut Bay**. The traditional activity here is to pig out on fresh oysters. For 75 years, the **Oyster Creek Inn** (2190 Chuckanut Drive; noon–9pm; tel: 360 766-6179) has offered diners fresh oysters in a treehouse setting high above the scenic waters. Alternately, **The Oyster Bar** (2578 Chuckanut Drive; 5–9pm; tel: 360 766-6185), with a fine view of the bay, has won several "Best Seafood" awards. It has as it's slogan *"The oyster you eat today slept last night in Samish Bay!"* **Chuckanut Manor** (3056 Chuckanut Drive Bow; Tues–Sun noon–9pm; tel: 360 766-6191) is also a popular stop. All three restaurants also serve meat dishes.

If snack-packs of freshly smoked oysters in flavors such as *jalapeno* float your boat, stop by the **Taylor Shellfish Farm** (2182 Chuckanut Drive; tel: 360 766-6002). They sell big, fresh Dungeness crabs too.

Perched on the northeast corner of the Olympic Peninsula, where the waters of the Strait of Juan de Fuca and Puget Sound create muscle-bound riptides, is the lovely town of **Port Townsend** ⓱. Heir to a fine British title, Townshend was an aide to General Wolfe in the Quebec campaign of 1759 and commanded British forces after Wolfe was killed. Townshend lived for 83 years, but never set eyes on the Pacific, let alone learned of the town that now bears his name (somehow misplacing the "h" along the way).

Port Townsend delights

Known for its historic downtown district, art galleries and bed-and-breakfast inns in artistically preserved Victorian homes, Port Townsend is the home of Centrum, an arts and education foundation presenting jazz, blues, fiddle tunes and classical music festivals. During the summer months, performances are held at **Fort**

BELOW: a nostalgic view of La Conner and snow-covered Mount Baker.

Map on page 114

Worden State Park (fee) on the north side of town. One of three forts built in 1896 to protect the Puget Sound from an enemy naval attack, it houses the educational **Marine Science Center** (Sat–Sun noon– 4pm; free); the **Coast Artillery Museum** (Sat–Sun 1–4pm; free); and the **Fort Worden Theater**. The movie *An Officer and a Gentleman,* starring Richard Gere and Debra Winger, was filmed here.

The position of Port Townsend could not be more picturesque: jagged Olympic peaks stand guard to the south, cliffs soar on nearby Whidbey Island and the elusive "Great White Father," the Skagit Indian name for Mount Baker, shadows the horizon. This location convinced pioneers Alfred Plummer and George Bachelder of the town's prosperous future.

In the mid-19th century, they believed it would become the greatest port on Puget Sound. However, when the Union Pacific's transcontinental railroad failed to connect, Seattle soon emerged as the port of entry for the Sound. Overnight, a town designed

to hold 20,000 residents was left with a mere 3,500. Seventy years later, in 1961, Port Townsend residents – working under their own initiative – refurbished the Victorian homes of years past, and rekindled the town's dormant sense of civic pride.

Beautiful homes

The downtown district, centered on **Water Street**, encompasses about four blocks of graceful turn-of-the-19th-century brick buildings. Here, between glimpses of the Strait and nearby islands, are relics of bygone years such as the **Jefferson County Historical Museum**, housed in the 1898 City Hall on Madison Street; an 1890 **Bell Tower**, and the stately **Customs House**. Tours of historic homes (May 20–Oct 20 daily; tel: 260 385-1967; exteriors only; donation) include tales of Shanghaied sailors, underground tunnels and juicy tidbits not found in history books.

The 1858 **Rothschild House** (Apr– Sept daily; Nov–Mar Sat–Sun; closed:

BELOW: Port Townsend has many Victorian homes.

Dec; tel: 360 385-1003; fee), built by a local merchant, is a fully restored Victorian home with original period furnishings and a garden. At the restaurant called **Manresa Castle** (7th and Sheridan on Castle Hill; tel: 360 385-5750; reservations), baked cranberry King Salmon served with red potatoes is one of the most popular dishes. Another favorite is roasted pork tenderloin stuffed with a special mixture of apples and herbs swimming in Applejack brandy sauce.

Just a few of the elegant bed-and-breakfast inns around town include the **Ann Starrett Mansion B&B** (744 Clay Street; tel: 360 385-3205), with a floating spiral staircase leading to a Solar Calendar; the **F.W. Hastings House Old Consulate Inn** (313 Walker Street; tel: 360 385-6753), sitting high on a bluff with commanding views; **Heritage House B&B** (305 Pierce Street; tel: 360 385-6800); and the **James House** (1238 Washington Street; tel: 800 385-1238) furnished with fine period antiques. Almost all of Port Townsend's

B&Bs in historic homes are extremely popular, so if you are traveling around the islands in the summer months, be sure to book far ahead.

Compelling islands

Maybe it's the eagles soaring overhead that cast a blissful spell, but whatever the reason is, the **San Juan Islands** are certainly compelling. Hunkering down prettily in the dry rain-shadow of the Olympic Peninsula, these islands receive more sunshine than nearby but often-cloudy Seattle.

Temperatures average 68°F (20°C) in summer and 34°F (1°C) in winter; with rainfall averaging 29 inches (73 cm) annually. Many of the 172 San Juans are privately owned, accessible only via private craft. Washington State Ferries stop at four of the largest islands: San Juan, Orcas, Lopez and Shaw.

Reservations for accommodations on these popular islands should be made well in advance; the **San Juan Visitor Information Service** (tel: 360 468-3663) acts

BELOW: starfish on the shore, a noted Puget Sound visitor.

Map on page 114

as a clearing house for reservations. As well as whale-watching, sea kayaking and exploring the far corners of the islands on bicycles are popular with athletes as well as amateurs (bikes can be easily rented).

San Juan Island

The commercial center for the San Juan archipelago is **Friday Harbor** ⓲ on San Juan Island itself. The marina and village are fun to explore. The **San Juan Island Historical Museum** (405 Price Street; May–Sept Thur–Sat 10am–4pm, Sun 1–4pm; Oct, Mar and Apr Sat 1–4pm; closed: Nov–Feb; tel: 360 378-3949; fee), near the ferry terminal, presents a view of life here in 1894.

The **Whale Museum** (62 1st Street North; June–Aug 9am–5pm; tel: 360 378-4710; fee), a non-profit organization, seeks through education and research to encourage responsible stewardship of local whales. Between late April and September, orcas, also known as killer whales, are regular visitors to the surrounding waters. Glimpse them a designated whale-watching park like **Lime Kiln Point** (1567 Westside Road; daily 8am–dusk). Or hook up with one of the whale-watching tour boats such as **San Juan Safaris** (tel: 360 378-1323).

Snug Harbor and its little "resort" (1997 Mitchell Bay Road; tel: 360 378-4762), about 8 miles (13 km) from the ferry terminal, is another center for marine activities. **Roche Harbor** ⓳ and its **Seaside Village** (248 Reuben Memorial Drive) and listed on the National Register of Historical Sites, is situated about 10 miles (16 km) northwest, a quaint harbor with cobbled streets and rose bushes.

Its history as a lime and cement quarry can be savored during a stay at the historic 1886 **Hotel de Haro** (tel: 360 378-2155), which has plain but comfortable rooms or a new condominium. There is a traditional "Colors Ceremony" at sunset every evening in summer, where flags are lowered to the sounds of various national anthems. Anyone with sensitive ears should beware

BELOW: music room of the Robert Moran House, Rosario Resort on Orcas Island.

the super-loud bang from the cannon. If you would like to send a surprise announcement to someone during this event, you may do so by entering the message in a book kept at the hotel's front desk; it will be read out on the evening of your choice. Even if you can't stay, at least be sure to take in a sunset. **Duck Soup Inn** (Roche Harbor Road; tel: 360 378-4878) or **Friday Harbor House** (130 West Sreet; tel: 360 378-8455) provide romantic overlooks from which to watch the light show before dining or staying the night on San Juan Island.

Orcas Island

The tallest mountain in the San Juan islands, mighty 2,000-ft (610-meter) **Mount Constitution** is topped by a replica 12th-century fortress, which penetrates the early morning fog. From the peak and well worth the long, winding drive, a 360° view encompasses the Canadian Coastal Mountains, the Cascades, the Olympic Peninsula, the San Juans and Vancouver Island. Bald eagles soar above and below. Located entirely within **Moran State Park ㉕** (tel: 800 452-5687; camp reservations required; fee), the mountain sports almost 30 miles (48 km) of hiking trails built by the Civilian Conservation Corps in the 1930s.

The towns of **Eastsound**, **Olga** and **Deer Harbor** offer shops to explore that brim with local items from the island's multitude of cottage artists: check out the pottery, the jewelry and the weaving.

The famed **Rosario Resort** (tel: 360 376-2222) and marina offers luxurious lodging with all the trimmings. The inspiration of Robert Moran, photographer, writer and humorist, the resort's foundation is cut into solid rock, 16 ft (5 meters) deep. Doors of solid Honduran mahogany are so heavy, Moran invented a special butterfly-hinge. Windows are thick plate glass, while the roof was covered with 6-tons of copper sheeting. Teakwood floors, mahogany paneling, original furnishings and Tiffany details contribute to the

BELOW: Hotel de Haro at Roche Harbor, San Juan Island.

Map
on page
114

resort's luxury. The upper three floors are paneled in mahogany with floors in Indian teak. The showcase Music Room features a stained-glass window imported from Brussels and a magnificent 1,972-pipe Aeolian Pipe Organ. Stop by the Rosario for dinner – at the very least.

Musicians and writers, boat builders and fishermen, sewer diggers and potters, corporate retirees and cannabis growers are said to be a few of the odd assortment who live on **Lopez Island**. The island is a sleepy, rural place popular with cyclists for its flat terrain; most rental companies will deliver bikes to your place of lodging. Camp overnight by contacting the **Visitor Information Service** (tel: 360 468-3663). **Shark Reef Park** has 40 acres (16 hectares) of fragile forest.

South Puget Sound

South of Tacoma, **Steilacoom** ㉑, one of Washington state's oldest towns, sits on a high bluff with a sweeping view of Puget Sound and its islands. The tidy town has a museum, a vintage drugstore with old-fashioned soda fountain, and streets of historic homes and retail buildings.

On the nearby grounds of Western State Hospital, volunteer craftsmen have restored the four remaining military buildings from **Fort Steilacoom** (8714 87th Avenue Southwest, Lakewood; tours June–Aug Sun 1–4pm; tel: 253 588-6090; free), a regional center of military activity between 1849 and 1868. The officers' quarters are in front of the hospital administration building; re-enactment battles from the Civil War take place here from time to time.

Olympia ㉒ rests at the southern end of the Sound. Besides the state capital's tree-lined **Capitol Campus** and historic government buildings, attractions include waterfront **Percival Landing** park, with its humorous statues and mile-long boardwalk; serene **Capitol Lake**; and the **Washington State Capitol Museum** (211 West 21st Avenue; Tues–Fri 10am–4pm, Sat noon–4pm, closed: Sun, Mon; tel: 360

BELOW:
an orca
(killer whale),
Orcas Island.

753-2580; fee). The museum provides interpretations of Washington's political history, and is probably best visited after a stroll through the capitol.

Tours of the impressive, marble-lined **Washington State Capitol** (Legislative Building, Capital Way; drop-in tours Mon–Fri usually 10am–3pm; tel: 360 586-8687; free) meander through a building similar in design to the United States Capitol in Washington, DC. On a clear day, it is well worth the climb up to the brick and sandstone dome. Measuring 287 ft (87 meters) to the top of the cupola, the capitol's roof is one of the tallest masonry domes in the world. From the top, it's possible to enjoy sweeping views of Mount Rainier and Mount St Helens.

Additionally, there are guided tours of the **Executive Mansion** or feel free to walk around on your own through the **gardens** and **conservatory**, or past several **war memorials**. **Chief William Shelton's Story Pole** is on a grassy slope in front of the General Administration

Building on the Capitol Campus. Elders from various tribes continue to teach their stories to young people who wish to participate in their tribe's culture.

Olympia's **Farmers' Market** (700 North Capitol Way; Apr–Oct Thur–Sun 10am–3pm; Nov–Dec Sat–Sun 10am–3pm; tel: 360 352-9096) on historic **Budd Inlet** is the state's second-biggest open-air market and offers great produce: baby *bok choy* and a variety of juicy berries, meats and seafood. A rarity is the golden raspberry, a well-kept secret for some of the sweetest jams. It's fun to have lunch in the market and listen to live music.

Returning visitors will remember Tumwater and its famous slogan "it's the water." Tumwaters has been replaced by the equally exuberant **Miller Brewing Co.** (Exit 103, 100 Custer Way, Tumwater; ongoing tours and tastings, Mon–Sat 9am–4:40pm; tel: 360 754-5000; free; must be 21 years old), the second-largest brewer in America. Adjacent to the brewery are well-landscaped paths along the waterway at **Tumwater Falls Park**.

Vicinity of Olympia

South of Olympia is **Millersylvania State Park** (Exit 95), a restful park with a small lake and huge trees. **Nisqually National Wildlife Refuge** (100 Brown Farm Road; tel: 360 753-9467; free), not far from Olympia, is a relatively unpolluted delta on the west coast. Great blue herons, golden eagles and hawks soar overhead. There are walking trails, but it's much more fun to rent a canoe or kayak and explore its many inlets.

Another unique wildlife experience is **Wolf Haven International** (3111 Offut Lake Road, Tenino; daily guided tours 10am–5pm, closed: Feb; tel: 360 264-4695; fee), a sanctuary that cares for nearly 40 wolves. Each year, over 25,000 visitors tour this important site, a pre-release facility for the Federal Mexican Gray Wolf Recovery Program.

The **Howl-In** (tel: 360 264-4695; reservations required; fee) takes place on summer Saturday evenings. This is where campers throw back their heads and howl, and the wolves howl back. ❑

LEFT: the Washington State Capitol at Olympia.
RIGHT: St Paul's Church, Port Townsend

COASTAL WASHINGTON

*This remote, windswept coastline is home
to fantastic mountains, Native American reservations,
oddly shaped rocks and a kite museum*

Map
on page
132

The Olympic Peninsula, which encompasses Washington's coastal regions, juts out like an oversize thumb from the fist of Washington state. Within the lower 48 states (that is, not counting far-flung Alaska and Hawaii), there is no farther western point; this is the frontier's end. From here, the US looks out across the Pacific Ocean toward Asia. Along the outer length of the thumb, wilderness meets the sea in a roaring jumble of coves and bays, beaches and foaming breakers.

Native American land

Some of this remote, storm-swept shoreline is Native American land, where travel is restricted. Around 50 miles (80 km) of the coastline becomes part of Olympic National Park *(see page 180)*. The rest is beach, bay and forest, though along certain stretches of this coastline, beaches are less accessible than along the Oregon coast. The average summer high temperature is 68°F (20°C), with winter lows averaging at around 34°F (1°C).

Yes, it does rain a great deal, but how else could its legendary rainforests grow lush? Try to absorb the annual rainfall figures: 137 inches (347 cm) as reported in the Hoh rainforest and a significant 82 inches (209 cm) at Long Beach. Port Angeles on the northern edge, closer to the San Juan Islands, reports a more tolerable 26 inches (66 cm) a year.

Despite change and development, portions of this Olympic-shadowed region look just as they did when early explorers declared claims for them to the monarchies of Spain and England. That occured more than two centuries ago, when sailing ships sought routes to the region's wealth of natural resources.

In 1788, after many attempts to pilot his ship across the treacherous Columbia River bar, British fur trader John Meares gave up. Looking across the tossing surf

at the rain-lashed headland north of the river, he named it **Cape Disappointment**. The name seems appropriate to visitors who come here seeking balmy weather and discover instead the endless rain of the **Long Beach Peninsula ❶**. However, the storms can be an attraction here. Watching wind-whipped waves from the comfort of the **Lewis & Clark Interpretive Center** (daily, weather permitting) provides a certain kind of thrill.

The interpretive center is perched on a cliff in **Fort Canby State Park**, where yurts and cabins are available for overnight stays (tel: 800 452-5687 for reservations or 360 642-3078 for information). The center makes the explorers' 1804–1806 journey enthralling by using original journal entries

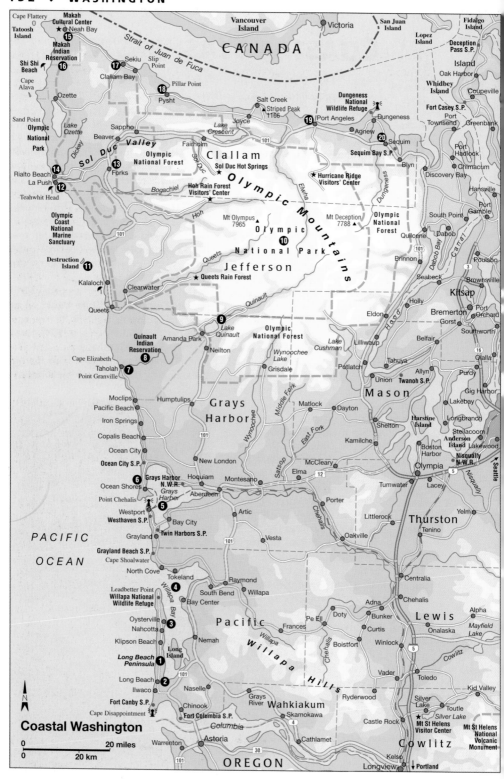

Cape Flattery
Tatoosh Island
Makah Cultural Center
Neah Bay **15**
Makah Indian Reservation **16**
Shi Shi Beach
Cape Alava
Sand Point
Olympic National Park
Ozette
Lake Ozette
Sekiu
Slip Point
Clallam Bay **17**
Pillar Point
Pysht **18**
Joyce
Salt Creek
Striped Peak 1166
Victoria
Vancouver Island
CANADA
San Juan Island
Lopez Island
Fidalgo Island
Deception Pass S.P.
Oak Harbor
Whidbey Island
Coupeville
Dungeness National Wildlife Refuge
Port Angeles **19**
Dungeness
Fort Casey S.P.
Port Townsend
Greenbank
Sappho
Beaver
Sol Duc Valley
Fairholm
Lake Crescent
Agnew
Sequim **20**
Sequim Bay S.P.
Blyn
Port Hadlock
Chimacum
Discovery Bay
Hansville
Clallam
Olympic National Forest
Sol Duc Hot Springs
Hurricane Ridge Visitors' Center
Forks **13**
Rialto Beach **14**
La Push **12**
Teahwhit Head
Bogachiel
Hoh Rain Forest Visitors' Center
Hoh
Olympic Mountains
Mt Olympus 7965
Elwha
Mt Deception 7788
Olympic National Forest
Quilcene
Dabob
Port Gamble
South Point
Olympic Coast National Marine Sanctuary
Destruction Island **11**
Kalaloch
Clearwater
Queets
Queets Rain Forest
Olympic National Park
Jefferson
Quinault
Lake Quinault
Poulsbo
Brinnon
Dabob Bay
Seabeck
Brownsville
Kitsap
Eldon
Holly
Bremerton
Port Orchard
Gorst
Southworth
Quinault Indian Reservation
Taholah **7**
Amanda Park
Neilton **9**
Olympic National Forest
Wynoochee Lake
Lake Cushman
Lilliwaup
Belfair
Cape Elizabeth
Point Granville **8**
Grisdale
Potlatch
Union
Tahuya
Allyn
Twanoh S.P.
Purdy
Olalla
Gig Harbor
Moclips
Humptulips
Grays Harbor
Matlock
Dayton
Mason
Lakebay
Longbranch
Harstine Island
Pacific Beach
Iron Springs
Copalis Beach
Ocean City
Ocean City S.P.
Middle Fork
Wynoochee
East Fork
Shelton
Kamilche
Steilacoom
Anderson Island
Lakewood
New London
Grays Harbor N.W.R. **6**
Ocean Shores
Point Chehalis
Westport **5**
Westhaven S.P.
Hoquiam
Grays Harbor
Aberdeen
Montesano
McCleary
Elma
Satsop
Porter
Chehalis
Tumwater
Boston Harbor
Olympia
Nisqually N.W.R.
Seattle
Lacey
Thurston
Bay City
Artic
Vesta
Oakville
Littlerock
Yelm
Grayland
Twin Harbors S.P.
Tenino
PACIFIC OCEAN
Grayland Beach S.P.
Cape Shoalwater
North Cove
Tokeland **4**
Raymond
Willapa
Centralia
Leadbetter Point
Willapa National Wildlife Refuge
South Bend
Bay Center
Adna
Chehalis
Lewis
Alpha
Oysterville
Nahcotta **3**
Pe Ell
Doty
Frances
Bunker
Curtis
Onalaska
Mayfield Lake
Klipson Beach
Long Island
Nemah
Willapa
Boistfort
Winlock
Cowlitz
Long Beach Peninsula **1**
Long Beach **2**
Ilwaco
Wahkiakum
Willapa Hills
Vader
Toledo
Fort Canby S.P.
Cape Disappointment
Naselle
Chinook
Fort Columbia S.P.
Grays River
Skamokawa
Ryderwood
Castle Rock
Silver Lake
Toutle
Kid Valley
Silver Lake
Mt St Helens Visitor Center
Mt St Helens National Volcanic Monument
Coastal Washington
N
0   20 miles
0   20 km
Columbia
Warrenton
Astoria
Cathlamet
Kelso
Longview
Portland
OREGON

Map
on page
132

matched with photo murals and artwork. Lewis and Clark ended their historic, adventure-filled journey at this spot. There are also several exhibits in the center devoted to local Native American tribes.

A duo of lighthouses

In the park are two lighthouses. The 1856 **Cape Disappointment Lighthouse** – also known as "Cape D" (short, steep walk required, with no entry into the building) and still in operation by the United States Coast Guard – was considered inadequate when 59 additional wrecks occurred after it was built.

As a result, 42 dangerous years later, the **North Head Light** (summer, daily tours; winter Fri–Sat 9am–4pm; tel: 360 642-3078; small fee) was constructed to warn sailors of the treacherous sands all around. The lighthouse keeper's quarters can be rented overnight (see the phone number above for reservations).

Pillow lava headlands at North Head and Cape Disappointment are excellent examples of natural lava formations. The nearby **Coast Guard Lifeboat Station and Surf School** teaches boat handling and rescue operations in rough surf; over the years it has been instrumental in curbing various smuggling operations. Farther south, on top of historic **Chinook Point** promontory, Fort Columbia was once a coastal defense site. Completed in 1904, armed with rapid-firing guns, it never had to fire a shot. In 1950, it became **Fort Columbia Historical State Park Interpretive Site** (Hwy 101, a couple of miles east of Chinook; June–Sept Wed–Sun 10am–5pm).

North of the Cape is the port village of **Ilwaco** (pronounced *ill-wahco*). At the turn of the 19th century, knives and rifles often made a statement about rights to fishing grounds here. Today's tourists are guaranteed less controversy, so consider taking a fresh-water or sea-fishing trip. The sturgeon fishing season is all year round, without the need to cross the turbulent bar where the Columbia River and

BELOW:
the US Coast Guard still uses the lighthouse at Cape Disappointment.

the Pacific Ocean collide. For more information, contact the **Ilwaco Charter Association** (tel: 360 642-4943).

After posing for a trophy photo, head for the **Portside Café** (303 Main Street; tel: 360 642-3477) to gaze at the harbor through steamy windows. When locals began asking for jars of pie-filling to tide them over during the times Nan Holme (its owner) wasn't baking: a new business was born. You can have a cup of joe, then take a tour of **Nan's Pantry and Fruit Packing Kitchen**.

In the late 19th century, the Olympic Peninsula was a summer playground for people from Portland, who would ride a steamer down the Columbia River, then board the *Clamshell,* a narrow-gauge train that ran all the way to the peninsula's base. In 1881, promoter Jonathan Stout had big plans for the little town of **Seaview**, but during the 1893 depression, fire destroyed his hotel and real estate sales fell through. Time heals, and since 1896 – when the **Shelburne Country Inn** (4415 Pacific Way; tel: 360 642-2442) opened its doors – the inn has received rave reviews. Reputedly serving the best clam chowder in the west, **My Mom's Pie Restaurant** (4316 South Pacific Highway; tel: 360 642-2342) is a good choice for lunch.

The longest beach

Said to be the "world's longest beach," a wide uninterrupted stretch of sand extends a full 28 miles (45 km) in length. This is, of course, Long Beach. There is also a town called **Long Beach ❷** (Visitor's Bureau, tel: 360 642-2400), which leans heavily on tourism with a tacky carnival touch, including go-carts, kiddy rides, miniature golf and bizarre attractions such as the "world's largest frying pan." Just outside the reach of the mighty Pacific, the **Long Beach Boardwalk** stretches way off into the distance. Offering displays, ocean views and picnic areas, the boardwalk is a short stroll from most attractions.

The **Discovery Trail** winds through dune grasses from 17th Street South to

BELOW: the coastline at Rialto Beach, Olympic National Park.

Map on page 132

16th Street Northwest, a distance of about 2 miles (3 km). The **World Kite Museum and Hall of Fame** (112 3rd Street Northwest; June–Aug daily; Sept–Oct Fri–Mon; Nov–May Sat–Sun 11am–5pm; tel: 360 642-4020; fee) is dedicated exclusively to the history of kites. The museum presents fun facts as well as scientific uses for its flying fantasies, interspersed with more than 1,400 samples. A major kite festival is held here in late August.

Visitors can relive the *Clamshell* train's journey aboard a **green and gold trolley** (tel: 360 642-4421; fee). Built in 1988, the trolley adds a special memory to the grass-covered dunes and hard-packed sand. Boating, beachcombing and surf-fishing are popular pastimes here, but when freshwater fish is the quarry, anglers head for **Loomis Lake** and its tasty rainbow trout.

Banner of the Bogs

About 550 acres (223 hectares) of cranberries, altogether yielding about 40 percent of Washington's consumption, are presently under cultivation on the peninsula. That's a lot of cranberry sauce. Cranberry festivals, a flag – Banner of the Bogs – and guided tours of a research center show how the tart red berry is grown and harvested.

A century ago, cranberry vines were shipped in from the state of Massachusetts, and the industry was born. In winter the fields take on a muted burgundy tint; by June blossoms turn them light pink. During October's harvest, "blooms" containing tens of thousands of marble-sized berries paint the flooded fields a bright crimson. A former research station north of Long Beach on Pioneer Road is now the **Cranberry Museum and Gift Shop** (Apr–Oct daily 10am–5pm; tel: 360 642-5553; free).

The town of **Nahcotta**, nestling on the shores of **Willapa Bay**, received the rail terminus its northern neighbor Oysterville coveted. The narrow-gauge lines enabled Nahcotta – named after Chinook Indian Chief Nahcati – to become the peninsula's

BELOW: Long Beach stretches for many miles.

transportation hub for logging, fishing and oyster shipping. Small, native oysters were once in great demand, especially in San Francisco during the Gold Rush era. An observer at the time wrote "I have seen forty sailing boats at one time loaded with oysters… two and three schooners loading at one time, each of which would carry from 4,000 to 5,000 bushels of oysters."

Today, the oyster industry here is "a shell of its former self," but a replica of an oyster station house transports visitors back to the boom times. Known as the **Willapa Bay Interpretive Center** (May–Sept Fri–Sun; free), the building has walls covered with quotes and anecdotes, along with a film about the industry and bay ecology. Center visitors can also walk to rocky shores and the bay.

Elk and bears

Across the bay, the nearby heavily forested estuarine island is home to bears and elk, but **Willapa National Wildlife Refuge** can be reached only by boat. For a special overnight or dining experience, try the **Moby Dick Hotel and Oyster Farm** (25814 Sandridge Road; tel: 360 665-4543), a restored hotel that once housed the US Horse Patrol. The hotel has comfortable rooms, a Japanese-style dry sauna plus outdoor showers. Cuisine from the **Ark Bayfront Restaurant** (tel: 360 665-4133; reservations required) has been on the menu at the White House.

Founded on its bivalve namesake, today **Oysterville ❸** is a sleepy village on the marshlands of a bay. Once a booming oyster center, harvesters exhausted the native supply, the railroad line opted to bypass the town, and South Bend got the county seat. Oysterville somehow persevered, and the entire community was placed on the National Register of Historic Places.

Many of the community's century-old homes were constructed from Northern California redwood that was shipped in as oyster-schooner ballast. The **Long Beach Peninsula Visitors Bureau** has tour maps of the area's fine homes.

BELOW: Neah Bay.

Map on page 132

The northern tip of the peninsula is the stopover site for more than 100 species of birds, including sandpipers, yellowlegs and sanderlings. **Leadbetter Point** is also the northern limit of the Snowy plover's breeding range. This small shore bird nests on the upper ocean beach from April through August and, as they are a threatened species, part of the dunes are closed during their five-month visit.

Leadbetter State Park (tel: 360 642-3078) – named after a lieutenant of the US Coast Survey who later became a general in the Confederate Army – is part park, part wildlife refuge. Local activities include surf fishing, driftwood collecting, studying the wildlife and, of course, clamming.

Oyster capital

US highway then wends 101 turns east where the **Willapa River** joins the bay toward the tiny towns of **South Bend** (Chamber of Commerce, tel: 360 875-5231) and **Raymond**. South Bend's estimated population used to be 1,795. In 1974 the population was 1,850. It hasn't grown much – and they haven't bothered to take a census since.

In South Bend, the **Pacific County Courthouse** (open for self-guided tours), dubbed a "gilded palace of extravagance" when it was built in 1911, contains carvings, murals and an illuminated stained-glass dome of green, lavender and gold.

Fried, stewed or eaten plain, the oysters from **Willapa Bay** ❹ are world famous for their exquisite flavor. The brisk waters here provide the ideal habitat for these tasty mollusks. In fact, one out of six oysters consumed in the United States is grown and harvested in Willapa Bay, thereby allowing the locals to lay claim to bragging rights as the "Oyster Capital of the World."

Several establishments in the area serve oysters daily, including **Coast Seafoods Company** (1201 West Robert Bush Drive, Hwy 101; tel: 360 875-5557), well-known for its raw oyster-eating contest in May. Crab, salmon and Manila clams are also harvested in this seafood-lovers area.

Probably the most unusual emigrant ever to arrive in Washington Territory was 19-year-old Willie Keil from Bethel, Missouri. During his incredible journey west, he may have been responsible for saving the lives of many other emigrants – although he died in 1855, before the touring party actually ever left Missouri.

William Sr mourned the loss of his son, and refusing to leave young Willie behind, arranged to have his son's body placed in a black, lead-lined coffin and liberally sprinkled with Golden Rule whiskey. Placed in a wagon open at the sides, and given a place of honor at the head of the wagon train, it is said that at least four times during the 2,000-mile (3,000-km) trek west, Keil and company escaped trouble largely because of the presence of Willie in his hearse. **William Keil's gravestone** can be seen off Hwy 6, between Menlo and Raymond.

For 12 miles (19 km) along Hwy 105, the section of coastline between North Cove and Westport is known variously as **South Beach** or the **Cranberry Coast** (Chamber of Commerce, tel: 360 267-

RIGHT: mussel shells in a local coastal tidal zone.

2003). Berries are grown, harvested, processed and honored with special events here. **Tokeland**, at the southern end, is a dreary seaside village named for Chief Toke of the Chehalis tribe, who used the area as his family summer home. Today it is home to the **Shoalwater Bay Indian Reservation**. The **Tokeland Hotel** (tel: 360 267-7006), built in 1886, operates the only full-service restaurant in the area.

Bogs and beaches

Near the community of Grayland is **Grayland Beach State Park** (6:30am–10pm; closed: Nov–Mar; tel: 800 452-5687; reservations) with 60 campsites, a self-guided nature trail and 7,499 ft (2,285 meters) of ocean frontage.

In a nod to its red-berry industry, south of town the **Furford Cranberry Museum** (2395 Hwy 105; Fri–Sun 10am–5pm; tel: 360 267-3303; donation) is an old cranberry warehouse with some funky equipment. The bogs themselves are to the east off Cranberry and Larkin roads. In the

other direction, a few miles north of town, **Twin Harbors State Park** (Apr–Oct 6:30am–10pm; tel: 800 452-5687; reservations) has 249 campsites among the ferns near an open beach. There, the **Shifting Sands Nature Trail** meanders through huckleberry patches and woody areas over the dunes.

Busy **Westport** (Chamber of Commerce, tel: 360 268-9422) is at the terminus of a short arm of land that marks the entrance to **Grays Harbor ❺**. A jetty and marina filled with sport and commercial fishing boats dominate. During the 1940s the jetty was built to protect the harbor. With additional dredging, the dock area and the land on which it stands have been reclaimed from the ocean. Charter boats are available at the 800-slip marina, for whale-watching or deep-sea fishing: one among several is Coho Charters (tel: 360 268-0111).

A 1,000-ft (300-meter) walking pier (Float 20 at the marina) is worth a look, and a blue steel observation tower (Westhaven Drive) stands at one end of the boat basin. Visitors are allowed to climb it, and at the top are views of the pounding surf. On a particular day in a lucky season, you might see a whale migration.

At **Westhaven State Park** (open during the day only) – also known as **Agate Beach** – activities are low-key. Watching surfers and collecting shells, driftwood and agate is, as they say locally, "nature's own tranquilizer." The **Westport Lighthouse** and **State Park** (lighthouse closed to the public) is only about a mile away; a concrete boardwalk traverses the main dune area. The Nantucket-style **Westport Maritime Museum** (Wed–Sun 10am–5pm; tel: 360 268-0078; donation) was once a Coast Guard Station.

During summer months, a passenger-only ferry runs between Westport and **Ocean Shores** (Float 10, 2453 Westhaven Drive; May–mid-June and Sept Sat–Sun; mid-June–Aug daily 10am–6:30pm; tel: 360 268-0047; fee). The **Westport–Hoquiam Passenger Ferry** (tel: 800 562-9730) also operates in summertime. It's a short journey as the crow flies, but a long one (50 miles/80 km) on the road all the way around the harbor.

LEFT: the Shelburne Country Inn dates from 1896.

Shore birds and tall ships

Map on page 132

Scenic coastal beaches, towering stands of ancient firs, spruce and cedars, and mysterious rainforests top the list of natural wonders found on the western side of the Olympic Peninsula. State highway 105 passes the twin cities of **Aberdeen** and **Hoquiam** (pronounced *ho*-qwee-um; Chamber of Commerce, tel: 800 321-1924). These are shipping and milling ports at the tip of triangular Grays Harbor. Aberdeen, home of the clamburger and the Chokers – its Community College team – is peppered with inland waterways.

Bowerman Basin (adjacent to Hoquiam-Aberdeen airport) consists primarily of the **Grays Harbor National Wildlife Refuge** and the **Hoquiam Sewage Ponds**. This is where birdwatchers can enjoy the spectacle of resting and feeding birds in a staging area during their annual migrations. Grays Harbor is one of four major staging areas for shorebirds in North America, and has one of the largest concentrations of shorebirds on the west coast, south of Alaska.

The best viewing times for shorebirds are two hours before and two hours after high tide. Birds of a dozen species number in the thousands in the spring, and up to half a million during the autumn. This arresting sight is very popular with both local and visiting amateur ornithologists.

The castle

Hoquiam's Castle B&B (515 Chenault Avenue; tel: 360 533-2005; reservations) is listed on both the National and State Historic Registers. Built in 1897 by lumber tycoon Robert Lytle, it was quite a contrast to the sawmills and bar rooms of the lusty, booming timber town. The Lytle family lived in this unique home until they moved to Portland in 1910, then gave it to their niece Theadosia Bale as a generous wedding gift. Theadosia lived in "the castle" until the late 1950s.

Upon her death, almost everything in the house was auctioned off; the house itself was put on the market for $14,000. A 600-piece crystal chandelier and a rosewood grand piano are currently among the house's elegant furnishings, although it should be noted that, in a nod to local

tastes, there is a tacky saloon on the third floor. The B&B has five restored bedrooms with private baths, a formal parlor and a dining room, tearoom, den and grand ballroom. Full breakfast and complimentary beverages and desserts in the afternoon are included in the overnight price.

Also in town is the **Arnold Polson Museum** (1611 Riverside Avenue; June–Labor Day Wed–Sun; Sept–May Sat–Sun; tel: 360 533-5862; fee), another mansion paid for with timber money. This 26-room house now holds historic memorabilia of the Grays Harbor area. A rose garden and a 1910 Shay Three-Spot locomotive are displayed in the adjacent park.

Grays Harbor Historical Seaport (guided tours; tel: 360 532-8611; fee) is home to a replica of the *Lady Washington*, the tall ship that Captain Robert Gray sailed in 1788, and the first American vessel to land in the Pacific Northwest. This meticulously crafted replica sometimes ventures out to sea, so check to see if it's in port when you are there.

North Beach

Back at Grays Harbor, Hwy 115 curves through heavily logged and replanted forests, ending at a wide, flat peninsula running southward. From Ocean Shores to Taholah is known as **North Beach**. Somewhat shabby beachside resorts give way to timber-dominated lands with prominent clearcuts.

Ocean Shores ❻ (Chamber of Commerce, tel: 360 289-2451), conceived in the 1960s to become a sprawling resort development with nightclubs and wide boulevards, has since backed away from that ambitious approach. It is now an area of summer homes in various stages of repair scattered over 6 miles (9 km) of ocean dunes. There are motels and restaurants, an 18-hole golf course and opportunities to fish, clam and beachcomb. There are also marked bike routes; some of the best and most scenic are on the bay side. Take a map with you.

For accommodations, **Ocean Shores Reservations Bureau** (tel: 360 289-2430)

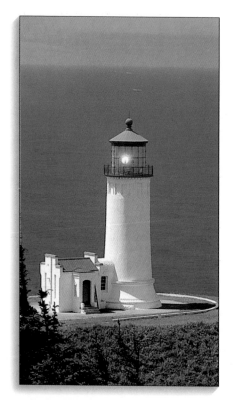

or **Ocean Front Beach Rentals** (tel: 360 289-3568) both act as clearing houses. **North Jetty** is considered a great place to watch storm waves or the sunset. But be careful: winter storms can bring 25-ft (8-meter) seas, and high winds can be dangerous. At the end of the peninsula on the bay side, the **Ocean Shores Environmental Interpretive Center** (1013 Catala Avenue Southeast; summer only, Wed–Sun 10am–4pm; tel: 360 289-4617; free) at the marina displays the local area's marine life in two aquariums, with additional exhibits on birds and shellfish. **Damon Point** (also known as Protection Island; Mar–Sept, parts off-limits) is a nesting site for the Snowy plover. You'll also see brown pelicans, Peregrine falcons, herons and dozens of other species.

Fog and mist

North of Ocean Shores, near the confusingly named Ocean City, is the 112-acre (45-hectare) **Ocean City State Park** (daily 6am–8pm; tel: 800 452-5687; reservations), a large camping park with a beach, dunes and dense thickets of shore pine. The historical availability of razor clams makes this an important destination for enthusiastic diggers during the appropriate season, but do note that permits are required. Migratory birds are prevalent and beachcombing is a popular activity.

There are plenty of strolling opportunities along the wide-open sandy beaches that extend north from the Ocean Shores jetty nearly 20 miles (32 km) to **Moclips**. The drive north up Hwy 109 takes in a more remote section of the coastline. The sand is a fine, dark gray color piled with driftwood and is a resting place for seagulls.

Fog and mist drift through the landscape, muting the sky against the wind-twisted dark green forests. **Pacific Beach**, a run-down village off the highway, offers decent camping facilities in a state park; otherwise it is mostly a center for oceanographic research. Its northern neighbor Moclips has a more prosperous appearance, with homes, resorts and restaurants on cliffs overlooking the sea.

Eleven miles (18 km) beyond Moclips on the coast is **Taholah** ❼, an Indian vil-

LEFT:
North Head
Lighthouse,
near Ilwaco.

Map
on page
132

lage that is the last settlement accessible by road in this area. Crystal Sampson, great-granddaughter of a Quinault chief, was one of ten children born in her grandmother's cabin in Taholah. At the age of 19, she left the reservation and moved to Portland to attend business school. Now she's back in Taholah as a health manager.

Beyond Taholah lies the **Quinault Indian Reservation ❽**, where travel is restricted. Some maps show a coastal road through the reservation, but it is not passable. Visitors may fish on the reservation if given a permit from the tribe; sometimes the Indians, excellent fishermen and boaters themselves, will take tourists for canoe trips up the **Quinault River**.

Lakeside or seaside

To continue up the coast, travelers must retrace their route to Moclips. On its way north, Hwy 101 passes **Lake Quinault ❾**, a serene, cold-blue lake where the highlight is **Lake Quinault Lodge** (345 South Shore Road; tel: 360 288-2900; reservations). Built in 1926, the handsome lodge has 92 rooms, from suites with fireplaces to rooms where pets are allowed. Full dining and lounge facilities, plus an indoor pool and spa, make this a good stopover in an area with few accommodation choices. Service, however, can be slow.

The sweep of grassy lawn down to the waterfront is particularly wonderful. Be sure to explore the lake by kayak or canoe (rentals on site), or hike through the surrounding old-growth timber. The lodge is at the edge of **Olympic National Park ❿** *(see page 180)*.

The highway angles west again, toward the mouth of the **Queets River** and the long strip of National Park that borders the coast. This segment is the only place where Hwy 101 touches the coast in Washington; from here onward, the ocean is ever present, but mostly out of reach.

Also near the National Park, the highway is dominated by **Kalaloch Lodge**, (pronounced *clay*-lock; 157151 Hwy 101;

tel: 360 962-2271; reservations required). It's shabby appearance is caused by the constant onslaught of onshore winds. Inside, the accommodations are plain but comfortable. The lodge, with cabins and a restaurant, overlooks the ocean and Kalaloch Creek fronting onto a picturesque section of wave-dashed shoreline. It is popular with visitors eager to hit the beaches, then return to a sumptuous salmon dinner in the dining room while watching the sunset.

There's a campground nearby with good walking opportunities: drive along the coast past Beach 3. **Kalaloch Campground** (tel: 360 962-2283) has 175 sites and a summer nature program that is open to all. Seven beach access points, each a short hike from the highway, are within 6 miles (10 km) of Kalaloch. It appears easy to walk from one beach to the next, but this impression is deceptive.

Outgoing tides are hazardous, and incoming tides have caused more than one explorer to be marooned on a rock for many hours or worse. There are also problems with the surf torpedoing rogue logs back onshore. This is no joke and is to be taken seriously as there are fatalities each year. To avoid these hazards, visitors should first obtain a tide table, available free at information centers and businesses. It charts the daily highs and lows of this dangerous surf.

Destruction Island ⓫ with its picturesque **Light** was named by beleaguered 19th-century sailors whose compatriots were murdered by less-than-welcoming Native Americans. The history of this wild and photogenic shoreline is full of harrowing tales, but in spite – or even because – of this ambiance, this part of the coast is particularly compelling.

The repetitive rumble of surf rolling over sand and stones is mesmerizing; the briny smell of the blue-gray ocean is primal and poignant; wind-twisted Sitka spruce forests line the bluffs. Oddly shaped seastacks (tall, offshore rocks) project from headlands; in a near prehistoric scene, they resemble a line of gray dinosaurs marching into the ocean. At times, when the spruce trees creak in the wind, the entire coast seems haunted by ghosts of shipwrecked sailors, warring Indians and desperate settlers.

Quileute tribe

Off-the-beaten-path, diminutive little **La Push** ⓬ is owned by the Quileute tribe and often sought out by photographers. It fronts a charcoal gray beach strewn with driftwood – the "bones of the forest, picked clean by the sea," as the descriptive panels say. High breakers roll in from the northwest, and the mournful moan of warning buoys is constant.

Near La Push are **Second** and **Third Beach**, both picturesque spots. At the latter, a seastack and rugged **Teahwhit Head** are landmarks that make the beach especially popular. But neither Teahwhit Head or Taylor Point can be rounded at any tide; people have been killed in the attempt. Most coastal streams in this vicinity have a tea-stained appearance originating from tannin leached from leaves, so do avoid the tea.

LEFT: Quileute salmon fisherman, La Push.

Map on page 132

After years of decline, there is cautious good news for the seafood industry. In the first years of the 21st century, North Pacific ocean temperatures dropped a few degrees, with positive results. Fishermen are catching more salmon out of Ilwaco, Westport, La Push and Neah Bay than they've caught in years.

They're also starting to catch large numbers of steelhead along the Columbia River and its tributaries. Sardines are back in quantity along the Oregon and Washington coasts after an absence of years. Oysters are reappearing along the Oregon coast. All this bodes well for an industry concerned about its survival.

Heading inland, **Forks** ⓫ (Chamber of Commerce, tel: 360 374-2531), a sizable lumbering community, is a good place to stop at a service station and pick up tourist information. Take a quick spin around the comprehensive little **Timber Museum** (mid-Apr–Oct daily 10am–4pm; tel: 360 374-9663; donation) located prominently roadside in the center of town.

Continuing north and turning westward toward the point farthest west in the lower 48 on Rt 112, **Clallam Bay County Park**, on an agate-strewn saltwater beach, offers views on a clear day of Vancouver Island and **Sekiu Point**. Farther along, seastacks form wildlife refuges, which provide sanctuary for puffins, murres, guillemots and auklets.

Lake Ozette hikes

Between **Rialto Beach** ⓮ and Sand Point along the North Olympic Coastal Wilderness, the **Ozette trailhead** (north) is a hiker's dream, covering coastal forest and ocean beaches. Creeks must be forded and log jams may be slippery, so be sure to seek advice before setting out.

Lake Ozette is the third-largest lake in Washington and is part of the **Lake Ozette Triangle Trails** (backcountry permit required, fee). The ranger station (tel: 360 963-2725) is staffed only seasonally, but year round there is a self-service kiosk, public telephone, picnic area and boat

BELOW: old shipwreck along a wild stretch of beach.

ramps. There is a small store with camping and canoe rentals adjacent to the park boundary.

The total hiking time is two days for the entire Lake Ozette loop, although there are shorter variations if you arrange a shuttle to pick up your car and deliver it to your destination point (tel: 360 374-2501).

People who live by the rocks

Considered the scenic starting point of the **Strait of Juan de Fuca Highway**, Rt 112, **Neah Bay** ⑮ is the home of the **Makah Indian Reservation** ⑯ and is known for its saltwater fishing. The little fishing village is 13 miles (20 km) west of Sekiu and 72 miles (115 km) west of Port Angeles.

It's worth making the side trip to visit the noteworthy **Makah Research and Cultural Center**, located at the farthest northwestern point of the contiguous US, (Bayview Avenue, Hwy 112; late May–Aug daily 9am–4pm; then Wed–Sun; tel: 360 645-2711; fee). Built in 1979, it traces the history of these "People of the Cape" calling themselves *Kwih-dich-chuh-ahtx* or "people who live by the rocks and seagulls." The Makah are said to have lived at this tip of land for more than 2,000 years. The museum was built to house ancient artifacts uncovered near Lake Ozette. It now showcases a scale model of an 18th-century Makah village, a fine whaling canoe with harpoons, samples of clothing, implements, hooks and tools, and intricate weavings of cedar, bird feathers and animal hair. There is also a wealth of detail on traditional whale-hunting methods. Totem poles include a thunderbird with a clever transformation mask.

The museum shop sells carvings and jewelry made by Makah artists and a wide selection of prints, books and cards. The Makah still weave handsome baskets, with prices starting at $200.

Neah Bay itself is a fishing center and has several motels, simple cafés, boat launches and charter fishing companies, like Big Salmon (tel: 360 645-2375). For the past several years, the tribe has been featured in the local and national news for its decision to engage in whale hunting.

Next stop: Asia

The sometimes muddy trail near the museum includes a cedar boardwalk built by the Makah tribe and has a 30-minute walk with spectacular views of crashing surf and 18-acre (7-hectare) **Tatoosh Island** and **Light** at the entrance to the Strait. Tatoosh Island is the only piece of land between Cape Flattery and Asia. Great waves crash deep into cliff caves carved by centuries of sea action.

The cape was named in 1778 by British explorer Captain James Cook, who spied "a small opening which flattered us with the hopes of finding an harbour."

South of Cape Flattery, another of the state's scenic wonders borders national park land. **Shi-Shi** (pronounced Shy Shy) **Beach**, 3 miles (5 km) of sand between **Portage Head** and **Point of Arches**, is considered Washington's true wilderness beach. Getting there demands a rugged hike rewarded with the dramatic spectacle of jagged, offshore rocks and a smooth beach with myriad tidepools.

LEFT: sun, sea, sand and shells.

Map on page 132

The peninsula's north rim

The drive back from Neah Bay, east on Hwy 112, passes close to the gentle waters of the Strait of Juan de Fuca. Protected by the huge landmass of Canada's Vancouver Island, the surf crawls to shore, rather than crashes as it does on the western side. The strait is a dramatic glacial fjord connecting Puget Sound to the Pacific Ocean.

With complex rocky shorelines, and the magical combination of soft northwest light and water, it is a place where eagles soar above the water. Smoke from woodstoves drifts lazily, and farms and cattle dot the landscape. The Canadian island across the strait looms on the horizon, hazily green and peaked with frost. **Sekiu** ⓱, a harbor-facing community nestled against a hill, has more boats than houses and some people return here year after year.

Past Clallam Bay, **Merrill and Ring Pysht Tree Farm Interpretive Tour** is a self-guided tour with informative signs promoting resource management and reforestation; **Pysht** ⓲ takes its name

from a Clallam Indian term meaning "wind from all directions." The **Joyce General Store**, built in the early 1900s, still has the old false front, beaded ceiling, oiled wood floors, and original fixtures. There is a simple museum.

The county park at **Salt Creek Recreation Area** (tel: 360 928-3441) and its 196 acres (79 hectares) was originally used as a World War II harbor defense site. Called **Fort Hayden**, the military reservation concealed camouflaged, bomb-proof batteries. After the war, Clallam County bought the military reservation and created a 92-site campground (tel: 360 417-2291) with a marine life sanctuary and hiking trails. Like Pysht, it has an interesting geographic name: Tongue Point.

Striped Peak

Another 2 miles (3 km) up a steep, pot-holed road is **Striped Peak**, also the location of old Batteries 131 and 249, where the only man-made touch is a picnic table. The drive is worth the trouble for the view

of the Olympic Mountains to the south, Vancouver Island to the north, and expansive coastal vistas to the east and west.

The Elwha River was once home to a famous run of Chinook salmon reputed to be large enough for Native Americans to use a single skin as a ceremonial robe. The scenic river's glacier-fed water and deep gorge remain splendidly intact.

Port Angeles

Port Angeles ⓵ (Chamber of Commerce, tel: 360 452-2363), the major stopping point in this part of Washington, bustles with ferry traffic going to and from Victoria, British Columbia – proof of how close the town is to Canada. An observation tower at **City Pier** provides a good vantage point to watch the ferries, freighters and pleasure boats sailing the strait.

A short walk from City Pier, Port Angeles' **Clallam County Historical Museum** (138 West 1st Street; Mon–Fri 8:30am–4pm; tel: 360 452-2662) shows various aspects of the region's history displayed

beneath an art-glass rotunda. Port Angeles is the gateway to Canada, and also provides an entrance to the **Hurricane Ridge** area of beautiful Olympic National Park (*see page 180*).

Black Ball Transport (tel: 206 622-2222) offers a car-ferry service crossing the Strait of Juan de Fuca to Victoria, sailing three or four times a day, depending on the season. The **Victoria Express** (tel: 800 633-1589) passenger-only ferry has a fast, one-hour service from Port Angeles beginning late May and ending October 1.

Farther east, near the town of **Sequim** ⓴ (pronounced *skwim*, rhymes with "swim;" Chamber of Commerce, tel: 360 683-6197) is in a rain shadow, a region of relatively low rainfall that occurs downwind of a mountain range. Meaning "quiet waters" in local Indian dialect, the place is distinguished for having the lowest annual rainfall in western Washington, only 11–17 inches (27–43 cm); climatically, a desert island surrounded by water.

Dungeness

Puget Sound waters supply exquisite seafood. Dungeness crab, Latin name, *Cancer magister,* is native to the Dungeness Spit, and is known by its distinctively sweet flavor. At the **Three Crabs** (101 Three Crabs Road; tel: 360 683-4264), the crab is so fresh it practically jumps straight from the ocean onto your plate. Patrons dine on a medley of crab salads, crab cakes, boiled crab or crab served in the shell, slathered with lemon butter.

The **Dungeness National Wildlife Refuge** is a favorite destination for birdwatchers, affording a 5-mile (8-km) hike along an impressive sandy hook of land – **Dungeness Spit** – the longest, natural sandspit in the United States. The narrowest portions of the spit measure only 50 ft (15 meters) wide during high tides, and breaches have been known to occur. A great walker's destination is the 1857 lighthouse.

The spit was visited by the distinguished British sea captain George Vancouver in 1792. It was named for Dungeness, a harbor in Great Britain. **Cline Spit** to the east is popular with windsurfers.

LEFT: the crabs were discovered here in the 1800s.

Map on page 132

The drive-through or walk-through **Olympic Game Farm** (1423 Ward Road; daily 9am–dusk; tel: 800 778-4295; fee) is home to bears, tigers, spotted leopards, lions, zebras and yaks. In 1996, mammoth fossils were uncovered near Sequim. Persistent elementary school students persuaded the state legislature to designate a new official category and name the *Columbian Mammoth* as an official state fossil. The pupils were successful, and the mammoth has earned its place in fossil history.

Dry red wine

Two hospitable wineries offering tastings are located nearby. **Olympic Cellars** (255410 Hwy 101; daily; tel: 360 452-0160) is in an old barn. **Lost Mountain Winery** (June–Sept daily 11am–5pm; Oct–May Sat–Sun; tel: 360 683-5229; free tastings), a family owned place producing dry red wines, is situated in the serenity of forested foothills.

Established in 1967, **Cedarbrook Herb and Lavender Farm** (1345 South Sequim Avenue; Mar–Dec Mon–Sat 9am–5pm, Sun 10am–4pm; tel: 360 683-7733), in a charming century-old building located in the "Bell House," is a pleasant diversion with the accent on spicy scents, herbs and gifts. The restaurant is the **Petals Garden Café.**

A certain actor often vacationed on the property he owned here; that's why the boat basin at Sequim Bay is called the **John Wayne Marina**. Good seafood is available at the **Marina Restaurant** (tel: 360 681-0577), which – naturally – overlooks the marina. **Sequim Bay State Park**, 4 miles (6 km) east of town, has rustic benches and moss in a green setting of cedars and ferns. Trails lead through the trees to a beach and boat launch.

The final part of the peninsula's northern rim heads east back toward Puget Sound and Seattle. The lovely old town of Port Townsend, nestled in a sheltered cove, is a popular destination known for its Victorian homes, shops and art galleries *(see page 122).*   ❑

BELOW: sunset and seastack.

Map
on page
150

WASHINGTON CASCADES

*Just a couple of hours from Seattle are mountains
to conquer, rivers to raft, slopes to ski,
wildlife to watch, and hot springs to soak in*

Rather than hibernating throughout the notoriously wet months, on-the-go Northwesterners extract excitement from their surroundings. Within one to two hours from Seattle – in all directions – there are peaks to conquer, rivers to run, slopes to ski, wildlife to watch, hot springs to soak in. Even during Seattle's winters there are places with sunny skies – the eastern side of the mountains is generally less wet than the western side.

The two primary mountain ranges in Washington state are the Olympics *(see Coastal Washington, page 131 and Olympic National Park, page 180),* and the mighty Cascades. As the Japanese current from across the Pacific bumps up against the North American continent, Washington's Olympic Peninsula is the first to see its water-logged clouds. This results in rain-drenched western shores and a moss-draped rainforest.

The Cascade Mountains are the next obstacle. Just east of Seattle, this continuous ridge forces moisture-laden clouds ever higher. Up the western side of the Cascades, the air becomes increasingly dry, sweeping over the summit as cold winds. By the time the winds crest the mountains, their moisture has been transformed into rain or snow.

Rain gear and suntan oil

As these weather systems continue down the Cascades' eastern slopes, they warm up quickly. Known as the "rain shadow," this constant pattern of weather results in regions of relatively low rainfall on the eastern side of the mountain range.

Consequently, the west side of the Cascades, appropriately labeled the "wet side" by author Bill Speidel, is gray, drizzly and necessitates rain gear, while the east side *(see page 159)* is dry, sunny and calls for suntan oil. The ever-present Casacdes are a reminder to Seattleites

that the wonders of nature are only an hour away. On winter evenings and weekends, damp city dwellers burst out of their concrete walls with a craving to attack the ski slopes. In summer, when warmer weather prevails, hiking, fishing and outdoor pursuits capture the attention. The North Cascades, in the northern part of the state, are described in *North Cascades National Park and Mount Baker (see page 190).*

Accessible slopes

Although not as lofty as its North Cascade neighbors, **Snoqualmie Pass ❶**, only 47 miles (75 km) east of Seattle on Interstate 90, offers magnificent wooded ridges and Alpine lakes. Since it is an easy getaway from the city, it is particularly popular, and

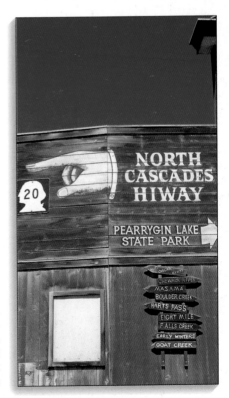

LEFT:
Snoqualmie
Falls.
RIGHT: there
are Cascades
to the north,
south, east
and west.

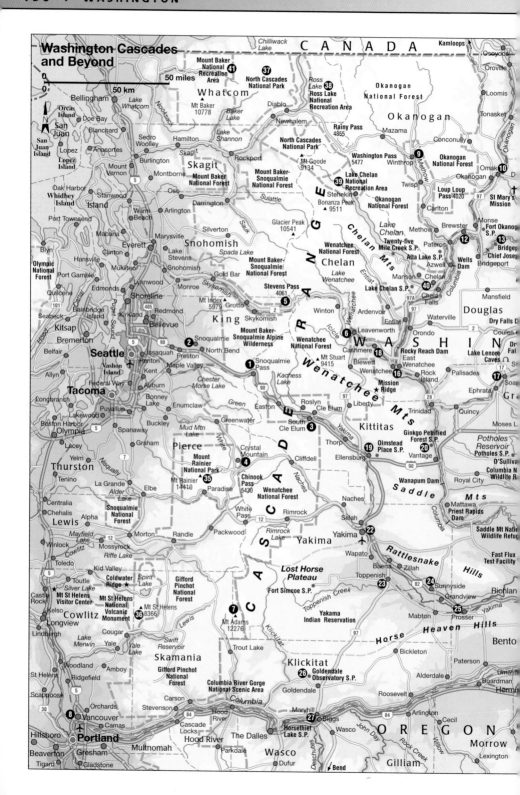

Washington Cascades and Beyond

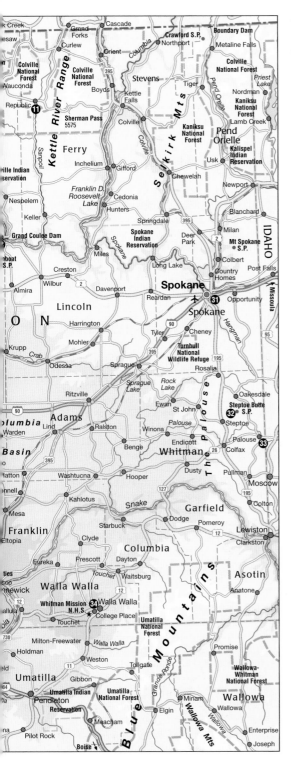

finding a peaceful spot demands a fair amount of research. At the top of Snoqualmie Pass are several ski areas. With a drop of 2,200 ft (67 meters), the **Summit-at-Snoqualmie** lies in the very heart of the **Mount Baker-Snoqualmie National Forest** and consists of six base areas offering what they consider the best night skiing in the United States (tel: 206 236-7277 for information.)

Annual snowfall is around 405 inches (10 meters). Considered one of the best areas to learn how to ski, the Summit has a variety of terrain that accommodates beginners to intermediate levels. There are also miles of cross-country trails.

While they do not always have the best snow in the state of Washington, the convenient drive and night skiing guarantee crowds on the weekends. Clustered on the edge of the snow level, the snow conditions here are often called "Seattle Cement." During the summer months, the Summit Mountain Bike and Hiking Center (open weekends only) offers recreational opportunities.

The summit actually consists of four mountains: **Summit Central**, **Summit East**, **Summit West** and **Alpental**, each with its own appeal. The giant among them is Alpental, with a drop of 2,200 ft (670 meters); this is where Olympic gold medalist Debbie Armstrong began racing. It is best suited to expert skiers with its 50 percent advanced terrain. There's also a Nordic center for get-fit skiers.

Summit Speedway is a "daredevil" track where kids get on mini-snowmobiles and ride around the course in energetic 10-minute sessions.

Scenic Byway

Each year, over 20 million vehicles travel over the Cascades, making this 100-mile (160-km) route along Interstate 90 – called the **National Scenic Byway** – a popular gateway from Seattle, then east over the Cascades to the dry plateaus of eastern Washington. Along the way there is a complete turn-around in climate, geology, and hometown style.

After passing through **Issaquah** *(see page 118),* it's an easy drive north to the town of **Snoqualmie** ❷ (Chamber of Commerce, tel: 425 455-1962) with its vintage railroad museum and cute shops. Highly recommended is a trip to 268-ft (81-meter) **Snoqualmie Falls**. The falls can be viewed from a roadside overlook on the south side of Rt 202.

Twin Peaks

David Lynch's surreal TV show *Twin Peaks* was based around here, and locals are used to fans looking for familiar sites. **Preston** was once a thriving mill town, while **North Bend** is a truck stop dominated by 4,157-ft (1,267-meter) **Mount Si**.

Derived from the Spanish term *madroño*, meaning "strawberry tree," the fairly rare Pacific Madrone tree with its papery bark grows throughout this area. In spring, the madrone produces white, fragrant flowers that mature into orange-red berries. Northwest native peoples were known to use its bark and leaves to treat colds, stomach problems and tuberculosis.

The highway continues through the

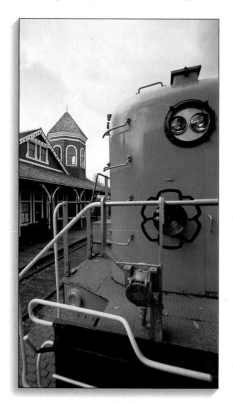

3,022-ft (921-meter) Snoqualmie Pass, then passes **Keechelus Lake** and **Cold Creek Pond**. Scenic Hwy 970 in **Cle Elum**, just east of the Cascades, winds through sleepy-looking **Teanaway River Valley**. Here, many species of native wildflowers grow unencumbered; visitors tend to seek out the demure yellow bell, beautiful balsamroot, camas lilies and wild iris.

Hidden Valley Guest Ranch (3942 Hidden Valley Road, Cle Elum; tel: 509 857-2344; reservations), the state's oldest dude ranch, lies deep within the sun-washed valley. Here, guests can sleep in rustic cabins and ride horses along trails that offer splendid mountain views.

The **John Wayne Trail and Iron Horse State Park** are located near Easton, at a major cross-state link on the old Milwaukee Railway. The level grade of the trail makes it ideal for mountain bikers, equestrians and walkers.

The highway continues past **Easton** and **South Cle Elum** ❸ (Chamber of Commerce, tel: 509 674-5958), a former railroad, coal and logging town. The Cle Elum Bakery (501 East 1st Street) first opened in 1906 and continues to be a popular stopping place for snacks. The Brick Tavern, in the town of **Roslyn**, tel: 509 649-2643, is built of stone, not brick, and has a water-fed spitoon that runs the length of the bar at foot level. Note that there is a notorious speed trap patrolled by aircraft on the open stretch of Interstate 90 east of town. The Scenic Byway trundles on past **Thorp** with its historic 1883 **Thorp Grist Mill** (tel: 509 964-9640; free) and continues to **Ellensburg** *(see page 166)*.

Sloping off

Located in the Mount Baker-Snoqualmie National Forest, **Crystal Mountain** ❹ lies on the northeast corner of **Mount Rainier National Park** *(see page 182)*, 76 miles (122 km) southeast of Seattle. Higher elevations mean abundant, lighter snow here. When the clouds blow free of 7,012-ft (2,137-meter) Silver King, **Crystal Mountain Ski Area** (33914 Crystal Mountain Boulevard; mid-Nov–mid-Apr 9am–4pm Sat–Sun 9am–8pm; tel: 360 663-2265) and its visitors come face to

LEFT: the vintage railro museum in Snoqualmie.

Map
on page
150

face with the mighty Mount Rainier. Panoramic views sweep past several other magnificent volcanic cones in the Cascade chain, including Mount Hood, Mount St Helens and Mount Baker.

Not only winter skiers, but summer visitors may catch the **scenic chairlift** (late June–Oct Sat–Sun only; tel: 360 663-2265; fee) to take in the fine vistas. Hotel and condominium accommodations are available in Crystal Mountain's village, complete with restaurants, bars, swimming pool and saunas.

Located between Mount Baker and Snoqualmie near **Skykomish**, an hour and a half north of Seattle on Hwy 2, and stashed in the middle of the North Cascades spires, is the **Stevens Pass** ❺ ski area (daily: late Nov–Mar 9am–10pm; mid Mar–season close 9am–4pm; tel: 206 812-4510; fee). Its geographical elevation of 4,061 ft (1,237 meters) is combined with dry winds from the east and 450 inches (11 meters) of snow annually. The ski resort was built in 1936, and the area

has aged like a fine bottle of wine. New lodges and lifts do not detract from the friendly hometown atmosphere. Variety and a vertical drop of 1,800 ft (550 meters) ring every skier's bell here.

Ski with the stars

The terrain ranges from tricky, double black diamond chutes and couloirs to smooth, wide-open cruising runs for all levels; and from a triple chair on the beginners' slope to some of the most demanding expert runs. A number of slopes are lit until 10pm for night skiing, and there are miles of cross-country trails.

For summer visitors, the 105-mile (170 km) **Stevens Pass scenic byway** winds through the rugged, forested Cascades and runs beside the **Skykomish** and **Wenatchee rivers** along most of its length. Summer recreation opportunities in the area include white-water rafting and very good hiking.

Mission Ridge ski area (late-Nov–mid-Apr Mon–Fri 9am–4pm, Sat–Sun 9am–

BELOW:
everything is
or sale in this
Snoqualmie
shop.

9pm; tel: 509 663-6543) in **Wenatchee**, east of Seattle on Interstate 90, has a diversity of terrain, from groomed runs to powder bowls, and a 2,100-ft (640-meter) vertical drop. Great snow and hardly ever crowded, the very short or non-existent lift lines contribute to the pleasant experience.

Both downhillers and cross-country skiers use **White Pass** (tel: 509 672-3101), southeast of Mount Rainier on Hwy 12, with a drop of 1,500 ft (460 meters), 350 inches (9-meters) of annual snowfall, miles of cross-country trails and wonderful views. The **Village Inn Condominiums** (tel: 509 672-3131; reservations) are located just steps away from the ski slopes and Nordic trails. **Loup Loup** is a smaller hill between Twisp and Okanogan near **Omak**.

Leavenworth

Leavenworth ❻ (Chamber of Commerce, tel: 509 548-5807), located directly east of Stevens Pass, and a 3-hour drive from Seattle, attracts both summer and winter visitors. Constantly styling itself on a Bavarian theme, Leavenworth has non-stop summer entertainment in the downtown band shell; theater performances of various light-hearted plays; non-stop festivals, and plenty of beer drinking.

Nordic-theme shopping includes The Tannenbaum Shoppe (735 Front Street; tel: 509 548-701), which carries an array of souvenirs like Hummel, Disney classics and Swarovski; a display of lighted houses, and some fine glass ornaments shipped over from Germany, Poland and the Czech Republic.

The surrounding area is noted for good skiing and ice climbing in winter, and good hiking or rock climbing in summer. The **Bavarian Nordic Club** maintains many miles of cross-country tracks located just outside the town, and many are lighted for night skiing.

Located at the edge of Washington's fruit-tree territory, the **Leavenworth Farmers' Market** (June–Sept Tues only), brings in an array of fresh produce from the Wenatchee Valley. There are also tasty baked goods and local crafts.

Among the many pleasant lodgings are: Bavarian-style **Haus Lorelei** (347 Division Street; tel: 509 548-5726) in an historic mansion; and **Abendblue Pension** (12570 Ranger Road; tel: 509 548-4059), an Austrian-style chalet with marble showers and fireplaces in some of the rooms. Leavenworth and Wenatchee, both east of the mountains, are also popular with climbing enthusiasts. The enormous number of nearby peaks and cliffs offer a variety of exciting routes.

White-water thrills

Washington's Cascades rivers are diverse, changing from season to season. They can flow in a white-water rampage part of the year, and end up in a bottom-scraping trickle at other times of the year. For rafting purposes, these rivers are graded Class I to Class IV – easy to difficult.

Rivers like the **Cowlitz** and the **Skagit** are easy, while the **Wenatchee, Green River Gorge** and **Skykomish** run to Class III and more. Most beginners

LEFT: the Cascades are popular with hikers and skiers.

Map
on page
150

choose a "float" – an easy river, which allows them to get their feet wet without major incident. A "rafting" experience is the next level up. At the top of the scale are the "paddlers" – athletes who choose a river or a section of river in keeping with their high level of experience.

For river adventures on the Wenatchee and Methow rivers, All Rivers Adventure (tel: 509 782-2254) provides both catering and white-water adventures; Leavenworth Outfitters Outdoor Center (tel: 509 763-3733) has rentals or scenic river floats starting near Lake Wenatchee. Additionally, Chinook Expeditions (tel: 800 241-3451) can provide days of adventure in the Cascade Loop or the Skykomish River.

There are a number of particularly safety-oriented outfitters including Riverdrifters (tel: 800 226-1001), operating on seven Washington rivers from March through October, and Downstream River Runners (tel: 360 805-9899), operating on the Wenatchee, Sauk, Suiattle, Skagit and other rivers.

BELOW:
the non-stop
summer
entertainment
has a Bavarian
theme.

Hot springs

With limited access, **Goldmyer Hot Springs** (GHS; tel: 206 789-5631; reservations) is owned and operated by a Washington state nonprofit corporation, and is nestled in the foothills of the Cascade Mountains about 25 miles (40 km) from the town of North Bend. It's a good idea, not only to call in advance for reservations – access is limited to just 20 people a day – but also for exact route directions, as the place is well hidden. Use of the springs can include camping in one of several wilderness campsites overlooking the river.

The springs are located at a low elevation in an area that is part of an ancient forest ecosystem, now a wilderness preserve. The upper **Middle Fork Snoqualmie Valley** beyond Goldmyer has never been logged, so is home to species of plants and animals found nowhere else. Giant western red cedar and Douglas fir up to 10 ft (3 meters) in diameter and over 900 years old can be found in this valley.

Mount Adams ❼ is one of five volcanos in Washington's Cascades. Although less familiar to many people due to its remote location, 12,276-ft (3,741-meter) Mount Adams is actually higher than the more famous Mount Baker, Mount St Helens and Mount Hood. It lies some 30 miles (50 km) east of Mount St Helens and 30 miles (50 km) north of the Columbia River. The peak marks the western extremity of the Yakima Indian Reservation *(see page 170)*; the surrounding area forms the **Mount Adams Wilderness** (USDA Forest Climbing information, tel: 360 891-5015). A Cascades Volcano Pass is required for climbers who want to visit between April 1 and October 31.

Because of the high elevation, all climbs can be difficult and dangerous. Weather on Mount Adams can change rapidly; sudden snowstorms can occur above 6,000 ft (1,800 meters) in any month of any year. What appears to be a fairly straightforward route can change drastically during these storms, so be aware and come prepared.

Vancouver, Washington

Captain George Vancouver did not leave his mark here, except in name, but he did on a large island further north, in Canada. Vancouver was born in 1758, joined the Navy at age 13 and served as a midshipman on Captain James Cook's third voyage. In 1791, he was picked to command a voyage to complete Cook's work, charting one of the last unexplored coasts on the globe. He was instructed to find the Northwest Passage, linking the North Atlantic and Pacific oceans; instead, he proved it did not exist. Vancouver was respected for his skills in navigation and charting, but disliked for his dour temperament. He died aged 40 in 1798.

The prosperous city of **Vancouver ❽**, Washington, just north of Portland, Oregon, was a major outpost along the Columbia River, and named for the captain by a officer serving under him. Although George does not feature strongly in the city's history, Vancouver does have a number of attractions relating to its past.

The buildings on the **Fort Vancouver National Historic Site** (1501 Evergreen Boulevard; daily: Nov–Feb 9am–4pm; Mar–Oct 9am–5pm; closed: holidays; tel: 360 696-7655; free) were originally a fur trading post; in 1825 it became the headquarters of the Hudson's Bay Company, which moved here from Astoria on the Oregon coast *(see page 244)*.

Although British, the primary languages were Canadian French and Chinook. The fort represented British interests, yet made American settlement in the area possible. The Blacksmith Shop is open Thursday through Monday; the Carpenter Shop is open on Tuesdays and Wednesdays. **Pearson Air Museum** (1115 East Fifth Street; Tues–Sun; tel: 360 694-7026; fee) has vintage aircraft.

Vancouver's Charthouse (101 East Columbia Way; no lunch on weekends; tel: 360 693-9211) presents diners with good seafood, good service and a wonderful view of the water as well as outdoor dining during the summer months.

For a description of the Columbia River Gorge on both the Washington and Oregon state borders, *see page 217.* ❏

Map on page 150

LEFT: reenacting a fur trappers' life at the Fort Vancouver National Historic Site.

Bigfoot

From the dense forests of Washington and British Columbia to Northern California, legends of Sasquatch – also known as Bigfoot – have been handed down over the ages. It's a Northwest version of a fearsome fable – from the Grendel of Beowulf to the Himalayan Yeti – as old as the forest and the night. There has always been some degree of anecdotal evidence, but since the dawning of the Internet, ever more stories about yeti-like creatures are amassing daily. Encounters always take place in the world's most remote forested mountain areas, including the wilderness of North Cascades National Park.

Two of the most highly educated cyptozoology researchers live in the Northwest: Dr. Grover S. Krantz, a Seattle-based anthropology professor, and John A. Bindernagel, a wildlife field biologist from Canada. Krantz estimates there have been a quarter of a million Bigfoot "events" over the past 40 years. He has tracked nearly identical reports from the Northwest to western China, supporting his theory that the ancient *gigantopithecus*, the greatest ape that ever lived, some 8 or 9 ft (2.5 or 3 meters) tall – did not die off in Asia 400,000 years ago. He believes it crossed over into North America, and survives in small numbers.

Bindernagel's research analyses the content of thousands of stories. He surmises that most encounters go unreported because people are afraid of ridicule. But 90 percent of those that are reported correctly describe typical ape behavior: appearance, calls and sounds, bedding sites, locomotion and gait, upright stance and hunched posture, even odor. Bindernagel concludes, "the Sasquatch is a very real wildlife species, and is, indeed North America's great ape."

And so the tales of the Cascade Mountains continue: large, human-like footprints found along a creek; screaming sounds heard late at night by mountain campers. Old Native American stories tell of a fearsome hairy creature called Tsonoqua (So-no-kwa) who stole fish and sometimes kidnapped children. Pioneer fur trader David Thompson recounted finding a bedding site as long ago as 1828, while in the 1860s, there were reports of

huge "man-creatures" skulking around homesteads throughout Washington and Oregon.

One famous story took place at Mount St Helens in the 1880s. A hairy creature, later dubbed "Skookums," pelted a prospector's cabin with rocks, resulting in the so-named Ape Cave area. Putting aside the fanciful stories of aliens that make up 2 percent of the sightings, researchers continue to seek conclusive, preferably DNA, evidence. "The tests," says Oregon zoologist H. Henner Fahrenbach, "could legitimize, to my mind at least, the sightings, the footprints, everything...." But so far that evidence has been hard to find.

"As an evolutionist, I'd love to see the thing. But to my knowledge... they prove to be hoaxes of one type or another..." says Daris Swindler, professor at the University of Washington. Whatever the doubts, years after much of the forest gave way to suburbs, Sasquatch stories are in resurgence all over the Northwest, a cultural phenomenon that is at least as remarkable as any scientific evidence uncovered in DNA labs. ❏

RIGHT: stories of Bigfoot are as old as the forest itself.

EAST OF THE CASCADES

*Ponderosa pine forests on gently sloping hills, orchards growing
Washington apples, and the wide-open wheatfields of
The Palouse characterize Eastern Washington*

Map on page 150

Two-thirds of Washington state lie east of the Cascade Mountains, which includes additional ranges like the Blue Mountains and the Selkirks. There are many routes and many choices to make for anyone who wishes to see this vast and glorious region. For the purposes of this chapter, central Washington is described by traveling from north to south; eastern Washington is described in the same way; central Washington regions are: Okanogan Country, Wenatchee Valley, Columbia Basin, Yakima Valley, Columbia Gorge and Tri-Cities; eastern Washington regions are: Ponderosa Pine Country (northeast corner), the Spokane area, The Palouse and Walla Walla (southeast corner). In practice, visitors often meander between these regions, choosing any number of delightful combinations.

Central Washington

Encompassing the Colville Indian Reservation and the Okanogan National Forest, dry and rolling pine-forested hills climb a mile in elevation into the upper reaches of the **Okanogan Highlands**. Numerous lonesome valleys, the silence broken by an occasional bird call, eventually give way to larger valleys. Cattle ranching and fruit production are the principal occupations.

The town of **Winthrop** ❾ (Chamber of Commerce, tel: 888 463-8469) has remade itself into a favorite stop for many travelers unable to resist the chance to walk past false-front stores that resemble the set from a western movie. Think "cowboy," grab a sarsaparilla and listen to old-time fiddlers or blues players, all the while wandering around the well-conceived Old West-style shops and restaurants. If time is limited, at least check out the ice-cream shops and try the black walnut variety.

Winthrop is also the place to join a pack-horse-train through the hills, or fish, camp and explore the Methow River valley. This tributary of the Columbia River originates along the eastern slope of the Cascade Mountains, making it particularly popular with rafters. Its waters offer different levels of sporting challenges, from serene family floats to consistent rapids such as Hurricane Rapids, Cinder Block Drop or the notorious Black Canyon.

In keeping with the western feel, upscale **Sun Mountain Lodge** and **Dining Room** (Patterson Lake Road, Winthrop; tel: 509 996-2211; reservations recommended), perched on top of Sun Mountain 10 miles (16 km) from Hwy 20, has panoramic views of the North Cascades and trails for hiking and horseback riding. The lodge's award-winning dining room

LEFT AND RIGHT: the grasslands known as The Palouse were named by early French fur traders.

present tasty specials such as Dungeness crab chopsticks with a ginger curry emulsion, or shredded Daikon salad and roast Maine lobster on a lobster rouge cream.

On the way out of town, stop by to read the plaque at the **Smokejumpers' base**. The highly trained smokejumpers' job is to attack small wildland fires in remote areas before they grow too dangerous, or to assist larger firefighting efforts. First on the scene, they jump out of an airplane and parachute to the ground, prepared to do battle *(see photograph on page 303)*. BLM smokejumpers use ram-air square parachutes, while Forest Service jumpers use round parachutes.

Nearby **Twisp** (Visitor Information, tel: 509 997-2926) is home to the **Confluence Gallery** (104 Glover Street; closed Mon) for all sorts of one-of-a-kind objects made by local artisans and craftspeople. **Methow Valley Farmers' Market** (mid-Apr–Oct Sat only 8:30am–noon) is the place to buy locally grown fruits and vegetables (some organic), baked goods,

cheeses, spring plants and handcrafted items. Continuing through the 4,020-ft (1,280-meter) **Loup Loup Pass** brings travelers to the county seat and the **Okanogan** community. The **Okanogan County Historical Museum** (1410 2nd Avenue North; May–Sept daily 10am–4pm; tel: 509 422-4272; fee) displays a series of dioramas, models and photographs plus a replica of an Old West town of the early 1900s. There is also the **Firehall Museum**.

Suicide race

The town of **Omak** ❿ (pronounced *oh-mack*; visitor information, tel: 509 826-4218) is both famous and infamous for its horseback-riding event, traditionally held the second weekend in August. The **Omak Stampede and Suicide Race** (tel: 800 933-6625) starts atop Suicide Hill, on land owned by the town of Omak. With a 120-ft (36-meter) running start, as many as 20 riders on horseback – mostly from local tribes – send their horses plunging 210 ft (64 meters) downhill, on a slope Stampede organizers have boasted is an "almost verticle *(sic)*…62° angle."

More than a football field's area of water awaits them, the may-be-deep, may-be-shallow Okanogan River. Horses with riders must swim across the river. After a sprint of roughly 500 ft (150 meters) more on Colville Indian land, surviving horses and riders enter Stampede Arena in the hope of collecting one of the race's modest prizes.

Started in the 1930s, this extreme race has proved to be as controversial as it is popular, as injured horses (and there are many) are immediately euthanized. A full-fledged rodeo accompanies the event.

Omak's **St Mary's Mission**, with its church dating from 1910, was founded by Jesuit Father Etienne de Rouge in 1886 to minister to the 11 bands of the Colville Federation. The adjacent Paschal Sherman Indian School, Washington's only Indian boarding school, is managed by the Colville Confederated Tribes.

State Highway 155 meanders to the southeast, past a trunk road to **Omak Lake**, then to **Nespelem** on the Colville

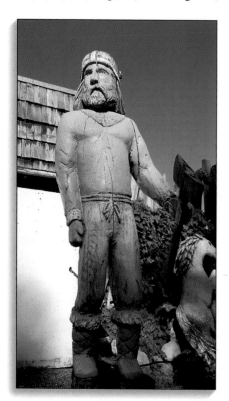

LEFT: logger figure made of finest Washington wood.

Map
n page
150

Indian Reservation. The **grave of Chief Joseph** of the Nez Perce tribe *(see page 63)* is close by.

Fifty million-year-old roses

Republic ⓫ (Chamber of Commerce, tel: 509 775-2704) is the county seat and another western-style, false-front town. Of particular significance is the presence, in the upland *lacustrine* fossil beds around Republic, of the earliest known records of the *Rosaceae* (rose family) and *Aceraceae* (maple family). The **Stonerose Interpretive Center** (North Kean Street; tel: 509 775-2295; fee) displays fossils of plants, insects and fish discovered at the nearby **Ecocene Fossil Site**.

Visitors are encouraged to dig for fossils on the site, which is made up primarily of slate. Chisels and hammers are available for a fee. Up to three fossils a day may be kept. Fossil diggers and would-be ranch hands might like to stay in one of the four rooms at the **K Diamond K Guest Ranch** (15661 Hwy 21 South; tel: 509 775-3536;

reservations recommended), where everyone, even tenderfoots, join in the Wild West activities.

Anyone traveling Hwy 97 north of **Brewster** ⓬ notices 39 huge satellite antenna dishes. This is the **Brewster Earth Station Verestar** (tel: 509 689-1000). Once part of the Comsat satellite communications project, today US Electrodynamics Inc (USEI) is in charge. Systems here are used for a variety of purposes: to transmit temporary data services for military maneuvers during disasters such as typhoons in the Pacific Ocean; to host an FAA system that allows airplanes to establish their position within 6 ft (1.82 meters) anywhere in the United States; to host one of 12 Earth stations for satellite telephones; to carry news events for all four major television networks; and to provide various internet transmission capacities.

The station hosts a large percent of Internet traffic to China, and provides both Internet and LAN/WAN services to Russia, Korea, Taiwan and the Pacific Islands. It

LOW: the
ak Suicide
ce, in which
esmen ride
rses down
almost
tical slope.

also connects remote installations such as oil rigs, construction sites and cruise ships with the McMurdo Sound research base in Antarctica. Finally, the Brewster Earth station is the communications center for the Sea Launch program, which puts commercial satellites in orbit from a platform located in the Pacific Ocean near Christmas Island.

The **Chief Joseph Dam** at Hwy 174 in **Bridgeport** is part of the chain of dams that harnesses the power of the Columbia River from Grand Coulee Dam to the Columbia Gorge. **Bridgeport State Park** ⓭ (tel: 360 902-8608) with its lake, lawn, golf and shady trees in the midst of a desert terrain is a pleasant place to camp overnight or simply to have a picnic lunch. "Haystacks" – unusual, large volcanic formations – are the park's unique feature.

Four other dams in the Big Bend region of the Columbia River also offer recreational facilities for visitors: **Wells Dam** south of Brewster on Hwy 97; **Rocky Reach Dam** north of Wenatchee on Hwy 97; **Wanapum Dam** 6 miles (10 km) south of the I-90 crossing of the Columbia; and **Priest Rapids Dam** on Hwy 243. North of Bridgeport State Park is **Fort Okanogan State Park** (day-use only), which is set on a bluff overlooking the Columbia River. This was the site of the first settlement in what is now the state of Washington.

Onsite is the **Fort Okanogan Interpretive Center** (mid-May–Aug Wed–Sun; tel: 509 923-2473), which has historical information about fur trading and riverboats. The fort was established in 1811 by David Stuart for the Astor Fur Company and in 1821 it was purchased by the Hudson's Bay Company. The name is a derivative of the word the local Indians had for themselves, "Okinakane." South of Okanogan is the popular Lake Chelan area *(see North Cascades National Park, page 190)*.

Grand Dam

The mighty **Columbia River**, once formidable with many treacherous rapids, flows 1,270 miles (2,040 km) from its source in the glaciers of British Columbia to the Pacific Ocean. In this, the early section of the river's course, its energy is harnessed by mammoth **Grand Coulee Dam** ⓮, and backed with the reservoir, **Franklin D. Roosevelt Lake**. Altogether a total of 11 dams have been built on the river, but Grand Coulee is the keystone. Additionally, gigantic pump-generators move water into **Banks Lake** to form a complex irrigation system.

To appreciate one of the great wonders of the west, the **Grand Coulee Dam Visitor Arrival Center** (VAC; self-guided or 30-minute guided tours; June–Sept 8:30am–9:30pm; tel: 509 633-3074; free) offers a wealth of information in a concrete building on the hill just off Hwy 155. Round in design and two stories high, it looks remarkably like a bottle cap.

Watch the short film, then go to the other side of the dam to take a free **incline elevator ride** (every 30 minutes; 10am–5pm) into the bowels of the dam itself. The all-glass-front elevator travels 465 ft (140 meters) on a dramatic 45° incline.

LEFT: fishing for Washington's finest.

Map on page 150

On summer nights, a free **laser light show** (June–July 10pm; Aug 9:30pm; Sept 8:30pm) plays colorful images across the entire span of the leviathan structure, narrated with music and an uplifting patriotic finish. Viewing bleachers are available, but visitors can also just stand and watch.

Nearby, the small **Colville Tribal Museum** and **Gift Shop**, (512 Mead Way; May–Sept daily 10am–6pm; tel: 509 633-0751; fee), in an A-frame structure that was once a church, portrays the history of the region's Native American tribes. These tribes include the Okanogan, Nespelem, SanPoil, Nez Perce, Chelan, Wenatchee, Entiat, Methow, Lakes and Palouse. The reservation is home to many fine artists, whose work is represented in the museum, though the **Casino** is the main tourist focus here.

East of the dam is the **Coulee Dam National Recreational Area** (tel: 509 633-9441) encompassing the Franklin D. Roosevelt Lake. Twenty-two campgrounds offering 524 sites dot the area:

some are open year-round and most have boat-launching facilities. Many species of waterfowl are attracted to this region making it a rewarding stop for nature lovers. Visitors should check with area headquarters in the town of **Coulee Dam** (Chamber of Commerce, tel: 509 268-5332) for more details and information.

Flat-topped lava buttes

Steamboat Rock, near the mid-point of Roosevelt Lake and a well-known landmark to First Nations and early fur traders, is 1,000 ft (300 meters) in elevation. A side road from the highway leads to **Steamboat Rock State Park** ⑮ (call Reservations Northwest, tel: 800 452-5687 for information) a huge camping park with 50,000 ft (1,500 meters) of freshwater shoreline at the north end of Banks Lake. Dominating the landscape is the great columnar, basaltic rock itself, which has a surface area of 600 acres (245 hectares).

In the middle of apparent desert, sweeping green lawns – protected from winds

BELOW: Grand Coulee has been called the eighth wonder of the world.

GRAND COULEE DAM

Sometimes called the "eighth wonder of the world," the Grand Coulee Dam is the largest hydroelectric project in America, and the third largest producer of electricity in the world. Its base covers four times the area of the Great Pyramid in Egypt, and is higher, too. The dam is second only to the Great Wall of China as the largest man-made structure in the world. Its construction required almost 12 million cubic yards (9 million cubic meters) of concrete – enough, it has been said, to build a sidewalk that would completely encircle the world. It is as high as the Washington Monument and twice as high as Niagara Falls.

The monumental size of the Grand Coulee (*coulee* is from a French word meaning "to flow") created colossal problems – obstacles many said could not be overcome. When bedrock was exposed, a huge volume of clay began seeping forward, threatening to swallow the dam's foundation. After frantic deliberations, engineers froze the clay, and work was able to continue. The Grand Coulee took 13 years of political maneuvering to achieve, and nine years to construct, which began in 1933 when President Franklin D. Roosevelt authorized $60 million. As this was during the Depression years, thousands turned up for work, and the town of Grand Coulee sprang up virtually overnight.

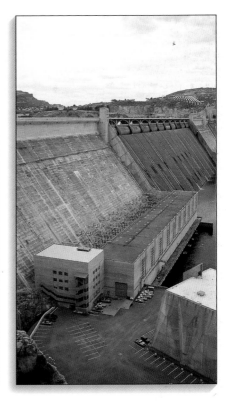

by tall poplar trees – compliment the surrounding areas carpeted with wildflowers. All this adds to the gray-green brush of the so called "Scablands." A hiking trail leads to the top of the butte and a wildflower preserve. The lake is the summer home of western grebes. A hiking trail leads to **Northrup Lake**, within natural forest, open 24 hours a day.

Lakes and caves

Southwest of Coulee City, geologic **Dry Falls** was created when the ice age-era Lake Missoula – then covering much of present-day Montana – overflowed its ice dam and surged westward. **Dry Falls Interpretive Center** (May–Sept daily 10am–6pm; tel: 509 632-5583) is located at the top of the canyon. Farther south are **Lake Lenore Caves** (tel: 509 766-1699), accessible via a 3-mile (5-km) hiking trail. These seven caves, formed by the rush of meltwaters during the ice age, were used by prehistoric man for temporary housing during hunting and food-gathering trips.

East of **Wenatchee ⓰** *(see below)* is **Soap Lake ⓱** (Chamber of Commerce, tel: 509 246-1821). With its high mineral content, the lake's waters are thought to be of therapeutic value. Lake water is piped into many of the town's hotels, including **Inn at Soap Lake** (tel: 508 246-1132; reservations recommended), and public beaches and swimming pools are conveniently located; some have therapeutic mud baths.

Apple facts

Wenatchee (Chamber of Commerce, tel: 509 663-2116) sits on the banks of the Columbia River at the junction of Hwys 97 and 2. Dry air, hot days and cool nights, an ample water supply and excellent soil make ideal growing conditions for the crisp apples that have made Washington – and Wenatchee – famous.

The **Wenatchee Valley** lays claim to the title "apple capital of the world." Washington has led the nation in apple production every year since the early 1920s. In 2001, the state apple crop was estimated at 90 million boxes. Each box holds 42 lbs (15 kg) of apples making a total of about 3.78 billion pounds (1.4 billion kg). More than half of all eating apples in the US come from this state, and in independent surveys, more consumers ranked Washington apples as of a better quality than apples from any other state. Per capita, Americans eat approximately 19.6 lbs (7.3 kg) of apples annually, compared to about 46 lbs (17 kg) by residents of European countries.

In Wenatchee, waterfront orchards produce crisp varietals: Red Delicious, Golden Delicious and delectable Galas. In season, fruit stands line the roads. And tree-ripened cherries, apricots, peaches, pears and nectarines are usually ripe in early July.

Apples are grown all around this region: in the Okanogan, Lake Chelan, Columbia Basin, Yakima Valley, the Skagit Valley and around the town of Spokane. For a juicy look at America's favorite fruit, the **Washington Apple Commission Visitors Center** (2900 Euclid Avenue; Mon–Fri 8am–5pm; May–Dec Sat 9am–5pm, Sun 10am–4pm;

LEFT: the Wenatchee Valley claims ▸ be the world's apple capital.

Map on page 150

tel: 509 662-3090) in Wenatchee has good displays, a video about apples and their production, as well as samples. At the accompanying gift store are a selection of fresh fruits, ciders, syrups, jams, jellies and candies.

At a nearby **interpretive orchard** (Cascade Loop; weekdays 8am–5pm; tel: 509 662-3090), up-to-date planting technology and frost-protective wind machines are demonstrated.

Fruit and a farmers' market

Fruit lovers should not miss the **Blossom To Bearing tour** (Green's Home Outfitters; Apr–Oct daily; tel: 509 782-3564; reservations; fee), which covers the history of Wenatchee Valley orchards, visits a working family orchard and a commercial packing house, features samples including dry apple cider; and includes lunch where lots of apple products are served in various guises.

Wenatchee Valley Farmers' Market (Riverfront Park at 5th Street; June–Oct

Wed and Sat only, 8am–1pm) sells an array of farm-fresh fruit and vegetables, homemade goodies, arts and crafts. Of note is the particularly fine locally grown produce, which ranges from summersweet Musk melons, cling peaches, heirloom salad greens and boysenberries to fire-hot peppers and fragrant herbs like thyme, sage, fennel and dill.

Founded in 1939, the **Wenatchee Valley Museum and Cultural Center** (127 North Mission; Mon–Fri 10am–4pm, Sat–Sun 1–4pm; closed: Jan; tel: 509 664-3356; fee) displays local pioneer and Native American items – including petroglyphs from the Columbia River – an operating railroad diorama, and an exhibit about the apple industry.

As well as 15 acres (6 hectares) of lawns and gardens, **Rocky Reach Dam** (Hwy 97A north) includes the **Gallery of the Columbia** (mid-Feb–Dec daily 8am–dusk; tel 509 663-8121; free), which has a variety of river-related exhibits. Included are a pilothouse from an 1800s steamer;

BELOW: a farmer's friend, plus flowers.

the Gallery of Electricity; replicas of Indian dwellings; plus logger and railroad worker's tools. You can also visit the Powerhouse and watch fish as they pass by the dam.

Acclaimed **Ohme Gardens County Park** (3327 Ohme Road; mid-Apr–mid-Oct daily 9am–7pm; tel: 509 662-5785; fee), north of Wenatchee on Hwy 97 overlooking the river, is a garden well-known for its Alpine rockeries. Established in 1929, its good-looking grounds are a blend of conifers and alpine meadow flowers planted around pools of water.

Cashmere

Nestled between Leavenworth and Wenatchee is the town of **Cashmere ⓮**. The **Cashmere Fruit Exchange Farmers' Market** (99 Aplets Way; daily 10am–5pm; tel: 509 782-7700) offers gift baskets and boxes of fruit and vegetables as well as hand-selected gifts. In town, with its old-fashioned street lamps and covered walkway, **Cashmere Pioneer**

Village and Museum (600 Cotlets Way; Mar–Dec 15 daily 9:30am–5pm; tel: 509 782-3232; fee) is an assemblage of 20 original pioneer structures dating to the late 1800s. Said to be the tastiest tour in Washington, **Liberty Orchards Aplets and Cotlets Candy Kitchen** (off Hwy 2; continuous tours; May–Dec Mon–Fri 8am–5:30pm, Sat–Sun 10am–4pm; Jan–Mar Mon–Fri 8:30am–4:30pm; tel: 509 782-2191) offers delicious free samples. Candy lovers take note.

College town

The college town of **Ellensburg ⓳** (Chamber of Commerce, tel: 509 925-3137) is located in the geographic center of the state. About 110 miles (170 km) east of Seattle and 170 miles (275 km) west of Spokane, it is a popular hub for concerts at the **Gorge Amphitheater**, waterskiing on the Columbia, golf, fly fishing, river rafting, snowmobiling and cross-country skiing. Ellensburg's historic shopping district has eclectic shops, pubs and restaurants. It began as a trading post in the 1870s, when pioneer John Shoudy bought 160 acres (64 hectares) and a store, plotted the future city and named it after his wife Mary Ellen.

The railroad arrived in 1886 and in 1889 prospering Ellensburg had high hopes of being named the capital of the new state of Washington. Unfortunately, on July 4 that year, a huge fire destroyed most of the town. Although reconstruction began within days, the town of Olympia was chosen as the capital. Undaunted, Ellensburg continued to flourish, its attractiveness enhanced by handsome brick buildings and early Victorian architecture. Cattle- and horse-ranching, corn and grain production are all major players here.

Ellensburg is home to the tree-lined **Central Washington University** campus. A fascinating stop is the world-famous **Chimpanzee and Human Communication Institute** (14th and D boulevards; tours Sat 9:15 and 10:45am; Sun 12:30 and 2pm; tel: 509 963-2244; fee), a tour that is unusual to say the least. Five adult chimpanzees live in a sanctuary where

LEFT: Ellensburg is a friendly town with lots of college kids and activities.

Map
on page
150

they communicate with humans and each other using American Sign Language. "Chimposiums" are frequently held; these are a combination tour and educational workshop.

More mainstream but still interesting is the **Olmstead Place State Park Heritage Site** (East on Mountain View, south on North Furgeson Road; daily 8am–5pm; tel: 509 925-1943; free) with its interpretive trail and 19th-century log buildings giving visitors an idea of how early settlers lived.

Columbia River Basin

Numerous gigantic lava flows of unbelievable force engulfed the landscape here over a period of several million years, covering much of eastern Washington and parts of Idaho and Oregon with black basalt. One of the deepest areas of basalt in the world, this region is known to geologists as the Columbia Basin basalt field. In the years between flows, soils developed and supported plant life. Even an untrained observer can see soil layers sandwiched between lava flows.

In some parts of Washington, layers of basalt buckled to form ridges, plateaus, gentle valleys and broad, shallow basins. The **Umtanum** and **Menashtash ridges** and the **Saddle Mountains** south of Ellensburg were formed in this way. The accumulation of various sediments in the basin soils at the foot of these uprisings has helped to make these areas the rich agricultural regions they are today.

From Ellensburg, Interstate 90 passes large cattle and horse ranches, then houses framed by cottonwoods and lilacs, and continues on through sagebrush country. Three hours east of Seattle on Interstate 90, the river comes into view at the crest of rolling hills near **Vantage**. For visitors new to the region, the biggest thrill might well be the first sighting of the great Columbia River. There are several paved viewing areas for gazing at the river as it passes beneath spectacular basalt cliffs. Outstanding at sunset is a series of metal sculptures, *Grandfather Cuts Loose the Ponies,* featuring life-size horses running over the hills.

Feeling hungry? Washington-reared buffalo makes for mouthwatering burgers or steaks around these parts; try the **Fort Wanapum Restaurant** (Holiday Road; tel: 509 856-2808). Marinated in a tangy sweet and sour sauce, the buffalo meat makes the taste buds tingle.

Ginkgo Petrified Forest State Park [20], 28 miles (45 km) east on I-90, consists of three separate parts: the **Heritage Area**, housing the park's **Interpretive Center** (mid-May–mid Sept 10am–6pm; free); the **Natural Area**, with a short interpretive trail following a prehistoric lake bed where petrified wood deposits occur; and the **Wanapum Recreation Area** (Oct–Mar 8am–dusk; Apr–Sept 6:30am–dusk; tel: 509 856-2700) located 4½ miles (7 km) south, with camping by a reservoir.

Perched on a bluff high above the Columbia River, with splendid views of the water, the interpretive center displays 50 cut and polished sections of petrified wood. Ginkgo is one of the rarest forms of fossil wood. Although the Ginkgo tree

RIGHT: autumn is a perfect time to walk through the forests.

became extinct on this continent, it survived in Asia, and now grows in North America through reintroduction as an ornamental plant. Below the Interpretive Center is a collection of Native American petroglyphs that were moved here from a now-submerged site along the river.

Striking columns of basalt, formed as lava cooled and contracted, rise sentinel-like from the earth in various parts of central and eastern Washington. Some of the most arresting are found along the south side of **Frenchman Coulee**, a few miles east of Vantage. If you're walking along any of these trails, cover up from the sun, carry water and watch out for rattlesnakes.

Bird-watching central

The sprawling desert-oasis town of **Moses Lake ㉑** (Chamber of Commerce, tel: 509 765-7888), located on the shore of a natural claw-shaped shallow lake, seems exceptional in the dry landscape of east-central Washington. Ever since the Columbia Basin Project has been in effect,

there has been more than enough water in the area. The **Farmers' Market** (Civic Center Park; mid-June–mid-Oct Sat morning and Wed afternoon) sells farm fresh produce and handmade arts and crafts. **Potholes Reservoir area**, about 4 miles (6 km) south, takes its name from the numerous glacial depressions formed in ancient sand dunes. Seepage from irrigation and nearby **O'Sullivan Dam** has created many small ponds in this area.

Across the dam is Mardon Resort and **Potholes State Park**. Millions of birds use the marshes, lakes, potholes and puddles for feeding and resting on their annual migration along the Pacific Flyway. During spring and summer, yellow-headed blackbirds, kingbirds, meadow larks and several species of hawks and owls can be seen along the road. Coyotes, jackrabbits and a variety of smaller mammals are all residents of these lands.

Over 200 different species of birds have been noted at the **Columbia National Wildlife Refuge** (tel: 509 488-2668; free), a wintering area with an average population of more than 100,000 ducks, mostly mallards, and Canada geese. Some mallards, redheads and cinnamon teal nest on the refuge along with various song, water, marsh, and shorebirds, while hawks, owls, ravens and cliff swallows can be observed in the cliff areas. Local wetlands provide shelter to herons, American avocet and other shorebirds. Pheasants, quail and magpies are found in the upland areas.

The Yakima Valley

With 300 days of sunshine per year, fertile volcanic soil, hot days and cool nights, the **Yakima Valley** is a fertile stretch of land that has flowered from the water of the Yakima River and irrigation projects that date to almost 100 years ago.

More than 200 different agricultural commodities are produced here: vegetables from asparagus to zucchini, herbs from dill to mint, livestock from cattle to dairy cows. Being leading growers of apples and hops, as well as cherries, pears, grapes, peaches, mint, corn and other garden produce, summertime roadside stands are well worth stopping for.

LEFT: the Columbia National Wildlife Refuge has a winter population of more than 100,000 ducks.

Map
on page
150

The city of **Yakima** ㉒ (Visitors Bureau, tel: 509 575-3010) is the commercial center of the valley. Take a step back in history with a stroll along the boardwalk of **Track 29** and visit the restored 1912 **Northern Pacific Depot** that now houses the very modern **Grant's Brewery Pub** (tel: 509 575-1900; ask for a tour). As early followers of the American microbrew movement established in 1981 – according to *America's Best Brews* – Grant's are rated one of the top 25 breweries in the country, based on the appearance, aroma and palate of their cask-conditioned ales.

In addition to a collection of horse-drawn carriages, including a Conestoga wagon, **Yakima Valley Museum** (2105 Tieton Drive; Mon–Fri 10am–5pm, Sat–Sun noon–5pm; tel: 509 248-0747; fee) has exhibits pertaining to the Yakima Native Americans. Also here is a depiction of a 1930s soda fountain, where ice-cream treats are home-made.

The Japanese garden, Trees of Washington, Wetland Trail and the Jewett Visitor

and Interpretive Center (1401 Arboretum Drive; tel: 509 248-7337; free) together make up the **Yakima Area Arboretum**, a greenway collection of more than 2,000 species along the river.

Washington's Fruit Place Visitors Center (105 South 18th Street; tel: 509 576-3090; free) tells the story of the fruit industry with hands-on displays, free samples, room-size photo murals, and interpretive services. Fruit stands are found throughout the area in season; one of the best is **Johnson Orchards** (4906 Summitview Avenue; tel: 509 966-7479).

Indian Pictographs

The **Indian Painted Rocks** just off Hwy 12 about 2 miles (3 km) west of Yakima – just before the Fred Redmond Memorial Bridge – are reached via a short walk; 80 pictographs are on display. The age of these images is unknown to both archaeologists and regional Native Tribes. They appear to depict religious subjects or records of hunts and meetings with other tribes.

ELOW:
ncy dancer
om the
akima tribe.

Pastoral **Birchfield Manor Country Inn** (tel: 800 375-3420) offers delightful rooms, with dinners prepared by trained chef/owners and served with Washington wines in the casual atmosphere of a gracious home. Roast rack of lamb with apple and Dijon glaze is a favorite, or the baked king salmon filet wrapped in puff pastry drizzled with Yakima Valley Chardonnay sauce.

In 1800, a member of the Gasperetti family once served the family's famous chicken *cacciatore* dish to Pope Pius VI. Today, fifth-generation family members at **Gasperetti's** (509 248-0628; reservations recommended) serve notable Italian fare – with a French twist.

City of murals

A real cowboy-and-Indian site, the town of **Toppenish** ㉓ (Chamber of Commerce, tel: 509 865-3262) is dominated by 55 building murals depicting the region's history, including all of its Mexican-American influences. The best way to see the murals is by taking a **horse-drawn wagon** (1550 Gibson Street; tel: 509 697-8995), complete with a narrated tour. Toppenish's **American Hop Museum** (22 South B Street; May–Sept daily 11am–4pm; tel: 509 865-4677; donation) focuses on this brewing industry from 1805 to the present day, including old photographs, memorabilia, antiques and a gift shop.

Located on the edge of the **Yakima Indian Reservation**, the now-expected gambling **casino** is very much in evidence. Also of interest is a stylized version of an ancient Yakima winter lodge – 12,000 sq. ft (1,115 sq. meters) in size, the **Yakima Nation Cultural Center** (Mon–Sat 9am– 5pm, Sun 10am–5pm; tel: 509 865-2800; fee) includes a meeting hall, museum, theater and library.

The **Toppenish National Wildlife Refuge** (daily, daylight hours; tel: 509 865-2405) about 6 miles (10 km) south of town on Hwy 97, is a fine place for bird watching, with a nature trail and an inter-

BELOW: one of 55 murals in the town of Toppenish.

Map
on page
150

pretive center that displays natural history exhibits. From Toppenish, Hwy 220 leads 30 miles (50 km) to **Fort Simcoe State Park** (day use only; tel: 509 874-2372; fee), a restored military fort with 10 historic buildings that also served as an Indian agency and a school. In this case, "simcoe" is a translation of the Yakima word *sim-qu-ee*, the native name for a type of saddle.

The **Rocky Mountain Chocolate Factory** (daily; ask for a tour; tel: 509 829-3330; free) in **Zillah** uses old-fashioned techniques and tools. Visitors to the factory watch as the hot mixture is poured onto a thick granite table and moved around with a giant wooden paddle, gradually being coaxed into creamy fudge.

Views and brews

South of downtown **Sunnyside ㉔** on Alexander Road, **Darigold's Dairy Fair Visitor Center** (tel: 509 837-4321; free) is a large working facility with self-guided tours of its cheese-production process. Follow up with free samples (try the

squeak cheese) and a quick lunch at **Snipes Mountain Microbrewery and Restaurant** (905 Yakima Valley Hwy; tel: 509 837-2739). Located in a massive log cabin, Snipes offers the views and brews that one would expect in Washington. Few people realize that 75 percent of America's hops are grown in the vicinity. A walled patio shows off fine natural surroundings but unfortunately that includes the aromas from a nearby dairy farm.

Farther south, **Prosser ㉕** (Chamber of Commerce, tel: 509 786-3177) is centrally located between Yakima and Tri-Cities and less than a four-hour drive from Portland, Seattle or Spokane. Thousands of acres of wheat, barley and other dry-land crops are grown on **Horse Heaven Hills**. Lovers of chocolate-covered cherries will be interested to hear that the Pacific Northwest is also the number-one producer in the world of delicious fresh and dried cherries.

In Prosser, the **Chukar Cherry Company** (320 Wine Country Road; daily

10am–5pm, closed: holidays; tel: 509 786-2055; free samples) creates scrumptious dried specialties as well as "create-your-own" gifts. The warm summer days, cool nights and rich soil also enable local farmers to grow fine wine grapes here; there are 15 **Washington Wineries** within a 30-mile (48-km) radius. Touring the area for its wineries alone has become an increasingly popular vacation occupation.

One among many is **Columbia Crest Winery** (Hwy 221, Columbia Crest Drive, Paterson; daily 10am–4:30pm; tel: 509 875-2061; free tastings) located on the rise of the Columbia River. Fashioned after a French country chateau, it lies at the same latitude as France's Bordeaux and Burgundy regions. Picnickers can also enjoy the winery's landscaped grounds, scenic pond and courtyard with tables.

Washington's Columbia Gorge

Located at latitude 45°, 50 minutes, 20.104 seconds and longitude 120°, 48 minutes, 49.787 seconds, at an elevation of 2,100 ft

(640 meters), the **Goldendale Observatory State Park ㉖** (north of Goldendale; Apr–Sept Wed–Sun 8pm– midnight; donation) caters to stargazers. The observatory has a number of telescopes including a 24½-inch (65-cm) Cassegrain used in the evenings for **public viewing**.

After a stop here most visitors continue on to an exceptional museum. Receiving more than 10,000 visitors a month is the **Maryhill Museum of Art ㉗** (Mar 15– Nov 15 daily 9am–5pm; tel: 509 773-3733; fee). Near the Columbia River on the Washington side, and dedicated in 1926 by Queen Marie of Romania, the museum is housed in the castle-like mansion of eccentric road-builder Samuel Hill. Born in England in 1875, Queen Marie took a liking to this part of the world. Her mother, also called Marie, was the only surviving daughter of Tsar Alexander II of Russia and her father, Alfred, was the second son of Queen Victoria. To complement the coronation gown and royal furnishings given by Queen Marie, arts patron Alma de Bretteville Spreckels donated much of the furniture, embroideries, sculptures and paintings.

The museum's collection is exceptional: European and American paintings; a collection of Auguste Rodin watercolors and sculptures (originals); 19th-century French art glass; and 18th-century Russian icons. Serendipitous exhibits include Hill memorabilia, Native American basketry and the Theatre de la Mode French mannequin gallery. In 1918, on finding a spectacular panoramic viewpoint overlooking the Columbia River 3 miles (5 km) east of Maryhill, Samuel Hill built a **memorial** (daily 7am–10pm; free) to those who died in World War I. The memorial is a full-size replica of Britain's Stonehenge.

Horsethief Lake State Park is a camping park with 7,500 ft (2,300 meters) of freshwater shoreline – an impoundment of the Columbia River. Power surveyors gave the present name to the canyon in the 1950s. To them it had the appearance of a movie hideout for horse thieves; now **Horsethief Butte** dominates the skyline. Some of the oldest picto-

LEFT:
a checkerspot butterfly rests in one of Washington's many parks.

Map on page 150

graphs in the Northwest are in this state park; the best known is called "She Who Watches" or *Tsagaglalal*. Unfortunately, because of vandalism, much of the area is now restricted, so visitors must arrange to see the pictographs via one of the **ranger-guided tours** (Apr–Oct Fri and Sat only, 10am; tel: 509 767-1159; free).

Three cities in one

The nearby cities of Richland, Pasco and Kennewick are usually referred to as the **Tri-Cities ㉘** (Visitors Bureau, tel: 509 735-8486), a group of towns clustered together along the Columbia at its junction with the **Snake River**. Pasco was founded as a railroad town in 1880 and Kennewick in 1892, yet the area remained relatively quiet until the 1940s.

Then, in 1943, for strategic reasons, the Federal Government founded the **Hanford Atomic Works** at **Richland**, and 60,000 workers appeared in a town with a former population of 250. The eventual expansion of atomic energy work and research at the plants, combined with the development of irrigated land, soon rocketed the population to 80,000. The facility was first administered by the United States Army Corps of Engineers, followed by E.I. du Pont de Nemours and Company, then the Atomic Energy Commission. In 1947, the General Electric Company assumed control.

In 1988, the US Department of Energy announced its permanent closure except for one massive concrete chemical plant. Concern continues about uranium isotopes, toxic solvents, plutonium contaminated equipment, and heavy metals buried in some 177 underground tanks or stored above ground. Nonetheless, in a highly surprising move, part of the region was designated an official **National Monument** in June 2000.

The 195,000-acre (80,000-hectare) **Hanford Reach** is a dry, undeveloped region that can be seen by jet boat: contact **Columbia River Journeys** (tel: 509 734-9941) to see it. This soon-to-be-developed area is located near the **Saddle Mountain National Wildlife Refuge**, along the last untamed free-flowing section of the

Columbia River. A shrub-steppe habitat, it is home to coyotes, deer and giant white pelicans. The area suffered a significant grass fire in 2000, but is expected – in time – to recover.

Dominated today by a large contingent of Latino workers, **Pasco** is a good place to sample authentic Mexican food. The **Pasco Farmers' Market** (4th and Lewis; May–Nov Sat only, 8am; tel: 509 545-0738) is one of the largest open-air markets in the state.

Located on Hwy 12, on the Snake River and Lake Sacajawea, **Ice Harbor Lock and Dam and Visitor Center** (Apr–Sept daily; powerhouse tours; tel: 509 547-7781; free) generates electricity as river traffic passes through the second- largest navigational lock in the world.

Kennewick

The city of **Kennewick ㉙** has repeatedly hit the international headlines since a 9,300-year-old skeleton was discovered in 1996 *(see page 174)*. The bones were

RIGHT: overlook above the busy and winding Snake River.

found in the center of town in **Columbia Park**, on the west bank of the Columbia River. Other Kennewick attractions include the *Tri-City Herald* (for a free tour of this newspaper office, tel: 509 582-1500), while the **Sacagawea Heritage Trail** (2503 Sacajawea Park Road; tel: 509 545-2361; free) commemorates the Lewis & Clark expedition's historic visit. Early morning or late evening visits are recommended to view the town's migratory waterfowl and wildlife. Kennewick's preserve is located in a wetlands delta with protected riparian habitat.

If you're feeling hungry, the **Blue Moon Restaurant** (tel: 509 582-6598; reservations recommended) serves seven-course meals from a menu that changes monthly. The choices are divine: start with wild boar chipotle, brie and garlic soup and fresh fruit sorbet. Follow that with sauteed ostrich medallions with wild mushroom demi-glace, then finish with a chocolate cinnamon cheese soufflé, and vanilla nut-roast coffee.

Nuclear Energy

The **Fast Flux Test Facility** (FFTF) **30** (tel: 509 376-8089; ask for a tour; free) is located 11 miles (18 km) north of Richland and is recognized as the most advanced test reactor in the world. This facility has established itself in the scientific community as very valuable in the production of medical isotopes used in pharmaceutical radiation therapy for the treatment of osteoporosis and cancer. Visitors must be US citizens and 18 years or older.

Energy Northwest Plant #2 (Thur–Sun; tel: 509 377-4558; ask for a free guided tour), located 12 miles (20 km) north, is the state's first operating electric-generating commercial nuclear reactor. Its Visitor Center has lots of energy information, related computer games, videos and interactive exhibits. Also available for special visits is the world's first large-scale plutonium production reactor, the **105-B Reactor**. Hanford employees who lived at this once top-secret site act as

BELOW: the site in Columbia Park where the 9,300-year-old Kennewick Man was first discovered.

KENNEWICK MAN

In 1996, two boat-racing enthusiasts stumbled across a skeleton near the Columbia River in Kennewick. This find has threatened to rewrite the history of the US, for the discovery challenges the assumption that the original inhabitants of the Americas were Amerindians. The bones of Kennewick Man are at least 9,300 years old. Six independent groups of scientists have now concluded that the bones are those of an Ainu person from Japan. The skeleton has also kicked off a series of legal battles. Teams are battling over legislation that gives Native Americans the right to claim back from museums their ancestors' remains for burial, while scientists are fighting to keep the bones for further study. Though the "who was here first?" question appeals to laypersons, the courts are wrestling with a different matter whether the oral tradition of Native Americans, in recent rulings accepted as factual, can continue to define issues in court matters. Paraphrasing a judge's recent finding, "If we happen to find a stray Viking skeleton here in North America, do we have to return him to Native Americans in the area where he was found because they claim… to be the only people here at the time?" Some say this issue goes beyond the question of First Peoples; that it's aboriginal oral tradition versus modern scientific method that's at stake.

guides (May–Sept; some Sats; tel: 509 376-7505; free). Tours are by advance reservation only.

Northeast corner

Taking the Columbia River as the rough western boundary, the part of Washington called, variously, the Inland Empire or the Ponderosa Pine Country, has the city of Spokane as its major urban center. This region – the far eastern side of the state – has more than 200 lakes, 76 of them within an hour or two of Spokane.

These eastern lakes range from tiny **Fish Lake** and **Liberty Lake**, barely outside Spokane's city limits, to the huge **Coeur d'Alene**, **Pend Oreille** and **Priest lakes** in the next-door state of Idaho. There are tour boats available on the larger lakes, as well as seaplane excursions.

Nestled in the foothills of the beautiful **Selkirk Range** of mountains, 107 miles (62 km) north of Spokane and just one mile south of the Canadian border, **Boundary Dam** (May–Aug daily 10:30am–4:30pm; tours by arrangement; tel: 509 446-3083; free) arches gracefully between two massive rock cliffs. Its safety gates retard the flow of the state's second-largest river, the **Pend Oreille** (pronounded *pond*-o-rye). At its peak, the dam generates 1,024 megawatts of power – enough energy to light a city the size of Seattle. Other area attractions include **Gardner Caves** at **Crawford State Park**, and herds of buffalo at the **Kalispel Indian Reservation**.

A place where Native Americans came to fish for thousands of years along the Columbia is remembered at the **Kettle Falls Interpretive Center** (tel: 509 738-2827; free) on the site of St Paul's Mission. In 1825, the Hudson's Bay Company set up a trading post here. Today it is part of the massive reservoir of the Grand Coulee Dam. The **Colville National Forest** (tel: 509 684-700 for backpackers' information) encompasses mountain forests and meadows north of Rt 20. Streams here teem with healthy, good-looking trout.

Spokane ③ (pronounced Spo-*can*; Visitors Bureau, 801 West Riverside. 301; tel: 509 624-1341) takes it name from the local Spokan tribe of Salish Nations; it translates as "Sun children." Averaging more than 170 days of sunshine each year, the city receives an annual rainfall of only 16.71 inches (42 cm).

Nicknamed "Lilac City," Spokane is the second-largest city in Washington and the largest metropolis between Seattle and Minneapolis, four states to the east. With a population of around 392,000, its metropolitan area stretches from west of Downtown all the way to the Idaho border.

Father's Day

In 1910, Mrs Sonora Smart Dodd founded Father's Day here; in 1916 President Woodrow Wilson proclaimed Father's Day as a national day of observance. That same year, when the railroad and mining barons of the Inland Empire discovered that they had created a thriving center, they hired the Olmsted brothers – sons of the man who designed New York's Central Park, – to devise a system of parks and scenic roads.

Map on page 150

RIGHT:
Spokane's
Riverfront Park.

City fathers followed most of the Olmsted brothers' advice. Prime examples are **Manito Park** (Grand Boulevard at 17th Street) and **Rockwood Boulevard**, but one idea they ruled out was the creation of a "gorge park" along the riverfront. Access to the river by rail was extremely important financially. The next 60 years saw the decline in rail and mining interests, however, and eventually economic changes made it possible to reclaim the riverfront.

World's Fair

Spokane emerged with a new image for the World's Fair Expo '74 – the smallest city to host this exposition. The Fair's legacy at the heart of the city is the pleasant 100-acre (40-hectare) **Riverfront Park** (Spokane Fall Boulevard and Washington; tel: 509 625-6600) covering the islands, both sides of the **Spokane River** and highlighting **Spokane Falls**, two sets of cascades, one 60 ft (18 meters) high, the other 70 ft (21 meters high). In ancient times, salmon gathered at the falls and a native village was located here. Children and adults delight in feeding the ducks, geese, swans and marmots, while other park visitors thrill to the ride across the falls on the **Riverfront Park Gondola Skyride**. The **Park Tour Train** offers a narrated journey, and there are amusement rides and mini-golf in the **Park Pavilion** (all charge fees). More than 250,000 riders reach for the brass ring annually on the majestic 1909 carousel.

One survivior of the city's face-lift is the **Great Northern Railroad Clocktower**, built in 1902. The massive station is now gone, but the Italianate clocktower still stands in Riverfront Park, a monolithic reminder of the dynasties that once created fortunes. **Finch Arboretum** (3404 West Woodland Boulevard; tel; 509 624-4832; free), west of Downtown, is a 65-acre (26-hectare) collection of more than 2,000 trees, flowers and shrubs.

Directly south of the park, 10 blocks of Spokane's leading department stores, specialty shops and restaurants are connected by covered, street-spanning **skywalks**. Colorful **streetcars** connect the **Spokane Arena** with the city's pedestrian mall on **Wall Street**. Visitors are encouraged to park at the Arena and ride the streetcar to Riverfront Park or Downtown. Vehicles run every ten minutes and stop at the **Spokane Transit Plaza**. From there, the Transit System provides access to every area of town.

Spokane looks like it was planned to be clean, safe, pretty, friendly and middle-class. The city center comprises restored brick-and-stone buildings from the 19th century, several bridges, a castle-like county courthouse and modern buildings.

You can enjoy roasted onion gorgonzola ravioli sautéed with arugula, walnuts and olive oil and topped with chilled tomato-fennel gazpacho at **Mizuna** (214 North Howard; tel: 509 747-2004). The city's only production brewery is the **Northern Lights Brewing Company** (to schedule a free tour, tel: 509 244-4909), which brews draft beers that are distributed throughout the state and Northern Idaho. There is no pub on the site, but there are fresh samples

LEFT: eastern Washington has rich soil perfect for farming.

Map on page 150

in the hopper. The city is also noted for its medical and educational facilities.

Spokane was the home of crooner Bing Crosby. He attended **Gonzaga University** (502 East Boone Avenue; tel: 509 328 4220 ext 2234; free) and his family home is now its Alumni Center. Tours of the **National Weather Service** (near Fairchild Air Force Base; daily; schedule a tour; tel: 509 244-0110, ext. 223; free) convey details of how forecasts are made and observations taken of air conditions. The cornerstone of this equipment is the interactive weather system that issues active warnings.

Mount Spokane Ski and Snowboard Park (tel: 509 443-1397 for a snow report), 25 miles (40 km) northwest of Spokane, is a favorite spot with locals. With few chairs, the lines are short and the terrain is fun. In summer, hikers, campers and mountain bikers take advantage of **Mount Spokane State Park** (tel: 509 238-4258), which contains two mountains – the most southerly peaks in the Selkirks.

Now listed on the National Historic Register, **Mount Spokane Stone Vista House** was built in 1934 by the Civilian Conservation Corps. The view from the top of the 5,883-ft (1,793-meter) elevation includes the surrounding states all the way to the Canadian border.

The Palouse

South of Spokane, The Palouse is a broad area of low hills and wide-open land with an occasional fringe of trees and rich soil up to 100 ft (33 meters) deep. The name for this area of green grasslands is a corruption of the word *pelouse*, meaning "lawn." It was named by early French fur traders. For centuries, Native peoples fished for salmon and eel in the rivers and cultivated the soil, which was rich with volcanic ash. A land of amber waves and warm-hearted people, the long, peaceful roads are perfect for leisurely cycling.

Climb to the top of pyramid-shaped **Steptoe Butte** about 50 miles (80 km) south of Spokane, and peer south, toward the steep Blue Mountains, over seemingly

BELOW:
the name The Palouse comes from the French word for "lawn."

thousands of square miles of undulating terrain. Starkly dramatic **Steptoe Butte State Park** ㉜ (no water; tel: 509 459-3551), near the state's eastern border, has this thimble-shaped, 3,612-ft (5,812-meter) granite butte looming in bald grandeur over the prevailing flatlands. From the top, visitors reputedly can see for 200 miles (300 km). It's named for Colonel Edward J. Steptoe, who was soundly defeated in a running battle with the local Cayuse Indians in 1858.

Vintage printing and glass

Native Americans were the first to arrive here, followed by explorers Lewis & Clark, who passed through nearly two centuries ago on their way to the mouth of the Columbia River. They were probably the first non-indigenous people ever to set foot in Washington. In the fall of 1805, while traveling west, the expedition arrived at the junction of two great rivers. One was the mighty Snake River; the other was the Clearwater, on the banks of which

the expedition established a camp. They also camped on the banks of Patit Creek, a short distance from **Palouse** ㉝ village.

Modern-day visitors usually enjoy the **Boomerang Newspaper and Printing Museum** (tel: 509 878-1309; donation) that maintains equipment used by early printers. **Kamiak Butte County Park** provides good opportunities to spot rare or unusual birds. The **Pine Ridge Trail** is a loop of about 3 miles (5 km). Tiny **Garfield** is home to the New Morning Glass Studio (weekends; tel: 509 635-1263), where visitors can watch glass blowing first-hand. Just east of **Oakesdale** is Hanford Castle B&B (tel: 509 285-4120), a hilltop mansion that has fine sweeping views.

Colfax (Chamber of Commerce, tel: 509 397-3712) is the site of **Perkins House** (North Perkins Avenue; tel: 509 397-3712; donation), listed on the National Historic Register and furnished with items from the late 19th century. This funky college town is also the home of **Washington State University** with the on-campus **Charles R. Conner Museum of Zoology** (Sept–May daily 8am–5pm; tel: 509 335-3515; free) – a fine collection of stuffed birds and preserved invertebrates.

Known for its wheat fields, The Palouse also produces billions of lentils, making it the "lentil capital of the world." From this quaint corner of Americana, millions of pounds of lentils are shipped to Europe, South America and the Middle East.

Clarkston (Chamber of Commerce, tel: 800 933-2128) has a green and pleasant valley walkway called the **Greenbelt** and is surrounded by fields of grass. The 1.4 million-acre (567,000-hectare) **Umatilla National Forest** (tel: 541 278-3716), with its rugged backcountry of peaks and canyons, is ideal for hiking, mountain biking, and horse packing. Rocky Mountain elk, bighorn sheep, deer, cougar and black bear are common here. If skiing is a passion, you can swoosh through deep powder on the slopes of the nearby Blue Mountains. The second-highest base elevation in the state is located here, along with – on most winter days – clear skies and short lines at the ski lifts.

LEFT: the famous sweet onions of Walla Walla

Southeast corner

Founded on the site of a Nez Perce Indian village, delightful **Walla Walla** ㉞ (Chamber of Commerce, tel: 509 525-0850) is well maintained. Its centerpiece is not the locally known but uninteresting penal institute, but the pretty campus of **Whitman College**.

The surrounding countryside, famous for its asparagus and vineyards, is also renowned for its "so sweet, you can bite 'em like an apple" Walla Walla Sweet Onions. Simply called "Sweets," these really are mild enough to eat as a tasty and refreshing snack – although it may take a while to get used to the idea.

The Walla Walla area is also home to at least 18 wineries, enough to justify a couple of days touring between them (with a designated driver, of course). One among many is **3 Rivers Winery** (5641 West Hwy 12; daily 10am–5pm; tel: 509 526-9463; free sampling) in a dramatic setting overlooking vineyards.

In another vein, the **Fort Walla Walla** Museum (755 Myra Road; Apr–Oct Tues–Sun 10am–5pm; tel: 509 525-7703; fee) is a collection of 14 pioneer buildings, a railroad museum and old machinery. For aficionados of the Oregon Trail, **Whitman Mission National Historic Site** (daily 9am–5pm, closed: holidays; tel: 509 522-6360; fee) preserves the site of Waiilatpu Mission, a Presbyterian mission for the Cayuse Indians from 1836 to 1847. During the 11-year period of the mission, the site also became a way-stop for Oregon Trail pioneers.

The mission was destroyed in violence in November, 1847, after an outbreak of measles killed half the Cayuse tribe. Marcus Whitman and 12 others were killed by the Cayuse. The park preserves the foundations of the mission buildings, the Mill Pond, a short segment of the Oregon Trail, and the sad grave of the victims. Other exhibits highlight the pioneer life. From the Whitman Mission, many visitors go on to **Hell's Canyon** in Northeast Oregon *(see page 305).* ❑

Map on page 150

BELOW: the Fort Walla Walla Museum relives pioneer days.

OLYMPIC NATIONAL PARK

*Snuggled deep within the Olympic Peninsula,
this park of rainforests and glacier-capped
mountains remains remarkably undeveloped*

Few, if any, other regions in North America combine the natural whimsy, gentle wildness and infinite variety of **Olympic National Park**. Often referred to as "three parks in one," it encompasses three ecosystems, all within a day's drive of each other. These include magnificent stands of old-growth and temperate **rainforest**; rugged glacier-capped **mountains** and 60 miles (100 km) of Pacific coast – the last **wilderness ocean beaches** in mainland USA. Eight kinds of plants and five kinds of animals found in this park live nowhere else in the world.

Native American tribes had bestowed the region's high country with enough legends and mystery to discourage travel, so it wasn't until 1889 that an exploration party, sponsored by the *Seattle Press*, headed west and crossed the Olympic Mountains. The early logging industry spotted choice opportunities, and timber fellers swiftly cut their way through the low-elevation rainforests. In 1897, however, concerned naturalists lobbied to maintain the Olympic Forest Reserve. This evolved into Olympic National Monument (1909), and then Olympic National Park (1938).

The **Hoh Rainforest** is the area's most-visited spot. Olympic National Park is recognized internationally as a Biosphere Reserve and World Heritage Site because of this temperate rainforest. The preternaturally fertile forest thrives because of a mild coastal climate, infrequent winter

BELOW: the Hoh Rainforest, the park's most beautiful and popular spot.

Map on page 132

frosts and summer temperatures that rarely go above 80°F (25° C).

In the moss-draped rainforest, colonnades of virgin spruce and hemlock rise to form an evergreen lattice; under them, vine maples spiral from pillowy forest-floor coverings of club moss. Relatively easy walking trails include the **Hall of Mosses Trail** and the **Spruce Nature Trail**. Self-guided or guided tours can be taken; contact the **Park Service Interpretive Center** (tel: 360 374-6925).

Another beautiful area, the **Quinault Rainforest**, can be reached by taking either the North Shore or South Shore Road northeast from Hwy 101 in the southwest corner of the park.

The **Olympic Mountains** are a cluster of lofty canyons, flowered ridges and glaciated peaks. The highest is **Mount Olympus**, which stands at 7,980 ft (2,430 meters) – high enough, icy enough and rugged enough to challenge even world-class climbers. Much of the park's trail system weaves through high country past up to a dozen glacial lakes. From late June through August, blacktail deer graze belly-deep in avalanche lilies, and marmots scurry from rock to rock.

The Olympic's wild ocean beaches are memorable. Wildlife includes bald eagles, harbor seals, shorebirds and migrating whales. Highway 101 runs along the southern-most region near **Kalaloch**, with a number of beaches just a few hundred yards from the car. At **Ruby Beach** – famed for its red pebbles – sentinel trees and oddly shaped rocks called seastacks *(see picture, page 141)* stand guard over tiny **Abbey Island**. If you plan to walk from beach to beach, be sure to take an up-to-date tidetable, as the coastal tides can be changeable and dangerous.

There are 17 park campgrounds, all booked on a first-come, first-served basis (tel: 360 565-3130). Summers are crowded, so it's an idea to arrive early, especially on weekends. **Olympic National Park Visitor Center** is at 600 East Park Avenue, Port Angeles (tel: 360 565-3130). ❏

ELOW:
ake Crescent s seen from yramid Peak the Olympic Mountains.

MOUNT RAINIER NATIONAL PARK

*Mount Rainier, an active volcano almost permanently
topped with snow, receives about 2 million visitors a year
and its towering summit has long attracted serious climbers*

Rich in topography, wildlife and plants, 14,411-ft (4,392-meter) high, glacier-clad **Mount Rainier ③** is clearly visible from Seattle and Tacoma. It was established as a natonal park in 1899. When Captain George Vancouver sailed into Puget Sound in 1792, he could not help but note the mountain's snow-covered magnificence, and named it for his friend, Rear Admiral Peter Rainier.

Though the Admiral sailed several times to the East Indies, and captured an American ship during the Revolutionary War, he never saw the Pacific Northwest, nor the mountain that bears his name.

The mountain had, however, been known for centuries by the First Nations – the Nisqually, Cowlitz, Yakama, Puyallup, and Muckleshoot – who hunted and gathered berries in its forests and meadows. They called it *Tahoma*, *Tachkoma*, *T'chakoba* plus 40-other variations on this name, with interpretations running from "nourishing breast" to "rumbling noise." To them all, the mountain was an entity of power and fear.

Unlike Mount St Helens, a young stud of the Cascade range at 40,000 years, Rainier is around half a million years old. St Helens is a tidy mountain, a nearly symmetrical cone until 1980, having been built by alternating layers of lava, ash and vol-

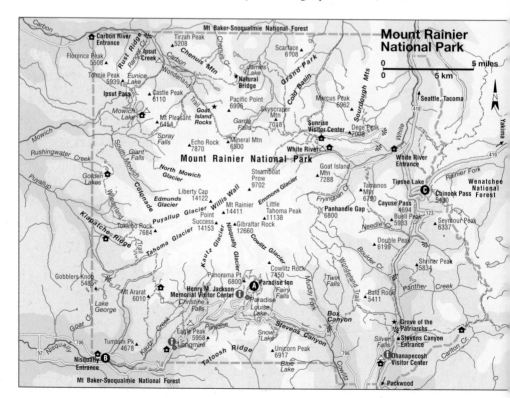

Maps,
page 150
& 182

canic debris. Rainier is a mishmash, a mound of many layers of lava and blast fragments. But – like Mount St Helens – Rainier is an active volcano. It is encased in over 35 sq. miles (140 sq. km) of snow and ice, surrounded by old-growth forest and stunning wildflower meadows.

Directly in the path of any future mud-flows will be the town of **Orting**. In the wake of St Helens' 1980 eruption, Orting's relationship to Rainier has become like a marriage tinged with distrust. But new residents don't seem to mind; Orting is one of the fastest-growing communities in Washington state.

Lodging in the park is most prized at historic **Paradise Inn** Ⓐ (summer only; tel: 360 569-2275; reservations; book months in advance). In 1919, Hans Fraehnke, a German carpenter, designed and built much of the decorative woodwork that exists today, including a rustic piano and a grandfather clock. The inns's voluminous dining room serves the establishment's celebrated Bourbon buffalo meatloaf.

Other lodging is at the **National Park Inn** at Longmire (year round; tel: 360 569-2275; reservations), located 6 miles (10 km) from the southwest entrance. For lodging near Rainier, but outside the national park, contact the **Mount Rainier Visitors Association** (tel: 877 617-9950).

One unique recommendation is the **Cedar Creek Treehouse** (tel: 360 569-2991, reservations compulsory) near **Ashford**, Each cabin is 50 ft (15 meters) up a giant cedar tree, with a fantastic view of Mount Rainier from every single bed. The two-level eyrie is reached via a 77-step staircase.

Weather patterns at Mount Rainier are strongly influenced by the Pacific Ocean, elevation, and latitude. If half a million Seattle residents drank and bathed only in meltwater captured from Rainier's snow and ice fields, the water supply would last 200 years. The climate around the mountain is generally cool and rainy, with summer highs of 60–70°F (15–20°C). While July and August are the sunniest months,

BELOW:
sunrise,
Mount Rainier
National Park.

rain is possible any day, and very likely in spring and autumn. From November through April, there is heavy snowfall, an average of 620 inches (1,575 cm) annually. Raingear is recommended year-round. The park offers a variety of recreational and educational activities, from easy guided walks with park rangers to mountain climbing to car touring. Trails are steep, but well-maintained in summer; in winter they are snow-covered and difficult to follow.

Backpacking and photography are popular summer activities, while winter offers cross-country skiing, and snowshoeing opportunities, plus a limited amount of camping. There are no ski areas with lifts on the mountain.

Visitors without a car might like to consider Gray Line of Seattle (mid-spring to mid-fall; tel: 206 626-5208), which does bus tours to Rainier leaving from a couple of different sites in Seattle. This is a great way to sit back while learning about the park's history, wildlife, plants and Native American heritage.

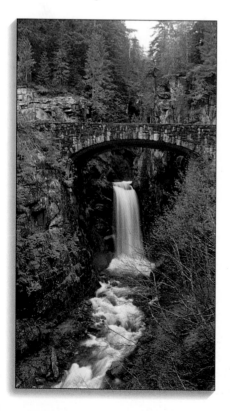

People in cars most frequently utilize the **Nisqually entrance** ❸, on Hwy 706, in the southwest corner of the park (open year-round; vehicles pay a national park fee). One of the best and most accessible drives takes about 3 hours one-way, on narrow scenic roads that invite lingering.

A first stop might be the **Longmire Wilderness Information Center** (May 22–Oct 15; tel: 360 569-4453). The original site of mineral springs found by James Longmire in 1883, it is open daily fto personal callers for hiking and backpacking information, wilderness permits and wilderness reservations. Anyone who intends to camp needs to obtain a permit, which can be done from here.

The nearby **Longmire Museum** (daily 9am–6pm, closed: holidays; free), the park's oldest operating interpretive museum, has exhibits on its natural and man-made history. Next to the museum is a fine transportation exhibit.

The road then winds up to the 5,400-ft (1,647-meter) area called **Paradise**, located on the south face of Rainier. Besides the stupendous view, visitors can take in the **Henry M. Jackson Memorial Visitor Center** (May–Oct; tel: 360 569-2275; donation), which has exhibits on geology, glaciers, flora and fauna, as well as mountain climbing.

There are various walking trails near here: **Nisqually Vista Trail** is a vigorous ¼-mile (2-km) hike. The easiest is **Skyline Trail**, which travels the half-mile circumference of the meadows. Common flowers in these parts are the Indian paintbrush, daisies, lupins and beargrass, which are at their most beautiful during the months of April, May and June. Please do not disturb or pick the flowers.

From Paradise, motorists can return to Seattle or continue east along **Stevens Ridge** (road open June–Oct) to Hwy 123 south, or continue past the **Ohanapecosh Visitor Center** (May–mid-Oct). This route emerges from the east side of the park at about the midpoint on the historic **Mather Memorial Parkway**. Roads are sometimes closed in winter, so contact Washington State Transportation (tel: 800 695-7623) for information. Some of the

LEFT: Christina Falls a favorite Rainier spot.

Maps, page 150 & 182

road entrances to Rainier allow access to only small sections of the park, so do check before heading off on one.

Rainier is a hiker's dream. There are no limits on the size of a party, or what trail to choose for a hike, and there is no charge (beyond the park entrance fee) for hiking during the day – although day hikers are required and requested to stay on designated trails. It's a good idea to keep hiking plans flexible, because some trailhead parking lots may be full, especially in the summer, and overflow parking is not permitted. Paradise, Sunrise and **Tipsoo Lake** ❻ meadows are the most popular with hikers. Bicycles are allowed on the roads in Mount Rainier park, and cyclists will find opportunities that are both challenging and scenic.

For more than a century, mountain climbers have been drawn to the towering summit of Mount Rainier. Many American mountaineering expeditions train here for the challenges of its steep slopes and glaciers. Going to the top is rigorous, dangerous and requires proper equipment and training. Reaching the summit involves an elevation gain of more than 9,000 ft (2,800 meters) over a distance of 8 miles (13 km). All climbers going above 10,000 ft (3,000 meters) or climbing glaciers must register at a ranger station and check in and out.

Guide services, including one-day climbing instruction, two-day summit climbs, and five-day seminars, are available through Rainier Mountaineering Inc. (tel: 360 569-2227). Visitors do not need mountaineering experience to climb Mount Rainier, but it is imperative to be in good shape and well-equipped; the trip is physically strenuous. Each year about 10,000 people attempt to climb to the top; only half of them make it.

For information on any aspect of Mount Rainier, contact **Mount Rainier National Park** (tel: 360 569-2211). The park is open year-round, but access is limited in winter. Try to schedule your visit for mid-week in summer, if possible, since parking is limited in many areas on the weekend. ❑

BELOW: Paradise Inn under cover of new snow.

MOUNT ST HELENS NATIONAL VOLCANIC PARK

*Many people in the Pacific Northwest remember
exactly where they were on May 18, 1980 –
the day that Mount St Helens erupted*

An explosion with the force of an atomic bomb blew the top off of **Mount St Helens** 36 in 1980, sending rock and debris hurtling at 500 mph (800 kph) into the atmosphere. Shaken by an earthquake measuring 5.1 on the Richter scale, the north face of this previously symmetrical mountain collapsed in a massive rock avalanche. In just a few moments, an enormous slab of rock and ice slammed into **Spirit Lake**, crossed a high ridge and roared 14 miles (22 km) down the **Toutle River**.

The avalanche released pressurized gases stored within the volcano. A tremendous lateral explosion ripped through the

avalanche and developed into a turbulent, stone-filled wind that swept over ridges and toppled trees. By nightfall, over half a million sq. miles (1.3 million sq. km) in three US states were covered in ash, and the impact, or the fall-out from the impact, was felt around the world. The once 9,677-ft (3,000-meter) mountain was 1,300-ft (400-meters) shorter, a huge bite gone from its northern slope.

The initial eruption lasted 9 hours, but Mount St Helens and the surrounding landscape were changed within minutes. Nearly 60 people died, buried under ash and mud slides. The toll on wildlife was severe: later estimates put the casualties at 5,000 black-tailed deer, 1,500 elk, 200 black bears, 15 mountain goats, together with unknown numbers of mountain lions, bobcats, small rodents, birds, fish and insects. According to biologists, the region's rare spotted-owl population was also wiped out.

Mount St Helens park takes in 1,110,000 acres (500,000 hectares) of trees, plants and wildlife, revealing nature's amazing ability to regenerate. The eruption of this volcano remains one of the largest natural disasters in recorded American history. Visitors today can travel to Mount St Helens – about three hours drive from Seattle – and straight into the heart of the blast zone, learning about the violent eruption and witnessing at first hand the chaotic results of earth's catastrophic forces. Anyone without a car can take a one-day tour from Seattle with Cowlitz Coach Tours (tel: 877 274-0385), or from Portland through Ecotours of Oregon (tel: 503 245-2428).

The well-documented death and destruction, the 57 people smothered in hot ash, the northerly blast of hot rock and gas that scorched and bent mighty

LEFT: the eruption of Mount St Helens remains one of America's worst natural disasters.

Map
on page
150

Douglas fir trees like so many blades of grass: all are clearly recounted at a series of five visitor experience centers.

State Highway 504, starting at **Castle Rock**, offers a day of exceptional viewing. First stop is the privately run Mount St Helens Cinedome Theater in Castle Rock itself. The presentation in the blue and red theater, with its huge screen, is vivid and explosive, owing as much to Hollywood effects as to history. It's an excellent, wide-awake introduction to the day, as most of the media shows in the park are serious and small screen.

Continue east to **Mount St Helens Visitor Center** (tel: 360 274-2100) at **Silver Lake**. Purchase any Monument Passes here. If you fail to do so, they will catch up with you later (and be none too polite about it, either). Take a leisurely walk along the **Silver Lake Wetlands Trail** – where Mount St Helens can be seen in the distance – to discover how this lake was formed by a previous eruption.

St Helens was not an isolated event;

various Cascade mountains have erupted in the past; this is merely the most recent and the closest to the large cities of the Pacific Northwest.

Back on the road, views become more remarkable when traveling Hwy 594 up the north fork of the Toutle River. Stop at the designated viewpoints to note the 2-mile (3-km) wide mudflows and debris that crashed down the river valley in the largest avalanche ever recorded. Entering the "lateral blast zone," the hillsides remain littered with shattered trees and tree stumps: super-heated winds decimated everything to the north up to 17 miles (27 km) away.

On a clear day, this new highway, built 3,000 ft (1,000 meters) above the valley floor in case of future eruptions, offers colossal views of the surrounding mountains and valleys.

Bypass the next two visitor centers – Hoffstadt Bluffs and the Weyerhauser Forest Learning Center – and catch up with them on the way back.

BELOW:
the eruption
of Mount St
Helen's lasted
only 9 hours,
but the effects
will last at
east a lifetime.

About 43 miles (70 km) east of Castle Rock is the **Coldwater Ridge Visitor Center** (daily; tel: 360 274-2131; free with a park pass). This center paints a picture of the plants and animals that survived and are recolonizing the blast zone. Elk are returning and wildflowers are blooming. Scientists are monitoring these events closely: trapping, measuring and even weighing hundreds of small animals. Botanists crawl through bushes and timber to categorize dozens of plants and trees, which are now growing in places where a few years ago there was only volcanic ash.

The scientists' laboratory is huge, and their findings extremely important. As well as being alert to other potential explosions, the lessons learned from Mount St Helens are being applied to timber management and some of the other problems associated with the Cascade volcanic mountains.

At Coldwater Ridge, the short, easy **Winds of Change Interpretive Trail**

illustrates how a stone-filled wind blasted the forests into wastelands. There are panoramic views of the volcano, plus newly formed lakes, toppled trees and the debris-filled Toutle River Valley. As well as the usual facilities, there is a simple restaurant with a selection of sandwiches and soups. Talks held at the center are usually very informative.

The most interesting aspect of any trip up Mount St Helens is the $10.5 million **Johnston Ridge Observatory** (May–Oct 10am–6pm; tel: 360 274-2140), located at the end of Hwy 504, 52 miles (84 km) east of Castle Rock, in the heart of the blast zone. The Center's state-of-the-art interpretive displays portray the sequence of geological events that transformed the landscape, and there are eyewitness accounts from eruption survivors. This explosion ushered in a new era of monitoring an active volcano and predicting eruptions.

The **wide-screen theater presentation** is a "must-see," with a surprise at the end. Services include interpretive exhibits, an information desk and books for sale, but note there is no food on sale here.

Take a short walk on the **Eruption Trail** to see how the eruption shaped the surrounding landscape. On a clear day, visitors can expect to see views of the lava dome, crater, pumice plain and the landslide deposit. Forest interpreters share the geological events through formal talks and guided walks.

On the way back down the mountain, stop in at the stunning **Weyerhaeuser Forest Learning Center** (May 15–Oct only) to walk through a realistic-feeling recreated forest, and to experience the Eruption Chamber. The story of reforestation is told here; after the events of 1980, millions of Douglas fir, noble fir, lodgepole pine and black cottonwood trees were replanted. Look for elk on the landscape.

Hoffstadt Bluffs Visitors Center (tel: 360 274-7750) at Milepost 27, is a facility that looks like an Alpine lodge. Inside, there is a family-style dining room, a deck and a gift shop. Helicopter rides are available from here to Spirit Lake or the volcano's crater.

LEFT: along the road to Windy Ridge 57 people died here.

Map on page 150

Adventures other than the one-day driving tour are also available. Forest Roads 25 and 99 on the east side give access to the blown-down forest and views of the remains of Spirit Lake. Viewpoints and ranger stations are open during the summer months.

On the south side, Hwy 503 and Forest Roads 83 and 90 pass through lava flows and mudflows from earlier eruptions (Forest Roads open during the summer only; 503 open all year). Guided lantern walks are conducted at **Ape Cave** (Forest Road 83; lanterns available to rent). The cave is named after a supposed Sasquatch (Bigfoot) encounter.

Other trails lead to **Lava Canyon**, which is spanned by two high suspension footbridges over a narrow gorge, complete with lovely waterfalls and pools.

Mount St Helens Eco Park (tel: 360 274-6542; reservations) is an environmentally sensitive campground sprawling over 90 acres (36 hectares) that allows visitors to experience the ecosystem, leaving only a soft footprint on the environment through using alternative life solutions. The eco park has log cabins, yurts, RV or tent sites to rent.

For hikers, the Mount St Helens region is truly diverse, with trails crossing not only into the stark landscape of the blast zone below the crater, but also through intact old-growth ecosystems, past ancient lava flows, or near to high mountain lakes surrounded by dead "ghost trees." Many of these trails can be covered by mountain bike.

Climbing permits (tel: 360 231-4276; fee) are required year-round to climb above a 4,800-ft (1,460-meter) elevation. Each person must display the permit during a climb. From May 15 through October 31 climbing is limited to 100 people per day. Entry into the crater of Mount St Helens is strictly prohibited.

Climbing the volcano is not a trail hike, it is a rugged, off-trail scramble and definitely not for everyone; be sure to arrive with proper equipment. ❏

BELOW: landsat (satellite) view of the St Helen's site; landsat is a joint venture between NASA and the US Geological Survey.

NORTH CASCADES NATIONAL PARK AND MOUNT BAKER

The North Cascades have glacier-covered volcanoes,
miles of hiking trails, rain-soaked forests and rushing rivers.
The Mount Baker Recreation area is perfect for skiing

The North Cascades National Park Complex sits deep within the wild, nearly impenetrable northernmost reaches of the Cascade Mountain range. Damp forests and rushing rivers surge through sharp valleys; volcanoes are covered in glaciers and dusted with ash. The complex is composed of three main areas each with their own access points: **North Cascades National Park ③**, plus **Ross Lake National Recreation Area ③**, and **Lake Chelan National Recreation Area ③**. To make the most of a visit, it's a good idea to consult a map before setting out and plan a route between them. A true land of plenty, only an invisible boundary separates the North Cascades park from two official National Recreation areas, adjoining National Forest lands, and the Provincial park and Crown lands of neighboring Canada. Surrounding these national areas are wilderness and recreation areas of outstanding natural beauty, chief among them the extensive **Mount Baker-Snoqualmie National Forest**.

The Cascades rank among the world's great mountain ranges. Extending from Canada's Fraser River south beyond Oregon, they shape the Pacific Northwest's climate and vegetation. This remote part of the United States is also the homeland of the elusive, mythical and sometimes controversial Sasquatch, or Bigfoot *(see page 157)*.

The usual route through the park is State Route 20 (SR20) – the paved **North Cascades Scenic Highway** – to the **North Cascades Visitor Center** (tel: 206 386-4495 ext 11). The best weather occurs between mid-June and late-September. Snow has melted from all but the highest trails by July, though summer storms can occur. Some 93 percent of the park complex is wilderness, with 386 miles (625 km) of hiking trails and numerous defined climbs. For information about climbing or hiking, contact the **North Cascades National Park Service Complex** (tel: 360 856-5700 ext. 515).

The **Skagit River** is the water-jewel in the park, offering enough waves and wildlife to keep children interested without seriously testing their swimming skills. The best months to visit are July and August, but for salmon and bald eagle migrations, try September and October. Guided tours, interactive exhibits, and a video of the mammoth generators at the **Skagit Hydroelectric Project** are offered during the busy summer months.

LEFT: Mount Shuksan and reflection in Picture Lake near Mount Baker Lodge, Mount Baker-Snoqualmie National Forest.

Map on page 150

Just outside the park and stretching fjord-like for 55 miles (90 km) into the remote northwest end of the Cascade mountains is **Lake Chelan**. Peaks here range up to 8,000 ft (2,400 meters) in height; **Bonanza Peak** at 9,511 ft (2,900 meters) is the tallest non-volcanic peak in Washington. The southeast section of the lake, is, surprisingly, one of the hottest spots in the state of Washington. The town of **Chelan** ④⓪, with its fine setting at the south end of the lake, is a favorite with sun-seekers.

Mount Baker National Recreation Area ④① sits at the edge of the wilderness complex in the heart of the Cascades. Volcanic **Mount Baker** stands at 10,778 ft (3,285 meters), the fourth-highest summit in the state and the dominant landscape feature in the area. It is named for Joseph Baker, Captain Vancouver's lieutenant and the first crewman to spot the snow-clad peak as Vancouver's British ship *Discovery* sailed into the Strait of Juan de Fuca in the early 1790s.

The **Mount Baker Ski Area** (mid-Dec–late Apr; tel: 360 734-6771) receives an average of over 600 inches (15 meters) of snow each year, making it one of North America's top resorts for snowfall. The most snow ever measured in the US at any one time fell at the Mount Baker Ski Area during the winter of 1998/99 – an astonishing 1,124-inches (28.55 meters). The **White Salmon Day Lodge** offers views of spectacular **Mount Shuksan** (*see photograph on page 82*).

On the southern side of North Cascades National Park, **Glacier Peak Wilderness** (tel: 206 470-4060) and **Alpine Lakes Wilderness** (tel: 206 470-4060) are ideal hiking spots; serious walkers should make sure they get a permit for each area. **Mount Index** is a welcoming beacon in a spectacular area as hikers head up **Stevens Pass**, considered the heart of the North Cascades range, with towering **Glacier Peak** as its centerpiece. Most years this part of the national park is buried under snow until May. ❏

BELOW: he North ascades cenic ighway near Washington ass.

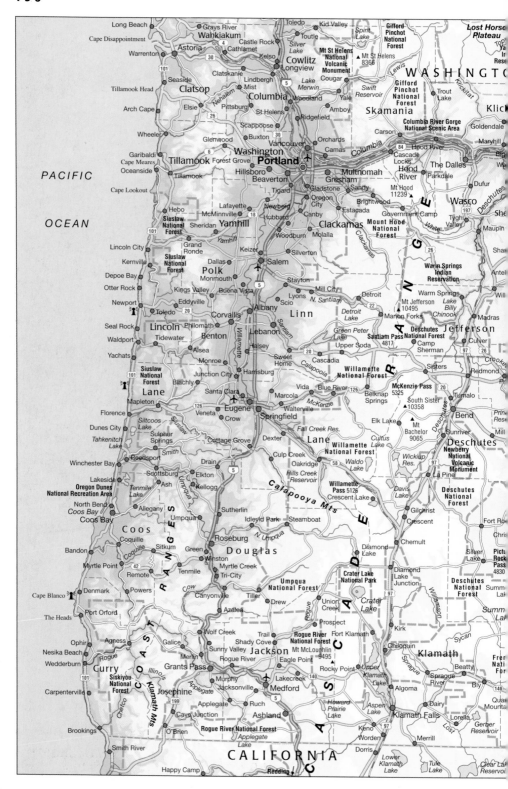

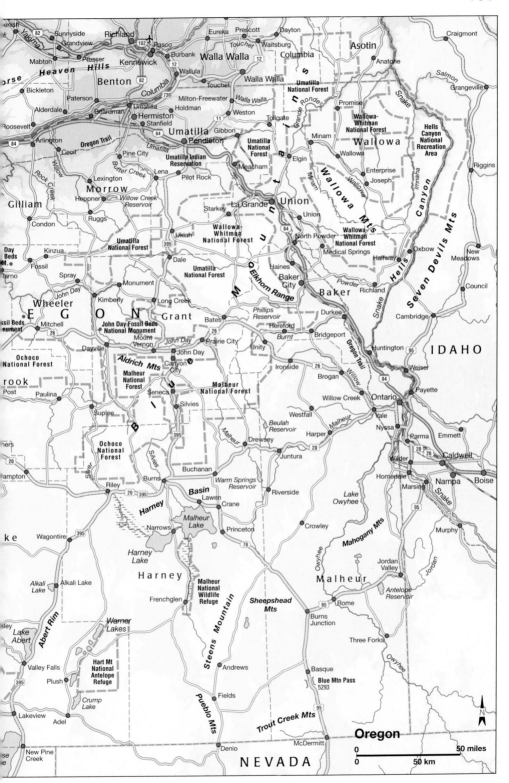

Oregon

0   50 miles

0   50 km

OREGON

A detailed guide to Oregon State, with principal sites clearly cross-referenced by number to the maps

Oregon is a state divided by mountains, but not by ideas. Although it celebrates its cultural diversity, the underlying experience is wrapped up in the discovery that it is a land that delivered on its promise. Thousands came to find a place of abundance at the end of the Oregon Trail, and abundance is exactly what they found. This optimism continues to imbue the spirit of the state's inhabitants. Perhaps it's because every Oregon schoolchild studies the words written in the tattered journals of Lewis and Clark, or sees the actual ruts of the covered wagons that are still etched across the landscape.

Collectively, Oregonians are not only devoted to furthering their own prosperity, but also to making that promise productive in other ways. The state regularly spawns new ideas about protecting the environment; acts as a leader regarding urban renewal; searches for a balance between individual rights and group pressures; and integrates a flourishing art world into everyday life. Oregonians do, however, insist on accomplishing these things their own way. Perhaps that's the reason they react with unusual tension to California immigrants. What *didn't* work for its neighbor state to the south is something they passionately strive to avoid.

Oregonians love to read. Bookstores are not only places to buy books, they are also places to meet like-minded people – or places to find out how to dry potpourri, or make a quilt during the rainy season. The state has brought to a fine art the celebration of its cultural differences: one week it might be a grand production of the opera, the next it might be a rip-roaring Wild West rodeo.

Ever-present among all this is the land. It's difficult not to wax lyrical about the countryside, which in its own way is as diverse as the medley of people thronging its landscape. In the space of a few hours' drive are endless beds of black lava; bone-dry desert peppered with twiggy sagebrush; rushing rivers brimming with recreational possibilities; majestic snow-capped volcanic peaks; foamy breakers crashing onto sandy shores; rich green pastoral beauty; and timbered mountain passes.

The response to all this beauty is an implicit protectiveness, a determination to pass on the legacy, not only of the land but also the dream of success. That's why the pioneers endured that harsh, soul-destroying Oregon Trail: not to dwell on past dreams, but to put into practice the way forward that Oregonians are living today. ❏

PRECEDING PAGES: Oregon's Willamette Valley is well known for its wines; the Sea Lion Caves along the rugged Oregon coast attract visitors and mammals alike. **LEFT:** the Yaquina Bay bridge and South Beach marina, Newport, Oregon.

PORTLAND

*An easy-going, wealthy, lovely and eminently livable place,
Portland likes to think of itself as "the city of
beers, bikes and blooms"*

Map on page 202

Portland has traditionally been called "The City That Works," but the new Portland (pop. 1.6 million) is a city that knows how to enjoy itself, too. Some say the secret of Portland's renaissance is the blossoming of its once-dull neighborhoods, Downtown, the Pearl District and Nob Hill. All are trendy, pedestrian-friendly enclaves with fun cafés and glamourous gallery-goers. Some say it is Portland's economic success that makes it desirable: it is home to three Fortune 500 companies: Nike, Pacificorp, and Willamette Industries, plus the steady-on Tektronics and its own silicon forest anchored by the giant, Intel.

Magnificent setting

Others say it is Portland's magnificent setting *(see picture, page 64)*, when, early on a clear day, morning light glows pink on the West Hills and the sun slowly rises behind Mount Hood. Often visible from the city, the Cascade Mountains with their Fuji-like peaks literally define the surroundings: Mounts Hood and Jefferson on the Oregon side; Adams and St Helens in Washington on the north side. The city's premium on protecting the environment springs from the fact that the so-called "City of Roses" is a beautiful place, worth saving and savoring. The town's setting and temperament are intimately interwoven. It likes to call itself the city of "beers, bikes and blooms."

Portland's downtown area is lively, clean and easy to traverse on foot or by free public transit, though it's not so easy by car. One place to start is the **Portland Oregon Visitors Association** (701 Southwest 6th Avenue; Mon–Fri 9am–7pm, Sat 10am–4pm, Sun noon–4pm; tel: 503 275-8355), located in the heart of Downtown at **Pioneer Courthouse Square Ⓐ**. A gathering spot for people from all walks of life, the square is bordered by glazed terra-cotta towers and 1920s style facades. It is known locally as the city's "living room," and hundreds of events take place here, including concerts at noon, city celebrations, political rallies and presidential speeches.

Unusual among public spaces, the $2.7 million **interior "underground" lobby** at the square houses four useful visitor services: the Visitors Association; a money exchange; the public transit system information center (tel: 503 238-4949) and a place to buy events tickets (tel: 503 275-8385).

The latter is also the place for complimentary tickets to **Theatre on the Square** (every 30 minutes; free). Presented in a 75-seat surround theater, a 12-minute show called *Perfectly Portland* is a commercial, but a perfectly OK introduction to the city.

LEFT: the Portland Building.
RIGHT: the Arlene Schnitzer Concert Hall.

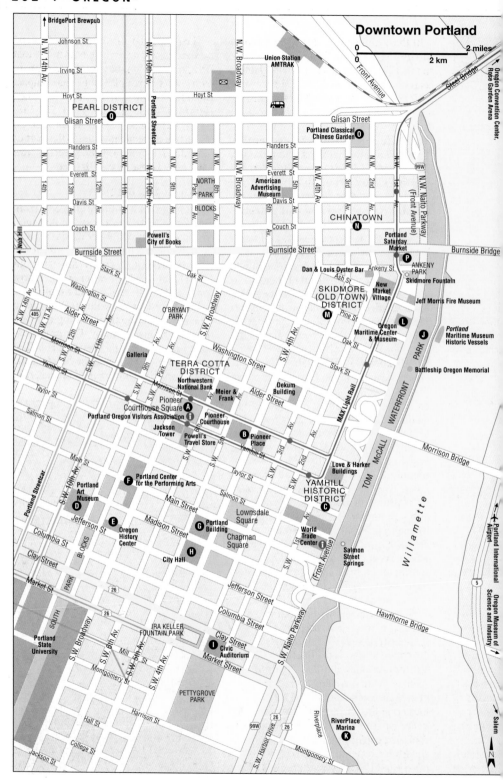

Downtown Portland

Map on page 202

In the 19th century, this square block was the site of Portland's first public school and in 1890, the majestic Portland Hotel, heart of the city's social life. A mechanical 25-ft (8-meter) **Weather Machine** sports three weather creatures to announce the daily forecast at noon each day. A whimsical **Mile Post** shows the distance to Portland's nine sister-cities, and so-called stoa columns with little sculptured roses line Yamhill and Morrison streets.

A local, respected retail outlet is Powell's, who have a travel bookstore on Yamhill Street opposite the square. Anyone serious about the city and/or serious about books, though, should head a few blocks north to **Powell's City of Books** (1005 West Burnside; Mon–Sat 9am–11pm, Sun 9am–9pm; tel: 503 228-4651) for a free walking map of Downtown. Occupying an entire city block, Powell's is reputed to be the world's largest independent bookstore. The literary atmosphere is heady in the Anne Hughes Coffee Rooms, and authors often hold readings in the shop.

BELOW: Downtown Portland with Mount Hood in the background.

The American Institute of Architects' executive vice president points out that Portland is a "model for the nation in terms of its urban planning." Its compact Downtown historical district is fun when viewed by **Vintage Trolley** (tel: 503 238-RIDE), but is also accessible on foot. So distinctive is the architecture in this part of Downtown that it has been given its own name: the **Terra Cotta District**.

Terra Cotta District

The lovely terra cotta **Meier & Frank Building** (621 Southwest 5th Avenue), constructed in 1909–1932, is a huge department store. **Pioneer Courthouse** (555 Southwest Yamhill Street), constructed in 1873, now serves as a post office and has several outdoor sculptures.

Pioneer Place ❸, with 70 shops and a four-story atrium connected by a pedestrian sky-bridge, is nearby. The atrium fills the building with light even on the dullest days; there is an information booth on the ground level and a food court on the lower

level. The 1928 **S.H. Kress Building** (Southwest Morrison Street, 4th and 5th avenues) is constructed of cream-colored terra cotta; the 1913 **Northwestern National Bank** (Southwest Morrison Street, Broadway and 6th avenues), another glazed terra cotta offering, was built for newspaperman Henry Pittock, whose fabulous Pittock Mansion high above the town is open to the public *(see page 213)*. The 1925 **Dekum Building** (519 Southwest 3rd) is a Romanesque structure with carved faces constructed of Oregon sandstone and embellished with floral terra cotta friezes.

The **Yamhill Historic District** ❻, which occupies the area around 1st, 2nd and 3rd avenues, adjoins the Terra Cotta District. Ride public transit to the Galleria Station to find the handsome Olds, Wortman & King department store (1910), which has now been remodeled and renamed **The Galleria** (921 Southwest Morrison Street and Alder between 9th and 10th avenues). The first retail store in

the Northwest to occupy an entire block, today The Galleria is Portland's smallest shopping center and has suffered a little from competition with the flashier Pioneer Place. Still, it offers an interesting range of shops, including a large Made In Oregon store and a Jantzen outlet packed with the company's trademark, its nationally known bathing suits.

Jackson Tower (Southwest Broadway and Yamhill Street), constructed in 1912 and an early headquarters of the *Oregon Journal*, is a glazed terra cotta structure lit by 1,800 lightbulbs. These were switched off from World War II until its restoration in 1972, when the store reopened in a blaze of glory.

The 1878 **Willamette Block** (722–28 Southwest 2nd Avenue) is a cast-iron palace that once housed shops and a dance hall. It is now occupied by the University of Oregon. **Strowbridge Building** (built 1878; 733 Southwest 1st Avenue), a modest cast-iron building, once contained shops and a furniture manufacturer. And the

BELOW: Powell's City of Books is one of the largest independent bookstores in the world.

Map on page 202

1878 **Van Rensseiser, Love and Harker buildings** (Southwest 1st Avenue and Yamhill Street) is a unified block of three cast-iron commercial storefronts. Between 3rd and 4th avenues, the sidewalk is engraved with entertaining phrases.

Arts and history

The **Oregon Art Institute** (an alternative name to this area is **Museum Plaza**) consists of the **Portland Art Museum** ❶ (1219 Southwest Park Avenue; Tues–Sat 10am–5pm, Sun noon–5pm; tel: 503 226-2811; fee) and the **Northwest Film and Video Center** (tel: 503 221-1156).

The three-level art museum features American, European and Asian galleries, plus the **Center for Native American Art**. The film center's **Guild Theatre** is one of the few places to view Academy Award nominated documentaries; if time is limited, many are as short as 20 minutes, so you can dash in, view a favorite, then continue touring. Be sure to book.

The **Oregon Ballet Theatre** (818 South-east 6th Avenue; tel: 503 227-0977 for tour information) invites visitors to watch dancers perform or rehearse through a specially designed glass studio window.

The **Oregon History Center** ❺ (1200 Southwest Park Avenue; Mon–Sat 10am–5pm, Sun noon–5pm, closed: Mon in winter; tel: 503 222-1741; fee) has an R. Haas *trompe l'oeil* mural on the Madison Street wing depicting the Lewis & Clark expedition. The center also has an interesting bookstore, library and museum with permanent and visiting exhibits on the West; its archives include manuscripts and 2 million photographs.

The **Portland Center for the Performing Arts** ❻ is located in three adjoining buildings.These are the **Arlene Schitzer Concert Hall**; **Keller Auditorium**; and the **New Theatre Building** (Southwest Broadway and Main; guided tours; free). Once a vaudeville hall, it is now home to the Oregon Symphony Orchestra.

Nearby are the buildings of **Portland State University** (PSU). The college's

BELOW: Pioneer Courthouse Square is known as "Portland's Living Room."

pleasant campus is punctuated by small, grassy urban parks.

The 15-story **Portland Building**  (1120 Southwest 5th Avenue) was built in 1980. One of the first postmodern structures in the US, it remains the most controversial of architect Michael Graves' love-it-or-hate-it landmarks *(see picture, page 200)*. The 36-ft (10-meter) tall figure known as *Portlandia* is said to be the second-largest hammered copper statue built – second only to the Statue of Liberty.

For a nearly eye-to-eye view of this kneeling goddess, go across the street to the **Standard Plaza Building** (which, by the way, is also a good place to exchange money). Take the elevator up to the enclosed landing; from here the Portland Building, adorned with rosettes and pink-and-blue tiling, is said to look like a gift-wrapped box.

Next door is **City Hall** ⬤ (1220 Southwest 5th Avenue), pink-marbled, a small jewel, and listed on the National Register of Historic Places. First constructed in

1895, it was renovated at a cost of $30 million in 1988. The **east courtyard** contains the oldest of Portland's artworks – basalt **petroglyphs** estimated to be around 15,000 years old.

On hot summer days in front of the **Civic Auditorium** ⬤ (Southwest 3rd and Clay Street), workers eat picnic lunches on the sweeping green lawn park, and children wade in the **Ira C. Keller Fountain**, a multilevel water sculpture with voluminous misty falls and rectilinear pools. The *New York Times'* architecture critic described this place as "perhaps the greatest open space since the Renaissance" – no faint praise for public works.

Downtown Riverfront Park

Early Portlanders strung their town along the Willamette River, and the city prospered as the first clipper ships made their way upstream carrying grain and lumber. **Governor Tom McCall Waterfront Park** ⬤ (Southwest Naito Parkway from Clay to Glisan) provides up close and personal access to the river, along with grassy areas and a 2-mile (3-km) jogging trail that extends the entire length of Downtown. Named after a 1960s Oregon governor credited with giving the state its "green" reputation, the park is home to big summer festivals.

The southwest end is occupied by handsome **River Place Marina** ⬤ (1510 Southwest Harbor Way), a complex that includes an elegant hotel, condominiums, a public marina and **specialty shops** along an esplanade. Perhaps the best known of Portland's fountains, **Salmon Street Springs** is particularly popular during hot weather. The intermittent center power-jet is so forceful it can knock down an adult; kids delight in running through its constantly changing waterspouts.

The world's smallest dedicated park is situated in the middle of a traffic island at Naito Parkway and Taylor Street; **Mill Ends Park** is a mere 23 inches (58 cm) in diameter. Boarding nearby, the luxury yacht *Portland Spirit* (daily narrated cruises; tel: 503 224-3900; reservations required) offers a variety of scenic cruises. One of the most popular includes Northwest

LEFT: a vintag trolley serves downtown Portland.

Map
on page
202

cuisine, singing wait staff, grand pianos with live performers, and a marble dance floor. Always a memorable way to spend an evening in Portland, *Willamette Star* and *Crystal Dolphin*, its sister ships run by the same company, deliver similar cruises from their berths at River Place Marina.

Near the Burnside Bridge is the formerly hard-working **USS** *Oregon*, berthed at the **Battleship Oregon Memorial** (1000 Southwest Naito Parkway), which commemorates the 1893 ship. Sealed in the base of the memorial is a time capsule, to be opened on July 5, 2076.

The **Oregon Maritime Center and Museum** ● (113 Southwest Naito Parkway; Sept–Apr Fri–Sun 11am–4pm; May–Aug Wed–Sun 11am–4pm; tel: 503 224-7724; fee) is hidden in an ordinary storefront at the east end of Skidmore Square. The museum is filled with artifacts, manuscripts and photographs, as well as being the caretaker for several full-size historic vessels which reside prettily on the water.

Skidmore

The **Skidmore Old Town District** ⓜ, north along the river between the Steel and Burnside bridges, is where the city was founded in the 1840s. A fire in 1872 leveled much of the town, although it was quickly rebuilt. The district is notable for its early ornate buildings and antique road-signs, but has so far resisted gentrification, though galleries and brewpubs are starting to find their way into the old buildings. Across the square, the **Skidmore Fountain Building** (1st and Ankeny) has been remodeled and has a few tourist-oriented shops.

At the east end, the small **Jeff Morris Fire Museum** (55 Southwest Ash; daily; tel: 503 823-3700) next to Portland's **Central Fire Station** displays vintage horse-drawn fire engines from the early 1900s. Across the angular plaza, an ornamental colonnade stretches alongside the **New Market Village**, which was originally built to house the combination of a produce market and an opera house. It is now

the site of several cafés. A venerable Portland tradition, **Dan and Louis Oyster Bar** (208 Southwest Ankeny Street; Fri–Sat 11am–11pm, Sun–Thu 11am–10pm; tel: 503 227-5906) was founded in 1907. Today, the founders' grandchildren and great grandchildren still run the place, preparing raw oysters to order at the famous bar, and Louis' seafood stews.

Along 1st Avenue and Pine Street are an intriguing variety of fine arts, photographic and poster shops. Along with other city galleries, these establishments observe First Thursday (the first Thursday of each month) where, during the early evening hours, galleries open their doors and often launch new artists.

Smith's Block (Southwest Naito Parkway), with its fine cast-iron filigree, is beautifully restored. The **American Advertising Museum** (211 Northwest 5th Avenue; Wed–Sun noon–5pm; tel: 503 226-0000; fee) presents some of the country's groundbreaking advertising, and shows how it affected contemporary soci-

ety. Among the collection's highlights are a montage of vintage television commercials.

At Northwest 3rd Avenue, Old Town blends into diminutive **Chinatown ⓝ**, Portland's second-oldest neighborhood. Reputed to be the largest classical Suzhou-style Chinese garden outside of China, the **Portland Classical Chinese Garden ⓞ** (Northwest Everett and Flanders and 2nd and 3rd avenues; Nov– Mar 10am–5pm; Apr–Oct, 9am–6pm; tel: 503 228-8131; fee) and tearoom is a wonderful walled garden occupying an entire city block. Serenity is achieved through its serpentine walkways, Moon Gate and Garden of Awakening Orchids reflected in ponds or arranged around rock groupings.

Market forces

Arguably the city's most loved weekend event, the **Portland Saturday Market ⓟ** (Southwest 1st Avenue and Southwest Ankeny Street; Mar–Dec 24, Sat 10am–5pm, Sun 11am–4:30pm) packs the area around the west end of the **Burnside**

BELOW: the Saturday Market is one of the best weekend events.

Maps
pages
02 & 211

Bridge with craft stalls, street musicians, spicy foods and lively crowds. Reputed to be the nation's largest open-air craft market continuously in operation within the US, the market is an extravaganza of more than 250 craft booths, as well as an international food court and a venue for live entertainment. This is the best place in Portland to shop for one-of-a-kind gifts.

Pearl District

The district north of Powell's City of Books and known as the **Pearl District** ❶ (north of Burnside to Marshall Street between Northwest 8th and 15th avenues) keeps city planners and developers busy constructing offices, storefronts and trendy loft apartments. The **Main Post Office**, one of Downtown's largest employers, occupies a 12-acre (5-hectare) site in the heart of the Pearl, though it faces redevelopment.

The name suggests an old oyster-canning factory sat amidst aging warehouses, but the real story is, in fact, modern: more than a decade ago, Thomas Augustine, a local gallery owner, suggested that the buildings were like crusty oysters, while the emerging galleries and artists' lofts hidden within were like pearls.

Today, the artistic infusion crackles during the first Thursday of each month when the trendy galleries along **Northwest Glisan Street** crack open their doors and their wine bottles until 9pm. The Pearl breathes life in the daytime too; the **Portland Streetcar** (daily scheduled operations; tel: 503 478-6404; fee), its electrified vehicles manufactured by Skoda in the Czech Republic, runs through the heart of it.

The redevelopment of a mammoth five-block project within the Pearl is known as **Brewery Blocks** (1133 West Burnside Street), marking Portland's emergence as a true 24-hour city. The area is getting the ultimate scrub down – the scheduled arrival of yet more luxury condominiums, artists' lofts and high-profile boutiques.

The huge **Gordon Biersch Brewery restaurant** (tel: 503 968-8787) occupies the first two floors of the old Blitz Weinhard Brewery; before his death in 1904, Portland brewer Henry Weinhard Biersch

personally designed this brick building.

If "new" is not your thing, a well-established place is **Bridge Port Brewpub** (1313 Northwest Marshall; Mon–Thur 11am–11pm, Fri–Sat 11am–midnight, Sun 11am–8pm; free brewery tours; tel: 503 241-7179), a big, former warehouse. On fine evenings, the old loading dock becomes a patio. The focus is on top-fermented ales, from the palest copper-color to the darkest black, and in the appropriate season, strong Old Knucklehead barley wine. Near the Pearl District, **Widmar Gasthaus** (955 North Russell; tel: 503 281-3333) is the place to enjoy German food with northwestern flair.

Arenas

Public transit Fareless Square runs over the Steel Bridge across the river to the **Oregon Convention Center** ❶ with its distinctive twin towers. The center is of interest to convention delegates but not particularly for casual visitors. The next major transit stop is **Holladay Park**,

named for Ben Holladay and the horse-drawn streetcar line he built. This is the exit place for the **Lloyd Center Mall**, the first covered shopping mall in the United States. There are around 125 enclosed shops and an indoor ice rink. Between the Broadway and Steel bridges, **Rose Garden Arena** (tel: 800 927-2770 for tickets) is a multi-purpose facility for sporting events and concerts.

Notable neighborhoods

Anyone who wears tie-dyed clothes will feel right at home among the eateries, shops and specialty coffeehouses of the **Hawthorne District** ❷, Portland's own little Haight-Ashbury. Hawthorne Boule-vard (between Southeast 32nd and 39th avenues), and Sellwood (Southeast 13th Avenue between Malden and Clatsop) teem with funky boutiques selling vintage clothes, herbal teas and patchouli oil.

One of Portland's three important rose gardens, the **Ladd's Addition Circle, Squares and Rose Gardens** ❸ (South-east 16th and Harrison; daily; free) covers four neighborhood blocks and appears on the National Register of Historic Places. It's gloriously planted in precise designs, with more than 3,000 roses.

Surrounding it are period homes and the **Hosford Abernethy neighborhood**. Des-ignated a National Conservation District, this is a prime example of turn-of-the-19th-century urban planning.

The best people-watching in Portland is reputed to be **Nob Hill** ❹ (also known as the **23rd Avenue District**), located between Burnside and Lovejoy. This is a neighborhood of elegant Victorian and Georgian homes, many refurbished as retail outlets. The area got its nickname in the 1880s from a grocer who likened it to San Francisco's upper-crust Nob Hill area. Portland's Nob Hill buzzes with activity around the clock, filled with middle-class trendies who live in apartments above retail shops or in restored homes along the nearby streets. Restaurants are small and fun, shopping is in one-of-a-kind stores. Parking is notoriously difficult, however, and the area is better visited using the Portland Streetcar.

A must-see educational and entertain-ment complex dedicated to science and technologies, the **Oregon Museum of Science and Industry** ❺ (1945 South-east Water Avenue; June 15–first week-end Sept daily 9:30am–7pm; in winter Tues– Sun 9:30am–5:30pm; tel: 503 797-4000; fee) is known affectionately as "**OMSI**" (pronounced *om-zee*).

Allow at least a half-day to explore the six immense exhibit halls and **Hands-On Labs**, which include **Engineer It!**, **Inno-vation Station** and **Turbine Hall**. Sub-jects range from the mechanics of moving liquids to the science of lighter-than-air flight. The **Changing Exhibits Hall** pre-sents science displays from both here and around the world. The **OMNIMAX theatre** (tel: 503 797-4640; additional charge) features ongoing showings on a five-story domed screen. If action is your thing, the **Motion Simulator** (tel: 503 797-4000; additional charge) accommodates 15 pas-sengers in an enclosed capsule that makes horizontal pitches, longitudinal rolls and

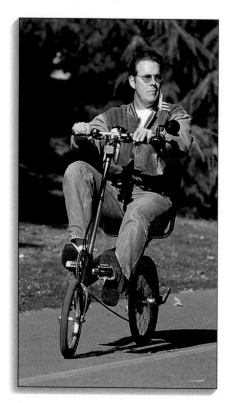

LEFT: getting around by bike is a favorite way to travel.

Map on page 211

vertical lifts. Look skyward for **Kendall Planetarium** and the **Murdock Sky Theater** (tel: 503 797-4610; additional charge) with its advanced technology Digistar II star projector displaying nearly 10,000 stars and the illusion of 3D space travel. Outside the complex is the Navy's last non-nuclear submarine, the **USS** *Blueback* (tours; daily 10am–5pm, tel: 503 797-4000; additional charge).

Samtrack (1-hour excursions; June–first weekend Sept daily, closed: Mon; tel: 503 659-5452; fee) is a red-and-white open-air train that takes in the scenery between OMSI and **Oaks Amusement Park ⑥** (mid-June–first weekend Sept Tues–Thur noon–9pm, Fri–Sat noon–10pm, Sun noon–7pm; tel: 503 233-5777; fee). Offering flashy thrill rides and an old roller coaster, the park's two notable landmarks are **Oaks Skating Rink**, established in 1909, where roller skaters romance to the sounds of a Wurlitzer pipe organ, and the antique **Noah's Ark Carousel** that continues to go round and round.

BELOW: set aside at least a half day for the huge, fascinating Oregon Museum of Science and Industry.

Back at OMSI, two riverboat companies offer cruises that depart from the OMSI dock (1945 Southeast Water Avenue) on the east side of the Willamette River.

Washington Park

Overlooking Downtown Portland, the Willamette River, the Cascades and the east side is expansive (546-acre/220-hectare) **Washington Park ⑦** (Southwest Park Place from Southwest Vista Avenue; dawn to dusk; tel: 503 823-7529) among the city's **West Hills**. This park is the site of seven major tourist attractions.

A light rail station is convenient to most of them, and an additional postage stamp-size rail line, the **Metro Washington Park Zoo Railway** (35-minute loop; tel: 503 226-7627; fee) runs onward to the Rose Garden. Alternately, ART The Cultural Bus, (Tri-Met transit, tel: 503 238-7433; fee), painted by a local artist, also covers these attractions.

Among notable works of park art is the **Lewis & Clark Memorial**, a granite shaft

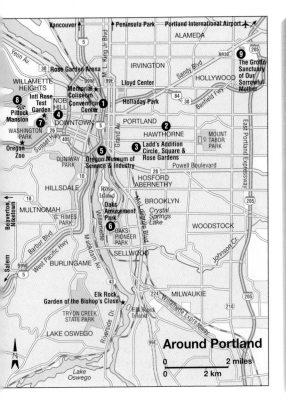

Around Portland

0 _____ 2 miles
0 _____ 2 km

with the seals of the states of Oregon, Washington, Montana and Idaho mounted at the base – a symbol of Oregon Country. Theodore Roosevelt laid the foundation stone on May 21, 1903.

The combined **Oregon Zoo** and **Lilah Callen Holden Elephant Museum** (4001 Southwest Canyon Road; daily except Dec 25, May–Sep 9:30am–6pm; Oct–Apr 9:30am–5pm; tel: 503 226-1561; fee) come together to form an internationally recognized center for breeding Asian elephants.

Established in 1887 with the gift of an animal collection from eccentric Portland pharmacist Richard Knightpretty, the zoo's animal population is remarkably fertile. More Asian elephants have been born here than in any other North American zoo. During the summer, the premises serve as a music venue, where jazz and bluegrass artists perform free concerts.

Across from Oregon Zoo, the **World Forestry Center Museum** (4033 Southwest Canyon; daily 10am–5pm; tel: 503 228-1367; fee) first opened in 1971 to enlighten visitors to the diversity within the region's forests. Uphill from the center, the **Vietnam Veterans' Memorial** (daylight hours; free) is a tribute to the sacrifices of a generation. Situated on 11 acres (4 hectares), the memorial honors the 57,000 Oregonians who served in Southeast Asia.

With 700-plus species of trees and shrubs, 175-acre (70-hectare) **Hoyt Arboretum** (4000 Southwest Fairview Boulevard; free) is cool in summer, lush in spring and ablaze with color in the autumn. One section of the 10-mile (6-km) ambling trail is paved for wheelchair access. Also opposite the zoo is the **Children's Museum 2nd Generation** (4015 Southwest Canyon Road; tel: 503 223-6500; fee), with learning and art exhibits of interest to babies through to 12 years olds.

Impeccable gardens

The oldest official, continuously operated public rose test garden in the US, Washington Park's **International Rose Test Garden** (400 Southwest Kingston Avenue;

BELOW: mural in a hotel lobby traces the journey of early explorers Lewis & Clark.

Map
on page
211

daily, dawn to dusk; tel: 503 823-3636; donation) cultivates 9,000 rose plantings. Portland's defining image is the rose-framed view of the city skyline and Mount Hood as seen from this garden. In 1915, nurseryman Jesse A. Currey convinced city fathers to inaugurate a rose test garden on this panoramic 5-acre (2-hectare) hillside.

At the time, Portland had miles of rose-bordered streets, a strategy devised a decade earlier to draw attention to the 1905 Lewis & Clark Centennial Exposition. As a result, Portland was dubbed the "City of Roses."

Founding a test garden was the opportunity to enhance that reputation. Though World War I was raging, hybridists from Europe and the US managed to send cultivars for testing, and the garden was an immediate success. Twenty-four gardens across the US now test roses, and Portland issues its own internationally recognized awards *(see page 214)*.

The **Gold Medal Garden** within the International Test Garden displays each year's Portland Award winners, with national winners on view in the garden's center aisle. The best months to visit are May through September. Nearby is a **Shakespearean garden** displaying botanics mentioned in the bard's works. The Washington Park Rose Garden Store is located south of the parking area.

Directly uphill from the Rose Garden, the lovely **Japanese Garden**, established in 1963 (611 Southwest Kingston Avenue; 10am–4pm; fee) is sheltered within a 5-acre (2-hectare) site. Five traditional gardens form the basis of this formal area. Unlike other gardens, a Japanese garden is designed to offer solace year-round, and is especially attractive during one of Portland's infrequent snowstorms.

Pittock Mansion

In 1914, on 46 lush acres (18 hectares) high above the city, Henry and Georgiana Burton Pittock built a French chateau-style home, the **Pittock Mansion ❽** (3229 Northwest Pittock Drive; Feb–Dec

daily noon–4pm, closed: holidays; tel: 503 823-3624; fee). Henry Pittock crossed the Oregon Trail in his teens "barefoot and penniless," then prospered as the owner of *The Oregonian*, the city's daily newspaper. He was an astute business leader, a mountaineer and a family man. Georgiana, also a pioneer, was well known for her lifelong love for roses which eventually lead to the establishment of the annual Rose Festival, now a Portland tradition.

The Pittock Mansion is listed on the National Historic Register, and is a lovely place in which to take lunch or afternoon tea. Visitors marvel at the view of mountains and the city below, and admire the beauty of the carefully crafted details, like gilt mirrors, chandeliers, a china tea service and mullioned windows. Up a winding, elegantly proportioned staircase are the bedrooms – one with floral wallpaper and carpet to match, one containing a canopy bed awash with ruffles, flounces and frills.

The adjoining **Pittock Acres** includes walking trails maintained as an **Audubon Society Wildlife Preserve**. The pathways of **The Grotto ❾** (Northeast 85th and Sandy Boulevard; daily, closes at dusk; tel: 503 254-7371; lower level free) offer a serene place for reflection, contemplation and inspiration in a cliff-side garden lined with sequoia trees.

Known as **The Grotto Sanctuary of Our Sorrowful Mother** in official circles, this Catholic shrine and 62-acre (25-hectare) botanical garden are administered by the Friars of the Order of Servants of Mary. In addition to a Meditation Chapel and a gift shop is a fine replica of Michelangelo's *La Pieta*, strategically placed in a sepulchral fern-lined cave. There is an elevator (fee) from the lower level to the top gardens.

Heading out

Southwest of Portland is Beaverton, which is best known as the site of **Niketown** (930 Southwest 6th Avenue, Beaver-

BELOW: exotic blooms compete for "Portland's Best Rose" award.

CITY OF ROSES

Every year since 1919, horticultural judges have bestowed the Portland Gold Medal on a lucky, hardworking rose-grower. Today, Portland is the only authorized North American city to grant internationally recognized rose-of-merit-awards. Experts from around the world congregate here each June to select from thousands of blooms and to bestow upon one the title "Portland's Best Rose." (Do not confuse "Autumn Damask" roses – sometimes referred to as "Portland roses" – with these prestigious awards. Damasks were named long ago for Margaret Cavendish Bentinck, the 2nd Duchess of Portland, who was given a mysterious rose during her Grand Tour of Italy in 1770.)

The International Rose Test Garden in Washington Park – the oldest in the US and with a commanding view of the skyline and Mount Hood – is one of 24 All-American Rose Selections (AARS) Test Gardens. Specimens undergo two-year trial programs. Evaluations are submitted to Chicago, with the result being a new crop of AARS-winning roses. Only two receive the All-America Rose Selections award, commonly known as the "Oscar of Roses." Past winners include Love & Peace, and Starry Night. Fortunately, they do not make acceptance speeches.

Map on page 211

ton; Mon–Thur and Sat 10am–7pm, Fri 10am–8pm, Sun 11:30am–6:30pm; tel: 503 221-6453; free). Housed in a remodeled building, Niketown is the showplace for the international sportwear giant Nike. Merchandise glitz and gladrags – no bargains here – is mixed in with giant video monitors, sports memorabilia, live reptiles and a life-size cast of basketball hero and spokesman Michael Jordan in mid-jump.

Garden lovers look here

Perhaps the finest of Portland's three major public rose gardens, and at its best from May to September, **Peninsula Park's Sunken Rose Garden** (North Ainsworth between Kerby and Albina; daily, dawn to dusk; free) has 9,000 roses on 16 acres (6 hectares) of parkland. The **octagonal bandstand**, now a National Heritage structure, was once the site for World War I patriotic demonstrations.

If the month is right, four other gardens in and around Portland are worth visiting, but be sure to telephone ahead, as opening

hours vary. The **Cecil and Molly Smith Rhododendron Garden** (5065 Ray Bell Road, St Paul; select weekends; tel: 503 771-8386; fee) is a magnificent garden, incorporating native trees, shrubs and its signature flowers.

The **Jenkins Estate** (tel: 503 642-3855; fee), best seen in spring and summer, has gardens built around a 1900s horse ranch, which include rockeries, ponds and a herb garden. A French rose garden with 1,200 bushes, an English vegetable garden, a gazebo, stone ornaments, a lily pond and topiary all feature in **Tallina's Wedding Gardens and Conservatory** (15791 Southeast Hwy 224, Clackamas; tel: 503 658-6148; free).

Elk Rock, the Garden of the Bishop's Close (11800 Southwest Military Lane at Rt 43; tel: 503 636-5613; fee) is an impressive estate best seen in April and May for its magnolias. But throughout the summer, its views of the river in a landscaped 1900s English-style garden make the trip to see it worthwhile. ❏

BELOW: St Anne's Chapel at The Grotto is a place to escape the urban bustle.

COLUMBIA RIVER GORGE AND MOUNT HOOD

*A river canyon that straddles both Northwest states
and the highest mountain in Oregon are two of the spectacular
attractions just a drive away from Portland*

Map
on page
218

The largest to empty into the Pacific Ocean, the second-largest river system in North America, 1,200 miles (2,000 km) in length: these are some of the phrases that give credence to the term the "Mighty Columbia." Originating as meltwater trickling from frozen glaciers in Canada's Rocky Mountains, this legendary river gathers strength while draining an area of 259,000 sq. miles (670,000 sq. km), amassing a volume of water each year sufficient to cover both Washington and Oregon states – knee deep. Dammed, but never tamed, the river courses through the Columbia Gorge, a river canyon cutting the only sea-level route through the Cascade Mountains.

Just gorge-ous

This result of eons of continental ruminations is set against the backdrop of Fuji-look-alike Mount Hood and the competing snowcapped sentinel Mount Adams. "The Gorge," as it is known, is some 80 miles (130 km) long and up to 4,000 ft (1,200 meters) deep, with its north canyon walls in Washington state and its south walls in Oregon. In 1986, Congress designated the 450 sq-mile (1,160 sq-km) corridor a National Scenic Area to preserve its characteristics, even though it serves as a transportation corridor and is home to 70,000 people.

A National Scenic Area Act does not create a wilderness or a park. Instead, it allows for existing rural and scenic characteristics to be retained, while encouraging compatible growth and development within urban areas.

Technically, the gorge stretches from Troutdale on the outskirts of Portland to The Dalles 80 miles (130 km) upriver. For the purposes of this text, the usual daytrip following the **Columbia Gorge**

National Scenic Area does not complete the parameters of the gorge, but turns south to pick up the equally awesome Mount Hood Loop *(for travel to The Dalles, see page 226)*.

The 160-mile (257-km) Mount Hood Loop features viewpoints above the Columbia River and takes in rainforest wildflowers, rustic mountain lodges, gossamer waterfalls, old-growth forests and abundant orchards. This trip will take one long day, or ideally two days, to appreciate in its entirety.

The drive through the Gorge Scenic Area begins with the **Historic Columbia River Highway**, or the 24 miles (38 km)

of Rt 30 that is also referred to as the "scenic route." Start about 16 miles (25 km) east of downtown Portland, take Interstate 84 to Troutdale, then take exit 17 to the start of the highway.

The highway was an engineering marvel in its day; when it opened in 1916, President Teddy Roosevelt praised its scenic grandeur and remarkable engineering, while the *Illustrated London News* called it "the king of roads."

The first grand view of the gorge comes at the **Portland Women's Forum State Park ❶**, 9 miles (14 km) east of Troutdale at **Chanticleer Point**, the former site of the Chanticleer Inn, where the highway's masterminds convened in 1913 to plan its construction. Here, the legendary gorge winds bluster and blow almost constantly.

Photo Opportunities

Next stop is the highly picturesque two-tiered, octagonal **Vista House** (daily Apr 15–Oct 15 8:30am–6pm; tel: 503 695-

2230; free). Soaring 733 ft (210 meters) above the river on equally memorable **Crown Point ❷**, Vista House *(see photograph on page 223)* was built in 1916–17 as a memorial to Oregon's pioneers. Today it houses educational displays, a small gift shop and a coffee bar. Designed by Edgar M. Lazarus, a Portland architect, it's an example of *jugenstil*, the 1916 German equivalent of art nouveau. The interior rotunda is expertly sheeted in Tokeen Alaskan marble as well as cream and pink Kasota limestone.

Most arresting, however, are the sweeping views of the river as it slices through the surrounding Cascade Mountains. Toward the end of the last ice age, some 15,000 years ago, tremendous floodwaters carrying massive chunks of ice and rock scoured out this spectacular site.

A side road, 14 twisting miles (22 km) upriver from Crown Point, terminates at **Larch Mountain** (May–Nov; day use fee) managed by the US Forest Service. At an elevation of 3,256 ft (992 meters)

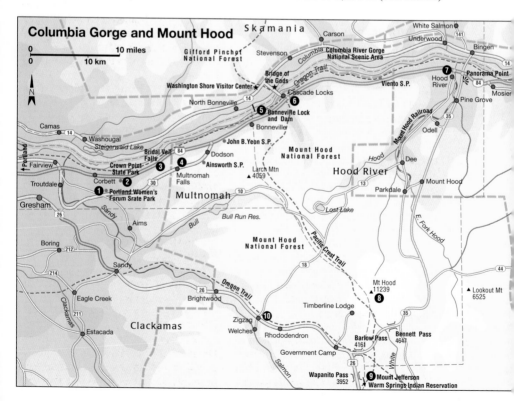

Map on page 218

are trailheads and picnic tables. At the end of a short paved walking trail, **Sherrard Point** offers a sweeping 360° view of Mount Rainier, Mount St Helens, Mount Adams, Mount Hood, Mount Jefferson, and the Three Sisters – as well as most of Portland. It's considered one of the best sunset-watching places in Oregon.

Fairytale falls

East from Crown Point, Rt 30 descends to an area with 11 waterfalls in as many miles (18 km). **Latourell Falls** is first, and a trail leads to its base. Just beyond, the falls at **Shepherd's Dell State Natural Area** cascade down steep cliffs into Youngs Creek. **Bridal Veil Falls ❸** is an elegant, graceful site best appreciated from a viewing platform. Picnic tables are dotted among large timber stands.

Upper Bridal Veil Falls Trail winds around precipitous cliffs, but is fenced in to allow all those gorgeous gorge views. Signboards point out wildflowers such as camas, lupin, trillium and bead lily.

The **Pillars of Hercules**, a 120-ft (36-meter) basalt tower, was once used as a training site for mountain climbing. **Bridal Veil lower trail**, a steep trail peppered with switchbacks, plunges downhill for a short way to the falls. Then comes **Wahkeena Falls**, the name taken from the Chinook word for "most beautiful." A walk to the tumble of water zigzagging down a narrow rock channel includes a complimentary blast of cool water mist.

The most famous, and the fourth highest waterfall in the United States is plummeting **Multnomah Falls ❹**, which drops a precipitous 620 ft (190 meters) from its lip on Larch Mountain to its lower plunge pool. Because of a rockfall in 1995, access to the upper plunge pool and its trails are now permanently closed, so from the parking area, head for historic **Benson arch bridge**. The flow over the falls is usually at its highest and most fulsome during winter and spring.

A Native American legend tells of a beautiful young maiden who threw herself from the precipice to save her father and her people from the ravishes of a great plague. **Multnomah Falls Lodge** (daily, 8am–9pm; tel: 503 695-2376), a National Historic Landmark at the base of the falls, was built in 1925 and houses a large restaurant with Northwest cuisine. Overnight accommodations are not available.

Inside the lower level, the USDA **Forest Service Information Center**, with its snack bar and gift shop, makes a good stop to pick up a free trail map to dozens of local walks and hikes. For serious hikers, not far away is a portion of the **Pacific Crest National Scenic Trail**, the famous long walk that connects Canada to Mexico.

The 45 overnight campsites in **Ainsworth State Park** fill up quickly. Camping or not, walkers can easily find the adjoining **Nesmith Point trail** with its splendid **St Peter's Dome**, a basalt monolith rising some 2,000 ft (600 meters) above the Columbia.

East from Multnomah Falls is **Oneonta Gorge**, a narrow mossy rift in the cliffs complete with stream flows that serve as the only pathway for walking to **Oneonta**

Falls. However, for those who favor dry feet, **Horsetail Falls** is accessible via a trail that merely ventures underneath the spray. From near here, Rt 30 then merges with Interstate 84. The **John B. Yeon State Scenic Corridor** (off I-84, exit 35) leads to the lower **Elowah Falls**, a 289-ft (88-meter) drop with odd angled cliffs, and the upper **McCord Creek Falls**. Unlike other falls, the trails to these two beauties are rarely crowded.

Power to the people

Bonneville Lock and Dam ❺ on Interstate 84, exit 40, straddles Oregon and Washington. The Bonneville Project is the US Department of Energy's key facility among 55 major hydroelectric projects on the Columbia and its tributaries. Of these, 30 are Federal dams and 25 are non-Federal installations owned by public and private utilities – all combining to serve 10 million people. This electric power grid gives the Northwest the largest hydroelectric system in the world.

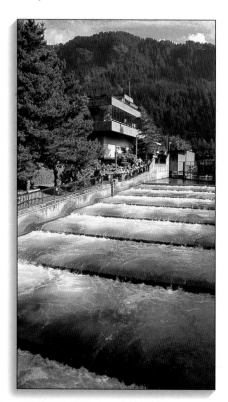

Named after the 19th-century hero of Washington Irving's book, *The Adventures of Captain Bonneville*, the 5-year dam construction project commenced in 1933. A visit to the 197-ft (60-meter) high, 2,690-ft (820-meter) long dam complex includes the **Navigation Lock Visitor Area**, **First Powerhouse** and **Fish Ladder**. On the Oregon side, **Bradford Island Visitor Center** (daily 9am–5pm, closed: Thanksgiving, Dec 25 and Jan 1; tel: 541 374-8820) celebrates explorers Lewis and Clark, who camped here on their return voyage. Wrote fellow traveler John Ordway, on April 9, 1806: "a number of these natives are moveing up to the Big Shoote (Cascades of the Clumbia River) to fish… we halted at a village at the foot of the 1st rapid… we purchased 2 fat dogs and crossed over to the South Shore and Camped." Both visitor centers provide interpretive presentations.

The **Bonneville Fish Hatchery** (daily, closed: holidays; tel: 541 374-8393; free) has a fish ladder with underwater windows to glimpse adult salmon as they return upriver to spawn. Interpretive displays include a viewing area to watch the energetic autumn spawn, at its most frenzied from mid-September to November, as well as an outdoor pool featuring "Herman the Sturgeon" – all 10 ft (3 meters) of him – pushing past 60 years old. Fish species under threat from such dams include Oregon's coastal cutthroat trout, Coho salmon, steelhead and the few remaining giant sturgeon.

Just east of I-84, at exit 41, the **Eagle Creek Trail** (trail fee charged on-site) passes a dozen waterfalls in a terrific 12-mile (19-km) round trip, complete with campground and picnic area. But it's not necessary to complete the entire loop if you want to take in just a few of the falls. An ascending trail climbs through verdant forests and leads along a short trail to **Metlako Falls**, named after a Native American "goddess," and **Punchbowl Falls** is about 2 miles (3 km) away.

Reached via the **Bridge of the Gods**, 2 miles (3 km) east and named after the huge rocks that lie beneath the water – remnants of a legendary natural bridge –

LEFT:
Bonneville Dam
was named for
a 19th-century
literary hero.

Map on page 218

is the second Bonneville Dam. **Washington Shore Visitor Center** off Rt 14 west of Stevenson, Washington, offers self-guided tours of the dam's **Second Powerhouse**, while the **Fish Viewing Building** contains underwater windows and regional history displays covering the fishing industry and fish lifecycles.

The Locks

On the Oregon side, **Cascade Locks ❻** is the passageway for ships traveling beyond the behemoth dam. Years ago, explorers, fur trappers, traders and overland settlers risked an exceptionally treacherous cataract at this point in their journey. Many perished. In 1896, construction began to tame the natural rapids, and today it is possible for ships to travel upriver for 188 miles (300 km).

In addition to **Cascade Locks Marine Park**, a National Historical Site off I-84, exit 44, the human story of the locks can be studied at **Cascade Locks Historical Museum** (June–Sept daily noon–5pm;

May Sat–Sun; tel: 541 374-8535; free), the residence of the original lock-tender. Alongside is the Northwest's first steam locomotive, the *Pony Engine*.

The **Port of Cascade Locks Visitors Center** (Marine Park Drive; Mon–Fri 8am–5pm; tel: 541 374-8619) is a source for Oregon travel information and the ticket office for boarding the triple-decker stern wheeler, the *Columbia Gorge* (2-hour excursions; mid-June–Sept daily ; tel: 541 374-8619; fee), which has frequent sightings of eagles, ospreys and cranes. Reservations are required for dinner and brunch cruises; onboard narration covers geology, local history and Indian legends.

Fruit Loop

The **Hood River ❼**, 62 miles (100 km) east of Portland on I-84, turns south to the Mount Hood Loop. The **Hood River County Visitors Council** (daily; tel: 541 386-2000) at Port Marina Park, exit 64, is the place to obtain detailed maps for the **Hood River Valley Fruit Loop**,

BELOW:
Rooster Rock State Park, on the Columbia River.

approximately 45 miles (72 km) of meandering country roads passing the valley's roadside fruit stands. In summer and autumn, you can expect to find strawberries, raspberries, cherries, apricots, blueberries, peaches, Gravenstein apples, pears and chestnuts.

After a disastrous frost killed thousands of fruit trees in 1939, regional farmers realized they had to plant other crops: today the county produces over 50 percent of the nation's winter pears – Anjou, Bosc and Comice, as well as 11 percent of all US-grown Bartlett pears. The volcanic soil, originating from Mount Hood's old eruptions, is also responsible for Newtown Pippin apples, reputedly the highest-quality apples in the world.

For another type of bounty, award-winning **Hood River Vineyards** (Mar–Nov daily 11am–5pm; tel: 541 386-3772; small charge) is located at 4693 Westwood Drive overlooking the valley. Their tasting room features traditional wines, plus pear and raspberry dessert wines.

Oregon collectors are famous for treasuring antique carousel figures. For aficionados, there is the **International Museum of Carousel Art** (304 Oak Street; Wed–Sun noon–4pm; tel: 541 387-4622; fee) dedicated to the preservation of the world's antique carousels. The Hood River is also the start point of Rt 35, which heads south to Mount Hood and onward to the Warm Springs Indian Reservation (*see page 273*).

The Hood River is one of the top three destinations for windsurfers from around the world; in first and second place are Hawaii and Australia. Winds through the gorge – best during the middle of the day – create ideal conditions for riding the waves. To see boardheads at play, follow any van piled high with equipment.

Alternatively, drive to the **Waterfront Center Event Site**, exit 63, or **Columbia Gorge Sailpark**, exit 64, at Hood River Marina. Downtown shops are ideal places to rent a board or arrange lessons. **Mayer State Park**, east on I-84, is a good spot to hang out, as is **Hood Vista Sailpark**, west of the Hood River Bridge in Washington.

The **Full Sail Brewpub** (506 Columbia, Hood River; summer daily noon–8pm; winter Thur–Sun noon–8pm; tours by appointment; tel: 503 222-5343) has a tasting room and pub. Beers range from pale Pilsner and golden ale, on through the amber, red, nut brown, and stout. Seasonal brews are also here, including Oktoberfest lager in the German style, and a fine, spicy Wassail in winter.

Around the Hood River

For touring the scenic Hood River area, the **Mount Hood Railroad** (2- or 4-hour excursions, brunch or dinner ride; late Apr–Oct; intermittent to Dec; tel: 541 386-3556; reservations recommended) departs from 110 Railroad Avenue. Designated a National Historic Site, a 1940s-era locomotive pulls restored railcars through the lush fruit-filled foothills of Mount Hood, with the added backdrop of Washington's Mount Adams.

Panorama Point, just south on Hwy 35, has the best highway viewpoint for Mount Hood's valleys. For another view,

LEFT: wildflowers of the gorge include camas lupine, trillium bead lily and bleeding heart.

**Map
on page
218**

travel east on I-84, exit at Mosier, and then travel onward to **Rowena Crest Viewpoint**, on old Hwy 30. There's a summer wildflower show in the **Tom McCall Preserve** maintained by the Nature Conservancy. West of Hood River, the restored, romantic **Columbia Gorge Hotel** (400 Westcliff Drive; tel: 541 386-5566; reservations recommended), a grand 1921 creation on a bluff, was originally built by the timber baron Simon Benson. This vintage hotel is noted for its elegant dining room, handsomely appointed rooms and its own waterfall.

Reigning monarch

Mount Hood ❽ – at 11,239 ft (3,421 meters) the reigning monarch in this section of the Cascade Mountains – is also the highest point in Oregon. First glimpsed in 1792 by the English navigator William Broughton, it was named for Admiral Lord Samuel Hood, who served in the British Navy during the American Revolutionary War. Hood's name apparently stumbled

into immortality merely by his signing the formal instructions for Captain Vancouver's voyage. Neither Rainier nor Hood ever set eyes on the landmarks that bear their names. Hood-the-volcano, however, remains a constant source of poetic inspiration for many. It is known to Native Americans as *Wy'east*, its name being derived from the legend of Wy'east and his brother Pahto (Mount Adams), powerful supernatural sons of the Great Spirit, who turned into stone to watch over the two shores of the great river.

Mount Hood is one of the major volcanoes of the Cascade Range, having erupted repeatedly for hundreds of thousands of years. There have been two major episodes in the past 1,500 years, the last of which ended shortly before the arrival of Lewis and Clark in 1805.

Today, Mount Hood is considered mainly dormant, but steam does still spew from fumaroles. Some scientists believe the mountain could erupt again within 75 years, this time more vociferously. In the

meantime, *jökulhlaups* – small glacial floods – periodically issue from Hood's crevasses, destroying sections of highways, bridges and trails. In 1805, Lewis & Clark, the first Americans to see the mountain, called it "Falls Mountain," until learning the British had already named it.

Take Hwy 35, then crest at **Barlow Pass**, which at 4,161 ft (1,268 meters) is the highest point on the Mount Hood Loop road. In 1845, Oregon Trail pioneers Samuel K. Barlow and friends founded the first wagon trail over the mountain's south side. While still difficult, the Barlow Trail was much preferred over the treacherous Columbia River rafting route to Oregon City. Take a short, quick side trip to picturesque **Trillium Lake** for a photo reflection of Mount Hood in the lake.

Hall of the mountain king

From **White River** it's just a few more minutes to Government Camp and the turnoff to **Timberline Lodge** (year round; tel: 503 622-7979; reservations recom-

mended), Oregon's "Hall of the Mountain King." Nestled midway to the summit at 6,000 ft (1,800 meters), Timberline was constructed in 1937 of mammoth local timbers. Dedicated in the same year by Franklin Delano Roosevelt, it was a flagship project of the Depression-era Works Progress Administration.

The lodge was built on a large scale to mirror the grandeur of the mountain, with lofty ceilings and a stone fireplace in the lobby that is 92 ft (28 meters) around; the front stairway leads to a half-ton (500-kg) door that opens onto a balcony with fine views of **Mount Jefferson ❾**.

Everywhere there is evidence of true craftsmanship: the ripples on the massive timbers reveal hand-shaping with broadax and adze; the light fixtures are the creation of skilled blacksmiths; woodworked newel posts are shaped like owls and eagles, and each room in the lodge has its own handpainted watercolor of the wild flowers native to the region, beautifully mounted next to the handmade furniture.

BELOW: Trillium Lake is the place for a photo reflection of Mount Hood

Map on page 218

In the main lodge, the **Cascade Dining Room** serves gourmet Northwest cuisine, while the Ram's Head and Blue Ox bars offer hearty mountain fare. In the day lodge, the Wy'east Kitchen for skiers on the run and the Market Café with its sundeck, offer quick-break choices. Though surrounded by meadows that burst into bloom midsummer, patches of snow can be found year-round.

The lodge is the trailhead for several pleasant summer walks including the **Timberline Trail**, a 40-mile (64-km) path that circles the mountain. Mount Hood is the second most climbed mountain in the world, second only to Japan's Mount Fujiyama. For serious climbing information, contact **Timberline Mountain Guides** (tel: 541 312-9242).

Ski the slopes

In winter, five ski areas in the region are active: **Timberline Lodge Ski Area**; **Mount Hood Meadows**; **Mount Hood Ski Bowl**; **Cooper Spur Ski Area**; and **Summit Ski**. Summer visitors can choose to be whisked along on the **Magic Mile Super Express Chairlift** (weather permitting: Mon–Thur 7am–2pm, Fri 7am–3pm, Sat–Sun 7am–4pm; tel: 503 222-2211; fee) up to the 7,000-ft (2,100-meter) level for a grand view of Mount Hood and the Cascades. Be prepared for rapidly changing mountain weather, however, and it never hurts to bring along a jacket and sturdy shoes.

Just down the mountain in the town of **Government Camp**, the **Mount Hood Brewing Company** (tours daily; tel: 503 622-0724) is a microbrewery offering pub-style fare and specializing in Ice Axe India Pale Ale – pale amber in color and aggressively hopped. In summer there's a fun **outdoor beer garden** (Mon–Thur 2–8pm, Fri–Sun noon–8pm), which is weather dependent.

Continuing along a short spur from the village of **Zigzag** ❿ is the **Green Canyon Campground** (Salmon River Road off Hwy 26; tel: 503 622-7674; call for

Map on page 218

conditions), where the **Old Salmon River Trail** winds through old-growth forest along the Salmon River, a designated Wild and Scenic river where salmon spawn in season. Also in Zigzag, travelers can turn north on **Lolo Pass Road** and take a 7-mile (11-km) side trip. A popular path leads to cool **Ramona Falls**, where the **Sandy River** splits into a multitude of falling ribbons as it pours prettily over a series of terraces.

For information on hiking the region, which encompasses 1.2 million acres (485,000 hectares), four designated Wilderness Areas, and over 1,200 miles (2,000 km) of hiking trails, contact the **Mount Hood Information Center** (65000 East Hwy 26, Welches daily 8:30am–4:30pm; tel: 503 622-4822). The people here can also provide advice on everything from microbrews to huckleberry picking.

While in **Welches**, stop by **Wy'east Bookshoppe and Art Gallery** (daily noon–8pm; tel: 503 622-4417), a little bit west of the stop light. It's a delightful enclave of books, beads, quilts and the fine works of more than 50 Northwest artisans. After sufficient rest, continue back to Portland via hwy 26.

The Dalles

Traveling east along I-84 from Portland along the Columbia Gorge and avoiding the Mount Hood Loop leads to **The Dalles ⑪** (Visitor Information, tel: 541 296-2231). The Dalles lies on a bend in the Columbia River where the water once tumbled over a series of sobering and rocky rapids. French voyagers named it "les dalles" or flagstones.

The Dalles main claim to fame is the so-called "Point of Decision" where the Oregon Trail branched out: some traveled over Barlow Road and Mount Hood; others continued down the Columbia, battling with its rapids. The change in precipitation between Bonneville Dam and here is astonishing: Bonneville receives 80 inches (200 cm) of rain each year; The Dalles just 11 inches (28 cm).

The **Columbia Gorge Discovery Center** (5000 Discovery Drive; daily Apr–Dec 10am–6pm; Jan–Mar 10am–4pm; tel: 541 296-8600; fee) is the official interpretive center for the Columbia River Gorge National Scenic Area *(see page 217)*. Exhibits demonstrate the volcanic upheavals and floods that gave form to the area. Beside it is the **Wasco County Historical Museum** covering Native American and pioneer life.

At exit 87 in summer and exit 88 other times are two attractions: the **Dalles Dam Visitor Center** (daily 8am–5pm; tel: 541 296-9533; free) and the one-hour trip to the fish ladder and **Dalles Dam Tour Train** (every 30 minutes: mid-Apr–Sept, daily 8am–5pm; Oct–Mar Wed–Sun 8am–4pm; tel: 541 296-1181; free). Not far away is the **Maryhill Museum of Art** *(see page 172)*.

Upstream from The Dalles, on the Oregon side of the **John Day Dam** (exit 109; open daily 9am–5pm; tel: 541 296-1181; free) is a fish-viewing room where visitors can see migrating salmon pass at eye level. The best months for viewing are April through October. ❏

LEFT: Oregon's Northern Spotted Owl is under threat. **RIGHT:** Multnomah Falls, Columbia River Gorge.

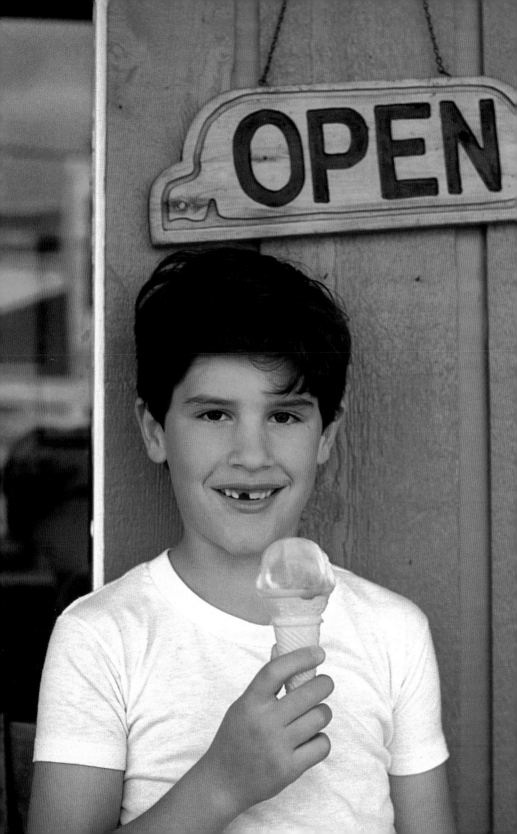

Map on page 230

WILLAMETTE VALLEY

*For thousands of pioneers who risked their lives on
the Oregon Trail, the rich and verdant Willamette
Valley seemed like the promised land*

Within minutes of Oregon's second and third largest cities, Salem and Eugene/Springfield, there is a landscape of pastoral charm laced with a sense of pioneer spirit. The Willamette Valley (pronounced wool-*am*-ut) takes its name from the river that flows through it. It is flanked by the Coast Range and the Cascade Mountains, and stretches from the headwaters of the Willamette River to its confluence with the Columbia River.

Historic cities and towns, settled more than a hundred years ago by emigrants from all over the world, are found throughout the valley, but it is best known for its agriculture, which includes the growing of vegetables, fruits, flowers, hops and even Christmas trees.

Since people first arrived in the Pacific Northwest – about 10,000 years ago – inhabitants have continued to benefit from the region's natural productivity. Then, too, there are the dense evergreen forests that at one time made the lower Willamette Valley the timber capital of the world, and the rich soil that moved pioneers to exclaim that "the crops never fail west of the Cascades."

Pleasant reward

This impressive landscape takes on a special character, thanks in part to the covered bridges, renovated and preserved historic buildings and old homes that date from the days of the Oregon Trail or earlier. Modern-day pioneers come to experience the abundance of recreational opportunities, to explore the area's progressive cities, or to tour the valley's wine country, which is now gaining attention as one of the Pacific Northwest's finest wine regions; more than 120 wineries are sprinkled across this valley.

A brief stop at any of these estate wineries can be a pleasant reward for an active day. Visitors from Portland who do not wish to rent a car can use the following tour services to visit a selection of Willamette Valley wineries for a day, half-day or evening: Grape Escape (tel: 503 283-3380) or Ecotours of Oregon (503 245-1428). Today, the Willamette Valley is home to over 7 percent of Oregon's 3.3 million inhabitants, and the number is growing. Oregon's two dominant educational institutions – Oregon State University and the University of Oregon – are both located in the valley.

Ecological concerns

Understanding the interaction between the land and its inhabitants is a major concern for many residents. With keen ecological antennae, watchgroups keep an eye on

LEFT: always open for ice cream. **RIGHT:** Salem's Mission Mill is a former textile factory.

how modern changes will affect future generations. One example of this is the Willamette Valley Livability Forum, a gathering of people seeking to clarify choices about the future of their valley. Created by Governor John Kitzhaber in December 1996, the forum's brief is to develop a vision for the valley; to enable wise decisions to be made; and to build partnerships to maintain and improve the habitability of the area.

The *Washington Post*'s Joel Garreau described typical October through April weather conditions in the valley as a "difficult-to-define balance that is moister than mist but drier than drizzle." Unappealing as this sounds, locals are quick to point out that the Willamette Valley's 40 inches (101 cm) average yearly rainfall does not appreciably exceed the totals reached in Miami. The average low temperature in January is 32°F (0°C); the average high temperature in July, 82°F (27°C). However, local sensitivities aside, this definitely is rain country.

End of the trail

To get a feeling for what it must have been like to reach the end of the old Oregon Trail, **Oregon City** ❶ (tel: 503 656-1619), just 30 minutes south of Portland, is one of the best places for history buffs to appreciate that sense of manifest destiny. It was this destination that welcomed a thousand "prairie schooners," the name for old covered wagons, and the place thousands of pioneer families in the 1840s grew to love.

The 8.5-acre (3.5-hectare) **End of the Oregon Trail Interpretive Center** (1726 Washington Street; Mon–Sat 9am–5pm, Sun 10am–5pm; tel: 503 657-9336; fee) is a living history museum where interpreters in costume relive the story. The **Oregon Trail Pageant**, an outdoor music drama, is performed in July and August. Historically accurate garden plantings compliment galleries, a craft workshop and a general store.

Closer to Portland, and on the crest of a hill, the **Kramer Vineyards** (26830

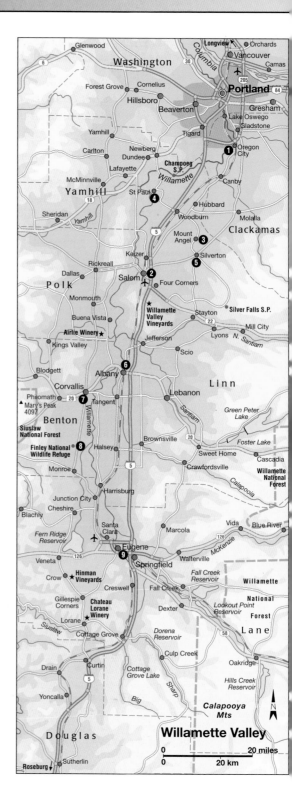

Olson Road Northwest, Gaston; June–Sept daily noon–5pm; Mar–Dec weekends noon–5pm; tel; 503 662-4545; small tasting fee) are easily reached from the suburbs of Hillsboro or Beaverton. Founded in 1984, Kramer produces Pinot Noir, Chardonnay, Muller-Thurgau, Pinot Gris and Riesling from their own vineyard and seem to attract hundreds of fans who share their last name.

Salem ❷, *circa* 1840, is one of Oregon's oldest cities and the state capital. The Calapooya Indian name for the area was *chemeketa*, which means "meeting or resting place." But the missionaries tweaked it a little and called it Salem. Sharing its name with several other US "Salems," in Hebrew the word means peace, *shalom*.

Salem is not served by commercial airlines, but those without vehicles can use the Greyhound Bus Lines (460 Church Street; tel: 503 362-2428). The local bus service is Intra-city Transit Cherriots (tel: 503 588-2877). Both body and soul will be rewarded by picking up two excellent lists from the **Visitors Association** (1313 Mill Street; 503 581-4325). One is of the local public gardens; the other of the dozen local wineries.

Gold-plated pioneer

Salem's **State Capitol** building (900 Court Street; tours daily; tel: 503 986-1388; free) has an unusual cupola and is topped with the gold-plated bronze statue of a bearded, ax-wielding pioneer. Oregon, admitted into the Union in 1859, was the 33rd state. Inside the capitol, ornate panels illustrate wagon trails along the Willamette and Columbia rivers. These panels are complimented by the neoclassical lines of the capitol's interior, built of gray Vermont marble.

Anyone who climbs the 121-step spiral stairway to the dome will be rewarded with a view of the Willamette Valley, as well as Mount Hood and other Cascade peaks over 40 miles (65 km) away. This area has been dubbed the **Emerald Empire**. There's no

BELOW: Deady Hall, University of Oregon at Eugene.
RIGHT: the State Capitol is topped by a gilded pioneer.

word on how Seattle, "the Emerald City," feels about this appellation. South of the Capitol complex and across State Street is **Willamette University** (tel: 503 370-6300), one of the oldest colleges in the western United States. It dates from 1842. Prominent buildings include the **Mark O. Hatfield Library**, with its campanile, **Walker Hall**, the **Putman University Center**, with a café, and the **Smith Fine Arts Center**.

Dance hall echoes

The tree-shaded campus has long been a training ground for aspiring polititians. The past and present come together Downtown on the corner of Court and Liberty streets northeast at the **Reed Opera House**. During the Victorian era this was the hub of Salem's cultural and social life. Today, specialty shops thrive amid an atmosphere evocative of a "gussied-up" dance hall.

Expectations of a laid-back "ecotopian" capital are initially put to rest in down-

town Salem by the spit-and-polish facade of its administrative buildings, and the no-nonsense demeanor of the people who work in them. But there is an ominous presence. Salem's **State Mental Hospital**, so prominently located, was the backdrop for the award-winning movie of Oregon novelist Ken Kesey's book, *One Flew Over the Cuckoo's Nest*.

The **State Penitentiary** and the surrounding drabness of the state office buildings compounds the superficial impression that legislation, and little else, goes on here. The hard edge of Salem is softened considerably, however, by a stroll through the many oases of urban greenery, or by a visit to the well-established **Honeywood Winery** (1350 Hines Street Southeast; weekdays 9am–5pm, Sat 10am–5pm, Sun 1pm–5pm; tel: 503 362-4111; tasting fee).

In 1840, the Jason Lee Mission moved from the Willamette River upstream to a site on **Mill Creek** in present-day Salem. There, in 1842, missionaries established "the Oregon Institute" and in 1844 they laid out a town site on the Institute's lands. Southeast of the Capitol are the second- and third-oldest buildings in the Northwest: the **Jason Lee House** and the **Methodist Parsonage**, both dating from 1841. They form part of the **Mission Mill Museum**, an historic brick textile mill and village (1313 Mill Street; Mon–Sat 9am–5pm; tel: 503 585-7012; fee) where yarn is still spun on antique equipment. Guides in period costume show visitors how it's done; there's also a pioneer herb garden.

Deepwood Estate

Waterpower from the Willamette meant Salem's wool and flour mills developed early, and later its iron works and lumber mills helped the city to flourish. In midsummer the Mission Mill area is a good place to see Oregon's state flower, and fine rose gardens are not far away. Tasty food can be found at Mill Creek Station.

The **Deepwood Estate** (1116 Mission Street; May–Sept Sun–Fri noon–5pm; Oct–Apr Tues–Sat noon–5pm; tel: 503 363-1825; fee), an 1894 Queen Anne-style house on the National Register of

LEFT: moon over Oregon.

Map on page 230

Historic Places, and its adjoining, sweetly scented **Deepwood Gardens** (daily, dawn-dusk; free). Designed in 1929 on a difficult site by noted landscape architects Elizabeth Lord and Edith Schryver, Deepwood features painted lattice fences and arbors, a wrought-iron pergola and lush plantings edged with precise borders. The gardens include a Chinese garden and a tea garden with summerhouse. The house itself displays many of Lord and Schryver's original watercolor plans for these gardens.

Oldest in the West

Down Mission Street from Deepwood Gardens, **Bush's Pasture Park**, on the grounds of an old pioneer home, includes an **old rose garden**. Many of the cultivars were brought West by pioneers in the 19th century. The **Conservatory** is one of the oldest in the West, dating from 1882. **Bush House** (600 Mission Street Southeast; May–Sept Tues–Sun noon–4:30pm; Oct–Apr Tues–Sun 2pm–5pm; tel: 503

363-4714; donation), an Italianate Victorian house completed in 1878, is also open to the public. Behind the house is the **Bush Barn Art Center**, a showcase for local artists. Exhibits and good-quality souvenirs include prints, ceramics, wood carvings, basketry, jewelry and handmade cards. For garden lovers, **Schreiner's Iris Gardens** (3671 Quinaby Road; tel: 800 419-4747 ext. 71; free) a commercial iris grower, has 10 acres (4 hectares) of fine display gardens; the flowers are at their best in June.

Prayer and Bach

A lovely, peaceful Benedictine Monastery, founded in 1882, sits on top of a butte near the town of **Mount Angel** ❸, 18 miles (28 km) northeast of Salem. Roman Catholic Mass is said every morning. The library is one of only two American buildings designed by Finnish architect Alvar Aalto. In July, there is a **Bach Festival** in the chapel utilizing the massive pipe organ.

The **Mount Angel Abbey** is not open

BELOW: farming has been a valley business since the 1800s.

to the public – it is a working house of prayer – but visitors are welcome at the **Abbey Bookstore** (closed: Sun; tel: 503 845-3030) in the **Retreat House**.

Champoeg

St Paul ❹, about 30 miles (48 km) north of Salem, is where the village now known as **Historic Champoeg** (pronounced sham *poo* ee) once stood. It was here in May 1843 that French-Canadian and American settlers voted to organize a provisional government for Oregon. When Oregon City was designated the home for this new government, Champoeg's political importance declined, but the town thrived as a commercial center until 1961, when it was destroyed by a severe flood.

Champoeg's **visitor center** (Mon–Fri 8am–4pm, weekends 1pm–4pm; tel: 503 678-1251; fee) is located near the entrance to **Champoeg State Park**. The history of the French-Canadian fur trappers is told here through paintings, photographs, films

and lectures. The name is thought to derive from *poeg* or *pooitch*, the Indian term for the camas flower bulb.

The **Champoeg Wine Cellars** (10375 Champoeg Road Northeast, Aurora; June–Aug and Labor Day daily 11am–5pm; tel: 503 678-2144; tasting fee) has vineyards planted on the south-facing slope of a hill known as **La Butte** overlooking the **French Prairie**. With elevations ranging from 200 to 450 ft (60 to 135 meters), the southern exposure provides the warmth and sunlight needed to ripen grapes to their fullest. Planting began on the site in 1974 with Pinot Noir. Soon after came Chardonnay and White Riesling. In 1990 Pinot Gris was added. Since the first harvest in 1978, the Champoeg vineyard has sold its wines only to Northwest wineries and to those who stop by.

Largest state park

A pleasant side-trip starting from Salem follows Rt 213 for 15 miles (25 km) to the old mill town of **Silverton ❺**, a place that prides itself on being the world's largest producer of bearded irises at **Cooley Gardens** (mid-May–early June; tel: 503 873-5463; free). It's also worth a stop at the **Oregon Gardens Project** (Apr–Sept daily 9am–6pm; tel: 503 874-8100; fee), a large botanical garden with a waterfall, a children's garden, a water garden and a two-centuries old oak forest.

The town has a swimming area, horse and bike trails and a nature interpretive center. An interesting stop is the **Thomas Kinkade Silver Falls Gallery** (202 North 1st Street; tel: 503 873-0511) featuring the work of artist Thomas Kinkade, the "Painter of Light."

Silver Falls State Park (tel: 503 873-8681; day use fee), is 26 miles (40 km) east of town via Hwys 22 and 214. Silver Falls is Oregon's largest state park. Within two densely forested canyons, 10 **waterfalls** cascade over the steep cliffs of Columbia River basalt that flowed as molten lava 14 to 16 million years ago. At **North Falls**, chimney-like holes in the overhanging rock were formed when hot lava flowed around and over standing trees. The 8-mile (13-km) walking trail

LEFT: this winery in Champoeg is one of more than 120 in the valley.

Map on page 230

among and behind the various falls is a treat during fall foliage season, and in winter the east winds transform the gossamer-like flumes into ice sculptures. Half of the falls are over 100 ft (30 meters) high, with the swirling mists of **South Falls** topping the group at 177 ft (54 meters).

Historic **South Falls Lodge**, built of native stone and logs and containing unique Oregon myrtlewood furniture, is now restored and used as the **visitors center** with displays of early logging pictures and tools. For anyone with a yen to stay in a little **cabin in the woods**, the park has spartan cabins for rent (contact the park coordinator, tel 503 873-8875, to find out about reservations).

Bacchus country

South of Salem, fields of strawberries, sugar beets, beans, broccoli and cherries alternate with regional specialties such as filberts (hazelnuts), peppermint and, of course, the acres of vineyards. Crops are nurtured by the mild climate and by the

blessing of what is usually gentle but persistent drizzle. The main route connecting the various Willamette Valley cities, Interstate 5, avoids the congestion of in-town, stop-start traffic. **Old State 99** parallels I-5, but runs through the small towns closer to the Willamette River. It is slower, but more interesting. Both of these routes are distinguished by year-round greenery, hawks perched on fenceposts, sheep in the pastures, and daffodils that chart a springtime yellow brick road through the Emerald Empire.

One way to savor the richness of the harvest is to stop at the **Willamette Valley Vineyards** (8800 Enchanted Way Southeast; daily 11am–6pm; tel: 503 588-9463; tasting fee). The winery and underground cellar here are carved into the top of an ancient volcanic cinder cone – **Ilahee Hill** – just south of Salem.

Well-drained volcanic soils appear red due to their oxidized iron content, setting the stage for fine hillside estate vineyards that yield intensely flavored grapes. The

BELOW: the Willamette Valley is known for its peaceful atmosphere and pastoral charm.

surrounding 50 acres (20 hectares) are planted to produce Pinot Noir, Chardonnay and Pinot Gris varietals. Bring a picnic and enjoy some of this fine local wine while lunching in a covered picnic area beside a pond.

Painted ladies

Situated between Salem and Albany on a side road, **Airlie Winery** (15305 Dunn Forest Road, Monmouth; Mar–Dec weekends noon–5pm; tel: 503 838-6013; tasting fee) overlooks the charming **Dunn Forest Vineyard**. It produces Maréchal Foch, Pinot Noir, Pinot Gris, Chardonnay, Riesling, Gewürztraminer and Müller Thurgau – all particularly suited to the coastal edge of the valley.

Just northeast of Albany, the primitive **Buena Vista Ferry** (Apr–Oct Wed–Fri, 7am–5pm, Sat–Sun 9am–7pm; tel 541 588-7979; fee), established in 1851 but now motorized, crosses the Willamette River. Within **Albany ❻** itself, an 80-square-block central neighborhood fea-

tures dozens of homes in architectural styles from colorful Queen Annes (the "painted ladies") to Craftsman bungalows including styles from the 1840s through the late 1920s.

Three districts are listed in the National Register of Historic Places: the **Monteith, Hackleman** and **Downtown Commercial Historic Districts**. These consist of 350 historic homes, all privately occupied at present. The motifs reflect an era of affluence when the Willamette River and the railroad combined to export timber and agricultural produce at great profit.

The **Albany Timber Carnival** is recognized as one of the largest logging shows in the world. Held annually on the Fourth of July weekend, the carnival includes novice and championship competitions in log chopping, bucking (sawing), speed climbing, tree topping, birling (log rolling in water), ax throwing, a queen coronation and fireworks.

Also of some interest are a number of **covered bridges**. Although these were built in the 1930s to protect their wooden platforms from Oregon's considerable rainfall, couples in search of a little privacy quickly discovered their charms, earning them the nickname "kissing bridges." Set out by car or bike (preferably with someone you want to kiss) on a self-guided tour of a dozen of Oregon's covered bridges, which are showcased on well-paved country roads just off I-5. You can pick up a map at the **Albany Visitors' Association** (300 Second Avenue Southwest; tel: 541 928-0911). There is a public park and swimming area beside **Larwood Bridge**, an ideal spot for a picnic.

Moo U

Situated between the Pacific Ocean and the Cascade Mountains, **Corvallis ❼** (tel: 541 757-1544) is a self-absorbed college town. Joseph C. Avery, one of the original settlers, made up the name of the town by compounding the Latin words for "heart of the valley." Lending the community a youthful vitality, **Oregon State University** (OSU) is set on a 500-acre (200-hectare) campus and specializes in agriculture and engineering.

LEFT: the End of the Trail Interpretive Center shows pioneer life on the Oregon Trail.

Map on page 230

Referred to as "Moo U," its presence is augmented by a high-tech industry dominated by **Hewlett Packard**, the granddaddy of Silicon Valley computer outfits. It's also the site of the **Linus Pauling Institute**, the premier research center on the benefits of Vitamin C. Oregon's oldest institution of higher education is the center of much of the town's activities, including all types of college sports. There are bookstores, restaurants, craft boutiques and other shops along the edge of the campus. On campus, the **Horner Museum** offers exhibits on Oregon's animal, mineral and human history.

University challenge

With two universities (one in Corvallis and one in Eugene) so close together – both with avid football fans – there is a constant search for a peaceful, demilitarized zone. For the spot where the flaming loyalties of the Oregon Ducks morph into a volcanic passion for the Oregon State Beavers, draw a line somewhere across

Main Street from George and Irene Daugherty's place in **Monroe** (pop. 480), which is the midpoint on Rt 99 between the two towns.

Corvallis has bike lanes on most streets, and lazy routes along the Willamette and Mary rivers. Great trails for hiking or biking are located in **Avery Park** or in OSU's **Peavy Arboretum** on Hwy 99W. **Michael's Landing** (603 Northwest 2nd Street; tel: 541 754-6141) is a restaurant known for its tasty chicken, seafood and steak in a former railroad depot overlooking the Willamette River.

Corvallis is also close to the **Siuslaw National Forest**, a 630,000-acre (255,000-hectare) woodland that includes the excellent **Oregon Dunes National Recreation Area** *(see Coastal Oregon, page 256)*. Camping, hiking, hunting and fishing can all be enjoyed in Siuslaw Forest.

Anyone who appreciates the forest might want to sign up for a free guided bus tour covering its geography, geology and history: contact **Starker Forests Inc**

BELOW: covered "kissing bridge" over the McKenzie River, dating from the 1930s.

(Wed only; tel: 541 757-1544). And for a look at one of the last steps in the production of lumber, **Hull-Oakes Lumber** (Hwy 99W south of Corvallis; ask for a tour; tel: 541 432-3112) is one of the last steam-driven sawmills remaining in operation in the nation.

Geese and woodpeckers

Finley National Wildlife Refuge ❽ (26208 Finley Refuge Road; limited access; Apr–Nov dawn–dusk; tel: 541 757-7236), situated 10 miles (16 km) south, 4 miles (6 km) west on Hwy 99W, has a number of observation posts where it's possible to scout for grouse, pheasants, quail, egrets, wood ducks, herons, plovers, sandpipers, hawks, and sandhill cranes. Finley Refuge was originally established to protect the winter habitat of the Canada Goose.

The **Woodpecker Loop** is a short hike that takes walkers through a diverse set of ecosystems while on the lookout for different species of birds. The trailhead is

located 3 miles (4 km) up Refuge Road, off Hwy 99W.

West from Corvallis on Hwy 34 is **Philomath**, a small lumber town nudging the Coast Range. Unending successions of cloud masses are blown here by the prevailing westerlies off the Pacific Ocean, so much so that Philomath is thought to be the cloudiest place in the Willamette Valley. Rain or shine, it's hard to ignore the 1865 Georgian brick structure that houses the **Benton County Historical Museum** (1101 Main Street; Tues–Sat 10am–4:30pm; tel: 541 929-6230; free).

Mary's Peak, 16 miles (26 km), west of Corvallis, is the highest mountain in the Coast Range at 4,097 ft (1,250 meters). From the top, which is easily accessible by car, there is a wonderful, wide-sweeping view, with the Pacific Ocean to the west and the Cascade Mountains to the east.

There are seven local wineries in Benton County. Between Corvallis and Eugene is **Alpine Vineyards** (25904 Green Peak Road, Monroe; daily June 15–Sept 15 noon–5pm; then weekends, noon–5pm, closed: Nov–Mar; tel: 541 424-5851; tasting fee.) Established in 1976, the Alpine is a 26-acre (10-hectare) vineyard and winery nestled in the scenic foothills of the Coast Range. All of the wines are estate-bottled and include Chardonnay, Pinot Gris, Pinot Noir, Riesling, Gewurztraminer, Cabernet Sauvignon and White Cabernet. Picnic facilities with a panoramic view overlooking the vineyards make for a very pleasant stop.

Sea level to ski level

Eugene ❾ (tel: 800 547-5445) is Oregon's second-largest city, and known as the "Jewel of the Emerald Empire." With its twin-city of **Springfield**, it rests in a garden-like setting with all manner of recreational facilities, from sea level to ski level. The Willamette River runs through the heart of the city, providing its own focus. With a distinct cultural mix, ranging from professionals and university students to counterculture and lumber company workers, it is definitely a community of contrasts.

LEFT: Eugene was the first city in the United States to make jogging popula[r]

Map on page 230

Over the past decade or so Eugene and Springfield have seen an ever-expanding high-tech manufacturing and support sector. While economic cycles do fluctuate from time to time, the landscape, architecture, historic buildings and cultural life continues unabated at the 280-acre (115-hectare) **University of Oregon** (**U of O**), (tel: 541 346-3014 for campus information), home of the Fighting Ducks. Architecturally pleasing buildings include the school's first building, **Deady Hall**, constructed in 1876. Anyone who drives here can get a temporary parking permit at the kiosk at 13th and Agate Street.

The U of O **Museum of Art** (1430 Johnson Lane; Wed–Sun noon–5pm; tel: 541 346-3027; fee) has a collection of Asian art, as well as African art, Russian icon paintings, Rodin sculptures and changing exhibits. Currently under extensive renovations, it reopens in 2003.

Graced by the bronze sculpture of a Native American woman with a spring salmon, the university's **Museum of Natural History** (1680 East 15th Avenue; Tues–Sun noon–5pm; tel: 541 346-3024; fee; free parking with permit from front desk) focuses on the state's ancient people and animals, as well as changing exhibits on other cultures. On display here is the oldest shoe ever unearthed, possibly 8,500 years old.

Tracktown, USA

Known for its cultural events, Eugene is the home to the **Hult Center for the Performing Arts** (1 Eugene Center; various presentations; free tours; Thur and Sat; tel: 541 682-5000) where ballets, symphonies and opera are performed in several halls. Among the shows to attend is the internationally known Grammy-winning **Oregon Bach Festival** (tel: 800 457-1486) in late June, featuring more than 40 concerts.

The campus projects its lifestyle onto the community. U of O's **Hayward Field** is the birthplace of Eugene's reputation as "Tracktown USA." This is where Bill Bowerman popularized the jogging regimen that swept the country in the 1970s. Even today, the city might well

have more joggers per capita than anywhere else.

Rated one of the top ten cycling cities in the US, Eugene has miles of cycle, walking and jogging paths along the Willamette River. These wind through parks and gardens, and even push up next to shopping malls. Canoes and kayaks can be hired for a pleasant day's boating on the river. For picnicking, **Fern Ridge Lake**, 12 miles (20 km) west of Downtown and part of an earth-dam project, is a good spot. If you prefer white-water rafting, Eugene is close to the **McKenzie River**, with Class II and Class III rapids: contact the McKenzie River Rafting Company (tel: 541 747-9231).

The young and the curious

Exhibits likely to appeal to the young and the curious can be found at the interesting **Willamette Science and Technology Center** (2300 Leo Harris Parkway; Wed–Fri noon–5pm, weekends 11am–5pm; tel: 541 682-7888; fee). There is

also a worthwhile **planetarium** adjacent to the center.

The somewhat plain **Oregon Air & Space Museum** (south end of Eugene Airport; Wed–Sun noon–4pm; tel: 541 461-1101; fee) is an educational, non-profit, aviation museum dedicated to the acquisition of historically significant aircraft. Its displays include a McDonnell Douglas F-4 Phantom, a Grumman A-6 Intruder, a North American F-86 Sabre Jet, a Fokker Dr 1 Triplane, a Taylor 2100 Bullet, a Mikoyan/ Gurevich MiG-17, and a Yakovlev Yak-50.

Store with nothing to sell

Want to visit a store that doesn't sell anything? **Energy Outlet** (409 East 4th Avenue; Tues–Sat 10:30am–5:30pm; tel: 541 683-5060; free) exists solely to demonstrate the latest energy-efficiency appliances and ideas that regular house-owners can apply in their own homes.

The kitchen displays the latest highly efficient appliances, including a refriger-

ator, a range, ovens, a washer, a dryer, lighting and a solar water heater. Huge displays on the wall illustrate the correct way to insulate and air-seal new construction or remodeling projects. Knowledgable staff are always on hand to answer questions.

Down by the riverside, the 9-acre (3.5-hectare) **George Owen Memorial Rose Garden** (North Jefferson; daily dawn–dusk; tel: 541 682-4824; free) has more than 4,500 All-America Rose Selections, which are in bloom from June to September. In the center of the garden is the impressive **Black Republican Cherry Tree** planted in 1847.

Nearby **Skinner's Butte Park** has a fine view of the Eugene skyline with the Coast Range visible on a clear day. **Hendricks Park Rhododendron Garden** (Summit Avenue; tel 541 682-5324), a 12-acre (5-hectare) woodland, displays 6,000 ornamental plants including rhododendrons, azaleas and magnolias under a canopy of Oregon white oaks.

Fifth Street Public Market (296 East 5th Avenue; daily 10am– 6pm; restaurants only 7am–9pm; tel: 541 484-0383) is a former chicken-processing plant in the restored **Historic District**, offering a choice of restaurants and boutiques selling the wares of local craftspeople. Whether it's freshly squeezed juice or a ceramic vase, the market can deliver a bite-size slice of Eugene life.

Chocolate to die for

The little **Euphoria Chocolate Company** (6 East 17th Avenue; Mon–Fri 10am–6pm, Sat 11am–5pm; July–Aug also Sun 11am–5pm; tel: 541 343-9223) is a delightful diversion for those who crave real-cream centers in extra-rich truffles and chocolate-covered cookies.

Another taste experience is the **Carte de Frisco** (Willamette and Broadway), worth the wait to line up at a vending-cart that looks like an oversize black phone booth. For what? For Eugene's famous "Chicken on a Stick" covered in a gooey, sweet and sour, tangy sauce. Be warned: one napkin is never enough.

A similar ambiance prevails, rain or

LEFT:
Eugene is one of the top ten cycling cities.

Map
on page
230

shine, among the 300 booths at the **Eugene Saturday Market** (8th and Oak streets; Apr–Dec 25). This weekly event features entertainment, fast food and crafts. And, of course, no self-respecting university town would be complete without its local beer. In a *Eugene Weekly* reader's poll, the town's favorite microbrewery and grub stop is **Mcmenamin's North Bank** (22 Club Road; tel: 541 343-5622) voted Best In-House Microbrew, Best Outside Dining and (second) Best Burgers.

Drink up and be happy

Fifteen minutes from Eugene, **Silvan Ridge/Hinman Vineyards** has tours and tastings (daily; tel: 541 345-1945; call for schedule; tasting fee). Established in 1979, Silvan Ridge is maintained in the tradition of a small European winery, with a well-landscaped property providing the backdrop for an afternoon picnic. Stop by on your way to the coast.

Another pleasant winery just south of Eugene is the 30-acre (12-hectare) estate

winery, **Chateau Lorane** (27415 Siuslaw River Road, Lorane; tasting room; June–Sept daily noon–5pm; Oct–Dec and May Sat–Sun noon–5pm; tel: 541 942-8028; tasting fee). Experimenting with grapes from Oregon State University vineyards, this facility produces several organic wines in addition to other vintages. Among these are Chardonnay, Pinot Gris, dry Gewürztraminer, Viognier, Pinot Meunier and Merlot. Be sure to try the fruit wines or sweet mead.

The relaxed atmosphere can be enjoyed from the tasting room or from the picnic area, where visitors overlook the private 24-acre (9-hectare) **Chateau Lorane lake**, enveloped in the dark green of the fir-covered Coast Range foothills.

Technically, communities located south of Eugene, such as Roseburg, Grants Pass, Medford and Ashland, are considered part of the Willamette Valley, but for the purposes of this book, these towns are described in the chapter entitled Rogue River Country *(see page 261).* ❑

ELOW:
he Oregon
ir & Space
Museum,
ugene.

COASTAL OREGON

Legislative action in 1913 set aside Oregon's coastline for "free and uninterrupted use." Nearly 100 years later, this is still the case

Map on page 244

With dozens of panoramic overlooks, crashing waves rolling in from the Pacific, old-fashioned seaside towns with streets of picturesque shops, galleries and restaurants, the 350-mile (550-km) long Oregon coast is a vast and (relatively) unexplored haven. The highway clings to the Pacific Coast, in places skirting the beach, then climbs high above the rolling breakers. The road is mostly two lanes, so traffic can move slowly, but no one seems to mind.

Legislative action in 1913 and again in 1967 set aside the coastline for "free and uninterrupted use." Beaches have numerous access points, billboards and advertising are controled, and its appearance is vastly different from the Washington or the Southern Californian coastline.

There are huge numbers of well-maintained state parks and waysides. Immense beaches, often hundreds of yards wide and stretching as far as the eye can see, have been public property since 1913.

Storm watching

Huge piles of driftwood marking the farthest reach of storm-tossed waves are testimony to the ever-changing weather. The area has a marine climate: summers are cool and winters are mild, with few freezing temperatures at night. Summer temperatures do not usually exceed 67°F (19°C); winter temperatures dip no lower than 36°F (2°C). The area gets about 70 inches (177 cm) of rain each year. Autumn is often an Indian summer of exceptional color, and September is the best month to visit for the often-clear skies.

Winter storms can be dramatic, with winds reaching some 70–100 mph (110–160 kph) on the ocean bluffs. Storm-watching is an unofficial "sport," and beachcombers rise early the following day to inspect the treasures deposited by the tossing surf and ebbing tides.

The coast road is US Highway 101, which runs north to south for more than 200 miles (325 km), from Astoria in the far north of Oregon to Brookings in the far south, near California – in other words, the full length of the state.

101 Miracle Miles

It's possible to drive this long and winding road – the **Pacific Coast Scenic Byway** – in a single day, but this would be pointless, as you would have no time to experience any of the breathtaking sights. It is not for nothing that this road is also referred to as the **101 Miracle Miles**.

Access to the coast from other parts of the state is easy. From the Willamette Valley, arteries head west to the coast.

EFT: Cape Foulweather, with lighthouse. **RIGHT:** the Astoria Column has 164 steps to the top.

US Highway 30 links up with Astoria with Portland. The so-called **Sunset Highway** is Hwy 26, connecting Portland with Seaside, a route ending in a major resort area.

There are over 60 state parks along Hwy 101, including some that preserve vestiges of the state's impressive coniferous forests. Everywhere, the parks beckon tourists to leave the car and actively enjoy the beach, the trails, the hillsides, the fresh and invigorating air. Anyone without a car can get to the major Oregon seaside towns using a service that departs from the Portland International Airport: the **Bay Shuttle service** (daily, scheduled departures; tel: 360 642-4196 or 800 376-6118).

Graveyard of the Pacific

Impressive **Astoria Bridge** crosses the mouth of the **Columbia River** and connects the state of Washington to the state of Oregon. Two **Welcome Centers**, one on Hwy 30 in Astoria, and one on Hwy 101 in **Warrenton** (Fort Stevens), serve tourist needs. The eddies and cross currents formed as the gaping mouth of the Columbia hurls itself into the Pacific – the infamous Columbia bar – can be felt many miles out to sea; would-be sailors are warned to seek expert advice here, and indeed all along the coast. Swimming can also be treacherous, due to undercurrents and rip tides.

It's known as the **Graveyard of the Pacific**, and the 1,500-plus shipwrecks that have occurred here are cited as evidence in the claim that this is one of the top three roughest river bars in the world.

The Astoria Bridge is the entrance to the town of **Astoria ❶**, which, by the 1870s, was a flourishing fishing and lumber center. It was also a place where drunken patrons of saloons and bawdy-houses could find themselves shanghaied to crew on sailing vessels bound for the Far East.

Considered the oldest American settlement west of the Rockies, the area was first visited by Captain Robert Gray in 1792, then served as the stopping place for the Lewis & Clark Corps of Discov-

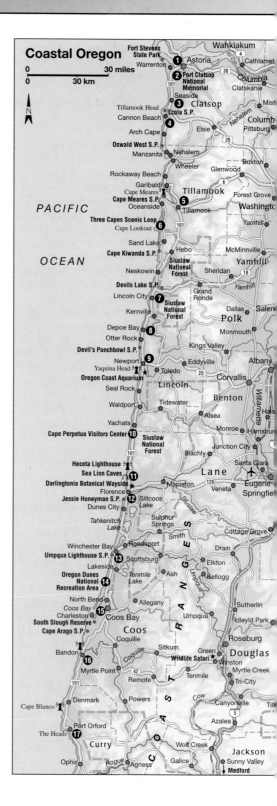

Map
on page
244

ery in 1805. Formally established in 1811 by John Jacob Astor (J.J.), the outpost was intended to develop Far East markets for the beaver-fur trade. But the War of 1812 blockaded the post, and Astor eventually sold it to the British.

Astor of Astoria

This did not stop J.J. The man most closely associated with the American fur trade, had, in fact, become involved in the business without ever setting a trap, and he continued to monopolize it until 1834, when he retired. Thereafter, Astor's earnings, plus investments in New York real estate, made him the richest man in the United States and the country's first recorded millionaire.

Astoria, the town that bears his name, is a very pretty place. Hundreds of Victorian-style homes cling to hillsides against a backdrop of misty rainforests. Astoria's extensive waterfront begins at the **6th Street Viewing Dock**, continues to the **14th Street Riverpark,** with its interpre-tive panels of river activity, and on to the **17th Street Pier**, where, often, visiting ships can be toured. Fishing charter operators offer the opportunity to land salmon, sturgeon or crab.

The **Astoria Riverfront Trolley** (Mon–Fri 3–9pm, Sat–Sun 10am–9pm; tel: 503 325-631; fee), with the loosest of schedules, is run by an eclectic army of volunteers. Old Number 300 clickity clacks its way along the town's tracks, and then crosses it, linking the Port of Astoria to the **East End Mooring Basin**.

Hollywood is fond of this area. Movies filmed here include *Kindergarten Cop*, with Arnold Schwarzenegger, and *Free Willy I* and *II* with Keiko as the films' whale hero. For *Free Willy's* climax, filmed at the **Hammond Mooring Basin**, a hot tub was installed to allow the actors, who were spending hours in freezing water, to warm up between takes.

The handsome **Astoria Column** (daily dawn to dusk; tel: 503 325-2963; donation), by architect Electus Ritchfield, is

BELOW:
sunset on the
Columbia River
near Astoria.

125 ft (38 meters) high and sits atop **Coxcomb Hill**. The column is patterned after Trajan's Column in Rome (built in AD 114). Now listed in the National Register of Historic Places, it was first dedicated in 1926.

Anyone who can bear to climb the 164 steps will be rewarded with a panoramic view of the Astoria Bridge, the Pacific Ocean, the Columbia River, Saddle Mountain and the Clatsop Plain. On the outside is a spiraling mural by Italian artist Atillio Pusterla depicting the westward expansion of Oregon settlers.

Columbia River Maritime Museum (daily, closed: Dec 25 and Jan 1; tel: 503 325-2323; fee) is host to more than 100,000 visitors annually who seek out its 7,000 sea-related artifacts. Displays cover lighthouses, shipwrecks, navigation, fishing and naval history. The largest artifact, a National Historic Landmark, is the lightship *Columbia*; from 1950 to 1980 it served as a floating "lighthouse" for ships crossing Columbia bar.

Fort Astoria

It was in 1811, only five years after the departure of Lewis & Clark, that John Jacob Astor sent fur traders aboard the ship *Tonquin* to establish a fur-trading post. They called the outpost **Fort Astoria**. This site is preserved as a roadside monument at what is now 15th and Exchange streets. Soon after an incident during the War of 1812, Fort Astoria was closed.

Captain Black, commanding the British *Racoon,* arrived at the fort on December 12. After dinner, the company ran up a British flag while Captain Black broke open a bottle of Madeira wine, loudly declaring that he was taking possession of the post in the name of His Royal Majesty. He followed by changing the name of Fort Astoria to Fort George. It didn't stick.

According to the *Narratives of David Thompson*, a famous Northwest fur trapper in 1817, 25 trappers left Canada. Due to deaths along the way, however, only 18 arrived in Astoria. The survivors included

BELOW: paddleboat on the river by Astoria.

Map on page 244

Andre Lachapelle and Louis Pichette dit Dupre. Captain J. Hickley and US Commissioner J.B. Prevost arrived at Astoria aboard the British frigate *Blossom* on October 6, 1818, and the British formally ceded Fort George at this time. The Canada Northwest Company, however, continued as the sole operators of the fort, which had become a trading post rather than a military outpost of Britain.

Wet, wet, wet

Listed in the National Register of Historic Places, Astoria's **Flavel House** (1618 Exchange Street; daily, closed: holidays; tel: 503 325-2203; fee) was built in 1885 by a Columbia River bar pilot and an early millionaire, Captain George Flavel. A fine example of Queen Anne- style architecture with period furnishings and artwork, Flavel House rests on park-like grounds covering a city block. The fourth-story cupola was designed as a vantage point to watch river traffic.

Near Astoria, **Fort Clatsop National Memorial** ❷ (daily in summer 8am–6pm, closed: Dec; tel: 503 861-2471; fee) is a National Park Service facility commemorating Lewis & Clark and their Corps of Discovery. It was on a wet Christmas Eve in 1805 that the party moved into a hastily built 50 ft by 50ft (15 meter by 15 meter) stockade fort surrounded by old-growth forest.

Visitors to the fort get a good idea of where the 33-strong party lived, but have to imagine the fleas, the rotting clothing and the rain that fell on all but 12 of the 106 days the explorers were here. Named in honor of the local Clatsop Indians, the fort offered much-needed refuge as the party rested from their arduous 2,000-mile (3,200-km) journey, and prepared for the return trek east to St Louis.

The original fort deteriorated in the wet climate, but in 1955, using Clark's sketches, local residents constructed a replica on the same site. Today, park rangers dress in buckskin coats, make candles, carve dugout canoes and fire flintlock muskets to reenact what life was like for the explorers. The fort is furnished with hand-hewn wooden bunks and

benches, and serves as an open-air museum.

Over 100 years ago, young soldiers dressed in Union blue stood watch over a fort at the mouth of the Columbia. A Civil War fortification in 1863, Fort Stevens was deactivated after World War II, and is now a state park. The **Fort Stevens State Park, Historic Area and Military Museum** (daily: May–Oct 10am–6pm; Nov–Apr 10am–4pm; tel: 800 452-5687 or 503 861-1671; fee) near the town of **Warrenton** has military artifacts, tours and history demonstrations.

Fort Stevens is the only military installation in the continental United States to be under fire since the War of 1812. On the night of June 21, 1942, the fort was the target of a Japanese submarine that fired 17 shells. The shelling caused no damage and Fort Stevens did not return fire.

Visitors can explore abandoned gun batteries and climb to the commander's station for a strategic view of the Columbia River and the **South Jetty**. During the summer, there are walking tours of the

underground **Battery Mishler** and tours of the entire complex aboard a US Army truck. Along the water's edge at Fort Steven lies the forlorn wreck of the four-masted, iron-hulled British schooner, *Peter Iredal*, which ran aground in 1906. The wreck emphasizes the importance of light-houses along this treacherous coast.

Down by the Seaside

A bronze memorial to Lewis and Clark stands gazing oceanward on the Prome-nade (the Prom) in **Seaside** ❸ (tel: 503 738-6391), a lively resort and convention area. At a salt cairn here in 1806, com-rades of Lewis and Clark boiled seawater for salt to preserve their food for the homeward voyage. The rollers from the Pacific Ocean are within walking distance of downtown Seaside with its shops, eateries and arcades.

From here, it's only eight blocks to Sea-side's **Factory Outlet Center** (Hwy 101 and 12th Avenue; tel: 503 717-1603), a shopper's delight with over 100,000 sq. ft

(2,800 sq. meters) of manufacturers' out-lets claiming to sell name brands at much less than retail prices. In addition to the usual mix of apparel and accessories, the center has a Northwest gift shop and a good wine shop.

The **Seaside Aquarium** (on the Prom; Mar–Oct daily 9am–dusk; Nov–Feb Wed–Sun 9am–dusk; tel: 503 738-6211; fee), established in 1937, has been a pop-ular attraction for generations. Underwa-ter animals in a starring role include a family of harbor seals, a 20-ray starfish, a wily octopus, a deadly Moray eel and a ferocious-looking Wolf eel. Visitors are encouraged to stroke star fish and prickly sea urchins in the "touch tank."

Postcards of the Oregon coast often show the view 2 miles (3 km) north of Cannon Beach at **Ecola State Park** (tel: 503 436-2844; day-use fee), a scenic park near **Tillamook Head** where waves roll in against craggy islands and secluded beaches. Framed by lines of breakers, the beach stretches to the horizon, punctuated by distinctive rocky outcrops called "sea stacks." Signs tell which of these unique features are safe to climb.

The park's miles of clean firm sand are very walkable; old-growth Sitka spruce and a western hemlock forest are prime habitat for elk and deer. Viewpoints acces-sible by car are at Ecola State Park and **Indian Beach** picnic areas. The **Tillam-ook Head Trail** (use Ecola State Park signs; May–Sept; tel: 503 436-2844; day-use fee; bring boots and waterproof jacket – even in summer) is a fairly easy 3½-mile (5.5-km) round-trip hike taking 2–5 hours. From the forest walk, there are peek-a-boo views of waves sweeping ashore. The Lewis and Clark expedition crossed Tillamook Head's crest in 1806 to buy the blubber of a stranded whale from Indians at Cannon Beach.

At a viewpoint along the way Clark marveled, "I behold the grandest and most pleasing prospect which my eyes ever surveyed." When Clark reached Cannon Beach he found the Indians had already carved up the whale and were loath to part with the rendered oil. The current trail across Tillamook Head not only follows

LEFT:
Haystack Roc
Cannon Beach

Map on page 244

the expedition's route, it passes a viewpoint known as **Clark's Point of View**. The headland itself is a tilted remnant of a massive, 15 million-year-old Columbia River basalt flow. Incredibly, the lava welled up near Idaho, flooded down the Columbia Gorge, and spread along the seashore to this point.

Situated a mile out to sea, **Tillamook Rock** is a bleak island with a lighthouse in operation from 1881 to 1957. Nicknamed "Terrible Tilly," the building was repeatedly swept by storms that dashed water, rocks and fish into the lantern room 150 ft (45 meters) above sea level. Funereal entrepreneurs bought the island, and urns of cremated remains arrive via helicopter.

Postcard-perfect

Marked by the picture-postcard monolithic **Haystack Rock** just offshore, the coastal village of **Cannon Beach ④** (tel: 503 436-2623) received its name from a cannon that washed ashore in 1846 after the US Navy schooner *Shark* ran aground.

Cannon Beach is packed with coffeehouses, bungalows, and gallery-shops, and is considered to be the arty counterpart to "kitchy" Seaside. **North by Northwest Gallery** (239 North Hemlock; tel: 800 494-0741) offers original art with an emphasis on regional art glass; **Fair Winds** (124 North Hemlock; tel: 503 436-1201) has old nautical artifacts, marine paintings and prints; **White Bird Gallery** (251 North Hemlock; tel: 503 436-2681) exhibits and sells local art-community paintings, sculpture, prints, photography, glass, ceramics and jewelry.

South of Cannon Beach stands 1,600 ft (490-meters) **Neahkahnie Mountain** in **Oswald West State Park** (tel: 503 842-5501; fee; if walking, bring a jacket). The road takes hair-raising curves as it climbs to a viewpoint 700 ft (200 meters) above the surf. Paragliders, with a flair for the extreme, find this daredevil place exhilarating. Indians thought this mountaintop was a viewpoint fit for gods and named it *Ne Ekahni*, "place of supreme deity."

BELOW:
Garibaldi Harbor at Tillamook Bay.

White men surrounded the peak with legend as treasure seekers sifted the beach at the mountain's base, spurred by tales of gold buried by sailors from a shipwrecked Spanish galleon. The discovery here of a strangely inscribed block of beeswax added to the speculation.

South of Neahkahnie is the quiet village of **Manzanita**, and then **Nehalem**, a small river town noted for its antique shops and good fishing opportunities.

A cheesy visit

During World War II, several giant blimps were based at **Tillamook ❺** (tel: 503 842-7525); their massive hangar, 1,072 ft (326 meters) long and covering over 7 acres (3 hectares), still dominates the horizon. Though blimps that once patroled the coast for enemy submarines are gone, there is a vintage aircraft museum, **Tillamook Air Museum** (6030 Hangar Road; daily 10am–5pm; tel: 503 8442-1130; fee)

What Tillamook is mostly known for, however, is its dairy products – particularly cheese and ice cream. It's almost impossible not to fill the picnic basket at one if not both of two cheese-making operations. **Blue Heron French Cheese Company** (daily: summer 8am–8pm; winter 9am–5pm; tel: 800 275-0639; free samples) offers samples of brie and camembert, plus tasters of Oregon wines, local mustards, jams, dips and other specialty foods. Outside in the picnic area is a petting corral. But it is cheddar, not brie, that represents the standard here.

With almost a million annual visitors, **Tillamook Cheese Visitor's Center** (4175 Hwy 101 North; daily: May 15–Sept 15 8am–8pm; mid-Sept–mid May 8am–6pm; tel: 503 815-1300) is a very popular stop and one of the largest cheese-making facilities in the West. After the self-guided tour with free samples, people line up in droves at the (not free) ice-cream counter.

The attraction here is ice cream in waffle cones, and it can take a little time for road-weary travelers to choose among the

BELOW: the Coquille River Lighthouse near Bandon.

40 appealing flavors. On a typical summer day, this one place can serve up approximately 4,000 ice-cream cones.

Tall forests and pounding surf

South of Tillamook, **Three Capes Scenic Loop** ❻ covers three jutting promontories: Cape Meares, Cape Lookout and Cape Kiwanda; each is a state park. Here the tall forests go right down to the pounding surf. Of particular note are the huge Sitka spruce with heartwood so light and strong it was used to make early wooden aircraft. The **Cape Meares Lighthouse** (tours May–Sept daily 11am–4pm; Oct, Mar and Apr Sat–Sun; tel: 503 842-3182; free), built in 1890, is definitely one of the highlights (no pun intended) here. Although it towers high above the ocean, its 38-ft (11-meter) tower is the shortest on the Oregon coast. The lighthouse's Fresnel lens is easy to photograph.

Walkways lead from the parking area to the lighthouse. Viewpoints overlook offshore islets inhabited by Steller sea lions and seabirds, common murres, peregrine falcons, tufted puffins and pelagic cormorants that nest on the cliff walls. Of particular note is the **Octopus Tree**, located a few steps south of the parking lot. Local Indian tradition says the eerie, giant Sitka is a burial tree; in olden times Natives put their dead in canoes, then placed the canoes inside specially prepared trees. Some people think this particular example is 2,000 years old.

Cape Lookout has a pleasant, year-round campground and an attractive strolling beach. There are two **Cape Kiwanda** state parks where the action of wind and waves on the sandstone has created a dynamic headland. The "other" Haystack Rock can be seen offshore; the more famous one is near Cannon Beach.

Between the beach and a lake

Southward, **Lincoln City** ❼ (tel: 541 994-3070) nestles between 7 miles (11 km) of sandy beaches and a 680-acre (275-hectare) scenic lake on the central Oregon Coast. Situated at the start of a well-publicized "Twenty Miracle Miles" – a strip of somewhat tacky coastal properties, it's crowded with mom-and-pop-owned establishments and emits a general "hey-let's-rent-a-moped" holiday feeling; there are 15 access points to the public beach.

Lincoln City was consolidated about 30 years ago when five smaller centers decided to amalgamate. In addition to a continuum of stores and motels, there are locations for wave-, whale-, sunset- and storm-watching. The beach is a treasure trove for driftwood, agates, shells and floats. Large rocks emerging from the sea create ideal pockets for tide pooling during low tides, and beach hiking, surfing, and fishing challenge sun seekers.

Sneaker waves

A few words of caution: Read the signs posted at every beach warning visitors to keep watch for bigger-than-usual "sneaker" waves and the incoming tide. You could become stranded on a rock – or worse – as the tide sweeps in. Wear shoes with grippy soles that you don't mind getting wet, and tread carefully. The rocks are often covered

Map on page 244

RIGHT: free samples of cheese here, but be sure to try the ice cream.

with sharp mussels and barnacles. And remember: look at these, but don't touch.

Voted the "Kite Capital of the World," Lincoln City receives steady winds; storm watching is best during the winter months. **Devils Lake**, deep only in terms of Indian folklore, is 3 miles (4 km) wide, 3 miles (4 km) long, and reaches a depth of only 22 ft (7 meters). Nine species of freshwater fish lure fishermen, while water sports such as windsurfing, waterskiing and jet skiing engage other enthusiasts.

Flowing from Devils Lake is the **"D" River**, which claims the title of the "World's Shortest River." From its source at Devils Lake, the river reaches its destination, the Pacific, in a mere 120-ft (36-meters). The **Connie Hansen Garden** (1931 Northwest 33rd Street; Tues and Sat, 10am–2pm, or by appointment; tel: 541 994-6338; donation) was created by one woman over a 20-year period and features hardy species that thrive in coastal climates, such as rhododendrons, azaleas, primroses and hybridized irises.

Lincoln has several galleries, plus opportunities to visit artisans at work. A few are: **Alder House II** (611 Immonen Road; tours Mar 15–Nov 30 daily 10am–5pm; 541 996-2483; free), Oregon's oldest glass-blowing studio; **Mossy Creek Pottery** (483 Immonen Road; tel: 541 996-2415), noted for porcelain and unusual glazes; **American Shadows Native American Images** (1800 Southeast Hwy 101; tel: 541 996-6887); and **Tom Thresher Stoneworks Gallery** (1293 North Bank Road; tel: 541 994-7342). Myrtlewood is found in only two places on earth: Oregon and Israel *(see page 257)*. Collectors travel from far and wide to visit **Swede's Myrtlewood** (1747 Northwest Hwy 101; tel: 541 994-5970).

Situated on its own decidedly non-tacky enclave is the **Westin Salishan Lodge** (tel: 541 764-2371; reservations recommended) at Gleneden Beach, recipient of the Centennial Medallion Award from the American Society of Landscape Architects in recognition for landscaping that preserves the natural environment.

In the middle of an unspoiled 750-acre (300-hectare) forest preserve overlooking **Siletz Bay**, Salishan is a luxuriously rugged resort offering fireplaces and panoramic views of **Cascade Head** from a number of private balconies. Dining is superb, and facilities include tennis courts, exercise rooms, hiking and jogging trails, plus a secluded beach. The 18-hole golf course resembles some of the finest Scottish links. Salishan's **Wine Cellar** is built in the old-world tradition with an extensive Pinot Noir collection. It is available for tastings, tours and small parties.

Whale capital

Depoe Bay ❽ (tel: 541 765-2889) claims to be the "whale-watching capital of the Oregon Coast" due to a resident pod of gray whales that makes its home here 10 months of the year. Interested visitors can **whale watch** from several on-shore observation spots or take a charter boat out to sea for a closer look. Charters run, weather permitting, every daylight hour seven days a week and there are several to choose from along the waterfront.

LEFT: the kayak were that-a-way.

Map on page 244

Considered the smallest natural navigable harbor in the world, an extensive sea wall runs the length of downtown Depoe Bay enabling visitors to shop or dine within view of the ocean. The waves here run beneath ancient lava beds forming natural tubes. During turbulent seas, wave pressure builds to spew geyser-like sprays as high as 60 ft (20 meters) into the air; this is particularly impressive at a place called **Spouting Horns**.

Cape Foulweather

Between Depoe Bay and Otter Rock, **Cape Foulweather** is one of the highest points on the Oregon Coast. This state wayside has good views but no facilities. Discovered and named in 1778 by Captain James Cook on his way back from Hawaii on his second voyage, it was at this point he first sighted mainland North America. A sudden storm greeted his arrival.

News of Cook's voyage to the Pacific Northwest stimulated American interest and years later led to the dispatch of the

Lewis & Clark Expedition. **The Lookout Observatory** and giftshop (tel: 541 765-2270), with a display of ships' wheels and driftwood characters, is perched atop this promontory, which rises 500 ft (152 meters) above sea level.

Midway between Depoe Bay and Newport, the aptly named **Devil's Punchbowl State Park** (tel: 541 265-9278; fee) gives a ringside seat on a frothy confrontation between rock and tide. Spread across a peninsula between the Pacific and Yaquina Bay is the effervescent town of **Newport ❾** (tel: 541 265-8801).

Newport is known for its picturesque harbor and graceful bridge, Dungeness crab and "let's-party-now" atmosphere. It is a budding upscale village, a strange bit of small-town Americana and a coastal treasure trove all in one. It's easy to get lost in the crowds and tourist traps, but then again it's not too difficult to find solace on a deserted section of beach somewhere not far away.

Late 19th-century charm is preserved

BELOW: Depoe Bay has a resident pod of gray whales.

in the **Old Bay Front**, a waterfront section of town that offers a mix of shops, galleries, canneries and restaurants. Particularly good are the latter, especially ones that serve local shrimp, oysters, crab and salmon. **Mariner Square** on Southwest Bay Boulevard is home to a waxworks museum, an undersea gardens attraction and Ripley's Believe-It-or-Not (tel: 541 265-2206). Cosmos Café and Gallery at 740 West Olive Street (tel: 541 265-7511) is a good place to savor the essence of the town. Both commercial and charter fishing boats sail from the harbor, and narrated whale-spotting tours are easy to find.

Window to the ocean

Across Yaquina Bay, the **Oregon Coast Aquarium** (2820 Ferry Slip Road; daily: July–Labor Day 9am–8pm otherwise 10am–5pm; tel: 541 867-3474; fee) promises to take up to three hours to view the 8,000 animals, including sharks and an inquisitive octopus. Four indoor aquarium galleries showcase coastal habitats via a

200-ft (60-meter) underwater tunnel; seals, sea lions and otters play in rocky pools. In North America's largest walk-through seabird aviary, birds soar and dive to the delight of all who watch them.

Within walking distance of the aquarium is the **Hatfield Marine Science Center of Oregon State University** (mid-May–early Sept daily 10am–6pm; Sept–mid-May Thur–Mon 10am–4pm; tel: 541 867-0100; fee), a window to the ocean for some 300,000 visitors each year. The center includes a public aquarium and hands-on exhibits offering one of the only places to touch a live tentacled octopus. The center houses many marine-related research projects.

The **Newport Performing Arts Center** (777 West Olive Street; presentations vary; tel: 503 265-9231) is set on 4½ acres (2 hectares) and hosts ballets, plays and special concerts.

Yaquina Bay and the 100-acre (40-hectare) **Yaquina Head** are at separate ends of town – both have lighthouses and **Interpretive Centers**. Gorgeous **Yaquina Bay lighthouse** (May–Sept daily 11am–5pm; Oct–Apr Sat–Sun noon–4pm; tel: 541 574-3116; donation) is a 40-ft (12-meter) tower with decorative light rising from a Cape Cod-style house, one of the few Pacific Coast lighthouses built with the lightkeeper's quarters inside the tower. It operated only from 1871 to 1874 before being replaced, though during that short interval it supposedly attracted hauntings by a young girl.

Tallest lighthouse

The **Yaquina Head Lighthouse** (daily noon–4pm, weather permitting; tel: 541 574-3116; fee) is active, having been lit continuously since 1873. Its tower is the tallest on the Oregon coast, soaring 93 ft (28 meters) into the air. Overall, the lighthouse stands 162 ft (50 meters) above sea level and can be seen by ocean-going vessels as far as 19 miles (30 km) away.

The two Yaquina lighthouses cap a host of interesting maritime sideshows battered and scoured by the waves. These help the region to be classified as an **Outstanding Natural Area**. Features include a man-

LEFT: hang gliding b the sea is unmissable.

Map on page 244

made tide pool, an experiment in the evolution of a small coastal ecosystem, and trails winding around a small mountain to its summit – where there are often few other humans; solitude seekers take note.

The high life

Between Newport and Florence, near the town of **Yachats** (pronounced *yah*-hotz; tel: 541 547-3530) is the highest point on the Oregon coast and its must-see interpretive stop, the **Cape Perpetua Visitors Center ⓾** (May Wed–Sun 10am–4pm; June–Labor Day daily 9am–5pm; then weekends only 10am–4pm; tel: 541 547-3289; free). While natural history information is delivered very nicely, the real attraction is the panoramic view. Nearby, the 2,700-acre (1,000-hectare) **Cape Perpetua Scenic Area** (daily; tel: 541 471-6500; fee) was set aside as part of the **Siuslaw National Forest** for its unique Sitka spruce rainforest. The most popular forest trail leads to the **Giant Spruce Tree** – a massive tree that's over 500 years old.

The **Heceta lighthouse** (tours by appointment; tel: 541 997-3851; fee) is 12 miles (20 km) north of the town of Florence. This working lighthouse is the brightest on the Oregon Coast, and is said to be the most-photographed lighthouse in the US. Built in 1894 and listed on the National Register of Historic Places, the **keeper's house** is an interpretive center and a bed-and-breakfast (tel: 541 547-3696; reservations required).

Sheltered by an enormous sea grotto, a rookery of non-migrating **Stellar sea lions** (*see page 259*) makes its home along the Oregon coast here. These often noisy and always smelly mammals shelter in the **Sea Lion Caves ⓫** (daily: July–Aug 8am–dusk Sept–June 9am– dusk; tel: 541 547-3111; fee) just north of Florence.

A different type of natural experience can be had at the **Darlingtonia Botanical Wayside**, 5-miles (8 km) north of Florence. It is best seen in early spring for the blossom or in summertime for the plants. The garden encompasses a short loop walk through a boggy area overlooking patches of *Darlingtonia*. These carnivorous plants, commonly known as

the "pitcher plant," trap insects with their sickly sweet smell.

Florence ⓬ (tel: 541 997-3128) is the City of Rhododendrons, exploding with vivid pink blossoms every spring. The area is good for hiking, bird-watching, horseback-riding and dune-buggy racing. The tastefully restored **Old Town** has interesting boutiques, and good coffeehouses and restaurants.

Other activities include fishing, swimming and boating at the 17 lakes surrounding the city. Jet-boat trips up the **Siuslaw River** are available during the summer. For a more leisurely pace, the *Westward Ho!* 1850s sternwheeler (Apr–Oct daily, 30- minute or 1-hour tours; tel: 541 997-9691; fee) cruises the river.

Jessie Honeyman State Park (tel: 541 997-3851; fee), south of Florence, is noted for its spring rhododendron blooms and sand dunes, which reach as high as 300 ft (90 meters). Among the 300-plus camping facilities are 10 yurts for overnight stays (tel: 800 452-568; reservations required).

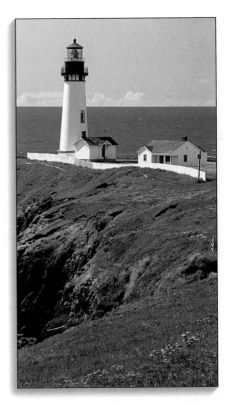

Umpqua Lighthouse State Park ⓭ sits in a stretch of towering sand dunes. The park includes picturesque **Lake Marie**; access to this small freshwater lake is provided for anglers, non-motorized boaters and swimmers. Two yurts and two log cabins (for reservations; tel: 800 452-5687; fee) are available to rent in the campground.

The **Umpqua River Lighthouse** (tours by arrangement; May–Sept; tel: 541 271-4631; fee) has a lens that emits a wonderful red and white flash.

Dramatic dunes

The **visitor center** at the **Oregon Dunes National Recreation Area** ⓮ (tel: 541 271-3611) is the place to gather information about amazing sand dunes that characterize the area, and also the dunes' fabulous recreational possibilities.

Higher than those of Africa's Sahara Desert, the Oregon dunes are the largest expanse of coastal sand dunes in the United States and stretch for 50 miles (80 km) between Florence and Coos Bay. Huge oceanfront dunes covering over 10,000 acres (4,000 hectares) and ranging up to 500 ft (150 meters) high form long banks up to 3 miles (5 km) deep. Facilities include the **Dunes Overlook**, 14 hiking trails, 11 parking areas within walking distance of 40 miles (64 km) of sandy beaches, nine day-use areas requiring a fee and three off-highway riding areas. **Dune buggy tours** can be arranged.

Scientists believe that most of the dunes were created in the last 10,000–15,000 years from erosion sediment that was transported by rivers and streams. Though the area's dunes make sand-boarding an obvious attraction, pounding surf, prolific estuaries, conifer forests and lakes teeming with fish make a perfect backdrop for anyone who loves sports, nature and wildlife viewing.

Oregon Dunes is a natural home to the Snowy plover (an endangered shorebird), egrets, bald eagles (themselves once threatened) and river otters.

BELOW: Oregon Dunes National Recreation Area.

Map on page 244

A trio of towns

South of the dunes, **Coos Bay ⑮** (tel: 800 824-8486) was founded in 1854 by J.C. Tolman of the Coos Bay Company and is known today as Oregon's "Bay Area." With the largest natural harbor between Seattle and San Francisco, Coos Bay is more than another quaint seaside tourist-town – it is a shipping and manufacturing center. **North Bend** is the sister city of Coos Bay, and the gateway to the fishing village of **Charleston**, 9 miles (14 km) west on Cape Arago Hwy.

Coos Bay is myrtlewood country. The myrtlewood tree grows only along the Oregon coast in a small, concentrated area, although a distant species of the same name does grow in Israel. At the **House of Myrtlewood** (1125 South 1st Street; tours daily 9am–5pm; tel: 541 267-7804), visitors can watch artisans saw myrtlewood logs, then use lathes to turn the wood into bowls and goblets.

Coos Bay Art Museum (235 Anderson; Tues–Fri 10am–4pm, Sat 1–4pm; tel: 541 267-3901; fee) contains nearly 400 artworks, many produced by local people.

Shore Acres State Park and Botanical Gardens (Cape Arago Hwy; daily 8am–dusk; tel: 541 888-3732; parking fee) was once the grand estate of pioneer lumberman and shipbuilder Louis B. Simpson, who built a luxurious summer home on a scenic bluff high above the Pacific Ocean. His home was destroyed by a fire in 1921 but its grounds today include a formal Japanese garden and beds of roses. The gardens were derelict until 1971, when they were lovingly restored.

Ghost shrimp

There are 4,300-acres (1,740-hectares) of tidal marshes, mudflats and open water channels preserved at **South Slough National Estuarine Research Reserve** (June–Aug daily 8:30am–4:30pm; Sept–May Sat–Sun 8:30am–4:30pm; tel: 541 888-5558; free) near Charleston. Great blue heron, elk and ghost shrimp are some of the unusual species found here.

BELOW: Sunset Bay State Park, near Coos Bay.

Around 14 miles (22 km) southwest of Coos Bay on a narrow coastal promontory, **Cape Arago State Park** (tel: 541 888-8867; free) is a fine place to whale-watch. Even if the gray ones decide not to make an appearance, this park and its coastal views are worth checking out, with wild vistas of pounding seas and glimpses of Oregon's distinctive seastacks.

Not far away and heading south is another lovely, camera-friendly warning beacon – the **Coquille River Lighthouse**. The lighthouse is not far from the small coastal town of Bandon.

Cranberries and cheese

Bandon ⑯ (also known as Bandon-by-the-Sea; tel: 541 347-9616) has sights and shops within walking distance of the renovated **Old Town** section, which is next to a boat basin. As Oregon's unofficial "Cranberry Capital," shops typically carry cranberry products harvested among the nearby 900 acres (350 hectares) of cranberry bogs.

The **Beach Loop** is particularly popular. It winds along the coast passing the **Garden of the Gods**, **Table Rock**, **Cat and Kittens Rock**, and **Elephant Rock**. The most impressive is **Face Rock**. This was reputedly the face of an Indian maiden frozen into stone by a spirit.

The **Bandon Cheese Factory** (on Hwy 101; tel: 541 347-2456; free samples) manufactures many kinds of cheddar, including those with added garlic, cajun spices, or onion. For a tour of the factory telephone ahead; for free samples drop in any time during opening hours.

Westerly points

South of Bandon, the Oregon coast reaches its westernmost point at **Cape Blanco**. The Cape was first noted by Europeans in the records of Spanish explorer Martin de Aguilar in January 1603. **Cape Blanco Lighthouse** (Apr–Oct Thur–Mon 10am– 3:30pm; tel: 541 756-0100; donation), built of brick in 1870, has been in use continuously since that time. The black sand at Cape Blanco is strikingly unlike the tan-colored sand along the rest of the coast.

Port Orford ⑰ (tel: 541 332-3681), the most westerly city in the contiguous United States, is considered Oregon's only true ocean harbor. A friendly and unpretentious town with panoramic ocean views, it has a long history as a fishing and lumber port. Fishing boats are unable to moor in the unprotected harbor so a daily activity involves hoisting fishing boats in and out of the wild ocean waves on a converted log boom.

The gigantic rock promontory of Battle Rock in **Battle Rock Park** dominates the waterfront shoreline. Site of a fierce battle between Indians and explorers, there is a steep trail to the beach, and to the top of the windy Rock.

Windsurfers have discovered the strong winds at **Floras Lake**, making it a popular location for boardheads. Ocean surfers ride the waves at **Hubbard Creek** and Battle Rock State Park. South of here, the coastal communities are considered the gateway to Rogue River Country (*see Rogue River Country, page 261*).

Map on page 244

LEFT: sunset o
❑ Bandon beach

Stellar Sea Lions

Stellar sea lions, also known as Northern sea lions *(Eumetopias jubatus)*, were once a common sight along the Oregon coast. Now, as their numbers decline, the Sea Lion Caves offer a rare chance to observe this, the largest of the sea lion species. Visitors descend fairly unobtrusively down a 208-ft (63-meter) elevator shaft, into a water-level sea grotto where these leviathans have sheltered for eons. At the bottom, they emerge inside a huge natural sea cave to encounter varying numbers of wild, decidedly odiferous, Steller sea lions, many with their black pups in tow.

The Stellar sea lion is named after George Wilhelm Steller, a German naturalist who accompanied Danish explorer Vitus Bering in 1741 on his second Alaskan expedition. Stellers have a bulky build and a thick neck resembling a lion's mane, hence the name. California sea lions, often confused with Stellars, live along the California coast and north as far as Canada's Vancouver Island. Various "Californias" do stop by the Sea Lion Caves, however, usually from late fall to early spring; they are smaller and darker in color.

The Stellar is a carnivore feeding on rockfish, sculpins, capelin, flatfish, squid, octopus, shrimp and crabs; sometimes a sea lion will even devour a northern fur seal. Biologists often find pebble-size stones in their stomachs; however it is uncertain whether the stones aid digestion, or are swallowed accidentally – possibly in play. They use their long front flippers for propulsion and their hind flippers for steering under water. On land, they pull hind flippers up under their body and "roll walk" on all four flippers.

The world population of Steller sea lions is estimated at 40,000, with about 500 living in California and 200 at the Sea Lion Caves. The overall population has dropped by 80 percent in the past 30 years. They have been a threatened species since 1990, with the Western US stock listed as endangered seven years later. Researchers believe one factor in the decline may be dwindling fish stocks.

Stellars breed and bear young in May and June; gestation is nine months. It was once assumed a Steller bore a pup each year much like its cousin, the Alaska fur seal. However, it appears that females bear every other year. Mothers stay with their pups for one or two weeks, then divide their attention between hunting and nursing. Pups nurse for a year, though some continue up to three years.

During the breeding season, bulls of up to 2,000 lbs (900 kg) lounge outside the caves, roaring and bleating. Breeding resumes 10–14 days after a pup is born. Driving weaker males away, dominant males maintain harems of 15 to 30 cows and breed with all. Until the harem structure dissolves, dominant bulls keep constant vigil over their females; bulls do not leave their harems – even for food – for up to three months.

Females display no such loyalty. When a storm breaks up a harem, the bull may never recover all his chosen mates. Therefore, much of his work is in keeping his females together. The ordeal causes the big bulls to lose weight, and by the end of the breeding season, they are exhausted. They generally spend the remainder of the summer by themselves, resting and regaining strength. ❑

RIGHT: both Stellar sea lions and California sea lions are visitors to Oregon's Sea Lion Caves.

ROGUE RIVER COUNTRY

*The Rogue is one of eight rivers protected by
the Wild and Scenic Rivers Act. Hike or take a jetboat to
Hellgate Canyon, Rainie Falls Trail and Whisky Creek Cabin*

**Map
on page
262**

The Rogue River flows 215 miles (346 km), from Lost Lake in the Cascade Mountain Range and through the Coast Range to the Pacific Ocean. One of the original eight rivers included in the Wild and Scenic Rivers Act of 1968, it is surrounded by forested mountains, rugged boulders and rock-lined banks. Steelhead and salmon fishing and extraordinary wildlife viewing have made the Rogue a national treasure. Popular activities include white-water rafting, jet-boat tours, scenic driving, hiking and picnicking.

Wild and scenic

To understand the river from a recreational perspective, think of it as a straight line divided into thirds. Each third of the river, for these purposes, runs from left to right (west to east). The first third starts in the west by Gold Beach on the Oregon Coast. It is designated the **Scenic Rogue** and is best traveled by jetboat.

The middle section is more challenging, and is known as the **Wild Rogue**. It passes through the Coast Range. Accessible by white-water floatboat or paddleboat or to experienced hikers only, this is the 84-mile (135-km) stretch designated by Congress as the "National Wild and Scenic" portion of the Rogue. Placesinclude Rainie Falls Trail, Hellgate Canyon, Whisky Creek Cabin, Mule Creek Canyon and Blossom Bar. This wild section extends from 11 miles (18 km) east of Gold Beach to 7 miles (11 km) west of Grants Pass.

The final section, which is known locally as the **Hellgate Recreation Area**, is accessible to everyone by road or jetboat. It ends near Grants Pass. Back-packing is popular in this area, and many companies have set up shop providing organized trips (for Rogue River backpacking information tel: 541 479-5301, or write to Siskiyou National Forest, PO Box 440, 200 Northeast Greenfield Road, Grants Pass, 97526). To ensure the company you select is a certified one – very important, as extreme sports are often part of the package – contact the Medford Bureau of Land Management (tel: 541 618-2273).

The light plays tricks

In southwestern Oregon, the light plays tricks. Moisture-laden air rolls in from the Pacific Ocean, and fog is a constant companion. It drapes the hillsides with a translucent blanket, painting the landscape like a movie scene shot deliberately out of focus. On the coast, Gold Beach gets an average of 81 inches (205 cm) of rain each year, while inland Grants Pass receives only 31 inches (78 cm); to stay

LEFT: Jacksonville is an old Gold-Rush town. **RIGHT:** Oregon residents claim to drink even more coffee than Seattleites.

dry while playing on the Rogue, approach it from Grants Pass. Viewed from a high vantage point, the succession of valleys seem to roll away toward the horizon. In the valleys, little communities – all enjoying the bounties of the land and the richness of rural living – offer diversions from the roar of the mighty river.

Scenic Rogue

Gold Beach ❶ (tel: 541 247-7526), just 37 miles (60 km) north of California, is situated along the Oregon coast at the western mouth of the Rogue River. Of the three river classifications – wild, scenic and recreational – this section is classified as scenic, meaning it is accessible by water, but is not wilderness.

Jet-boat trips from Gold Beach travel upriver to **Agness** (32 miles/50 km, the "short trip") or 104 miles (165 km) to **Paradise** and the notorious rapids of **Blossom Bar** (the "long trip"). The history of the short trip is part of postal service lore: mail boats still deliver the US mail to the

remote village of Agness, just as they have ever since 1895. For more information and scheduled departures, contact **Mail Boats Hydro-Jets** (tel: 541 247-7033).

Another popular operator is **Jerry's Rogue Jets** (tel: 800 451-3645), who call themselves "the original Rogue River Jet Boat trip and the first Jet Boat Tour in America."

Roseburg

South of Eugene on Interstate 5, **Roseburg ❷** (Chamber of Commerce, tel: 541 672-9731) is situated deep within commercial forest lands. It claims the largest old-growth timber stand in the world and is the gateway to two recreational areas: the **Hundred Valleys** of the **Umpqua National Forest** (tel: 541 672-6601) and the Cascade Mountains. **Downtown Roseburg**, located directly on the South Umpqua River, has art galleries and antique and gift shops, plus a series of original outdoor murals.

Nearby **Henry Estate Winery** has a

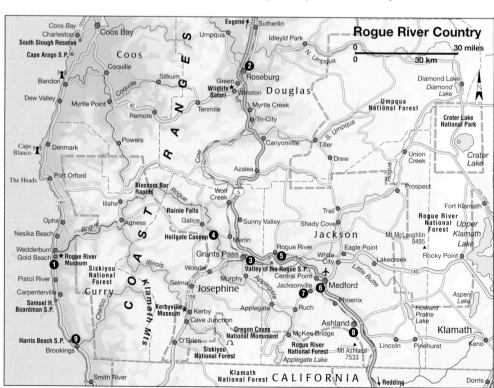

Map
on page
262

pretty flower garden, while **La Garza Cellars and Gourmet Kitchen** serves lunch and homemade bread with their vintages. Only 6 miles (10 km) from Roseburg, the 600-acre (240-hectare) **Wildlife Safari** (Safari Road, Winston; daily, hours vary; tel: 541 679-6761; fee) is a terrific drive-through park where the people stay in cages (cars) and the cheetahs, lions, tigers and bears roam around freely.

Continuing south on I-5, be sure to stop at the rustic **Wolf Creek Inn** (exit 76; tel: 541 866-2474), an old stagecoach pitstop built in the 1870s. Food is prepared with the freshest ingredients, meat is smoked by the hotel's owners, and the Oktoberfest celebration is legendary. Eight overnight rooms are perfect for travelers who enjoy the atmosphere of a bygone era.

The Wolf Creek is the oldest continuously operated hotel in the Pacific Northwest. Jack London completed his novel *Valley of the Moon* here. The hotel's register also includes the signatures of Hollywood stars Mary Pickford, Douglas Fairbanks, Clark Gable, Carol Lombard and Orson Welles.

White-water rafting

Known as the "white-water rafting capital" of Oregon, **Grants Pass ❸** (information, tel: 541 476-7717; events hotline, tel: 800 460-7700) is located directly on the Rogue River about 60 miles (100 km) north of the California border. The surrounding area inspired several Zane Grey novels. The downtown area recently earned a National Historic District designation for its fine older buildings and homes, plus its antique shops, ice-cream parlors and sidewalk espresso stands.

On Saturdays, the **Growers' Market** (4th and F streets; Mar–Nov Sat only 9am–1pm) has locally grown fruits and vegetables, plus crafts made by local artisans. **Riverside Park** is an unhurried place to picnic and walk along the river.

The **Wildlife Images Rehabilitation and Education Center** (11845 Lower

BELOW: boat afloat on the Rogue River.

River Road; tours daily by appointment; tel: 541 476-0222; donation) originally began as a rehabilitation station for birds of prey but now includes a program to aid injured or orphaned wild animals, including bears, cougars and raccoons.

Walkers can discover views of the Rogue River from **Valley of the Rogue State Park** (Exit 45B off I-5) and its mile-long hiking trail. Besides a jetboat, probably the most exciting way to view the surroundings is aboard a hot-air balloon: try **Oregon Adventures Aloft** (8959 Rogue River Hwy; tel: 541 582-2200).

The easiest place to experience the Rogue is along the stretch of river near Grants Pass called **Hellgate Canyon ❹**. It has 11 boat ramps on 27 miles (43 km) of river. One operator, **Hellgate Jetboat Excursions** (953 Southeast 7th Street, Grants Pass; tel: 541 479-7204) offers a 2-hour scenic canyon tour; a 5-hour rough water trip; or a 4-hour dinner trip, with the meal served downriver at an old homestead. There is a good café at their headquarters, too.

Wild Rogue

Dozens of outfitters offer various trips along the **Wild Rogue**, most of them starting from the nearby town of **Merlin**. This section of the river is usually traveled in three to four days, in row boats or paddle boats. Inflatable kayaks – called orange torpedoes by some – have become popular in recent years because they allow more freedom, maneuverability and thrills than a simple raft; they are also certain to soak occupants to the skin after the first serious rapids.

The wilderness has 33 miles (53 km) of Class III (or less) rapids. These include roaring **Rainie Falls**, plus the breathtaking scenery at **Mule Creek Canyon** and **Blossom Bar**. There are only two boat ramps, **Grave Creek** and **Foster Bar**, in this stretch of the river. Anyone planning a guided float trip must use a licensed commercial outfitter.

For information on running the Wild Rogue River visit the **Visitor Center** (14335 Galice Road, Merlin; tel: 541 479-

BELOW: jetboats are the speedy way to experience the Wild Rogue.

VORTEX HOUSE OF MYSTERY

Between Grants Pass and Medford is the curious community of Gold Hill. Since the 1930s, believers and skeptics alike have made the 4-mile (6-km) trek to the Oregon Vortex and House of Mystery (4303 Sardine Creek Road, Gold Hill; several tours daily June–Aug 8:30am–4:45pm; different opening times other months, so call before visiting; tel: 541 855-1543), to observe an alleged geophysical phenomenon. Within a small spherical area, twisted trees lean toward magnetic north, and compasses and light meters deviate from their true settings. In a quiet area devoid of wildlife, at an old, tilted office, brooms stand on end, tennis balls and bottles roll uphill, and normally straight-standing people lean 7° north.

Contrary to the laws of perspective, as a person on a level platform recedes toward magnetic south, they appear taller; as they come closer, toward magnetic north, they become shorter. Unlike in other "magnetic" areas around the world, it is claimed that these are not optical illusions, and photographs have been taken of the effects. Scientists have theories about why this magnetic activity occurs, but no one knows for sure. The Oregon Vortex and House of Mystery has been featured on various Discovery Channel programs and *The X-Files*.

Map on page 262

3735). From May 15 to November 15, each authorized outfitter may launch a trip only on specific days.

Trials and trails

The 40-mile (64-km) **Rogue River National Recreation Trail** lies at the heart of the National Wild and Scenic Rogue River Canyon. The average hiker takes about five days to complete it. The US Forest Service requires all hikers to obtain a Northwest Forest Pass (tel: 800 270-7504) and to read the instructions available at all Forest Service offices, before embarking on this trail. The trail runs from Grave Creek to Illahe. Hazards to look out for include bears, poison oak and rattlesnakes. **Affordable Shuttles** (1406 Southwestern G Street, #A Grants Pass; tel: 541 479-1042; fee) will take hikers to designated start points.

In the fall of 1846, the first emigrant wagon train from Fort Hall, Idaho, traveled the southern route of the Oregon Trail, which was known as the **Applegate Trail** *(see map on page 16)*. Martha Leland Crowley, a 16-year-old, died of typhoid fever during the encampment here and was buried on the north side of what was to become known as **Grave Creek**. The **Applegate Trail Interpretive Center** (I-5, exit 71; Wed–Sun 10am–5pm; tel: 541 472-8545; fee) in Sunny Valley, 14 miles (22 km) north of Grants Pass, tells this poignant story. The **Fireside Theatre** features a dramatic reenactment of the event, plus a more light-hearted interpretation of the stories of the pioneer settlers, the discovery of gold, the impact of the stage line, and the building of the railroad.

If history isn't your passion, you could instead choose to visit a winery in Southern Oregon's Rogue Valley, considered to be the oldest wine region in the Northwest. One such place is the **Valley View Winery** (1000 Upper Applegate Road, near Jacksonville and Ruch; Apr–Dec daily 11am–6pm; Jan–Mar Wed–Sun noon–6pm; tel: 541 899-1001).

BELOW: south of Gold Beach, with Cape Sebastian on the horizon.

The town of **Rogue River** ❺ (Chamber of Commerce, tel: 541 582-0242) is in the heart of a region where three mountain ranges meet: the Cascades, the Siskiyous and the Coast Range. Off I-5 east of Grants Pass, it is nestled along the banks of the Rogue – surprisingly placid here – and just 1,000 ft (300-meters) above sea level. This town is another good source of information and outfitters, the better to test the challenges of its namesake.

Palmerton Arboretum (tel: 541 776-7001; free) in West Evans Creek Road displays 40 species of trees and shrubs from around the world, such as cedars from the Mediterranean and redwoods from the Pacific coast. The collection, started in 1930, has trees from famous Civil War battlefields, bamboo from Hawaii, and specimens from England, Italy, Spain and Germany. The city's other parks – **Coyote Evans**, **Fleming** and **Anna Classick** – have facilities for playing horseshoes and tennis, or boat ramps for those missing the water.

Medford

Roughly 26 miles (40 km) southeast of Grants Pass, **Medford** ❻ (tel: 541 779-4847), an industrial, retail and professional center, is located on Interstate 5, just 27 miles (43 km) north of the California-Oregon border.

Situated in the heart of the attractive Rogue River Valley, this is where pear orchards bloom profusely in the springtime, surrounded by snow-capped peaks. Succulent pears have helped make the Rogue Valley famous the world over, and distributors have been packing and shipping gift baskets for more than 60 years.

The elevation is 1,380 ft (420 meters) above sea level; the average rainfall is 19 inches (48.2 cm); and temperatures vary from 31–41°F (0–5°C) in winter to 88–100°F (31–37°C) in summer. The timber industry, agriculture and tourism are basic to the local economy.

Years ago the Rogue River Valley was home to the Shasta, Takilma and Athabascan Indians. Then in 1852 word of gold

BELOW: framed.

brought a throng of pioneers in search of a fortune, followed by farmers lured by its fertile soil. Small towns sprang up overnight, and the California-Oregon Stage Road grew dusty with increasing loads of supplies.

It wasn't until 1883 that the Oregon & California Railroad reached Southern Oregon. Jacksonville, the county seat, expected to be the next station between Portland and Sacramento. But when the railroad company requested a $25,000 "bonus" for the privilege, the town fathers refused to pay. The railroad built a station at Middle Ford on Bear Creek instead. A new townsite was plotted and the name shortened to Medford.

By 1896, Medford was a major shipping and railroad center. The large **Southern Oregon History Center** (weekdays 9am–5pm, Sat 1–5pm; tel: 541 773-6536; free) has historic displays and research material; the **Crater Rock Museum** (2002 Scenic Avenue, Central Point; Tues–Sat 10am–4pm; tel: 541 664-6081; free)

displays samples of the county's rocks and minerals. For anyone who loves a hot-air adventure, the surrounding country is gorgeous when viewed via **Sunrise Balloon Adventures** (tel: 541 776-2284; reservations recommended).

Pears and roses

At **Butte Creek Mill and Country Store** (401 Royal Avenue, Eagle Point; Mon–Sat 9am–5pm, closed: holidays; tel: 541 826-3531; free), a water-powered grist mill, listed in the National Historic Register, still produces wholegrain flours and baked goodies. There is a museum, parks and a covered bridge nearby, dating mostly from around the 1870s.

Harry and David's Country Village (1314 Center Drive; scheduled tours, Mon–Fri 9:15am, 10:30am, 12:30pm, 1:45pm; tel: 877 322-8000 or 541 776-2277; fee refundable on a purchase) offers minibus tours of their premises. If you know H and D's catalogue, you'll love this tour: rich chocolate, velvety cheese-

cake, buttery fruit galettes – all with an emphasis on pears. The first stop is the packing house to view the company's high-tech automated pear sorter; next, the assembly lines where thousands of gift baskets are packed; last the bakery, where confections are made.

The singular **Jackson and Perkins** retail outlet store (tel: 541 776-2388) is right next door. **Jackson and Perkins Test and Display Garden** (2836 Pacific Hwy; tel: 541 776-2277), a 125-year-old mail-order nursery, has a lovely garden to stroll through. The country's largest suppliers of mail-order roses, a Jackson and Perkins rose is said to be planted somewhere in the US every 30 seconds.

The central location of Medford makes the town important to anyone wanting to explore the natural wonders of the region. It is the starting place to visit two of Oregon's scenic treasures: Crater Lake National Park *(see page 314)* and the Oregon Caves National Monument *(see page 318)*. It is also the entry point to the 630,000-acre (255,00-hectare) **Rogue River National Forest** (tel: 541 858-2200), which includes 40 campgrounds and picnic areas, plus 400 miles (650 km) of trails for hiking, mountain biking and horseback-riding.

The **Pacific Crest National Scenic Trail** runs the entire length of the forest, through the remote back country of **Sky Lakes Wilderness** along the spine of the high Cascades, and then extends westward along the crest of the Siskiyou Mountains. Other remote sections of the forest include the **Rogue-Umpqua Divide Wilderness** and, to the south, the **Red Buttes Wilderness** in the rugged headwaters of the Applegate River.

The town that gold built

Jacksonville ❼ (tel: 541 899-8118) is about 7 miles (11 km) west of Medford. In 1966, the entire town was put on the National Register of Historic Landmarks. "Living History" is reflected in the **Peter Britt House**, the **Nunan House**, the **Beekman House** (352 East California Street;

BELOW: Jacksonville church.

Map
n page
262

mid-May–early Sept daily 1–5pm; tel: 541 773-6536; fee) with interpreters in costume, and the **Jacksonville Children's Museum** (206 South 5th Street; June– Sept daily 10am–5pm; Oct–May Tues–Sun 10am–5pm; tel: 541 773-6536; fee) located in an old jail and containing artifacts from Indians and settlers. There are inns and B&Bs in historic houses that reflect the elegance of an earlier era; also in town are good bookstores and antique shops.

In 1851, gold was discovered at nearby Rich Gulch, and saloons and gambling halls quickly sprang up. Later, merchants – wealthy from supplying miners and, later, farmers – built grand mansions. After the town lost its position as a stop for the new railroad in 1883, Jacksonville remained relatively untouched and unchanged.

The long bar of California Street's **Bella Union** restaurant and saloon, backed by a wall mural depicting a street scene from Jacksonville's gold era, evokes the long-ago sound of miners' boots clumping into the boom town. The **McCully House Inn** (240 East California Street; tel: 541 899-1942) is a gracious place to eat a very good brunch, lunch or dinner.

Perhaps because of its proximity to Shakespeare-crazy Ashland, Jacksonville enthusiastically sponsors the Peter Britt Music Festivals (June–Sept; tel: 541 779-0847; fee) featuring classical, bluegrass and world music performed by nationally and internationally known artists in Jacksonville's **Britt Gardens**.

Ashland

The combination of tacos, juicy pears, country music, high tech and Shakespeare may seem unlikely, but in **Ashland ❸** (tel: 541 482-3486) just north of the California border, this is everyday life. The city is prettily sited 2,000 ft (600 meters) above sea level, with **Mount Ashland** looming above the city to the south, and the snow-capped Cascade Range lying about 30 miles (48 km) to the east.

Although this attractive town has fewer than 20,000 residents, it is quite ambi-

tious. As well as a $5 million plan to build a high-speed network from its existing 12-mile (16-km) fiber optic ring to connect schools, businesses and citizens, Ashland seems able to offer qualities of cultural life many small towns only dream about: a major Shakespearean theater company, several small theater companies, art galleries, museums and a "down home" feeling – all surrounded by mountain peaks.

Backstage tours

Ashland is known for its long-standing support of the arts. The **Oregon Shakespeare Festival** (OSF; season mid-Feb–Nov, 11 plays in three theaters; June–Oct, two plays in an outdoor Elizabethan-style theater; tel: 541 482-4331; fee) presents quality productions on an annual basis *(see page 271)*.

At the **Exhibit Center** (15 South Pioneer Street; tel: 541 482-4331; fee) visitors can review the OSF's history. Backstage tours, lecture series, informal talks, focus classes and pre-play prefaces provide additional opportunities to enrich the Shakespeare Festival experience. **Ashland's Bed-and-Breakfast Network** (tel: 800 944-0329) is a cooperative of 31 member inns which span a variety of architectural styles and decor, including rooms, suites, cottages and carriage houses. Be sure to book early if you're interested in staying in Ashland during the festival; many of these places are cute and desirable.

With its warm summers and year-round mild climate, Ashland is an excellent place for gardens and gardeners. The climate is also conducive to growing grapes, and there are a couple of good **wineries**. The 100-acre (40-hectare) **Lithia Park** (daily 8am–5pm; tel: 541 488-5340) offers an assemblage of native, ornamental and exotic plants, a Woodland Trail, a rose garden and a delicate, Japanese-style garden. The Ashland area is also on a flyway for thousands of gorgeous, migrating birds, and in the months from December to February, it is home to a large concentration of rarely seen bald eagles.

The lower left-hand corner

Brookings ❾ (tel: 541 469-3181), just north of the California border on the Oregon coast, calls itself "Oregon's banana belt" and is also the nation's major producer of Easter lilies and daffodils. Five varieties of azaleas can be seen at **Azalea City Park** east of Hwy 101. Choice locations for collecting driftwood and watching gray whales migrate are **Harris Beach State Park** and **Samuel H. Boardman State Park** (tel: 541 469-2021).

In addition, there are recreational regions for serious hikers venturing into the 180,000-acre (73,000-hectare) **Kalmiopsis Wilderness** (Chetco Ranger Disrict; tel: 541 469-2196). This wilderness – named for a unique shrub, the *Kalmiopsis leachiana*, a relic from before the ice age and one of the oldest members of the heath *(ericaceae)* family – is characterized by deep rough canyons, sharp rock ridges and clear rushing streams and rivers.

The **Chetco**, the **Illinois** and the **North Fork Smith** Wild and Scenic rivers flow through the Kalmiopsis, and offer opportunities for river-based recreation. ❏

Map on page 262

LEFT: downtown Ashland

The Bard of Ashland

But be not afraid of greatness: some are born great, some achieve greatness and some have greatness thrust upon them.
        – Twelfth Night, or *What You Will*,
                                        act 2, scene 5

When Angus Bowmer left Bellingham Normal School in 1923, he had a teaching certificate and an idea. After earning a University of Washington master's degree, he began teaching theater in a tiny southern Oregon town called Ashland. In 1935, he approached Ashland's city fathers with the idea of presenting not one, but two Shakespearean performances. City officials, nervous about this unorthodox request, pressured Bowmer into presenting a series of boxing matches during the daytime and at intermission to make sure the festival broke even.

Even then, Angus was not deterred. He insisted that the word "annual" be used in promoting the first festival. That first weekend, July 3–4, 1935, the revenue from *Twelfth Night* and *The Merchant of Venice* made up for the losses incurred by the boxing matches. From that unexpected beginning, the Oregon Shakespeare Festival (OSF) has become one of largest professional regional theater companies and enduring festivals in the US.

With its 1958 production of *Troilus and Cressida*, the festival completed the entire Shakespeare canon for the first time; with its 1978 production of *Timon of Athens*, it finished its second full cycle; with the 1998 completion of round three, the festival had entertained more than 8 million theatergoers. In 2000, during its nine-month season, the Tony Award-winning OSF presented a total of 764 performances of 11 plays; that year's attendance reached 380,101 or 95 percent of capacity. Its long years of success are due in large part to founder Angus Bowmer's conviction that the festival belongs to its audience; its spirit is also firmly rooted in the enthusiasm of the community.

From 1935 until today, audiences and artists have benefited from a style of theater now rapidly vanishing: rotating repertory. It

may have been just three performances of two plays in 1935, but they were produced by a single troupe. Today, plays are still produced by one acting company, but are now performed in a variety of different venues.

In 1959, an improved 1,188-seat outdoor Elizabethan stage opened; in 1970, the 600-seat Angus Bowmer Theater was inaugurated; in 1977, the intimate 140-seat Black Swan opened. In 2002, the latter became a rehearsal hall, replaced by the as-yet-unnamed $10 million new theatre with a capacity of 350. Local residents continue to participate in the theater's activities, acting as ushers and ticket sellers, and Ashland itself now has nine other accomplished theater groups.

Bowmer, known as "the Bard of Ashland," died in 1979, after producing all 37 of Shakespeare's plays and performing 32 Shakespearean roles. He earned three honorary doctorates in fine arts, was named to the National Council of the Arts and was recognized by the US Institute for Theatre Technology for his lifetime contribution to the performing arts. ❏

RIGHT: a scene from the Oregon Shakespeare Festival, held every year since 1935.

Map
on page
274

OREGON CASCADES

*A series of mountain journeys
takes in dramatic rimrock cliffs, volcanic formations,
sparkling Alpine lakes and vast, almost unimaginably empty spaces*

The Cascades form a mountainous north–south spine traversing the entire state of Oregon. They divide the state into the western "wet" side and the eastern "dry" side. This Oregon is a place of vast, almost unimaginable spaces, where enormous expanses of high desert stretch out to meet sky and land. It is also Native territory.

Warm Springs Indian Reservation ❶ comprises over 1,000 sq. miles (2,500 sq. km) of North Central Oregon. It extends from snowcapped Mount Jefferson and the summit of the Cascade Mountains to the deep canyons and rushing waters of the **Deschutes River**.

The reservation comes by its name honestly; as well as having springs, the average maximum temperature in July was and remains 92°F (33°C). The land today is but a small portion of the 640,000 acres (25,000 hectares) of territory ceded to the US government under the Treaty of 1855. The nearly 4,000 members of the Confederated Tribes who live here trace their ancestry to the Wascos, upper and lower Deschutes bands of Walla Wallas (Warm Springs) and Northern Pauite people, who established residence on the reservation more than 140 years ago.

These people have always derived their physical and spiritual sustenance from the region's rich resources – berries and roots, water, fish and game. They are committed to preserving these resources and the traditions that surround them for the well-being of future generations.

Kah-Nee-Tah

The main visitors' facility on the Warm Springs Reservation is the **Kah-Nee-Tah Lodge and Indian Head Casino** (tel: 800 831-0100; reservations recommended), a luxury lodge named after the Native woman, Kah-Nee-Tah, who once owned the site. "Bask in the warmth... of an ancient tradition," the brochure urges, though with so many modern conveniences, the word "ancient" is hardly appropriate. The arrow-shaped hotel is staffed by members of the Warm Springs tribe who have contributed to the decor with rugs and pottery, as well as lending a traditional touch to the food.

In addition to the 139-room lodge, accommodations range from the **Kah-Nee-Ta Village** recreational vehicle (RV) park to rentable apartments, cottages and camping spaces. If roughing it is your idea of fun, check into one of the 20 wood-frame, canvas-covered, unfurnished **teepees**. You can still pop over to the spectacular lodge to use the heated Olympic-size swimming pool.

LEFT: Middle Sister Mountain. **RIGHT:** Scott Lake, near McKenzie Summit.

Horseback riding, fishing and golfing are additional possibilities, and kayak float trips (tel: 541 553-1604; fee) can be organized. For centuries, the hot springs here were used for their soothing and healthy mineral waters. Today, **Spa Wanapine** offers aromatherapy, reflexology, facials and manicures. The resort staff also prepare salmon bakes, the food of the Columbia River tribes. Periodically, visitors are given a chance to experience ceremonial dancing and music. In the panoramic **Juniper Room** restaurant, the house specialty is bird-in-clay, a Cornish game hen with a bread and fruit stuffing encased in flour-clay and baked for three hours. It is presented with a mallet so that diners can crack it open.

All-Indian rodeo

In late June, during **Pi-Ume-Sha** (events; tel: 541 553-1196; fee) the tribes celebrate with a weekend of dancing, stick games, an endurance horse race and an all-Indian rodeo. The public is invited. Ceremonial events, including the **Root Feast** and **Huckleberry Feast**, are also open to the public, although it is best to seek an invitation from the tribes' Public Relations or Culture and Heritage departments (tel: 541 553-1338) before showing up.

The Root Feast is usually held the first Sunday in April; the Huckleberry Feast is celebrated in early August. The date of first-fruit celebrations are determined by the maturity of the roots and berries; feasts are declared by the tribes' Elder Woman as the time to give thanks and to begin the harvest.

These celebrations of life represent a layering of old and new, age and youth, cultural preservation and modern innovation. Perhaps it's the mountains that symbolize it best – their permanence and peacefulness, their raw beauty, the signs of upheaval and change. "Faith and patience have held our people together since the first contact with Europeans," a contemporary Wasco chief notes, "They have been our strength. I see a resurgence of traditional life. Faith and patience, together with technology, are bringing much of what we lost back to life."

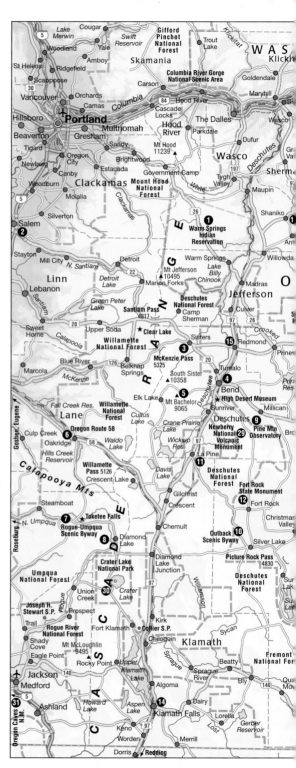

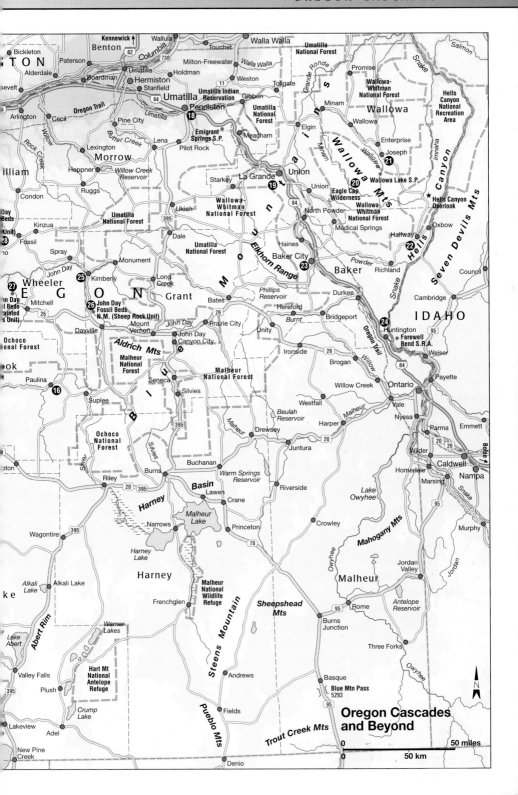

Oregon Cascades
and Beyond

50 miles

50 km

Medicine dances and storytelling revive spiritual needs in the shortened days of winter. To observe Native American culture outside of festival months, visit the **Museum at Warm Springs** (tel: 541 553-3331; fee). This $4.5 million facility offers a display of heirlooms, ceramics, baskets and photographs. Elsewhere on the reservation, any time from dawn to dusk, visitors can stop at the **Warm Springs National Fish Hatchery** (tel: 541 553-1692; free), where interpretive materials tell of the importance of salmon to the tribal community.

Some Warm Springs fishermen still catch salmon in the traditional way at **Shears Bridge**. In season, dip nets are lowered from platforms that are balanced precariously on the edge of the riverbank, while white water rushes below. At one time, immense runs of these silvery, darting fish enabled the tribes to survive.

Warm Springs makes a great base from which to explore the surrounding wilderness. The **Pacific Crest National Scenic**

Trail winds its way around the peaks of the Cascade Range at the very edge of the reservation, heading north into the wilds of **Mount Hood National Forest** and south into the fabulous **Three Sisters Wilderness Area**.

Salem to Sisters

The first mountain route starts in **Salem ❷** on **State Highway 22**, which threads through the Cascade foothills, past stands of Douglas fir the size of redwood trees and numerous reservoirs, all the while following the **North Santiam River**. This area could be considered a northern Cascades "Lakes District," with some four dozen mountain lakes scattered among scruffy pines. The region of lava buttes and alpine meadows is set against the snow-clad slopes of the mountains and planted with Christmas trees.

In the area is **Breitenbush Hot Springs Retreat** (tel: 503 854-3321), a consciousness-raising conference center nestled in an old-growth forest, where people come for the healing waters, to take a workshop or simply to experience the wilderness. In a place with trees as old as the ground they're rooted in, and a state where many people are more concerned with conservation that consumerism, it's not surprising to find a resort committed to holistic healing without the flash.

From here there is a good distant view of the second-highest peak in the Cascades, 10,495-ft (3,200-meter) **Mount Jefferson**. This peak is best viewed on a spur road past the small town of **Detroit** up the **Breitenbush River** in the **Ollalie Scenic Area** (tel: 503 630-6861; user fee). State Highway 22 then picks up Santiam Pass 20/126, part of the McKenzie Pass & Santiam Pass Scenic Byway, on its way to Sisters. This marks the end of the Salem to Sisters passage through the Cascades.

Two passes, one byway

The second scenic Cascade route consists of two connecting mountain passes forming a single route designated the **McKenzie Pass & Santiam Pass Scenic Byway**. It meanders through the Cascade Moun-

LEFT: fishing with dip nets Shears Bridge

Map on page 274

tains among 10,000-ft (3,000-meter) peaks, over jagged lava flows, along gurgling rivers, and through the old-growth stands of two national forests. This scenic 82-mile (132-km) loop is easily driven in 3–5 hours – unless, of course, you have your camera, fishing pole or tent in the car. Several parks and campgrounds are located along the route.

When you are about to drive these connecting passes, please do consider the following: **Oregon Route 242** is closed to vehicles over 35 ft (10 meters) long, and trailers are not allowed at all. It is often closed in winter. Medical services and hospitals are located only in the towns of Bend and Redmond; good vehicle services are available only in the town of Sisters. Be sure to start out with a full tank of gasoline, because you never know when you might need it.

The McKenzie Pass & Santiam Pass Scenic Byway is accessible from several cities west of the Cascades, including Salem, Albany, Corvallis and Eugene,

plus one location east of the Cascades – Bend. For the purposes of this description think of the route as a circle divided into quadrants. The start point, Sisters, is located at the right hand (east) point on the circumference. The route travels in a clockwise direction from here.

Gateway to the Cascades

Sisters ❸ (Visitor Center, 164 Northeast Alma Street; June–Sept daily; walking tours 2pm; free) is an enchanting Old-West-style village. At an elevation of 3,100 ft (944 meters), it offers knockout views of the **Three Sisters** peaks. Once a lumber- producing town, it is known as the "Gateway to the Cascades" and is famous for its handmade quilts. The downtown area has been artfully renovated, and is a fun place to shop, with many specialty stores and galleries.

Afterwards, rustle up a picnic lunch, fill up your tank, and head west past **llama ranches** on Rt 242 (closed in winter), ascending into the Deschutes National

Forest *(see page 281)*. The 242,400-acre (98,000-hectare) Three Sisters Wilderness (Sisters Ranger District, tel: 541 549-2111) lies partly in Deschutes and partly in Willamette National forests.

Sisters under the skin

Budding geologists will find it interesting to note that the Three Sisters area contains five large volcanic cones of Quaternary age – North Sister, Middle Sister, South Sister, Broken Top and Mount Bachelor. North Sister and Broken Top are deeply dissected and have probably been inactive for at least 100,000 years.

Middle Sister is younger than North Sister, and was active in late Pleistocene times, but not in post-glacial times. South Sister is the least dissected, and its basaltic summit cone has a well-preserved crater. Most of South Sister predates the late Wisconsin glaciation period and so is older than 25,000 years; however, eruptions have occurred as recently as 2,000 years ago.

Lava and lots of it

Oregon Route 242 follows an 1860s wagon route, emerging from the forest at **Windy Point** for a view of 7,794-ft (2,375-meter) **Mount Washington** and a 65-sq.-mile (168-sq.-km) lava flow. When you reach the summit of 5,325-ft (1,623-meter) **McKenzie Pass** you are literally surrounded by huge fields of lava that are around 2,700 years old.

Do not miss the easy walk to the **Dee Wright Observatory** (tel: 541 822-3381; free), a viewing tower that is itself constructed of lava rock. The view from the observatory takes in six Cascades peaks. The adjoining **Lava River Interpretive Trail** is an easy 30-minute walk along a paved surface through lava gutters and crevasses, offering spectacular vistas of the surrounding landscape.

Continuing west on Rt 242, catch more breathtaking glimpses of North and Middle Sister while descending into the 1.6 million-acre (682,343-hectare) **Willamette National Forest** (tel: 541 465-6521). A side road leads to picnic areas at **Scott Lake**, where glassy waters reflect the peaks. Nine miles (14 km) west of the summit, **Deadhorse Grade** drops nearly 1,200 ft (365 meters) in less than 4 miles (6 km). After a series of hairpin turns, look for the **Proxy Falls Trailhead** and hike the easy loop to two ethereal cascades: **Lower** and **Upper Proxy Falls**. The trail is heavily forested with wild rhododendrons, which bloom profusely in late spring; these shrubs alternate with open spaces and lava fields.

Oregon Route 242 ends here, so turn north on **Oregon Route 126**, about a mile from the **McKenzie Bridge Ranger Station**. From here the byway overlaps the **West Cascades Scenic Byway** along the Wild and Scenic **McKenzie River**. The McKenzie is ideal for first-time river runners (try Cool Runnings Rafting, tel: 877 389-5327). McKenzie's source is **Clear Lake**, which is fed by numerous springs. The 7 mile (11-km) stroll around the lake is rich in variety: lava crossings, big springs, old-growth forests. There is even a tiny stone fireplace in Clear Lake's primitive "resort" (tel: 541 822-3381;

LEFT:
Santiam Pass
runs thorugh
lava fields.

Map on page 274

summer only) and a good cup of coffee is always on offer. An excellent exercise for walkers is from **Ice Cap Campground** to graceful **Koosah Falls** and farther along to thundering **Sahalie Falls**. Both falls are roadside-accessible. The **McKenzie River National Recreation Trail** (tel: 541 465-6521) follows the river for some 26 miles (41 km).

A few miles north of Clear Lake, Rt 126 joins with **US Route 20** and Hwy 22, and heads back east to Sisters. Near Santiam Pass is a side road to **Hoodoo Ski Area** (tel: 541 822-3799), which features downhill and cross-country skiing December through March. In warmer months, the side road continues to **Big Lake**, a popular recreation area with a dramatic view of Mount Washington.

Shortly beyond the Hoodoo turn-off, the byway crosses the entrance to the **Pacific Crest National Scenic Trail**, a rugged cross-country trail, before the highway continues across the summit of 4,817-ft (1,468-meter) **Santiam Pass**. In an average year, precipitation in the Santiam Pass is 85 inches (215 cm); the average snowfall is 454 inches (1153 cm), and the snow depth 39 inches (99 cm).

Sliding down to Sisters

The eastern Cascades foothills are full of recreational possibilities. Year-round the primitive bring-your-own-bedding, outdoor toilet **Suttle Lake** "Resort" (tel: 541 595-6662; reservations recommended) offers boat rentals, a coffee shop with expensive food, camping, fishing tackle, and basic camping-type cabins. It is located on National Forest Land and operates under a special-use permit issued by the representatives of Deschutes National Forest. The **Metolius River** bursts into life as a full-fledged river from its spring source at the so-called "**Springs of the Metolius**." The observation area offers a commanding view of towering Mount Jefferson off to the west.

Farther down, another side road heads to **Camp Sherman**, where it's possible to

BELOW: the Dee Wright Observatory is made of lava rock; the view from it takes in six mountain peaks.

stay overnight at the **Metolius River Resort** (tel: 800 818-7688; reservations recommended) in one of 11 very comfortable cabins. Fly-fishing in the **Metolius River** is quieter now it is no longer stocked with rainbow trout, but the scenic beauty as it emerges full-force from underground springs near the base of Black Butte is still evident.

The first white people to live along the Metolius were homesteaders. Later, wheat farmers came here to escape the hot, dry weather of Sherman County, and to fish and rest in the cool river environment. Along the way, someone wrote the words "Camp Sherman" on a shoebox top to point the way, and the name stuck. The first building was constructed in 1917 and summer residents have been leasing land from the Forest Service ever since.

Cruising down the highway again, the 6,436-ft (2,000-meter) cone of **Black Butte** is just ahead on the left. Nestled among giant ponderosa pine trees just east of the summit, the impressive, expensive

Black Butte Ranch (tel: 800 452-7455; minimum 7-day stay; reservations required) is a destination-resort of 1,830 acres (740-hectares). It includes two championship golf courses that open onto peaceful meadows where cattle and horses graze against a backdrop of snow-capped Cascade Mountains peaks.

Guest accommodations range from deluxe hotel-type bedrooms to 1-, 2-, and 3-bedroom condominium suites and resort homes. The restaurants at Black Butte Ranch offer Pacific Northwest cuisine and are open to everyone. From here, it's an easy 8-mile (12-km) drive along Rt 20/126 back to the town of Sisters. This concludes the McKenzie Pass & Santiam Pass Scenic Byway circular route.

Cascade Lakes Scenic Byway

The best time for driving the **Cascade Lakes Scenic Byway** (tel: 800 800-8334) is from June through October. This 66-mile (108-km) highway travels southwest near Mount Bachelor, past a dozen sparkling Alpine lakes and ends near Crescent Lake in the Diamond Peak Wilderness. Named "one of the nation's 10 most important byways," it's possible to do the drive in one afternoon if you don't stop or tarry (which would be a pity).

Several parks and campgrounds are located along this beautiful route. Considerations before setting out on the Cascades Byway include the following: the road closes beyond Mount Bachelor in winter time; medical services and hospitals are located only in the town of Bend; vehicle services are available only in Bend, and, as always, start out with a full tank of gas.

Following the paths taken by historic figures Kit Carson and trapper Nathaniel J. Wyeth, this lake-filled journey begins in **Bend** ❹ *(for more on Bend, see page 290)*. The **Central Oregon Welcome Center** on **US Route 97** houses the Bend Chamber of Commerce Visitor and Convention Bureau, and presents a good overview of the region.

Before heading for the mountains and lakes, wander through Bend's downtown area and stock up on supplies, because

LEFT: Crescent Lake in the Diamond Peak Wilderness.

Map on page 274

this will be your best shopping opportunity, and many of the "resorts" are pretty basic. (Don't forget a flashlight, matches and poison-oak ointment).

Once you've done that, follow the signs toward Mount Bachelor and the Cascade Lakes. From the outskirts of town, **Century Drive** (also known as **Oregon Route 372**) climbs steadily into the **Deschutes National Forest** (tel: 541 383-4000). Besides providing natural commodities ranging from timber to mushrooms, the Deschutes, located in the high desert country, is one of most popular forests in the Pacific Northwest and attracts more than 8 million visitors each year.

Within the forest are five wilderness areas, six Wild and Scenic rivers, the **Metolius Conservation Area**, the **Oregon Cascades Recreation Area** and the **Newberry National Volcanic Monument** *(see page 312).* Just beyond the forest boundary, **Forest Service Road 41** leads to good hiking, fishing, rafting, kayaking, canoeing and camping spots along the Deschutes River. A few miles farther on, a **scenic viewpoint** with interpretive displays overlooks a vast lava flow that once altered the river's course.

Volcano playground

Mount Bachelor ❺ is the icon of Central Oregon, and is a major ski resort. Great snow typically lasts through June and the resort is considered one of the top "glade" areas in the US. Glade skiing areas are wide open patches lying between groups of trees, and typically offer wonderful, uninterrupted stretches of powder. During summer, the **Pine Marten chair lift** (July–Sept 3 daily, Sun–Thur 11am–4pm, Fri–Sat 11am–8pm; tel: 800 829-2442; fee) takes sightseers half way up the mountain, where a 360° view overlooks a volcanic skyline that stretches from California to Washington.

This view is a major attraction of the **Pine Marten Lodge** (tel: 541 382-2442), with its expansive outdoor decks. There are three other mountain restaurants between Mount Bachelor's base and the summit that offer hearty fare, fine dining or a beverage on the deck in the sun.

The view from **Dutchman Flat** at the base of Mount Bachelor should look familiar. This sweeping panorama of Broken Top and the Three Sisters has been featured in movies such as Disney's 1993 *Homeward Bound* and the 1975 John Wayne vehicle *Rooster Cogburn.*

A short drive and walk from the byway, **Todd Lake** is the first of many Alpine gems. Mount Bachelor and Broken Top loom at opposite ends of the lake.

Broken Top is the oldest and most eroded of the five major volcanoes in the Three Sisters region. Several hundred-thousand years ago its summit probably topped 10,000 ft (3,000-plus meters), but glacial erosion has now carved deep into the interior of the volcano, revealing its innermost structure. The highest remaining points form a horseshoe, surrounding what was once the crater of the original volcano.

As the byway drops to a large meadow, the route takes in **Sparks Lake**, chosen as the site to commemorate Ray Atkeson,

RIGHT: Diamond Lake with Mount Thielsen in the background.

Oregon's photographer laureate. Next along are the emerald waters of **Devils Lake**, a popular picnic and camping spot. **Devils Garden** is a meadow bordered by springs and covered with swaying grasses, lush moss, blue lupins and Indian paintbrush. A boulder in the meadow is painted with **pictographs**.

Probably between 50,000 and 10,000 years old, the towering **Devil's Garden lava flow field** contains excellent examples of inflated *pahoehoe* lava and covers an area of 45 sq. miles (117 sq. km). Features include kipukas, spatter ramparts, spatter cones and buriel mounds, but to see them all is a bit of a hike.

Lakes and lodges

Continuing south, 75-ft (22-meter) deep **Elk Lake** has a marina and a rustic, well-worn lodge; Elk Lake "Resort" (tel: 541 480-7228; reservations recommended) is operated under a special-use permit from the Deschutes National Forest, and serves as a mail drop for hikers. Neighboring

Hosmer Lake attracts fly-fishermen who catch and release its Atlantic salmon *(Salmo salar)*. It is one of only two lakes in Oregon stocked with this species.

As the Cascade Lakes Scenic Byway descends, there's **Lava Lake** for fishing, boating and camping, and **Little Lava Lake**, the apparent headwaters of the Deschutes River. **Lava Lake Lodge** (tel: 541 382-9443; reservations recommended) is a fairly spartan facility located on National Forest Land.

Lava Lake, informally known as "Big Lava Lake," is a spring-fed lake with a maximum depth of 34 ft (10 meters). Water levels fluctuate throughout the season and are dependent on snow melt. Some experts believe the lake is filled via underground tunnels from nearby Elk Lake. For serious hikers, great trails can be found in the **Three Sisters Wilderness** (Dechutes National Forest, tel: 541 383-5300), but a wilderness permit must be completed prior to entry.

Long before this area was designated as a wilderness, tribes of Native Americans roamed the forests and meadows here. They found food in the form of huckleberries and venison, and also came across a large supply of obsidian from which they fashioned arrow and spear heads. In the northern part of the wilderness, Felix Scott blazed the first trail (in 1863) to be used by white settlers in order to cross the central Cascades.

Elk and osprey

In the summer months, wildlife runs rampant through the wilderness. Be on the lookout for black-tailed deer, mule deer, and Roosevelt elk as well as yellow-bellied marmots, snowshoe hares, pine marten, mink, badgers, squirrels and pika. Wilderness visitors often hear and/or see many birds, including the Clark's nutcracker, gray jay, hairy woodpecker and dark-eyed junco. **Cultus Lake** and the 5,000-acre (2,000-hectare) **Crane Prairie Reservoir** (tel: 503 388-2715) represent one of the few osprey nesting grounds in the nation. Take the short trail to Crane Prairie's **osprey observation point** to view the nests from a safe distance.

LEFT: campfires keep the dark spirits away.

Map
on page
274

Beyond Crane Prairie, **Forest Service Road 42** heads east, past **Wickiup Reservoir** and **Twin Lakes**, to Rt 97. The Scenic Byway, however, continues south to **Davis Lake**, a large, shallow lake with dozens of campsites and even more species of waterfowl. The byway ends at Oregon Route 58, and the windy **Odell** lakes, near **Crescent**, two more favorite recreation sites.

The fairly basic **Crescent Lake Lodge and Resort** (tel: 541 433-2505; reservations required) offers rooms in the main lodge and 17 spartan guest cabins among tall Douglas fir, White fir and ponderosa pine trees. Hiking trails lead around the lake, which hook up with other trails to different lakes and streams.

Alternately, you could check out the **Odell Lake Lodge** (tel: 541 433-2540; reservations required), which has no-frills hotel rooms, cabins with wood-burning stoves and a small restaurant that overlooks the lake. This concludes the Cascade Lakes Scenic Byway.

Oregon Route 58

Picking up where the Cascade Lakes Scenic Byway ends is the fourth scenic route, **Oregon Route 58** ➏. It traverses the Cascades beginning at **Goshen**, which is located 7 miles (11 km) southeast of Eugene. The road sparkles with recreational reservoirs and lakes en route to **Willamette Pass** ski area (tel: 541 433-2505), about an hour from Eugene.

The **Elijah Bristow Historical Marker** located west of **Pleasant Hill** at milepost 4 commemorates a dour pioneer settler. Elijah Bristow was born in Virginia in April, 1788. He emigrated first to Kentucky, then to Illinois and California, before setting down in Lane County here in Oregon in 1846.

A sprawling park of the same name located along the Middle Fork of the **Willamette River** features 16 miles (25 km) of hiking, biking and horseback-riding trails, as well as several miles of waterfront, but – alas – no overnight camping is allowed.

BELOW: the ancient art of log rolling, seen here at a local festival.

A huge project of the US Army Corps of Engineers was the **Lookout Point Lake** and **Dexter Lake** project, which involved the building of two dams in 1954. **Oakridge** lies in the foothills of the Cascade with its nearby **Hills Creek Lake** offering good recreational facilities.

Some 16 miles (25 km) east, the 286-ft (87-meter) high **Salt Creek Falls** – the second highest waterfall in Oregon – is located above the highway in the **Willamette National Forest**. The waterfall is easier to photograph from the viewpoint above as the spray is often too heavy from lower vantage points.

Unidentified flying object

The moderately easy trail to **Diamond Creek Falls** begins at the bridge over **Salt Creek**, and the trail is marked with fun-to-follow diamond symbols. In November of 1966, a PhD scientist, returning to his California home from a business trip in Washington, was meandering through this part of Oregon and paused at a lookout point to photograph **Diamond Peak** in the **Diamond Wilderness**. Of the three photographs taken at this location, the last one included a strange object. This photo ultimately became the focus of a controversy among UFO investigators, and has been the subject of numerous articles as well as a book.

At present, conservation groups want the state to officially designate nine Oregon rivers and one lake as "outstanding resource waters" under the Federal Clean Water Act; **Waldo Lake** is the second-largest lake in Oregon and is reputed to be one of the purest in the world. It is accessible only to hikers, and is located at the headwaters of the Willamette River near the summit of the Cascades. Hikers who view the Willamette River headwaters from here are said to be awed at the feeling of being close to the hand that sculpted the Emerald Empire in the gorgeous Willamette Valley spreading out far below (see Willamette Valley, page 229).

Highway of waterfalls

The fifth passage through the Cascades is the **Rogue-Umpqua Scenic Byway** ❼, also called the Highway of Waterfalls. It starts in Roseburg (see page 262); from there **Oregon Route 138** ascends into the heart of the Cascades and passes Crater Lake National Park. The **North Umpqua River** is designated a state Scenic Waterway, so there are several parks and campgrounds located along this route. Note, however, that vehicle services are few and far between. The byway meanders through the Cascades and ends at Gold Hill, from where it is easy to get to the wild and woolly Rogue River Country and the cities of Medford, Ashland and Grants Pass.

Traveling east along Rt 138 leads through lush rural landscape and the community of **Glide**. Then comes a scenic stop at **Colliding Rivers**, where the North Umpqua and the **Little River** converge in thrilling tranquility. In pioneer days the area was not so serene, however, and tales of misadventure and hardship were commonplace.

LEFT: Elk Lake marina.

Map on page 274

According to the *Narratives of David Thompson* a fur trader writing about the winter of 1818–19, a frontiersman named Thomas McKay led a hunting brigade south toward the source of the Willamette River. His (mostly Iroquois) hunters killed 14 Indians of a different tribe. Most of the party fled, but Louis Labonte, Joseph Gervais, Etienne Lucier, Louis Kanota and Louis Pichette dit Dupre, all "free" trappers – that is to say, without affiliation to a specific company – decided to stay and, despite the fear of further Indian attacks, face the hardships.

Tales from the past

In a separate incident, in the late spring of 1835, a company of men and the family of John Turner, who was with his Native American wife, set out for Oregon from California; John Turner was making his second trip to Oregon. A couple of months later, an Indian attack at the Rogue River killed Dan Miller and one other (not named). All the survivors were severely wounded. An Irishman named Big Tom was left at the North Umqua River, too injured to move, and another called Saunders was abandoned at the South Umpqua. These two were reported dead by Indians visiting Fort Vancouver. What became of John Turner is unclear.

History feels close to home when standing at the old rustic forest service office, which was constructed in the 1930s by the Civilian Conservation Corps. It now houses a **Visitor Information Center** (tel: 541 496-0157), a bookstore and a nearby short botanical trail. If the schedule permits, why not spend the night at **Steelhead Run** (tel: 541 496-0563; reservations recommended), a Bed & Breakfast inn sitting on a bluff overlooking the North Umpqua River?

From Glide, the byway parallels the Wild and Scenic **North Umpqua** as it thrusts and rolls down a narrow canyon providing terrific **white-water rafting** (contact Oregon Ridge and River Excursions, tel: 541 496-3333). There are also numerous places where you can gain access to the scenic **North Umpqua Trail** (Bureau of Land Management, tel:

541 440-4930; user fee) for serious hikes that will test your strength, ability and endurance.

The shady route through the 1-million acre (405,000-hectare) **Umpqua National Forest** (tel: 541 496-3539) passes **Swiftwater Park**, **Toketee Reservoir (Lake)** and wonderful rock outcroppings including **Eagle Rock** and **Old Man Rock**. It is here that the highway delivers its promise: waterfalls. **Susan Creek Falls** (day-use fee) is a spectacular 500-ft (15-meter) waterfall that plummets over moss-lined volcanic rock cliffs. A short walk up the trail from the falls are the **Susan Creek Indian Mounds**.

Native Americans believed the moss-covered rocks were of spiritual origin, and spent nights fasting in order to summon guardian spirits. The stones were piled up in the hope that such a vision would be granted. (Caution: this upper section of the trail has lots of poison oak.)

There are many other falls in the area (tel: 541 498-2531 for information).

RIGHT: dress warmly in the mountains.

Spectacular **Toketee Falls** is an easy-to-reach tiered falls whose name means "pretty" in the Northwest Indians' Chinook language. A different short walk leads to the tallest waterfall in Southern Oregon, **Watson Falls**, a 272-ft (82-meter) plunge over a basalt lava flow. Also nearby is **Whitehorse Falls**. Depending on the time of year, wildflowers or outstanding fall foliage lead the way to most of these falls.

Crest of the mountain

Farther east is **Lemolo Lake**, with its own little threadbare "resort" (tel: 541 643-0750; reservations recommended). Here, Rt 138 heads south to **Diamond Lake ❽**, a scenic gem at the crest of the Cascade Mountains, nestled between **Mount Bailey** and the lightning-rod spire of **Mount Thielsen**. Diamond Lake's 24-carat fun includes the busy and well-maintained **Diamond Lake Resort** (tel: 541 793-3333; reservations required), also known as the "Gem of the Cascades."

Established in 1922 as a modest trout fishing lodge, it has grown into a year-round family destination including a marina and horse stables. In summer and fall, visitors can compete with osprey for rainbow trout, or cycle around the lake on a paved 11-mile (17-km) path. The side road to the **Mount Thielsen campground** has sensational lake views. In winter, the path turns into a cross-country ski trail and the lake becomes a giant ice rink.

At the south end of Diamond Lake, Rt 138 curves left and approaches the north entrance of Crater Lake National Park *(see page 314)*. The byway, however, turns right on to **Oregon Route 230** and offers a clear view of the remains of **Mount Mazama** at the **Crater Rim Viewpoint**.

Rogue headwaters

Oregon Route 230 then follows the ever-growing Rogue River *(see Rogue River Country, page 261)* and merges with Oregon Route 62 near historic **Union Creek**. From **Prospect**, travel on Rt 62 to one of several Rogue Gorge viewpoints. **Natural Bridge** is a fine walking loop that shows the river thundering through deep, narrow chasms (it should be called a tunnel rather than a bridge).

The gorge offers an interesting display of pothole formations – smooth depressions sculpted into solid rock by the continuous spinning of small rocks. Under a canopy of conifers between here and Prospect are several campgrounds along the Rogue River.

Lost Creek Lake Marina (tel: 541 560-3646) offers water recreation on a reservoir and **Joseph H. Stewart State Park** (tel: 541 560-3334; free). A little farther on, **Shady Cove** (tel: 541 878-2404) attracts anglers and river rafters. The Scenic Byway then heads west on Rt 234 past **Table Rocks** and meets the Rogue River again in the friendly town of Gold Hill, the byway's southern portal and home to the fascinating Oregon Vortex *(see page 264)*.

A visit to Gold Hill completes the Rogue-Umpqua Scenic Byway (Highway of Waterfalls) route. ❑

LEFT: taking in the view at Crater Lake. **RIGHT:** Toketee Falls; the name means "pretty" in Chinook.

Map on page 274

EAST OF THE CASCADES

*As you travel eastward through Oregon,
greenery and tall timbers are left behind in favor of
a hot, arid, near-desert landscape*

Map
on page
274

The huge tracts of land lying east of Oregon's Cascade Mountains are sparsely populated regions dominated by two anchor communities: Bend and Klamath Falls. Both cling to the eastern edge of the Cascades in a semi-arid desert landscape; within striking distance of mountain recreational facilities, while at the same time managing to avoid the uncertainty of mountain weather. The average annual rainfall here is about 12 inches (30 cm); the average high temperature in July is 85°F (30°C); the average low in January is 22°F (–5°C).

From mountains to desert

The 25-mile (40-km) highway between Sisters and Bend, just a hair's breadth east of the Cascades, showcases the transition from mountain range to high desert country. Pressing eastward through Oregon leaves behind shimmering Alpine lakes, greenery and tall timbers, to be replaced by a high-altitude arid land of sweeping vistas and waving grass. As a result of this "rain-shadow," leisure-oriented communities have sprung up, taking advantage of the cold, clear winters and the hot, but not humid, summers.

From 1850 until the early 20th century, the popularity of the town of Bend was as a result of Federal land giveaways to homesteaders. The past two decades' leisure boom has turned it into a tourist destination. Camp Abbott, a military base with 300 people, was transformed seemingly overnight into the community of **Sunriver**. The same leisure wave produced the **Inn at the Seventh Mountain** (tel: 800 452-6810; reservations recommended), a fine destination resort, and **Black Butte Ranch** just east of McKenzie Pass *(see page 280).*

The Federal government wisely created several wilderness areas *(see Oregon Cascades, page 273)* near these tourist meccas to spare the delicate forest ecosystems the fate of other loved-to-death paradises. With the exception of the upper right-hand corner of Oregon, most of the region farther east – beyond Bend and Klamath Falls – is a hot, relatively barren an unforgiving landscape.

But the area definitely has its charms. Oregon has a blowing geyser and its own version of Australia's Uluru (Ayers Rock); the scenic byway referred to as "the Outback" is a relatively quick way to discover them. There are also three fabulous national parks and monuments: the John Day Fossil Beds National Monument *(see page 308);* Newberry National Volcanic Monument *(see page 312)*; and Crater Lake National Park *(see page 314).*

LEFT: bald eagles like to spend their winters east of the Cascades.
RIGHT: llama at the High Desert Museum.

Bend in the river

Bend, where the Deschutes River slows down long enough to reflect snowy Cascade peaks, is one of the two main communities in the region *(see page 280)*. The **Central Oregon Welcome Center** on US Route 97 houses the Bend Chamber of Commerce Visitor and Convention Bureau (tel: 541 382-3221). A great place for souvenirs is the **Oregon Store** (tel: 800 541-5797), which is chock-full of regional delights like Pendleton blankets, myrtlewood items and locally made foods. The **Dechutes Brewery** (901 Southwest Simpson Avenue; tel: 541 385-8606) is a fun microbrewery stocking every kind of ale under the sun.

Before leaving town, be sure to enjoy **Drake Park's Mirror Pond**, a small lake with ducks and regal swans, reputed to be descendants of Queen Elizabeth II's Royal Flock in England. Green grass provides a counterpoint to the old brick buildings that make up Bend's galleries, restaurants, outdoor eateries and specialty shops.

For a panoramic view of Bend and the volcanic peaks around it, drive to the top of **Pilot Butte**. From the top of this 511-ft (155-meter) volcanic cindercone, a vista of the high desert region includes nine snowcapped Cascades peaks. The **High Desert Museum** (daily 9am–5pm; tel: 541 382-4754; fee) is a so-called "living" museum with live animals and exhibits on geology, pioneer life, and flora and fauna. There are shady paths among animal enclosures, settlers' cabins and a logging display. The Desertarium showcases live exhibits like lizards, a porcupine, bats, owls, kangaroo rats and other shy desert creatures.

A passion for recreation that brings many people here. Kayakers and rafters shoot through the triple waterfalls of the **Deschutes River**. Snowmobilers have 560 miles (900 km) of trails to explore in the **Deschutes National Forest** (tel: 541 383-5300 for permits), while fly-fishing enthusiasts have more than 500 miles (800 km) of streams and rivers stocked with trout and steelhead.

Golfers have 20 top-rated courses to choose from. Mountain-bikers can choose to ride through uncrowded forests, high mountain peaks, lava fields or arid desert. Alpine skiers have ten lifts to access 3,228 skiable acres (1,300 hectares) of slopes or 35 miles (56 km) of cross-country trails at **Mount Bachelor**. Rock climbers and walkers have miles of trails among interesting rock outcroppings at nearby **Smith Rock State Park** (tel: 541 548-7501; day-use fee).

Backcountry hikers and campers head into the solitude of the **Three Sisters Wilderness**, while others take a hike in the more than 2.5 million acres (1 million hectares) of **national forests** near Bend.

Bend to the south

Pine Mountain Observatory ❾ (tel: 541 382-8331; donation; no small children), 26 miles (42 km) southwest of Bend on a dirt road at an elevation of 6,500 ft (2,000 meters), owns some of the most advanced astronomical equipment in the Pacific Northwest. Operated by the University of Oregon Physics Department,

LEFT: near the Cascades, logging is still a major, if controversial, state industry.

Map
on page
274

the observatory consists of three Cassegrain reflecting telescopes, with mirrors of 15, 24 and 32 inches (38, 61 and 81 cm) in diameter, each in its own domed building. Visitors are welcome on Friday and Saturday evenings and Sundays on long holiday weekends from late May through September, weather permitting. Bring warm clothing, as observatories are unheated, and the desert cools down at night. At sunset, a guide gives a presentation on basic astronomy. If the sky is clear, visitors have been known to stay up all night.

Sunriver is an unincorporated, planned community consisting of interrelated villages. These villages contain single and multi-family residential, resort, commercial and industrial properties. Bordered by the Deschutes River and surrounded by attractive National Forest Land, the one stop visitors might like to see is the **Sun River Nature Center** (Apr–May Tues–Sat 10am–4pm; June–Aug daily 9am–5pm; tel: 541 593-4394; fee) located next to **Lake Aspen** on River Road.

The nature center includes a large-scale public **observatory** for both daytime (solar) and night-time viewing, a **botanical garden** and a **nature trail**.

Outback Scenic Byway

"Between the Cascade Mountains and the Continental Divide, there exists a dry, dry land of magic and mystery, a place where rivers run every which way but never to the sea. This is the Great Basin Country, a star-spangled landscape of mountains and rim rock, of seamless vistas and sage-scented dreams." So says writer Jonathan Nicholas of the dry area south of Bend that is traversed by the 171-mile (275-km) **Outback Scenic Byway ⑩**, a drive through rangeland and scrub.

In this vast high desert, peace and solitude have sounds and, some say, "colors" all their own. The ever-changing light – even the passing of a cloud – turns earthy browns, grays and greens into pastel blues, pinks and purples. In spring and autumn expect occasional snow; in summer plan

BELOW: Prairie schooner wagon at the High Desert Museum.

on temperatures in the region of 90°F (32°C) or higher; protect yourself from the sun and bring water. The minimum driving time is 4–6 hours. The closest medical services and hospitals are in Bend and Lakeview. There is a rest area at Summer Lake about half way between Rts 97 and 395. Vehicle services are few, so always set out with a full tank of gas. For information contact **Lake County Chamber of Commerce** (tel: 541 947-6040).

Shadow of the Cascades

To follow the Outback Byway, begin at **La Pine** ⓫, 30 miles (48 km) south of Bend. Then head 3 miles (5 km) south on Rt 97, then southeast on Rt 31, through stands of lodgepole and ponderosa pine. About 27 miles (43 km) east of Rt 97, the forest abruptly gives way to vast sagebrush plains reminiscent of the Australian Outback.

Like Australia's Ayers Rock, Oregon's **Fort Rock** ⓬ is a mysterious formation, a volcanic tuff rising 325 ft (99 meters)

above the desert floor and designated as a National Natural Landmark. It emerges from out of nowhere, and no one knows for sure what it symbolizes. Historians do believe, however, that a Native American population lived in the region about 10,000 years ago.

From Rt 31, **Fort Rock State Monument** is an easy 7 miles (11 km) along a side road. On the way, **Fort Rock Homestead Village** features a living history museum (summer months only). **Fort Rock State Park** (tel: 503 731-3411) is the site of **Fort Rock Cave**. It was here that artifacts dating back 9,000 years were discovered, including sandals woven in the manner of the ancient Greeks. They are said to be unlike the products of any known Native American culture.

Little is known of the lifestyle or appearance of the cave's inhabitants, but it is known that their "home" was sculpted by the waves of a huge inland lake that once lapped against the rimrock of the high desert. More Native artifacts have

BELOW: recreating the pioneer life.

Map
on page
274

been found here than in any other part of Oregon. The nearest town's namesake, **Silver Lake**, is actually a dry basin a few miles east that fills up with water every 30 years or so. It's the place for rockhounds, but watch out for rattlesnakes.

Christmas Valley

Take a detour to the wide-open spaces of **Christmas Valley**, a favorite with photographers and nature lovers. In addition to 15,000 acres (6,000 hectares) of sand dunes, it includes the **Lost Forest**, a 9,000-acre (3,600-hectare) stand of ponderosa pines that mysteriously grows in the middle of the desert east of the valley.

From Silver Lake, the byway – Rt 31 – turns south and climbs through **Picture Rock Pass**, named for the ancient Indian **petroglyphs** that decorate the rocks within walking distance of the highway. Sometimes the meanings of the petroglyphs are obvious, such as lightning and rain descending from a cloud, but often they are simply a mystery.

Over the pass is 18,000-acre (7,300-hectare) **Summer Lake Wildlife Area**, a long, shallow body of extremely alkaline water, which is a breeding and resting place for terns, gulls, swans and cranes pausing in their migrations along the Pacific Flyway overhead.

The little town of **Summer Lake** offers visitor services and has a way-side monument commemorating an 1843 expedition led by Captain John C. Fremont. Deep blue skies and crystalline air surround **Summer Lake Inn** (tel: 541 943-3983; reservations recommended), a nicely serviced inn built over 20 years ago with fine woods, Audubon art, local Indian motifs and attractive buildings.

A dozen miles beyond the lake, **Paisley** – named by an early Scots settler – is home of the annual Mosquito Festival and Air Show held in late July. The Pioneer Saloon has a 1905 bar that was built in Boston and shipped "round the Horn." And if handcrafted knives or powder horns are of interest, this is the place. The Feed and Supply

Store doubles as the ice-cream parlor. This community of fewer than 250 people offers the **Summer Lakes natural hot spring baths** (tel: 877 492-8554; fee) and choice spots to fish the trout-stocked **Chewaucan River**. From here, **Oregon Route 31** continues southeast to giant Lake Abert, whose placid alkaline waters reflect a palette of desert colors. Watch for coyotes.

Old Perpetual

After **Valley Falls**, Rt 31 joins **US Route 395** south. Here, the horizon is dominated by **Abert Rim**, a 30-mile-long (50-km) fault escarpment rising 2,000 ft (600 meters) above the desert floor. The rim's southern section is a popular launching pad for hang gliders. At the base is **Lake Abert**, the third-largest body of salt water in North America and home to a variety of birds. A scenic 27 miles (43 km) later, **Lakeview ⑬** at 4,800 ft (1,500 meters), calls itself Oregon's "tallest town."

A must-see here is the state's only naturally occurring geyser: **Old Perpetual** typically shoots 60 ft (20 meters) straight into the air. Also of interest is the presence of Oregon sunstone, the official state gemstone. Uncommon in composition, it is a large, brightly colored transparent gem in the feldspar family, now attracting collectors and miners from all around.

A long and interesting sidetrip from Lakeview is to spot Pronghorn antelope, bighorn sheep, mule deer, coyote, black-tailed jackrabbits, golden eagles and other wildlife on the **Hart Mountain National Antelope Refuge**. The refuge offers some of the best wildlife-watching opportunities in south-central Oregon. Even cattle aren't allowed to graze on this important reserve, which was established in 1936. In addition to wildlife, ancient art can be admired at **Petroglyph Lake** near **Hart Mountain**.

After Lakeview, the Outback Byway officially ends at the border town of **New Pine Creek** and the **Goose Lake State Recreation Area** (tel: 541 947-3111; fee) with its cool, shady grass.

BELOW: sunflowers in the market in the City of Sunshine.

GEOTHERMAL ENERGY

Oregon and the Northwest in general, and Klamath Falls in particular, have enormous geothermal potential. Some estimate that if Oregon's geothermal reserves were developed to their full potential, they could produce 2,000 megawatts of electricity, the equivalent of two nuclear power plants. By comparison, four Federal dams on the lower Snake River generate only about 1,200 megawatts. As the energy market heats up, so does the search for heat itself. The "rolling black-out" power cuts that hit California so comprehensively in 2001 sent shivers down everyone's spines, and in an area that depends to a great extent on energy-guzzling technology industries, the Northwest is particularly keen to pursue alternative sources. The same year as the black-outs, a Portland symposium on geothermal energy attracted utilities, businesses and government agencies, all with proposals to drill for heat. Plans are now in the works to probe the flanks of Newberry Crater, a volcano that is probably the most promising site for development, but the outcome hinges on contracts with utilities to buy energy generated by an eventual volcano-power plant. Geothermal energy is everything modern-day power is not: reliable, clean and attractively priced.

Map on page 274

City of Sunshine

Known as Oregon's City of Sunshine, today **Klamath Falls** ⑭ (tel: 541 884-5193) is a real hot spot. A local phenomenon is its underground supply of geothermally heated water used to heat homes, schools and businesses *(see page 294)*. At 4,100 ft (1,250 meters) in elevation, the town is located on the southern shore of **Upper Klamath Lake** (boating information, tel: 541 884-7237), a freshwater body covering 133 sq. miles (345 sq. km).

The surrounding **Klamath Basin National Wildlife Refuge Complex** (daily tours; tel: 541 667-2231; fee) contains six national wildlife refuges. These have been called "a western Everglades" because of the wonderful wetlands. The white pelican, one of the world's largest birds, can sometimes be seen here. The area also claims the largest wintering concentration of bald eagles in the lower 48 states. The eagles come to feed on injured waterfowl who have fallen, exhausted, from the sky when the great Pacific Flyway of migrating birds passes overhead.

Nearby Crater Lake National Park is only a day-trip away, but overnight adventurers who like a taste of the Old West may want to stay on a working ranch (**Box R Ranch**; tel: 541 482-1873; reservations required). Another unique escape, between Crater Lake and the region's seven National Wildlife Refuges has riverside cabins with full amenities, an original log cabin and a choice of **treehouses**. The Spaceship Treehouse is for stargazers, while the Eldin Treehouse – private and secluded – is for nature-lovers. Call **Retreat for Nature Lovers**, Chiloquin; tel: 541 783-2697; reservations required.

Back in Klamath Falls, **Favell Museum of Western Art and Native American Artifacts** (125 West Main; Mon–Sat 9:30am–5:30pm; tel: 541 882-9996; fee) showcases the work of more than 300 contemporary Western artists in a volcanic-stone building. The **Senator George Baldwin Hotel Museum** (31 Main Street; guided tours; June–Sept Tues–Sat 9am–4pm; tel: 541 883-4207; fee) covers the history of the region. It also doubles as the start point for a cute, modern **trolley** (fee) that runs in summer to the **Klamath County Museum** (June–Sept Mon–Sat 8:30am–5:30pm; Oct–May Mon–Sat 8am–5pm; tel: 541 883-4208; fee).

Tribes museum

Nearby, **Fort Klamath Museum and Park** (June–Labor Day Wed–Sun 10am–6pm; tel: 541 381-2230; donation) was established in 1863 to fend off Indian attacks. The **Klamath Indian Tribes Museum** (tel: 541 783-2218; inquire about hours) shows artifacts and data on the culture of the Modoc, Yahooskin and Klamath Indians. Although the museum is interesting, Natives would rather you pay a visit to their **Kla-Mo-Ya Casino** (tel: 541 552-6692), which is 22 miles (35 km) north of Klamath Falls.

Also out-of-town is the **Collier State Park and Logging Museum** (May–Oct daily 8am–8pm; tel: 541 783-2471; free), north on Hwy 97, featuring an historic log cabin and antique logging equipment.

RIGHT: much of life is lived out of doors in Oregon.

Bend to the north

North of the town of Bend, for those who love roadside curiosities and quirky sites, there is a "circle of oddness" encompassing the Oregon communities of Sisters, Redmond, Prineville and Madras. It takes effort to locate these whimsical finds, but aficionados take great pains to find these sort of attractions.

For starters, near **Redmond ⑮** town, **Petersen Rock Gardens** (South Canal Boulevard to McKay, follow signs; daylight hours; tel: 541 382-5574; fee) is a 4-acre (1.5-hectare) extravaganza with rock bridges, terraces and towers built half a century ago. A Danish farmer's obsession included collecting petrified wood, agate, jasper, obsidian and lava, and shaping them into a variety of remarkable statues and fairytale castles. His feverish folk constructions of stone and glass include an Independence Hall and a phosphorescent tribute to democracy.

Redmond is also home to **Operation Santa Claus** (4355 West Hwy 126 and Helmholtz Way; daily, daylight hours; tel: 541 548-8910; free), the home of a 100-strong herd of reindeer. Operation Santa Claus displays its reindeer teams at shopping centers across the country during the holiday season. Generally, reindeer are easy to handle and learn through repetition. They are inquisitive animals and can be much like people: some are nasty, some are nice. Reindeer dislike being alone; when excited or separated from the main herd, they make a noise something between a bark and a grunt.

The **World Famous Fantastic Museum** (daily; tel: 541 923-0000) is south of Redmond on Hwy 97 at Airport Way Road. The museum has over 1 million items of memorabilia, antiques and collectibles to go with its amusement park, go-carts, bumper boats, skittle bugs and miniature golf play area.

The area spawns weirdness, as evidenced by the **House of Rocks** (67288 West Hwy 20; daily; tel: 541 385-5200), about 5 miles (8 km) southeast of **Sisters**. It is set on the roadside, with a car and a trailer each crushed under a boulder. They sell rocks, of course.

The Funny Farm (Deschutes Market Road exit; daylight hours; tel: 541 389-6391; fee) is 7 miles (11 km) north of Bend. For some peculiar reason, no roadside signs are allowed, so watch for a field with a goat – a real one – running around and fainting. The parking lot is surrounded with folk art and homespun humor placards. Up on the roof of the "Buffet Flats" building, a sheepdog sits on an old couch. Next to him is a sign: "Hi. My name is Bear. Buy me a hot dog." On past the Pink Flamingo Nesting Area is the totem pole made out of tires. You get the picture.

Check your guns

Near the entrance of the **Ochoco National Forest** not far from **Prineville** is **Steins Pillar**, a giant basalt thumb protruding up out of an eroded hillside; it's a geological oddity. East of Prineville on the Paulina Hwy is the small town of **Paulina ⑯**, named for the creek nearby. In the town, a dance hall still has a sign by the front door requesting that patrons check their

LEFT: a farmer's obsession produced the Petersen Rock Gardens in Redmond.

Map on page 274

guns before entering. Abandoned homesteads along the route attest to the harshness of the climate; in 1825, Peter Skene Ogden's party were forced to eat their horses to survive while spending the winter along the upper **Crooked River** – certainly an appropriate name for the area.

Fun can be had by looking for the elusive **thundereggs**, Oregon's state rock. This part of the state is famous for its examples. The thundereggs' ugly outer shell masks true beauty hidden within.

The "World Famous" **Richardson Rock Ranch** (Hwy 97; daily 7am–5pm; tel: 800 433-2680), a store 11 miles (17 km) north of **Madras**, allows visitors to sift through its unopened agatized-thundereggs for a small fee; also selling in the store are finished spheres of polished rock, and rock-hounding paraphernalia.

A living ghost town

Continuing with the theme of eccentricity is the oxymoron embodied in **Shaniko** ⑰, Oregon's favorite "living" ghost town.

Located on Hwy 97, 70 miles (115 km) north of Bend, it was named for August Sherneckau, who came to Oregon after the Civil War and opened a stage station to profit from passing travelers, then bought a farm. The local Native Americans pronounced his last name "Shaniko" – hence the name. During its heyday in the early 1900s, the little town of Shaniko was on the rail line, a well-known stop for large shipments of wool.

Today, the old town has been reinhabited. Visitors can see jail cells, a Chinese laundry, the old City Hall, the pioneer church, a water tower and a school. The attractive **Old Shaniko Hotel** (tel: 541 489-3441; reservations recommended) is available for nights in old-fashioned bordello-style surroundings. A local ordained minister has performed over 300 marriages, both in the **Shaniko Wedding Chapel** (tel: 541 489-3446), and in **Shaniko Church**. There's life in the town yet, including old-time boardwalks, antique stores and a display of old wagons. ❑

BELOW: Shaniko's "ghost" school; you can get married in the town's wedding chapel.

NORTHEAST OREGON

This is an area of highs and lows, from snow-covered mountain peaks to the rattlesnake-infested depths of North America's deepest gorge. It's the landscape pioneers endured on the old Oregon Trail

Map on page 274

Beginning in 1841, around 300,000 people began an arduous 2,170-mile (3,492-km) migration from the East to the West, along what is now known as the Oregon Trail. It is estimated that more than 30,000 of these pioneers died: starving, falling out of wagons, being crushed under wagon wheels, being accidentally shot, drowning while crossing rivers, dying from snakebites, eating contaminated meat, freezing in the high mountain passes, succumbing to heat stroke in the deserts, contracting cholera, measles, typhoid, mountain fever or dysentery. Today, the region is much safer.

Fishing for the soul

Northeast Oregon is, literally, a place of highs and lows. Low places, like Hell's Canyon, are contrasted by the towering Blue and Wallowa mountains, which have 30 peaks over 8,000 ft (2,400 meters). Temperatures in the canyon summer heat average 92°F (33°C), while in the Wallowa Mountains the average highs are 82°F (27°C). The Eagle Cap Wilderness area is one of Oregon's largest; Hell's Canyon is remote, but truly "gorge-ous" with its deep ravine. There are around 5,600 miles (9,000 km) of clear, fast-rushing streams – some world-class, according to those who fish them.

Wallowa Lake, with reflections of Mount Joseph mirrored on the water, provides a serene fishing experience that is good for the soul. The "big" town of Enterprise has a population of just over 2,000, while Joseph, Oregon, has grown to accommodate around 1,200. No one worries about running a yellow – there are none to be found. The biggest danger facing drivers is running off into a ditch, which is what happens when there is too little traffic and too much jaw-dropping scenery. Starting along the busy Columbia Gorge, the sought-after "Wild West" feeling of Pendleton grows into a burst of beauteous back country at La Grande. It, plus Baker City, site of an 1860s Gold Rush, are the starting points for ventures into a vast scenic wilderness.

More deer than people

Wallowa County has a total population of 7,500. Compared to the deer, people are a minority here. Along Interstate 84 and near the town of **Hermiston** are two wildlife refuges. **Umatilla National Wildlife Refuge** (tel: 503 922-3232; fee) and **Cold Springs National Wildlife Refuge** (tel: 541 922-3232; fee) are home to mule deer, coyote, beaver, muskrats, raccoons, porcupines and badgers. Flocks of waterfowl such as mallards, grebes, Canada

LEFT: the Wild West town of Pendleton. **RIGHT:** modern-day pioneer.

geese, cormorants, American wigeon and American white pelicans can usually be seen in their proper habitat every day in season. Vehicles must stay on designated access roads; hunting is allowed from October to January.

Wild West town

Way back in 1910 a group of ranchers, farmers and local Natives gathered for wild bronc riding and greased-pig catching. They had so much fun, they decided it ought to become an annual event. The **Pendleton RoundUp** (second week in Sept; tel: 800 457-6336; rodeo reservations required) with its slogan, *Let'er Buck* now attracts some 50,000 spectators to four days of foot-stomping, high-kicking rodeo events, cowboy breakfasts, barbecues and parades. Vendors sell western-style curios while country bands twang. Since its inception, Native Americans from the **Umatilla Reservation** have contributed a unique costume-pageant entitled *Happy Canyon*.

When visiting the nearby town of **Pendleton** ⑱, one of the first stops should be **Pendleton Underground Tours** (daily, 90-minute tours; tel: 541 276-0730; fee). A tour here reveals once-secret passages that led to Hop Sing's Chinese Laundry, the Meat Market, the "Cozy Room" bordello and a 1920s Prohibition card room. Another stop should be to buy a famous Pendleton blanket.

Pendleton Woolen Mills (1307 Southeast Court Place; 20-minute tours Mon–Fri 9am, 11am, 1:30pm and 3pm; tel: 541 276-6911; free; no open-toed sandals allowed) is a dyed-in-the-wool American success story. From the 1909 purchase of a scouring mill through the Great Depression and war years, when the company produced blankets for the military, six generations of the Bishop family have produced these highly prized blankets. The mill here also makes womens' and mens' apparel and home decor items, perfect for Christmas gifts.

The **Tamastslikt Cultural Institute** (Hwy 331; daily 9am–5pm; tel: 541 966-9748; fee), a $9.9 million museum at the **Wildhorse Casino Resort** is operated by the Confederated Umatilla Tribes, and has exhibits depicting the history of local Native Americans.

Sleep in a log cabin

Back on Interstate 84, the cool old-growth forest at **Emigrant Springs State Heritage Area** (tel: 541 983-2277) near the 4,193-ft (1,278-meter) summit of the **Blue Mountains**, was once a popular stopover on the Oregon Trail. Here the wagons rested before starting the precarious descent. Today, visitors smart enough to reserve ahead can stay overnight in one of the tiny one-room log cabins here: **Cabin Camping in Oregon State Parks** (Reservations Northwest; tel: 800 452-5687; fee; no pets allowed).

Cabins include rudimentary electricity, beds, and a table and chairs; you need to bring bedding, cooking and eating utensils, plus a sense of ambiance. To get yourself in the spirit, you could first pay a visit to the Oregon Trail Visitors Park. This can be reached via the Blue Moun-

LEFT:
Wallowa
Mountains
Visitor Center.

Map on page 274

tain Scenic Byway. The byway, off I-84, 4-miles (7 km) northwest of **Meacham**, passes through the **Umatilla National Forest** (tel: 541 278-3716), a forest that includes three wilderness areas. Near the town of La Grande, among the pines, is the **Oregon Trail Visitors Park** (Spring Creek Road, exit 248; mid-May–Sept daily 8am–8pm; tel: 541 963-7186; fee). Here, the silence speaks powerfully of the human experience. At the **Blue Mountain Crossing**, actual tracks made by the wheels of pioneer wagons are visible; on summer weekends staff reenact the story of the pioneers' lives.

Visitors in a hurry can continue south along Interstate 84 straight to Baker City. A rural stop along the way in **Haines** is an excuse for a peek at the **Eastern Oregon Museum** (Apr 15–Oct 15 9am–5pm; tel: 541 856-3366; donation), a real "Grandma's attic" type of place with its household, farming, mining and pioneer artifacts. It is situated on the grounds of an old 1880s Union Pacific depot.

Blue Mountain Scenic Byway

The **Blue Mountain Scenic Byway** (tel: 800 551-6949) is an "All America" scenic road that leads through a region of extremes. This route provides a driving tour of the Northeast's high wilderness areas, showcasing mountain peaks, valley floors, undulating farmlands, plunging rivers and the deepest canyon in the United States. The stars seem brighter, the smiles friendlier here.

The byway consists of a loop that intersects Interstate 84 at La Grande, encircles the Wallowa Mountains and rejoins I-84 at Baker City. The route includes the Wallowa Mountain Loop Road, passes Eagle Cap Wilderness and traverses the Hell's Canyon Scenic Byway. Around 218 miles (351 km) long, it is best to allow a minimum of 8 hours, assuming sightseeing stops are made along the way.

The **Wallowa Mountains Visitor Center** (summer months Mon–Sat 8am–5pm; winter Mon–Fri 9am–5pm; tel: 503 426-4978) can provide lots of advice, and has

BELOW: the rowdy Pendleton RoundUp dates from 1910.

recreational information, exhibits and dioramas on the area's natural history.

The trip is not easy, so certain cautions apply: check road and weather conditions before setting out (tel: 800 977-6368); weather can change rapidly with temperatures varying as much as 50°F (10°C) in a day. There are no car services beyond Joseph. Part of the byway is on double-lane paved highway, but 50 miles (80 km) is the circuitous Forest Road, closed from November to February because of snow. In summer, vehicles in good condition should be fine.

In the Hell's Canyon section, rattlesnakes are common; also, bring your own supply of drinking water. Anyone planning to venture on foot into any of the wilderness is strongly advised to think ahead and arrive well-equipped, then stop at **Area Headquarters** (Mon–Sat 8am–5pm, Sun noon–5pm; tel: 541 426-4978) on the west side of the town of Enterprise for detailed maps, regulations, important precautions and on-the-spot advice.

Begin your driving adventure in the farming country around **La Grande** ⑲ (tel: 541 963-8588), northeast on Hwy 82, through the **Grande Ronde Valley**. Rimmed by the beautiful Blue and Wallowa mountains, the Grande Ronde is thought by many to be the largest completely enclosed circular valley in the world. The restored **Historic Elgin Opera House**, built in 1912, is pretty near acoustically perfect and continues to host concerts, plays and movies.

Cricket Flat – prime cattle country with broad open ridges and narrow, timbered canyon – is a prelude to the **Grande Ronde River** (white-water rafting experience, tel: 503 632-6836), part of the National Wild and Scenic River System.

Black bears and cougar

Hunting is popular here: deer, elk, black bear, cougar and bighorn sheep are the principal big-game animals inhabiting the cottonwood-lined river corridor. Hiking along side creeks and ridges is limited to day hikes, and vehicle access along the river is impossible.

The byway takes a long, steep climb up the **Minam Grade**, passing on the way the confluence of the Wallowa and **Minam rivers**, a popular launch point for rafting trips. The **Wallowa Range** – with some peaks as high as 10,000 ft (3,000 meters) – sneaks into visibility. The jagged peaks retain pockets of snow throughout the summer and are often compared to the Swiss Alps, although anyone who has actually experienced the Alps will find this something of an exaggeration. Baker City and the **Wallowa Valley** are at the mountains' base.

The **Wallowa River Rest Area** (tel: 800 551-6949) is located in a canyon alongside the **Wallowa River**. Flowers are abundant in the spring and add to the beauty of the river as it plunges down the mountainside. The 2.3-million-acre (930,000-hectare) **Wallowa-Whitman National Forest** (tel: 541 523-6391) offers hiking and recreational opportunities. Here, too, is the roadside Wallowa Mountains Visitor Center (*see page 301*), a very useful stop.

LEFT: the Eagle Cap Wilderness is called "Little Switzerland" because of its 60 Alpine lakes.

Map on page 274

Eagle Cap Wilderness

Wallowa County is the home on the range for a substantial herd of American bison. They move around depending on the season and are not kept together as a single group, but some of these slow-moving animals can be seen from the highway a couple of miles north of the town of **Enterprise**; there are also frequent sightings on the rural Ant Flat Road or Alder Slope Road to the northeast and west of town.

Passing Enterprise, the byway skirts the eastern boundary of a 360,000-acre (145,000-hectare) area interwoven with countless backpackers' trails. This is the well-known and well-loved **Eagle Cap Wilderness ㉒** (Wallowa-Whitman National Forest; tel: 541 523-6391; Northwest pass required). Sometimes referred to as the "Little Switzerland of America," (again an exaggeration), this region has almost 60 sparkling, crystal-clean Alpine lakes, which are in turn surrounded by open meadows, bare granite peaks and classical, U-shaped glacial valleys. The

air is intoxicating, almost literally. There are over 500 miles (800 km) of serious hiking trails, most of which require park passes (tel: 541 426-5546). Hunters come to the wilderness for elk, deer, mountain goats and bighorn sheep, while black bears, bobcats and mountain lions prowl these parts, too. High summer temperatures guarantee swarms of mosquitoes and horseflies in wet areas.

Tours by llama

Under a Special Use Permit, authorized guides and outfitters provide a quality service, safety and equipment. Opportunities are wide-ranging: there are fishing guides; horse-, mule- or llama-packers; jet boat and float tours; ski tours and aircraft tours. For the most up-to-date and reliable information, contact the Wallowa Mountains Visitor Center.

The dry-grass byway continues, set against views of the **High Wallowas** (as opposed, presumably, to the "Low Wallowas") on the drive to the picturesque

BELOW:
a challenging job: tracking down a forest fire (look through the door to see it burning).

town of **Joseph** ㉑ (tel: 541 432-1015). The tragic life of Chief Joseph of the Nez Perce tribe *(see page 63)* has spawned an industry here. The town is also noted for its bronzes, and several bronze-casting facilities are open to the public.

Valley Bronze of Oregon (tours May–Nov daily; tel: 541 432-7551; free) is just one that invites visitors to their casting foundry. A short "**Art Walk**" through Joseph to view its street-art bronzes and numerous art galleries is recommended.

Joseph the Older

The centrally located **Manuel Museum** (Nez Perce Crossing; tel: 541 432-7235; fee) is a striking log structure of Western design containing a large collection of Indian artifacts. The **Old Chief Joseph Monument**, south of town on the lakeshore, is a tribute to Chief Joseph's father, Tuekakas ("Old Chief Joseph"), the final resting place in the land he and his tribe, the Nez Perce, loved so well.

Six miles (10 km) north is the busy

village of **Wallowa**. Try **Vali's Alpine Delicatessen and Restaurant** (closed: Mon) for a pick-me-up meal or supplies. **Wallowa Lake Tramway** (May–Sept daily 10am–4pm; tel: 541 432-5331; fee) claims to be the steepest gondola in North America, with its 8,150-ft (2,500-meter) destination atop **Mount Howard**.

The 9,838-ft (3,000-meter) **Sacajawea Peak** (also known as **Matterhorn Peak**) is visible from Mount Howard. It stands only 12 ft (3.6 meters) lower than its Swiss counterpart, but that's where the similarity ends.

At **Wallowa Lake State Park**, in addition to campsites, there are two yurts and a primitive cabin to rent (Reservations Northwest: tel 800 452-5687; reservations required; fee). Backpacking and traveling with pack animals – horses, llamas, mules and even the occasional burro or goat – are popular pursuits here (Wilderness Pack Station; tel: 541 432-4145; fee). It is also pleasant to stay overnight at the **Wallowa Indian Lodge Motel** (tel: 541 432-2651; reservations recommended).

Journey to Hell and back

The twisting, turning **Hell's Canyon Scenic Byway** officially begins southeast of Joseph (remember to start out with a full tank of gas). At **Salt Creek Summit** (emergency tel: 541 426-3131) there is a snow-park and summer rest stop with an information kiosk. The Wild and Scenic **Imnaha River** is adjacent to Salt Creek; its clear waters offer camping and fishing opportunities even as it serves as a spawning habitat for anadromous steelhead and chinook salmon.

A **fish weir** for capturing salmon is located on the Imnaha River downstream from the mouth of **Gumboot Creek**. It is operated by the Bonneville Power Administration. The trapping of adult fish usually occurs from May through September; the facility is staffed full time then, only part time in other months.

The **Tenderfoot Wagon Road** once served the Tenderfoot Mine, built in 1903, but now serves as a horse and hiking trail in summer. For anyone with time, the **McGraw Lookout** is about 10

LEFT: grave of Old Chief Joseph in the town of Joseph.

Map on page 274

miles (16 km) north of the **Wallowa Mountain Loop Road** on **Forest Road #3965** which is slow and almost impassable in challenging weather. Although the structure is staffed only during emergencies, views are extremely impressive.

From the 5,400-ft (1,650-meter) high canyon rim at **Hell's Canyon Overlook**, visitors can take in sweeping grassland views and read about the canyon's formation. There are easy scenic paths nearby, but be warned: rattlesnakes are everywhere. This dramatic view includes **McGraw Creek**, Hell's Canyon and the very distant **Seven Devils Mountains** – a fortress constructed by demons, they say, which is all dark granite parapets, spires and ramparts. The latter forms the eastern wall of Hell's Canyon and its sculpted peaks have names like She Devil Peak, Devils Throne, Twin Imps, the Ogre and Goblin.

Deepest gorge in America

At a depth of 8,043 ft (2,451 meters) – measured from She Devil Peak to the Snake River floor – **Hell's Canyon** ㉒ is the deepest gorge on the North American continent. By comparison, the Grand Canyon is around 6,000 ft (1,800 meters) deep.

The Wild and Scenic **Snake River** winds for 110 miles (180 km) through its rocky heart, pumping at twice the volume of the Grand Canyon's Colorado River. The Snake can be treacherous, although white-water rafters find it exhilarating and its reservoirs are a mecca to both power boaters and rafters.

On average, the V-shaped canyon is about 10 miles (15 km) wide; on the canyon floor are places where bleak walls rise almost vertically, no more than 200 ft (60 meters) apart. Some of the exposed volcanic rock is estimated to be 250–300 million years old.

The **Hell's Canyon Wilderness Area** (tel: 541 426-4978; user fee) has acres of rugged ridges, grassy benchlands and deep canyons. The latter provides a habitat and winter range for the largest free-roaming elk herd in the US, as well as shelter for bighorn sheep, deer and mountain goats. Surroundings range from gen-

tle hillsides with peregrine falcons flying overhead, to rocky bluffs on which prickly-pear cacti, poison ivy and rattlesnakes are found. These areas of rugged terrain also offer an ideal habitat for a local species of partridge.

Within Hell's Canyon are old-growth boreal forests of ponderosa pine, Engelmann spruce, western larch, and Douglas fir – not to mention rare plants such as MacFarlane's four-o'clock; in fact, there are 24 plant species at the canyon found nowhere else on earth.

Farther along the scenic byway, 38 different layers of lava are visible. A long time ago this land was covered by lava up to 200 ft (60 meters) thick in some places. At **Columbia River Basalt**, columnar basalt forms an impressive pillar formation. The Columbia River Basalt Group is the youngest and most studied flood-type basalt. The province underlain by the basalt is loosely termed the **Columbia Plateau** and covers most of the states of Oregon and Washington. Here, very liquid

basaltic lava emitted from fractures perhaps 17 to 12 million years ago, has been sharply folded and broadly warped, so that its top varies in elevation from slightly below sea level in the Pasco Basin to more than 1½ miles (2½ km) above sea level here in the Wallowa Mountains.

Halfway to nowhere

Near the ragged town of **Halfway** is the **Hell's Canyon Bison Ranch** (year-round, 3-hour tours by arrangement; tel: 541 742-6558; fee). The ranch is a member of The Great Plains Buffalo Association, dedicated to studying the inter-relationship between bison and ecosystems.

Here's how they explain it: "They say the only people who can't handle bison are cowboys. We suspect it's a matter of respect. The old-timey cowboys weren't big on that. Here, we've gone to school to learn how to get the buffalo to want to go where we want them to go. We can share legends and explain what's happening now to the buffalo in America."

Perched on a hay wagon, visitors get close-up viewing and great photo opportunities of the beasts. And although the herds have been known to "thunder," as in cowboy folklore, they might instead be peacefully grazing. Some of the tours offer home cooking as part of the ranch experience; be sure to inquire at the time of booking. Halfway, Oregon, figures its name is about the most promising thing it has going for itself, and in 1999 briefly flirted with the idea of renaming itself "Halfway.com" to give itself more visibility on the internet.

Back along the byway, the roadside **Powder River**, the source of an early Gold-Rush boom, originates in the Blue Mountains and flows through **Powder Valley**. Wildlife viewing is a favorite activity here: beaver, geese and blue heron are all common. A major landslide, **Hole in the Wall Slide**, once temporarily dammed the river and now covers the original road.

Oregon Trail pioneers came through **Virtue Flat** on their way to the Willamette Valley and – poignantly – the ruts from their covered wagons are still highly visible. Within this vast expanse of rolling hills covered with sagebrush is a huge area popular with mountain bikers and drivers of off-road sports vehicles; in the spring it is open grazing land. The byway concludes here, with rugged little Baker City straight ahead.

Baker City

The exhausted pioneers first glimpsed the Oregon Territory from the Baker Valley at a place they called Flagstaff Hill. Renamed **Baker City** ㉓ (tel: 541 523-5855), the town is now equally popular with outdoor enthusiasts and history buffs. Both expert and amateur historians come to Baker City to visit the $11 million **National Historic Oregon Trail Interpretive Center at Flagstaff Hill** (daily: Apr–Oct 9am–6pm; Nov–Mar 9am–4pm, closed: holidays; tel: 541 523-1843; fee). The center focuses on six themes related to westward migration and settlement, including the discovery in 1861 of gold near the Powder River.

LEFT: one to watch: a "Dust Devil" storm near La Grande.

Map on page 274

As a result, within 20 years, Baker City became known as the "Queen City of the Mines," and was a thriving commercial center. By 1900, it was larger than Boise or Spokane, complete with elegant hotels, "bawdy houses," an opera house, trolleys, electricity and a telephone service.

There is access here to the John Day Fossil Beds National Monument *(see page 308)* but closer is the **Elkhorn Scenic Byway** (tel: 541 523-3356), a beguiling, well-marked 106-mile (170-km) loop through the Elkhorn Mountain Range on a two-lane paved road. It takes 4 to 8 hours to circumnavigate. The highest point is at **Rock Creek Butte**, with an elevation of 9,097 ft (2,800 meters).

Along the way, the old wood-burning steam engines of the **Sumpter Valley Railroad** (late May–Sept weekends and holidays three times daily; tel: 541 894-2268; fee) operate along a 3½-mile (6-km) narrow-gauge track. This all-volunteer project is recognized by the National Register of Historic Places.

Near the Idaho border

Back on Interstate 84, **Huntington**  is rather quiet now, but in the latter part of the 19th century this town was a center for hellcats and hell-raisers. As a stagecoach station and later a railroad center, it had its share of saloons, gunfighters and Chinese opium dens.

After following the Snake River for more than 330 miles (530 km), pioneers heading west on the Oregon Trail said farewell to this treacherous black-hearted river at a bend near what is now known as **Farewell Bend State Recreation Area** (year-round; tel: 541 869-2365; fee), not far from Huntington. An old pioneer wagon stands at the park entrance, and remnants of the trail are visible north of the park on Hwy 30.

As pioneers did before them, visitors to the 36-acre (14-hectare) park find an oasis amid the scrubby high desert. The terrain is rolling, rocky, verdant and, in spring, dotted with wildflowers. No trails are marked, but hikers and mountain bikers are free to roam around. The park has some unusual accommodations with a historical slant: choose between a modern re-creation of a **Plains Indian teepee** (sleeps up to a dozen people) or a rebuilt "prairie schooner" **pioneer wagon** (Reservations Northwest, tel: 541 869-2365 or 800 452-5687; fee).

Four rivers – the Snake, the Malheur, the Owyhee and the Payette – converge near here. They have attracted a constant flow of people, like Native Americans, Basques, Hispanics and Japanese, who have made this a rich and diverse region. Near the Idaho border and the confluence of rivers is the town of **Ontario** (tel: 541 889-8012) in the county of Malheur.

Most moving is a reconstructed barracks from a Japanese-American World War II Internment camp, which can be seen at the **Four Rivers Cultural Center** (676 Southwest 5th Avenue; tel: 541 889-8191; fee). The **Owyhee Recreation Area** is rich in geological formations, including an impressive canyon. The Owyhee River continues onward to flow through **Rome** – Rome, Oregon, that is. ❏

RIGHT: hoary marmot sunbathes on the rock.

JOHN DAY FOSSIL BEDS NATIONAL MONUMENT

With its flaming Painted Hills, 30 million-year-old fossils, ancient rock art and spectacular trails, this region continues to intrigue visitors

The 14,000-acre (5,700-hectare) **John Day Fossil Beds National Monument (JDFB)** is actually made up of three different areas scattered across the north central portion of Oregon. Each of these areas is called a "unit": the Sheep Rock Unit, the Painted Hills Unit and the Clarno Unit. The town of **Kimberly ㉕** is located at a connecting point for all three.

Established as a national monument in 1974, this region was the first in which scientists found fossils from five consecutive prehistoric epochs. Spanning more than 40 of the 65-million year duration of the Cenozoic Era, this prolific time was known as the "Age of Mammals and Flowering Plants." The fossils reveal Oregon's surprising past, a time when the high desert was the floor of an ancient sea framed by tropical forests no human ever saw. Responsibility for preserving and interpreting the fossils rests with the National Park Service.

Warm Springs *(see page 273)* makes a good starting point from the west, while the community of **John Day** or **Dayville** are good starting points from the east. To visit all three units, stopping to take in a few highlights at each one, takes about 10 to 12 hours. Two days are recommended, though the trip can be done in one.

BELOW: desert landscape of the John Day Fossil Beds.

Map on page 274

The monument's main **Visitor Center** is located in the historic (1917) James Cant ranch house at the **John Day Sheep Rock Unit** ㉖ (Mar–Nov daily 9am–5pm; Dec–Feb Mon–Fri 9am–5pm, closed: holidays; tel: 541 987-2333; park fee). The center is the place for fossil exhibits, a prehistory orientation film and interpretive talks and programs. Highly regarded are the ranger-guided Blue Basin hikes and Fossil Bed auto tours.

A short distance south of the visitor center is **Sheep Rock Overlook**. In the recent past, wild bighorn sheep and, later, a thriving sheep ranch both occupied this landscape, hence the name. The prominent dark-brown object halfway down the slope of Sheep Rock is a thick and extensive rhyolitic welded tuff. This was produced by a catastrophic eruption of ash from a vent in the **Ochoco Mountains** to the west.

The rock layers of Sheep Rock represent an ancient time, approximately 25 to 28 million years ago, when the region was covered by deciduous forests, and inhabited by three-toed horses, rhinos and saber-toothed cat-like animals.

The walls lining **Picture Gorge** display pictographs painted by an Indian culture centuries ago. Pictographs are rock art painted with pigments made from various minerals. (These differ from petroglyphs, a type of rock art scraped into a rock wall.) The red pigment paints here were derived from crushed iron oxide added to a binder such as eggs, blood, fat or plant juice. Typically applied by finger painting, the images depict human, animal and geometric designs. Evidence of indigenous peoples is provided by these pictographs, and other artifacts.

Seasonally, Native Americans used the John Day River basin as a means of subsistence and passage; the basin provided riparian rangeland, and forested habitat for fishing, hunting and gathering food. The Native Americans of the John Day Basin are the Northern Paiutes, Umatilla, Wasco and the Warm Spring Indians.

BELOW: John Day's Painted Hills in the winter snow.

Just north of Picture Gorge, **Wayside on Highway 19** is a pullout and exhibit describing how this impressive passageway was formed. **Goose Rock Cliffs**, thrust upward by a system of faults, reveal river rocks deposited at an ocean's edge 100 million years ago. Today they provide a nesting place for swallows and a stopover for migrating birds.

The lovely **Blue Basin** is a volcanic ash bowl transformed into a type of claystone by eons of erosion; most of the monument's fossils are found in this blue clay layer. These awesome blue-green canyons reveal fossils over 28 million years old. The short **Island in Time Trail** and the 3-mile (5-km) loop Blue Basin Overlook Trail are two ways to experience these vibrant badlands (off-trail hiking is strictly prohibited). Island in Time, a gently ascending trail, includes interpretive signs and fossil replicas. The dusty **Blue Basin Overlook Trail** is strenuous, but rewarding, leading to a spectacular vista overlooking the **John Day River Valley**.

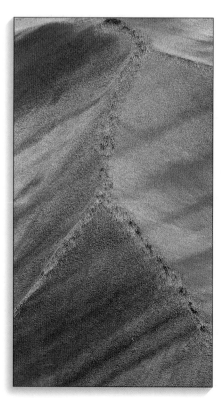

The tall spires of eroded claystone called **Cathedral Rock** create a natural cathedral formation along the river. This landform resulted from a large block of rock dislodging and sliding toward the river, diverting its flow.

The most photographed of the John Day units is the 3,132-acre (1,300-hectare) **Painted Hills Unit ㉗**, located 10 miles (15 km) west of Mitchell and 75 miles (120 km) east of the town of **Bend**. The yellows, oranges, reds and greens of the Painted Hills are sublime, and at their best in late afternoon near sunset.

With ever-changing light and moisture levels, tone and hue are in constant movement. Color changes reflect the ancient soils and vegetation present during a major global cooling event, approximately 33 million years ago. The volcanic ash that accumulated here and weathered into clays long ago also records the onset of Cascade volcanism. Most years, the peak days of wildflower season in late April to early May is outstanding. During the spring and summer, the Painted Hills Ranger Station provides a current report of what is in bloom; the wildflower hotline number is 541 462-3961.

A stunning viewpoint, **Painted Hills Overlook** is the gateway to an easy trail that permits visitors to see the landscape from different angles. Layers of claystone have been exposed and sculpted by water erosion. **Carroll Rim Trail**, a moderately strenuous trail, rewards hikers with an outstanding aerial view of the Painted Hills, surrounding canyons, and **Sutton Mountain**.

Painted Cove Trail is a short trail winding around a crimson-and-ochre hill, permitting a close-up view of popcorn-textured claystones that expand when wet, and a rhyolite flow that marks the transition between the John Day and Clarno Formations. A trail guide is available at the trailhead. Paleobotantists can trace changes in vegetation through the fossil records preserved in the ash.

The fossils of the upper John Day Formation indicate a climate much wetter than today's, in which oak, beech, birch and similar species flourished. The lower

LEFT: flower-accented drainage patterns in the Painted Hills.

Map on page 274

John Day formations speak of a still wetter climate. These changes occurred as the Cascade Mountains rose to the west, creating a rain shadow that precipitated the development of the high desert climate.

Leaf Hill Trail is a short, easy trail that circles a hill filled with the remains of a 30 million-year-old hardwood forest. Fossil leaf exhibits along the trail even show evidence of their veins. Stratifications here are an example of "inverted topography," as this present-day hill is made up of deposits that were once at the bottom of a lake. Leaf fossils preserved in lake deposits throughout the Painted Hills portray changing deciduous forest communities. Thousands of plant fossils have been removed for scientific study, and the research continues.

The **Clarno Unit** ㉘, 18 miles (28 km) west of **Fossil**, is 1,969 acres (800 hectares) in size. Vegetation here is typical of Central Oregon's near-desert environment with a variety of grasses, sagebrush and juniper. The cliffs of the **Palisades** were formed by a series of volcanic mudflows in a much different environment 44 million years ago. Volcanic debris saturated with rainwater once triggered enormous mudflows, called *lahars*, which in turn preserved a diversity of fossils.

At that time, the Clarno volcanoes dominated a landscape covered by near-tropical forest, with approximately 100 inches (250 cm) of rainfall per year.

Tiny four-toed horses, huge rhino-like brontotheres, crocodilians and meat-eating creodonts roamed these ancient jungles. **Trail of the Fossils**, a short walking trail, passes boulders where erosion has exposed glimpses of the fossil forest with its stony limbs, leaves, seeds and nuts.

John Day Fossil Beds National Monument has trails and picnic facilities open all year. The average high temperature in July is 88°F (31°C); the average low in winter is 21°F (–6°C). Camping is not allowed, and there are no facilities for lodging or buying food; be sure to bring your own water. ❑

BELOW: Painted Hills has easy trails and colors that change according to the light.

NEWBERRY NATIONAL VOLCANIC MONUMENT

It's only a matter of time before the volcano erupts again.
Meanwhile, the craters and calderas, lava lands and sparkling lakes
continue to fascinate geologists and tourists alike

Shaped by eruptions spanning more than half a million years, virtually every type of volcanic land feature can be seen at the **Newberry National Volcanic Monument** ㉙. These include cinder cones, spatter cones, tuff cones, ash flows, lava casts and tubes, gaseous vents and hot springs.

Newberry is a shield-shaped volcanic structure with its own huge caldera. Located about 10 miles (15 km) south of the town of Bend in Central Oregon, it is one of the nation's newest national monuments, established by Congress in 1990 in order to preserve its unique geologic structure and landforms.

The protected area includes more than 50,000 acres (20,000 hectares) of lakes, streams and waterfalls. An additional 10,300 acres (4,000 hectares) in special management units were included in the deal to allow current geothermal leases to continue. A wildlife refuge within the caldera rim is managed by the Oregon Department of Fish and Wildlife.

The **Lava Lands Visitor Center** (tel: 541 593-2421) is the central hub, where interpretive talks are given and a limited number of cars are allowed to approach the summit of Lava Butte. Behind the visitor center are two walking trails. One, the **Trail of Molten Land**, meanders over the

LEFT: trail winding through a lava river. **BELOW:** a lava tube shows volcanic forces at work.

Map on page 274

7,000-year-old lava flow from **Lava Butte**; the other, called the **Trail of the Whispering Pines**, wanders through a sharply scented pine forest. **Benham Falls** is a cascading waterfall on the Deschutes River, west of the visitor center.

Newberry Volcano is approximately 25 miles (40 km) in diameter. It is made up of ash, pumice, lava, cinders and mudflows, with deposits ranging from 700,000 to 1,300 years old. The volcano is expected to erupt again, both in a passive way – when lava flows occur – and explosively – when ash and pumice spew into the air. All activity is regularly noted, but no one can say exactly when the volcano will erupt. Nevertheless, modern monitoring methods are so advanced there should be ample warning.

At the 6,300-ft (1,920-meter) summit of Newberry Volcano is **Newberry Crater**, about 4 miles (6 km) in diameter, and filled with the water of two lakes. It is technically a caldera – the gaping hole left when a volcano collapses – rather than a crater. (A crater, on the other hand, can be created by violent impact, not just from implosion.) This caldera collapsed during a series of eruptions over a half million year period; the last of these probably occurred about 200,000 years ago.

A good overview of the monument can be seen by stopping at **Paulina Creek Falls** (which is actually two waterfalls), then driving on to **Paulina Lake Lodge** (tel: 541 536-2240; reservations recommended), with its lakeside cabins, food market, restaurant and fuel pumps. From the lodge, hike up **Paulina Creek** to **Paulina Lake**, on the lowest point of the Newberry Crater rim.

Serious hikers should push onward to 7,984-ft (2,433-meter) **Paulina Peak**, where they will be rewarded with an awesome view of the caldera and of most of Central Oregon. The 360° panoramic view sweeps from Washington to California, then takes in the Cascade Mountains and the Basin and Range region of eastern Oregon – three states in all. ❏

BELOW: obsidian flow above Paulina Lake in Newberry Crater.

CRATER LAKE NATIONAL PARK

*Lying in the collapsed caldera
of a volcano on Mount Mazama, this bowl-shaped
mountain lake has cobalt-blue waters and mysterious depths*

Crater Lake ❸ is so round, so blue, so perfectly tranquil that it seems unearthly. How odd that such an enchanting place is the byproduct of a violent explosion. It occurred some 7,700 years ago when **Mount Mazama** erupted and collapsed. The 1980 eruption of Mount St Helens pales by comparision.

According to a Klamath Indian legend, Mazama's demise was caused by a fierce battle between Llao and Skell, the spirits of the underworld and sky. Spurned by a human woman, Llao rushed to the peak of Mount Mazama and rained fire on her people in punishment. Skell took pity on the humans and, after an earthshaking confrontation, drove Llao back into the bowels of the volcano.

Geologists, of course, have a more prosaic theory as to how this came about. But the geologists *have* been useful. In August 2000, a sidescan sonar survey of the bottom of the lake was conducted, with the most detailed mapping to date. This new research revealed that Crater Lake is 17 ft (5 meters) deeper than was previously thought; the new official depth is 1,949 ft (594 meters). This makes it the deepest lake in the United States, and the seventh-deepest in the world.

Crater Lake's extraordinary depth, combined with a relatively small surface area – only about 6 miles (10 km) in diameter – coupled with its cobalt-blue water, make Carter Lake similar to few other lakes in the world.

LEFT: the Phantom Ship volcanic island.

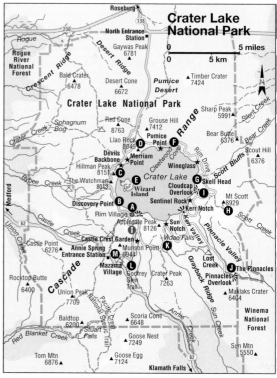

Maps, pages 274 & 314

The 33-mile (53-km) **Rim Drive** around Crater Lake features more than 20 scenic overlooks; the average height of the rim is 1,000 ft (300 meters) above the lake, so they are worth stopping for. Deer or icy conditions are potential hazards, and a slow, steady speed is advised.

Because of weather conditions, the Rim Drive around the east side sometimes closes earlier than scheduled (Oct), and may not open until July. Taking Rim Drive at a leisurely pace, with time set aside for a picnic and a few short hikes, requires a full day, although determined motorists could do the circuit in a few hours.

Rim Village Ⓐ makes a good starting point. Located on the southwest side of the caldera, it is the center of tourist activity. Stop first at the visitor center for a selection of books and maps, and to inquire about free campfire talks and ranger-led nature walks. Then take a quick stroll to the **Sinott Memorial Overlook**, where the sweeping views will help you get a feel for the lay of the land.

Seen under certain lights, a ghostly image appears to be sailing straight out of Samuel Taylor Coleridge's *The Rime of the Ancient Mariner*. **Phantom Ship**, a small island rising 167 ft (51 meters) above the water near Rim Village, was given its name by early explorers.

Driving northwest from Rim Village, there are several landmarks. The first, **Discovery Point Ⓑ**, is believed to be the spot where, in 1853, the first white men set eyes on the lake, which they named Deep Blue Lake. About 2 miles (3 km) up the road, a second peak, the 8,013-ft (2,442-meter) **Watchman**, overlooks the caldera. A short, steep trail leads to a fire tower atop the peak, affording the best views on the western shore.

Almost directly north, **Hillman Peak Ⓒ** is an ancient volcano, now sheared in half. Farther along the caldera wall, a formation known as the **Devils Backbone** – a wall of volcanic rock – juts into the water. Beyond that, **Llao Rock Ⓓ** is an ancient lava flow that hangs from the rim.

BELOW: Wizard Island in the wintertime.

The most prominent landmark on this stretch of the rim is **Wizard Island ⓔ**, a cone-shaped "volcano within a volcano." It rises more than 700 ft (210 meters) above the water level like a wizard's cap. The **Wizard Island overlook** offers the best view.

If you have plenty of time, you can also catch a tour boat to the island from **Cleetwood Cove ⓕ** on the northeast lakeshore. (Allow at least an hour to drive from Rim Village to the parking area, and then to hike down.) The trail to the boats, just under a mile in length, is fairly steep. If you are not too fit, or are in poor health, you may want to pass this up. Otherwise, bring water, sun block, a warm jacket and a camera.

A visit inside the caldera is spectacular, with stunning close-up views of the major formations. Contact Volcano Cruises (summer daily 10am–3pm, weather permitting; 105-minute cruises; tel: 541 830-8700). You can be dropped off on Wizard Island, and picked up later in the after-noon. Tickets can be purchased at the bottom of the trail, and reservations in advance are not allowed.

Back on the road, the eastern side of the lake features three extraordinary view-points. The first, **Skell Head ⓖ**, is an ancient volcanic formation that bulges toward the water. About 2½ miles (4 km) farther on, a steep trail climbs to the summit of **Mount Scott ⓗ**, at 8,929-ft (2,722-meter) the park's highest peak. The path makes a switchback ascent through dense stands of sub-Alpine fir and clus-ters of wildflowers before rising above the treeline, where bleached and gnarled whitebark pine manage to eke out an exis-tence under brutal conditions.

Mount Scott is easily the finest visual perch in the park; keep your eyes peeled for red-tailed hawks, golden eagles and other raptors who soar on the air currents above, looking for landing sites. The trees may appear no bigger than bushes but are often hundreds of years old.

Just beyond the Mount Scott trailhead, a spur road leads to **Cloudcap ⓘ**, the highest overlook on the rim. You can get good views of the Phantom Ship here. For a closer look, stop at **Kerr Notch**, a classic U-shaped valley carved by glaciers. If time allows, you can pick up the 7-mile (11-km) side road that leads straight out to the **Pinnacles ⓙ**. These are spiky, fang-like formations – some of them 100 ft (30 meters) tall or more – that have eroded out of a bed of volcanic ash.

Return to Rim Drive and turn left. The last leg of the journey takes you past **Vidae Falls ⓚ**, where you can picnic next to a stepped 100-ft (30-meter) cas-cade. About 3 miles (5 km) farther on, the **Castle Crest Wildflower Trail** is a pleas-ant stroll through a medley of blossom-ing flowers – lupins, shooting stars, Indian paintbrushes, phlox, gilias and oth-ers – during the summer months.

Interpretive signs point out the names of species that grow beneath the cool understory of old-growth fir and hemlock as well as those that prefer the sunny meadows. Hummingbirds spend the sum-mer in this area, and you can often see them busily collecting nectar.

LEFT: the Pinnacles have eroded out of a bed of volcanic ash.

Map on page 314

But Crater Lake National Park doesn't end with Rim Drive. There are several areas outside the caldera perimeter that are well worth visiting. And it's here that you're mostly likely to catch a glimpse of the park's shy wildlife, including elk, deer, pronghorn and black bears.

About 2 miles (3 km) south of park headquarters, for example, the **Godfrey Glen Trail**  makes a short, easy loop through a dense stand of fir and hemlock that grows at the edge of a weirdly eroded canyon of volcanic ash. Just a little farther down the road, at the Mazama Campground, the **Annie Creek Trail** enters yet another canyon carved out of ancient beds of ash, which are now embroidered with delicate wildflowers.

For longer hikes, a segment of the **Pacific Crest National Scenic Trail** runs the length of the park, swerving around the lake to the west and then flanking the stark, ash-covered **Pumice Desert**, reclining beneath Mount Thielsen just north of the park boundary. Several side trails make interesting trips along the way. It takes 2 to 3 days, possibly more, to cover the entire 33-mile (53-km) Pacific Crest Trail, but short stretches are accessible from Hwy 62 west on Annie Spring Station and the North Entrance Road.

The park is extremely popular with sports enthusiasts. Cyclists find the ride around the lake invigorating, especially when they are pedaling against the prevailing winds, which flow east to west. Runners converge here every August for a marathon race called the Rim Run.

Although many roads are closed in winter, cross-country skiing or snowshoeing can provide a magical way of seeing the lake and the surrounding countryside.

Rim Village has a couple of restaurants, plus the historic **Crater Lake Lodge** (summer only; tel: 541 830-8700; reservations required), built in 1915. **Mazama Village** has a store, a laundry, showers and gasoline. For information, contact **Crater Lake National Park** (tel: 541 594-2211 Ext. 402). ❑

BELOW: Crater Lake from Mount Scott, the park's highest peak.

OREGON CAVES NATIONAL MONUMENT

Oregon Caves – or cave, because there's only one – is low-key, off the beaten path and sparsely visited. This contributes to its charm

L ocated in the far southwestern corner of Oregon, just north of the California border, **Oregon Caves National Monument ❸** may be small in size – only 480 acres (194 hectares) – but it is extremely rich in diversity. Above ground, the monument encompasses part of an old-growth coniferous forest harboring a wide array of plants and a well-known **Douglas fir tree** which has, probably, the widest girth of any tree in Oregon. Three hiking trails lead deep into this green and lovely forest.

The verdant **Illinois Valley** lies at the western end of the Siskiyou Mountains, abutting the **Coast Range**. Hunting is popular in the valley, with hunters annually bagging more than 100,000 deer and 15,000 elk, as well as a number of antelope and bear. Bird hunters can be assured of a high showing of pheasant, quail, pigeon, geese and ducks.

A marble heart

Below ground is where all the action takes place, in a marble cave created by natural forces over hundreds of thousands of years. The **Cave Tour** (Mar–Nov; tel: 541 592-2100; fee) is the best way to understand this monument and its fantastical formations, but it is strenuous, with more than 500 stairs to negotiate, and visitors

BELOW: deer, antelope and elk roam the monument's Illinois Valley.

Map on page 274

must be accompanied by a guide at all times. Inside the caves are a myriad of calcite formations that decorate the marble heart of lofty monuments like **Mount Elijah**. The fine **Marble Halls of Oregon** has pillars, stalactites and canopies of calcite hanging from vaulted domes. **Paradise Lost** is a treasure of parachute-like flowstone in a room 60 ft (18 meters) high, while so-called **Banana Grove's** draperies resemble clusters of fruits.

The **Grand Column** is the junction of a stalactite and a stalagmite, forming the largest column in the cave. Named after a poet, **Joaquin Miller's Chapel** has a pleasing array of dripstone formations worthy of a cathedral.

The **Ghost Room**, the largest cavern, is about 250 ft (75 meters) in length. Evaporated water leaves a residue of bumpy lumps that locals call cave popcorn. A 7-ft (2-meter) calcite column with an imprint resembling a **whale's spine** compliments the **moonmilk** formation. Bats are fairly common at night.

Oregon Caves Chateau (tel: 541 592-3400; reservations required), also called **Oregon Caves Lodge**, offers accommodations right on the site. Built in 1934, the rustic, cedar six-story lodge has a huge fireplace made of local marble and a steeply pitched gable roof broken by gable dormers – a roofline as jagged as a mountain range.

Even non-residents can enjoy the 1930s **coffee shop** with its winding birch and maple lunch counter where you can order an old-fashioned ice-cream dessert. The **dining room**, a fine affair with linen cloths, has a section of a mountain stream diverted through it. Two mounds act as bridges, allowing guests to cross from one half of the room to the other.

Alternatively, you might prefer the amenities of a treehouse resort. **Out N' About Treesort** (tel: 541 592-2208) offers seven suites up in trees. "Treesort" aptly describes the labyrinth of roosts, all with refrigerators, some with baths, and a few connected by suspension bridges. ❏

BELOW: cactus on a wall of basalt.
RIGHT: Oregon Caves Chateau was built in 1936.

Travel Tips

CONTENTS

Getting Acquainted

Area & Features: The Pacific Northwest consists of Washington and Oregon states. Washington (not to be confused with Washington DC, America's capital city) is bounded on the north by the Canadian province of British Columbia, on the east by Idaho, on the south by Oregon, and on the west by the Pacific Ocean.

Its capital is Olympia, and its largest city is Seattle, which is long and narrow. Washington's 66,582 sq. miles (176,600 sq. km) make it the 20th largest state in the US and around half the area of Japan, three quarters of Great Britain, and 40 per cent of California. It is roughly rectangular in shape; its outside dimensions are about 235 miles (380 km) from north to south and approximately 345 miles (555 km) from east to west. The region has six national forests.

Elevations range from sea level to 14,411 ft (4392 meters) atop Mount Rainier, while Washington's coastline on the Pacific Ocean, often called the Olympic Peninsula, is 157 miles (253 km) long.

A series of ocean channels separate the state from Canada's Vancouver Island. Puget Sound, which is approximately one-fifth the size of Lake Erie, deeply indents the northwestern part of the state, and is a mixture of fresh- and saltwater. All these bodies of water contain numerous islands that also form part of the state.

The Columbia River forms much of the southern boundary, taking in the Columbia Gorge National Scenic Area on both the Washington and the Oregon sides.

Oregon, with its western border along the open Pacific Ocean, is immediately north of California. Its state capital is Salem, though the largest city – with over half the population – is the Portland Metropolitan Area. As the 10th largest state in land area, Oregon is 395 miles (635 km) wide and 295 miles (474 km) in length, covering a land area of 97,073 sq. miles (251,418 sq. km). Its highest point of 11,235 ft (3424 meters) is atop Mount Hood, and sea level is at the Pacific Coast. Oregon has 13 national forests, covering over 15.6 million acres. It has 889 sq. miles (2302 sq. km) of inland water and 296 miles (475 km) of wonderful coastline.

State Iconography: Washington entered the Union on November 11, 1889 as the 42nd state. Its state flower is the Coast Rhododendron, its nickname is "The Evergreen State," and the state fruit is the apple. State birds are the Willow Goldfinch or Wild Canary, and the state tree is the Western Hemlock. Washington was named in honor of former US president George Washington and has been confused with the East-Coast city of Washington DC ever since.

Oregon entered the Union before Washington, on February 14, 1859, as the 33rd state. Its state flower is the Oregon Grape, and its state nickname, "The Beaver State." The state bird is the Western Meadowlark, the state tree is the Douglas Fir, the state fish is the Chinook Salmon, and the state rock is the Thunderegg. The exact origin of the name "Oregon" is unknown, though it is generally accepted that the name, which was first used by explorer Jonathan Carver in 1778, was taken from the writings of English army officer Major Robert Rogers.

Population: Washington's estimated population at the end of 2000 was 5.9 million, making it the 15th most-populous state in the US. Its largest metropolitan area is

Seattle, with a population of around 3.4 million.

The entire state of Oregon has 3.2 million inhabitants (1.2 percent of the US population). Its largest city, the Portland Metropolitan Area, has a population of 1.6 million people.

Cultures: The area has a rich mix of cultures. Both Washington and Oregon have large populations of Scandinavian origin. Washington, in particular, has an active population from the Asia-Pacific region. Washington's 2000 census reports: white persons, 78.9 percent; persons of Hispanic or Latino origin, 7.5 percent; Asian persons, 5.5 percent; Black or African American persons, 3.2 percent; American Indian and Alaska Native persons, 1.6 percent. The 2000 Oregon census reports: white persons, 83.5 percent; Hispanic or Latino origin, 8 percent; Asian persons, 3.0 percent; Black or African American persons, 1.6 per cent; American Indian and Alaska Native persons 1.3 percent.

Weights & Measures: The US is one of the few industrialized countries that does not use the metric system. Though the metric system is familiar to American scientists and other specialists, most North Americans are only familiar with the imperial system of pounds, feet, inches, miles, etc. A conversion chart for clothing and shoe sizes is a useful tool for overseas visitors.

The nation is powered with an 110-volt alternating current. Foreign visitors with electrical appliances will need to bring both a converter and an adapter plug.

Time Zones: The Pacific Northwest runs on Pacific Standard Time. On the first Sunday in April, the clock is moved ahead one hour for Pacific Daylight Time. On the last Sunday in October, it is moved back one hour.

When it is noon in the Pacific Northwest it is: 10am in Hawaii; 2pm in Chicago; 3pm in New York and Montreal; 8pm in London; 6am (the next day) in Sydney.

For the local time, tel: 206 3612-8463 in Seattle, or tel: 503 976-8463 in Portland.

Telephone Codes

To place an international call from inside the US (except to Canada), dial "011" + the Country Code + the City Code, followed by the local number. Dialing "00" will get you a long-distance operator.

Ten-digit dialing (the area code plus a seven-digit number) is necessary for many local calls.

Access codes
MCI: 888 757-6655
Sprint: 800 877-8000
AT&T: 800 CALL-ATT

Climate

Climate varies significantly from west to east, as the spine of the Cascade mountain range creates two distinct weather patterns. A mild, humid climate predominates in the western part of the states, while a more extreme but dry climate prevails east of the Cascade Range. Moisture-laden clouds move inland from the Pacific Ocean, releasing precipitation mainly in the western half of the region. The Cascades also pose a barrier to prevailing westerly winds, leaving the eastern area dry and, in some areas, extremely arid.

The wet but generally mild climate west of the Cascades averages daily highs in July of 77°F (25°C), falling to an average of 55°F (13°C) at night. In January, the coldest month, daily high averages

State Area Codes

Washington
Seattle	**206**
East Seattle	**425**
Eastern Washington	**509**
Tacoma	**253**
Western Washington	**360** or **564**

Oregon
Portland Tri-metro	**503**
The Rest of Oregon	**541** or **971**

are 45°F (7°C), rarely falling below 35°F (2°C) at night.

From October through April, Seattle and Portland receive 80 percent of their annual rainfall, averaging 35 inches (900 mm) or more. During this time, the region has frequent cloud cover, periodic fog, and long-lasting drizzles. The far-western side of the Olympic Peninsula, on the Pacific Coast, receives as much as 160 inches (4,064 mm) of precipitation annually, which makes this the wettest area of the 48 mainland US states.

Economy

The Pacific Northwest is a prosperous region that derives its economic strength from a variety of sources. Washington is reliant on defense, aerospace, high technology, and the timber industry, with important additional economic generators including shipping, construction, mining, agriculture, and tourism.

Oregon has a large component of its labor force engaged in managerial service-industry roles and the retail trade, with a large sector devoted to shipping, warehousing, and transportation. Major industries include the lumber and wood products industry, the paper and allied manufacturing industry, and transportation equipment. Oregon's agricultural sector is fiercely proud. The finance, insurance, real estate, and leasing sectors are also large employers, followed by construction and manufacturing jobs including the making of silicon chips.

In both states, commercial forestlands support a major share of the region's economy, producing a third of the nation's softwood timber harvest. Foreign tourists annually spend $6.5 billion enjoying the region's various recreational opportunities.

Public Holidays

January 1st
New Year's Day
3rd Monday in January
Martin Luther King's Birthday
3rd Monday in February
Presidents' Day
Last Monday in May
Memorial Day
July 4th
Independence Day
1st Monday in September
Labor Day
2nd Monday in October
Columbus Day
1st Tuesday in November
Veterans' Day
4th Thursday in November
Thanksgiving
December 25th
Christmas Day

Business Hours

Shopping malls in major cities tend to be open Monday to Saturday from 10am to 9pm or 10pm, and Sundays from 10am to 6pm. Many (but not all) stay open on public holidays as well. Downtown areas of major cities close earlier than locations in the suburbs. Count on many downtown stores closing by 5 or 6pm, after the business crowd goes home.

Banking hours also vary from place to place but tend to be Monday to Thursday, 9am to 4 or 5pm; Friday, 9am to 6pm, and Saturday 10am to 1pm. Downtown banks tend to have abbreviated hours.

Government offices are typically open for business between 9am to 5pm Monday to Friday. Post offices open similar hours, as well as Saturdays from 9am to noon. Both facilities close on public holidays. Convenience stores are often open 7 days a week, 24 hours a day. Bank machines are available in many locations, 24 hours.

Planning the Trip

Visas & Passports

Please note that due to current world conditions entry requirements are subject to change at short notice. Generally, a citizen of a foreign country who wishes to enter the US must, in addition to a valid passport, also obtain a visa. Called a "nonimmigrant visa," this document is compulsory for any temporary stay for business or pleasure. Canadian citizens entering the US need only a birth certificate or passport. Travelers from certain countries may also be able to visit the US without a visa under the Visa Waiver Pilot Program *(see details below)*.

Customs

Every visitor over 21 years of age may bring in, free of duty, the following: (1) 1 liter of wine or hard liquor; (2) 200 cigarettes, 100 cigars (but not from Cuba), or 3 pounds of smoking tobacco; and (3) $100 worth of gifts. These exemptions are offered to travelers spending at least 72 hours in the US.

It is forbidden to bring into the country foodstuffs (particularly fruit, cooked meats, and canned goods) and plants (vegetables, seeds, tropical plants, and the like). For specific information regarding US Customs, call your nearest US embassy or consulate, or the US Customs office, tel: 202 927-1770. www.customs.ustreas.gov

Health & Insurance

It is recommended that before traveling to the United States all visitors separately purchase comprehensive emergency health insurance coverage. Special insurance is needed to protect you and those traveling with you in the case of an accidental or emergency medical need. Policies can cover everything from the loss or theft of your baggage and trip cancellation to the guarantee of bail in case you're arrested. Comprehensive policies should also cover the costs of an accident, repatriation, or death.

Currency & Tax

American-dollar travelers' checks are the safest form of currency. When lost or stolen, they can be replaced and they can be used as cash in most stores, restaurants, and hotels. Banks will generally cash large amounts of travelers' checks (be sure to bring your passport for proof of identity); hotels should cash a limited amount (picture-proof not usually

required). Be sure to bring some actual dollars to pay for your ride from the airport to your first hotel.

TAX

Washington
A retail sales tax of 8.6 percent or more is usually applied to items purchased by consumers. Untaxed items include most grocery store food items and prescription drugs. Generally, no sales tax is charged on utility services or most personal services (medical, dental, legal, barbers, etc). Restaurant meals are taxed. The combined state and local retail sales tax rates range from 7.0 percent to 8.8 percent throughout the state, depending on the local sales tax.

Oregon
Oregon is the only state in the US that does not have a sales tax on either goods or services, and the amount ticketed is the exact amount you pay. There is a non-refundable, hotel-occupancy tax; this varies throughout the state, but hovers around 12 per cent.

What to Wear/Bring

Residents of the Pacific Northwest are quite casual, so informal clothing is fine for most daytime activities. The cities and mountains are best explored on foot, making comfortable walking shoes essential. A light raincoat, umbrella, and sweater are good companions.

Elevation changes are likely to result in the greatest variation for visitors. Starting at lower elevations it may be mild to moderate and wet. However, with a trip into the mountains the weather can turn stormy and cold. Bring several layers of clothing, including a warm coat and hat.

The Northwest is home to several makers of outdoor gear, and travelers needing to buy such goods will find a good range. **Recreational Equipment Incorporated** (REI) is a good bet and has several locations. Tel: 1-800-426-4840 for stores.

Visa Waiver Pilot Program

Travelers coming to the US for tourism or business for 90 days or less from qualified countries may be eligible to visit without a visa. They must, however, present passports and may be required to show additional identification and validating documentation.

Currently, 29 countries participate in the Visa Waiver Pilot Program: Andorra, Argentina, Australia, Austria, Belgium, Brunei, Denmark, Finland, France, Germany, Iceland, Ireland, Italy, Japan, Liechtenstein, Luxembourg, Monaco, the Netherlands, New Zealand, Norway, Portugal, San Marino, Singapore, Slovenia, Spain, Sweden, Switzerland, the UK, and Uruguay.

Visitors entering on the Visa Waiver Pilot Program cannot work or study while in the US and cannot stay longer than 90 days or change their status to another category.

Tourist Offices

Washington

The main tourism site for Washington state is www.tourism.wa.gov.

A free Washington travel packet is available by filling out a form online or contacting a Washington State Travel Counselor, tel: 360 725-5052. You may also write or telephone the official Washington State Tourism offices, PO Box 42500, Olympia, tel: 800 544-1800, fax: 360 753-4470. Additionally in the Seattle area and in busy tourist areas there are designated "**Tourist Bureaus**," for drop-in visitors.

In Seattle, the Washington State Convention & Trade Center, 800 Convention Place, Galleria Level, is open year round (daily, 10am–4pm), tel: 206 461-5800.

Oregon

The Oregon Tourism Commission website is at www.traveloregon.com. A free copy of the *Official Oregon Travel Guide,* with helpful travel information, is available by filling out a form online. You may write or telephone the Oregon Tourism Commission located at 775 Summer St. N.E., Salem, tel. 800 547-7842 or 503 986-0000, fax: 503 986-0001. Additionally, in concentrated tourist areas such as Portland, Astoria, and Klamath, there are designated "**Welcome Centers**" for drop-in visitors. These are staffed with knowledgeable, helpful people, who assist visitors full-time.

A Downtown Portland Welcome Center is located at the World Trade Center (daily, 10am–2pm) 25 SW Salmon St, tel: 503 275-8355.

Throughout the Northwest

Visitor Centers are usually combined with local **Chamber of Commerce offices** and stocked with free brochures. Signs to visitor centers appear roadside near the entrance to most towns. Additional resources for visitors are listed within the main text of this book. There are no specific overseas tourist offices.

Airlines

Carriers serving the Northwest include (with telephone numbers):
Alaska Airlines, 800 426-0333
America West, 800 235-9292
Delta Connection, 800 221-1212
Frontier Airlines, 800 432-1359
Harbor Airlines, 800 359-3220
Horizon Air, 800 547-9308

Getting There

BY AIR

Seattle

The main airport for the region is **Sea-Tac** (an abbreviation for Seattle-Tacoma). For details, visit: www.seattleinsider.com/services/travel/cams/seatac_cam.html

Several major commercial carriers have services to Sea-Tac and connecting flights with the Portland International Airport, PDX.

Carriers serving Seattle include: **American Airlines**, tel: 800 433-7300; **British Airways**, tel: 800 247-9297; **Continental Airlines**, tel: 800 523-3273; **Delta Airlines**, tel: 800 221-1212; **KLM** and **Northwest Airlines**, tel: 800 225-2525; **Scandinavian Airlines**, tel: 800 221-2350; **United Airlines**, tel: 800 241-6522.

Portland

The major air hub for the Portland area and southwest Washington is the **Portland International Airport, PDX,** located next to the Columbia River in northeast Portland. The airport has undergone recent expansion. All major air carriers serving the Pacific Northwest connect here. International carriers land in Seattle and connect to Portland. To arrange your connecting flight between Seattle and Portland, contact Horizon Air, tel: 800 547-9308.

Carriers serving Portland include: **Alaska Airlines**, tel: 800 426-0333; **America West**, tel: 800 235-9292; **American Airlines**, tel: 800- 433-7300; **Continental**, tel: 800 525-0280; **Delta Air Lines**, tel: 800 221-1212.

By Train

Amtrak runs US-wide train services. The *Empire Builder* runs from Chicago to Seattle, Portland, and Vancouver, BC in Canada. Amtrak's daily premier *Coast Starlight,* connects the West Coast's most-popular destination cities, including Los Angeles, San Francisco, Portland, and Seattle, while offering guests "land cruise" travel experience, with superior scenery, fine dining and amenities.

Seattle's Amtrak station is at Third Ave and S. Jackson St, tel: 1-800-USA-RAI. Some trains run from King Station, a block away.

Portland's Amtrak station is historic Union Station, 800 NW Sixth Ave, on NW Broadway, near the Broadway Bridge and the central bus terminal, tel: 503 273-4866. Amtrak trains stop about 10 blocks from the heart of downtown Portland; although you could easily walk from the station into the heart of Downtown, you have to pass through a somewhat rough neighborhood for a few blocks. It's best to take a taxi instead.

Rail Passes for Visitors

International visitors can also buy a **USA Railpass**, good for 15 or 30 days of unlimited travel on Amtrak. The pass is available through many foreign travel agents. With a foreign passport, you can also buy passes at some Amtrak offices in the US, including locations in San Francisco, Los Angeles, Chicago, New York, Miami, Boston, and Washington, DC. Reservations (generally required) should be made as early as possible for each part of your trip. Amtrak also offers an **Air/Rail Travel Plan** allowing international visitors to travel by train and plane. For information, tel: 800 440-8202.

Amtrak

To contact Amtrak for information, reservations and schedules, tel: 1-800-USA-RAIL; 800 872-7245, visit www.amtrakwest.com, or email: service@sales.amtrak.com

Practical Tips

Mail

The US Postal Service has branches in major cities. Stamps can also be purchased from Postal Service vending machines in post office lobbies and other retail locations, or from many retail stores that sell stamps at face value on consignment. Look for the "EASY STAMP" logo in shops.

If you do not know where you will be staying, you may receive mail by having it addressed to you, care of "General Delivery" at the main post office of that town.

For more information, call the Postal Service's toll-free phone number, tel: 800 275-8777.

Seattle
US Post Office, Main Branch
301 Union Street, Seattle
Tel: 206 442-6340

Portland
US Post Office, Main Branch
715 NW Hoyt Street, Portland
Tel: 294-2300

Email

Email kiosk stations are available in hotel lobbies, tourist areas, and shopping malls.

In Seattle, there's also **Kinko's**, 1335 Second Avenue, tel: 206 292-9255, or the **Cherry Street Coffee House**, at 103 Cherry Street in Pioneer Square, tel: 206 621-9372.

In Portland, there's a **Kinko's** Downtown at 221 SW Alder Street, tel: 503 224-6550, and in Northwest at 950 NW 23rd Avenue, tel: 503 222-4133.

Both Seattle and Portland's main libraries have on-line facilities. These tend to be very good, but only a short time per person is allocated, and lines can be long.

Changing Money

Foreign-Currency Exchange
This service is available at major banks throughout the region and at a few (stress-few) Downtown hotels. In **Seattle**, currency-exchange services are at **Sea-Tac Airport** (Thomas Cook). At **Portland International Airport**, there is Travelex America, across from the United Airlines desk.
In Seattle, the American Express, Plaza 600 Building, 600 Stewart St, tel: 206 444-8622, is open Monday to Friday 9am–5pm. For card member services, tel: 800 528-4800.

In Portland, the American Express Travel Service Office, 1100 SW Sixth Ave, tel: 503 226-2961, at the corner of Sixth and Main, is open Monday through Friday from 9am to 5pm. You can cash American Express travelers' checks and exchange major foreign currencies here.

ATMS

Most banks have automated teller machines (ATMs) located at their branches as well as at other convenient non-branch locations for quick and easy withdrawal of American funds. Depending on your ATM card you may have to pay one or more fees for a cash withdrawal outside your home area. Check the logos on your card to see which ATM machines are compatible with your card.

Tipping

Tips are generally expected. The accepted rate for airport porters is $1 per bag or suitcase, similarly for hotel bellboys and porters. A doorperson should be tipped if he or she unloads or parks your car. It is not necessary to tip chambermaids, unless you stay several days. In restaurants, tip 15–20 percent of the total bill. Tip taxi drivers, barbers, hairdressers, bartenders, etc., 10–15 percent.

Security & Crime

Seattle
The least safe neighborhood you're likely to be in is the Pioneer Square area, home to more than a dozen bars and nightclubs. By day this area is quite safe, but late at night, when the bars are closing, extra caution should be taken. Also, take care against pickpockets at Pike Place Market. The area directly below the Space Needle at night is a favorite haunt of muggers.

Portland
Because of its emphasis on keeping Downtown alive and growing, Portland is still a relatively safe city, and strolling the downtown streets at night is pretty safe. Take extra precautions, however, when venturing into the entertainment district along West Burnside Street or Chinatown at night. Northeast Portland is the center of the city's gang activity, so before visiting any place in this area, be sure to get very detailed directions so you don't get lost. If you plan to go hiking in Forest Park, don't leave anything valuable in your car. This also holds true in the Skidmore Historic District (Old Town).

Medical Care

HOSPITALS

Find a hospital in Washington or Oregon by selecting that city at: www.doctordirectory.com/Hospitals/Directory.

Seattle
Hospitals in Seattle include:
Harborview Medical Center, 325 9th Ave, tel: 206 223-3000;
Northwest Hospital, 1550 North 115th St, tel: 206 384-0500;
Providence Seattle Medical Center, 500 17th Ave; tel: 206 320-2000;
University Of Washington Medical Ctr, 1959 NE Pacific St, tel: 206 598-6000; **Virginia Mason Medical Center**, 925 Seneca St, tel: 206 624-1144.

Portland

Hospitals in Portland include: **Legacy Good Samaritan**, 1015 NW 22nd Ave, tel: 503 413-7711; **Providence Portland Medical Center**, 4805 NE Glisan, tel: 503 215-1111; St Vincent Medical Center, 9205 SW Barnes Road, tel: 503 216-1234, off US 26 (Sunset Highway) east of Oregon Highway 217; and the **Oregon Health Sciences University Hospital**, 3181 SW Sam Jackson Park Road, tel: 503 494-8311.

PHYSICIANS

Locate qualified physicians in **Washington** or **Oregon** by visiting: www.doctor directory.com/Doctors/Directory. Alternately, to find a physician in **Seattle**, check at your hotel for a reference, or call the **Medical Dental Building**, tel: 206-448-CARE, or the **Virginia Mason** referral line, tel: 888 862-2737. If you need a doctor in **Portland**, call the **Medical Society of Metropolitan Portland**, tel: 503 222-0156.

DENTISTS

In **Seattle**, contact the **Dentist Referral Service**, tel: 206 448-CARE. In **Portland**, be sure to contact the **Multnomah Dental Society**, tel. 503 223-4731.

Emergencies

Dial **911** to get immediate police, ambulance, fire, or other emergency help. In some remote areas, where the 911 service is not available, dial **0** to get an operator, who will put you in touch with the emergency service required. Hospitals in the Northwest are good, and are typically staffed with physicians and/or nurses 24 hours a day, 7 days a week. Emergency rooms are almost always available, but you will have to pay – alot. Always take out insurance before traveling.

Getting Around

From the Airport

Upon arrival at Sea-Tac (Seattle) or PDX (Portland), there are **taxis**, **limousines**, or **bus services** available curbside at the Baggage Claim level. Ask for directions to the correct area of the airport. In both Seattle and Portland economical Greyline shuttle buses depart every 15 minutes to all major downtown hotels from the Baggage Claim Level.

Many hotels and off-airport car-rental companies provide **courtesy van services** for their guests and customers from their offices to the airport. See the lighted displays in the airport for a direct phone line to these facilities. No reservations are required.

In Portland, Tri-Met **public bus** no. 12 leaves the airport approximately every 15 minutes, from 5.30am to 11.50pm for the trip to downtown Portland. The trip takes about 40 minutes. The bus between Downtown and the airport operates between 5.15am and 12.30am and leaves from SW Sixth Avenue and Main Street.

By Road

Major land routes through the Pacific Northwest are **Interstate 5**, running north to south, from Canada to Mexico, **Interstate 90** running east to west, linking Seattle with Boston, and **Interstate 84**, running vaguely southeast, from Portland to Salt Lake City. Federal and state highways are well maintained and policed, and there are refreshment areas and service stations at

Buses

Both Seattle and Portland have excellent bus services. Most bus lines operate weekdays, weekends, and holidays, serving all major hotels, shopping areas, and other points of interest. Buses are free in specially designated downtown areas in both cities. You must have the exact fare when boarding, but monthly and daily passes are also available.

regular intervals. All highways are free, without tolls.

Note: Pedestrians always have right of way. In Seattle, jaywalking is prohibited and carries a stiff penalty for violators. Although picking up hitchhikers is legal except on freeways, it is potentially dangerous.

Information on Road Conditions

For road conditions or mountain-pass conditions within Washington, tel: 800 695-7623, or visit: www.wsdot.wa.gov/Weather. For the greater Seattle area, tel: 206 368-4499. For information on road conditions in Oregon, visit: www.tripcheck.com/RoadCond/road condindex.htm or, if calling from all areas within Oregon, by touch-tone phone toll free, tel: 800-977-6368. If calling outside of Oregon, tel: 503 588-2941.

CAR RENTAL

To hire a car a major credit card is required, and the driver must be over 25 years and have a valid driver's license. To be on the safe side, take along additional photo identification. Local rental firms or companies that store cars away from the airport (you access the car via a free shuttle bus) sometimes offer slightly less expensive rates than those where you collect the car from the airport. Check insurance provisions before signing anything.

Car-rental agencies at or near Seattle's Sea-Tac airport include:

On-site Counter and Cars

Alamo, tel: 206 431-7588 or 800 462-5266; **Avis**, tel: 800 331-1212; **Budget**, tel: 800-435-1880; **National**, tel: 800 328-4567. Always ask if there is a "discount rate."

On-site Counter, Off-site Cars

Advantage, tel: 800 777-5500 or 206 824-0161; **Dollar**, tel: 800 800 3665 or 206 433-5825; **Enterprise**, tel: 206 248-9013; **Thrifty**, tel: 206 246-7565.

Off-site Counter and Cars

Ace Extra Car Rentals, tel: 206 248-3452; **Century/Rent Rite**, tel: 206 246-5039; **U Save**, tel: 206 242-9778.

CAR-RENTAL TAXES

In **Washington**, there is not only a sales tax but also an additional 10 percent tax and a 10 percent airport concession fee, for a vast 28.3 percent. You can cut 10 percent of this by renting your car somewhere other than the airport.

In **Oregon**, there is a 10 percent tax on car rentals, plus an additional airport-use fee (usually 10 percent) if you pick up your rental car at the Portland airport.

By Floatplane

Small airlines service Puget Sound, the Olympic Peninsula, and the San Juan Islands. **Kenmore Air Seaplanes**, 6321 NE 175th Street, Seattle, tel: 425 486-1257 or 800 543-9595 provide daily scheduled flights from Seattle to Washington's San Juan Islands, British Columbia's Gulf Islands and to Victoria, BC. It also offers private charters for exploring remote islands or quick access to golf and getaways.

By Train

Amtrak's premier Coast Starlight Express
Tel: 1-800-USA-RAIL
www.AmtrakWest.com/coaststarlight
See "Getting There," page 325.

By Ferry

Washington State Ferry
The largest ferry system in the country, tel: 206 464-6400. Tickets are sold on the spot or by reservation, and the ferry system accepts both walk-on passengers and vehicle-and-passengers. The website is www.wsdot.wa.gov/ ferries/index.cfm. Some private ferry operations are passenger-only.

The Alaska Marine Highway System
Offers a passenger and vehicle ferry starting from Bellingham, 90 miles (145 km) north of Seattle, once or twice a week to Haines and Skakway in Alaska.

Water sightseeing
This is possible from Seattle, Portland, and along the Columbia River. See the main text of this book for details.

By Inter-City Bus

Genie Service's **Seattle Express Service** (tel: 509 967-2902 or 800 814-2902) travels between West Richland, Pasco, Richland, Sunnyside, Yakima, and Seattle on several days a week. Passengers with special needs are requested to tel: 509 967-2902, 24 hours in advance of time of travel.

Northwestern Trailways Service (tel: 800 366-3830 or 206 728-5955) travels between Everett, Seattle, Tacoma, and Wenatchee, Moses Lake, Spokane, Pullman, and Moscow and Lewiston, Idaho.

Olympic Bus Lines Service (information and reservations, tel: 360 417-0700) travels between Port Angeles (and other communities on the Olympic Peninsula) and Sea-Tac airport, King Street Station (Amtrak), Greyhound Depot, and hospitals in downtown Seattle.

Quick Shuttle Service (tel: 800 665-2122) travels between Sea-Tac airport and Vancouver, BC; also picking up BC-bound passengers from Seattle, Everett, and Bellingham.

By City Transport

Seattle

Metro, Rider Information Office, tel: 206 553-3000, or 206 287-8463; automated schedule info., tel: 800 542-7876; transit.metrokc.gov

Portland

Tri-Met, tel: 503 238-RIDE; www.tri-met.org/home.htm

By Taxi

In Portland and Seattle, there are taxi stands at large hotels, the bus depot, the train station, the airport, and some street corners. Taxis do not cruise the streets looking for customers as in other locales – when you wish to use a taxi, telephone for one instead *(see numbers below)*. Taxicabs are regulated.

Seattle

Farwest Taxi, tel: 206 622-1717
Gray Top Cab, tel: 206 622-4800
Yellow Cab, tel: 206 622-6500

Portland

Broadway Cab, tel: 503 227-1234
Radio Cab, tel: 503 227-1212
Portland Taxi, tel: 503 256-5400

Travelers with Disabilities

Pennco Transportation provides door-to-door service 24 hours a day, 7 days a week to and from Clallam and Jefferson counties for travelers with disabilities. The company serves Sea-Tac airport, Seattle and Tacoma rail stations, Greyhound stations as well as hospitals and hotels in both cities. They can provide one-on-one transportation for clients with special needs. For further information on their wheelchair van service, tel: 888 673-6626.

Driving Times

Seattle to:
Portland 3 hrs 15 mins
Tacoma 45 min
Vancouver, WA 3 hrs
Vancouver, BC 3 hrs
Olympia 1 hr
Spokane 5 hrs
Walla Walla 6 hrs
San Francisco 15 hrs

Portland to:
Salem 1 hr
Eugene 2 hrs
Mt Hood 1 hr 30 mins
Bend 4 hrs 45 mins
Eureka, CA 9 hrs

Organized Excursions

Coach and Boat Excursions
www.columbiarivercruise.com/cruise
/trips/ashore.html
Special short adventures in the
Pacific Northwest.
**Eating Excursions in the Pacific
Northwest**
www.nwpalate.com/write.html
A subscription to indulge your
palate throughout the Pacific
Northwest.

**Elderhostel Adventures through
Washington and Oregon**
www.elderhostel.org/progopt/
Adventures.Afloat/cat_a901w/
D228A901W.html
Special coastal journeys and
adventures for elders.

**Excursions Up the Columbia River
via the *Columbia Queen***
www.historyamerica.com/TEXT_01/
0120_CQPacificNorthwest.html
Take one of the Delta Queen
Steamboat Company's fleet of
riverboats up the Columbia,
Snake, or Willamette rivers and
discover the beauty and rich history
of the Pacific Northwest.

**Fun Excursions in the Great
Northwest**
www.northwestcharm.com/subjects
/excursions.htm
Ghost towns, airplane rides,
waterfalls, lighthouses and more.

**Guided Fieldtrip Excursions with a
Consulting Wildlife Ecologist**
www2.proaxis.com/~hunter/guiding
Bio-diversity adventures and
oceanic birding and nature
excursions.
**Islands and Wildlife of the Pacific
Northwest: Periodic Excursions**
www.worldwildlife.org/travel/listings
/pac_nw2.htm
World Wildlife Fund travel against the
dramatic backdrop of the Pacific
Northwest's mountainous coastline
and maze of magnificent waterways.

**Pacific Northwest Expeditions for
Young Adults**
www.williwawadventures.com/pages
/pacificnw.htm
Beach backpacking and wilderness
sailing adventures.

**Pacific Northwest Float Trips and
Excursions**
http://members.tripod.com/
davebutton/toc.htm
Raft adventures and eco-tours
throughout the region.

**Sea Kayaking in the San Juan
Islands**
www.crystalseas.com/
Paddle the Pacific Northwest's San
Juan Islands, witness the graceful
blow of an Orca whale, be
surrounded by a small group of
foraging porpoises, and watch as
a bald eagle glides peacefully
overhead against the evening sky.

Small Gauge Railroad Excursions
www.pnwc-nrhs.org/ or
www.northwestrailmuseum.com/
The National Railroad Historical
Society sponsor various excursions
throughout the Pacific Northwest.

**Sporttours in the Pacific
Northwest**
www.sporttours.com/
Will organize ski, dive, golf/spa
resorts, and spectator sports,
groups or incentive travel.

Terratrek
www.goterratrek.com/
Premier group bicycle tour
excursions through the San Juan
Islands, Washington.

**Whale Watching Excursions
throughout the Pacific Northwest**
www.physics.helsinki.fi/whale/usa/
washington/wa.html or
www.whaleguide.com/directory/
pacific_nw.htm
Choices for whale-watching
adventures.

Add-On Trips

Visitors to Seattle can travel to
Victoria, British Columbia, in
Canada within 5 hours. There are
several options available from
Victoria Clipper, Pier 69, 2701
Alaskan Way, tel: 800 888-2535,
206 448-5000, or, in Victoria,
tel: 250 382-8100.

Throughout the year, a
catamaran passenger ferry taking
3 to 5 hours and a high-speed
turbo-jet passenger ferry taking only
2 hours make the trip. This latter
ferry is one of the fastest
passenger boats in the western
part of the US.

The trip to Victoria is memorable,
threading its way through the
islands and headlands of upper
Washington, with a view of
mountains and water constantly on
the horizon. If you're interested in
standing out on deck, be sure to
take a sweater, as it will be chilly
outside, no matter the season. If
possible, plan to return to Seattle
around sundown – sunset over
Puget Sound from a boat in the
middle of it, is something to write
home about.

Also within striking distance is
the Canadian city of **Vancouver,**
3 hours by car, and its two notable
cruise ship terminals. From here,
all the major cruise lines ply the
waters to and from Alaska, one of
the world's great cruise itineraries.

Seattle also has good access to
Hawaii, via a 5-hour flight. Due to
its close access, airfares are often
low: Hawaiian Airlines, tel: 800
367-5320.

Where to Stay

Lodging Chains

At least one example of a chain hotel or motel such as those listed here can be found in almost any large community in the Pacific Northwest (although the islands of Puget Sound are exempted). These establishments offer a good standard of service, predictable comfort and very competitive rates. They are usually set a bit back from the highway to reduce highway noise, but are heavily advertised along the way.

Always ask for a reduced rate when arriving at these hotels. The desk clerk will often adjust rates downwards if he or she is asked.

• **Best Western:** Call one of the following toll-free numbers for reliable accommodations throughout the Pacific Northwest; within the US, tel: 800 780-7234; within the UK, tel: 0800 39 31 30 fax: 353-1 6612646; within Germany, tel: 0180 221-2588; within the Netherlands, tel: 0800 022 1455; within Canada, tel: 800 780-7234; within Australia, tel: 131 779, fax: 61 2 9264-2062; within New Zealand, tel: 0800 237 893.

Hotels Online

A list of accommodations available throughout the two states can be found at: www.ase.network. For hotel discounts online, visit: www.180096hotel.com/cgi-bin/citylist?SID=G57&LKF=G57&TRK=H1 or, in the US, tel: 800 715-7666. In Europe, tel: 00800 1066 1066, and in other countries, tel: 214 369-1264.

Best Western offers reasonably priced accommodation, often setting the standard for the small towns and cities where they have well located facilities just set back from the highways. www.bestwestern.com

• **Days Inn:** Within the US, tel: 800-DAYSINN. Motor hotels vary in size, age and price but offer a basic budget stay in a clean room. There's an emphasis on special programs and savings. www.daysinn.com

• **Doubletree Hotels** are usually spacious facilities located in or near major urban areas and offer an impressive array of amenities. Linked to Hilton hotels, they are unique to the Pacific Northwest. Within the US, tel: Toll-Free Reservations 1-800-984-4878; www.doubletree.com

• **Hampton Inn** and **Hampton Inn & Suites** offer good-value, comfortable, and predictable places to stay, usually with a continental breakfast. www.hamptoninn.com

• **Holiday Inn Express:** These often-new hotels have reduced the business components of regular Holiday Inns, adjusted prices downward, and are noted for well-priced specials. Call one of the following toll-free numbers for accommodations throughout the Pacific Northwest; within North America, tel: 800 238-8000; within Australia, tel: 1300 363 300; within Canada, tel: 800 238-8000; within Germany, tel: 0800 181 5131; within Ireland, tel: 1800 553155; within New Zealand, tel: 0800 801 111; within the UK, tel: 0800 897121; from other countries in Europe, tel: 31 20 60 60 222. www.sixcontinentshotels.com/holiday-inn

• **Ramada Inns** usually have conference centers as well as predictable and familiar facilities; they are the companion and slightly cheaper version of Marriott Hotels. Tel: 800-2-RAMADA. www.ramadahotels.com

• **Red Lion Hotels:** This chain offers a good standard of care and comfortable hotels, in key locations in the Pacific Northwest, although they have fewer properties than the other groups listed here. Reservations are handled by Hilton Reservations Worldwide (HRW). Primarily, Red Lion calls flow to the Vancouver, Washington location, but all of the HRW facilities are able to sell Red Lion reservations. There is a separate toll-free number within North America, tel: 1-800-RED LION.

• **Shilo Inns and Resorts** have more than 46 convenient locations in 9 western states. Their mission is to provide beautiful, clean, comfortable, and affordable accommodations with friendly, dedicated staff. Facilities vary quite a lot in luxury, and rooms are priced accordingly. Call toll free within North America, tel: 800 222-2244.

• **Westcoast Hotels**: Generally romantic getaways, situated throughout the Pacific Northwest. Tel: 800-325-4000 or visit: www.westcoasthotels

Bed & Breakfast Inns

Be sure to check the main text of this book for particularly well-placed, historical, or special accommodation. Also check the pages to follow in the specific "Where to Stay" sections of both the Washington and Oregon Travel Tips. **Bed & Breakfasts** as well as **small inns**, (a slight variation of B&B's) and both luxury and rustic **cabins** are placed within these listings.

The following associations represent groups of B&B owners in a particular area.

• **Bed and Breakfast Inns Online** Recommended sites include: www.bbonline.com www.bbdirectory.com www.bestinns.net Once online, select the state (Washington or Oregon) in which you want to stay. The listings generally offer good descriptions.

Holiday villas beyond indulgence.

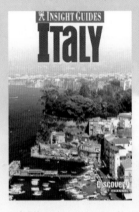

- **Washington State B&B Directory**
Features a selection of properties,
Tel: 800 647-2918; email:
info@Awbbg.com
- **Stash Tea's list of Bed &
Breakfast Inns**
www.stashtea.com/bbg-wa.htm
A directory of Washington inns that
participate in special offers and
apparently serve a good cup of tea.
- **Washington State Bed and
Breakfast Guild**
www.wbbg.com
Features inns that are licensed,
inspected, and approved to meet
high standards.
- **Bed and Breakfast Inns of North
America**
www.bestinns.net
A directory that lists several
good inns.
- **10,000 Inns**
www.10000inns.com/bb_us/or.htm
An Internet Guide to Oregon's Bed
and Breakfast Inns.

Western Style

Visit www.ranchweb.com for dude
ranches, fly-fishing resorts, working
cattle ranches, spa ranches, or Wild
West theme accommodations.

Hostels

**Hostelling International
Washington**
92 Union St, Seattle
Tel: 206 381-9926
www.hostelweb.com/washington/
hostels.htm
Six hostels in Washington offer
environmentally sensitive places for
budget-minded travelers. Locations
are in Blaine, Fort Flagler State
Park, Grays Harbor, Port Townsend,
and Seattle. **$**

Hostelling International Oregon
3941 SE Hawthorne Blvd, Portland
Tel: 503 239-0030
Fax: 503 232-2332
www.hostelweb.com/oregon/
hostels.htm
Five hostels in Oregon (in
Portland, Bandon, and Seaside)
offering environmentally sensitive
places for budget-minded
travelers. **$**

Shopping

What to Buy

Made in the Northwest
www.gonorthwest.com/store/
nwmade/nw_made.htm
Showcasing a variety of products
and services that are only produced
in the Pacific Northwest. Check out
Oregon and Washington.

Made in Oregon Stores
www.madeinoregon.com/
Features Oregon's best-smoked
salmon, berry products, Pendleton
Blankets, jewelry, and accessories,
all made in Oregon.

Made in Washington Stores
www.madeinwashington.com/
storeinfo.cfm
There are seven dedicated stores
throughout Washington featuring
glass art, pottery, foods and crafts
– all made in Washington.

**A Northwest Wine Buying Guide
from Wines Northwest**
www.winesnw.com/winebuying.htm
Information about a large variety of
Oregon wines, Washington wines,
and other wines from Pacific
Northwest regions.

**Reading List as a Guide to Buying
Indian Art in the Pacific Northwest**
www.sfu.ca/archaeology/museum/
nwcart/readlist.htm
Books to improve your
understanding of Northwest Coast
First Nations Art.

Sales Tax

In Washington there are variable
sales taxes on most consumer
goods ranging from 7.8 percent
to 8.8 percent. In Oregon there
is no sales tax on consumer goods.

Where to Eat

Eating Out

The aim of the restaurant listings
on the following pages is to point
out unusual places. This in no way
detracts from the good job done by
chain eateries, which can be found
dishing up harty American fare
at competitive prices throughout
the Northwest.

The restaurants listed here
may not be obvious during a quick
drive through the main street of
town, but it is worth the extra
effort to track them down as an
enhancement to a trip through
the Northwest. The listings
emphasize fresh, regional, well-
prepared food, wines, and
microbrews in restaurants with
great views or ambiance that
provide an experience to remember.

What to Drink

You must be at least 21 to buy
or consume alcohol. Liquor is
sold by state stores (closed
Sunday and holidays)
and licensed venues (until 2am
in Washington, 2.30am in
Oregon). Packaged wine or beer
is sold in grocery stores.

Local **microbrew beers** are
legendary and are sold both in
regular pubs and brewpubs
where they are made. For a guide
to good beer in Washington and
Oregon, visit:
www.nwbrewpage.com

Both states' **wine industries**
are growing in importance. Try a
local Washington or Oregon **Pinot
Noir**.

Throughout Pacific Northwest
cities, drinking **flavored coffees**
is *de rigor*.

Washington

SEATTLE/TACOMA

Seattle Airport/Sea-Tac

Courtyard Seattle Marriott, Sea-Tac Area
16038 West Valley Hwy, Tukwila
Tel: 425 255-0300 or 800 643-5479
Fax: 425 204-4975
www.marriotthotels.com
One of two Marriott hotels in the area; courtyard and comfortable sitting area, in-hotel- restaurant, swimming pool, whirlpool, exercise room; 4 miles from airport and about 12 miles from city center; comfortable guestrooms. **$$–$$$**

Econolodge Sea-Tac Airport South
19225 International Blvd
Tel: 206 824-1350
Fax: 206 824-8535
Basic clean rooms; a 24 hour airport shuttle will run any hour of the day, just telephone for pickup. 0.5 miles to airport. **$**

La Quinta Inn-Sea-Tac
2824 S. 188th St
Tel: 206 241-5211; 800 687-6667
Fax: 206 246-5596
Comfortable rooms, whirlpool spa and pool, close to restaurants, guest laundry, free airport shuttle available from 5.30am to midnight; 0.25 miles from airport. **$$**

Seattle

Alexis Hotel
1007 First Ave, Seattle
Tel: 866 356-8894 or 800 264-8482
Fax: 206 621-9009
www.alexishotel.com/
On the National Registry of Historic Places and near Pioneer Square, each luxurious room has an art collection reflecting local artists, complimentary wine tasting, gym, and valet parking. **$$$$**

Bed & Breakfast Association of Suburban Seattle:
www.seattlebestbandb.com
Each property, offering warmth and coziness, is in close proximity to the city, yet without the bustle associated with Downtown.

Best Western Executive Inn
200 Taylor Avenue N, Seattle
Tel: 206 448-9444 or 800 351-9444
Fax: 206 441-7929
www.bestwestern.com
Renovated traveler's motel with good access to Downtown attractions near the Space Needle and the Monorail. **$–$$**

Best Western Pioneer Square Hotel
77 Yesler Way, Seattle
Tel: 206 340-1234 or 800 800-5514
Fax: 206 467-0707
email: info@pioneersquare.com
www.pioneersquare.com/
Comfortable restored old brick hotel well located. Close to Underground Tour and waterfront, complimentary continental breakfast, but the parking fee is extra. **$–$$**

Gaslight B&B
1727, 1733 15th Ave, Seattle
Tel: 206 325-3654
Fax: 206 328-4803
www.gaslight-inn.com
Old buildings embellished with Northwest Native art and antiques, there's a garden and views. Simple breakfast, very friendly and surprisingly affordable. **$–$$**

Hampton Inn and Suites
700 Fifth Avenue N, Seattle
Tel: 206 282-7700
Fax: 206 282-0899
www.hamptoninn.com
Part of a chain of hotels in lower Queen Anne District, clean and spacious; near Seattle Center and Experience Music Project. **$–$$**

Inn at Harbor Steps
1221 First Ave, Seattle
Tel: 888 728-8910
Fax: 206 748-0533
www.foursisters.com/inns/innathar borsteps.html
Small, luxurious and comfortable hotel, heart of Downtown near Pike Place Market, many rooms with fireplaces, complimentary breakfast; homemade cookies. **$$$**

Inn at the Market
86 Pine Street, Seattle
Tel: 206 443-3600 or 800 446-4484
Fax: 206 448-0631
www.innatthemarket.com
A boutique hotel above Pike Place market with good access to shops, views of Elliott Bay and Olympic Mountains. **$$$**

Pacific Plaza Hotel
400 Spring St, Seattle
Tel: 206 623-3900 or 800 426-1165
Fax: 206 623-2059
www.pacificplazahotel.com
Value-for-money, European-style hotel within walking distance of Downtown, Pike Place Market and Pioneer Square. All rooms have cable, in-room movies and voice mail. The lobby offers a bit of privacy if needed for meetings, and the staff are helpful. **$–$$**

Renaissance Madison Hotel
515 Madison St, Seattle
Tel: 206 583-0300 or 800 278-4159
Fax: 206 624-8125
www.renaissancehotels.com
Upscale rooms with sitting areas in the heart of Downtown, with cafés, restaurants and lounges; good views. **$$$**

Seattle Bed & Breakfast Association: tel: 206 547-1020 or 800 348-5630. Obtain information on specific amenities, locations for member inns as well as referrals based on availability for particular dates and particular requirements.

Tacoma

Austrian B&B and Suites
723 N Cushman, Tacoma
Tel: 253 383-2216 or 800 495-4293/then dial 7097
www.travelguides.com/inns/full/WA/19718.html
Decorated with Austrian folk art and antiques and located in a residential neighborhood, all rooms have private entrances and can be found within 15 miles of Tacoma; economical. **$**

Commencement Bay B&B
3312 Union Ave, Tacoma
Tel: 235 752-8175
Fax: 253 759-4025
www.bestinns.net/usa/wa/cb.html
Colonial-style home with great views
of Elliott Bay and the lighthouse.
Romantic. **$$$**

Days Inn Tacoma Mall
6802 Tacoma Mall Blvd, Tacoma
Tel: 253 475-5900
Fax: 253 475-3540
reservations.lodging.com/servlet/P
ropertyInformation/DI_06315/hco
Renovated budget traveler's motel,
one of two Days Inns in the area,
continental breakfast, and only a
few minutes from downtown
Tacoma. **$$**

PUGET SOUND & THE SAN JUAN ISLANDS

**Go Northwest Directory of Puget
Sound Bed & Breakfasts:**
www.gonorthwest.com/Washington/
puget/pugetbandb.htm

Anacortes on Fidalgo Island/Puget Sound
Hasty Pudding House
1312 8th Street, Anacortes
Tel: 360 293-5773 or 800
368-5588
Fax: 360 293-5773
www.hastypudding.net/hasty/
Craftsman-style home *circa* 1 913;
antiques, abundant breakfast,
peace and quiet, great beds; great
excuse to take the ferry, no kids.
$-$$

Bainbridge Island/ Puget Sound
Agate Pass Waterfront Bed & Breakfast
16045 305 Poulsbo
Tel: 206 842-1632 or 800
869-1632
www.agatepass.com
Located between Bainbridge Island
and Poulsbo with ferry and road
access to Seattle and Tacoma;
there are four beachside rooms and
gardens, including the unique
"Lighthouse" room, 35 feet up with
a sweeping view of the water; no
smoking. **$-$$**

Island Country Inn
920 Hildebrand Lane, Bainbridge
Island
Tel: 206 842-6861 or 800
842-8429
www.nwcountryinns.com/island
Quiet retreat with guestrooms or
suites; complimentary continental
breakfast. **$$**

Hotel Prices

Prices are generally per room per
night in high to mid-season
(though in some cases they are
"per person" at the discretion of
the hotel). Low season rates may
be considerably reduced. In many
cases (but not all) these prices
include a better-than-average
continental breakfast.

$$$$	over $201
$$$	$150–200
$$	$100–149
$	under $99

Bellevue/Puget Sound
Courtyard Seattle Bellevue by Marriott
14615 NE 29th Place, Rt 250 Exit
148, Bellevue
Tel: 425 869-5300 or 800
321-2211
Fax: 425 883-9122
www.marriott.com
Comfortable rooms close to the
Overlake Shopping Center,with its
own restaurant. No smoking. **$$**

Hyatt Regency Bellevue
900 Bellevue Way NE, Bellevue
Tel: 425 462-1234 or 800
233-1234
Fax: 425 698-4281
www.hyatt.com/usa/bellevue/hotel
s/hotel_belle.html
High-rise hotel with enclosed garden
across from huge shopping mall,
restaurant; 10 miles
to Seattle, 17 miles to Sea-Tac
International Airport. **$$**

Bellingham/Puget Sound
The Castle Gate House Bed and Breakfast,
1103 15th St, Bellingham
Tel: 866 756-2224
www.castlegatehouse.com
Three-story Victorian home with

warmly furnished interior rooms and
sweeping views of the San Juan
Islands, Fairhaven and Chuckanut
Mountains. Nice flower gardens.
Great as a romantic escape from
the hectic world. **$$**

Hampton Inn Bellingham Airport
3985 Bennett Dr Bellingham WA
Tel: 360 676-7700
Fax: 360 671-7557
Four-story property with fitness
center, convenient to shopping,
local business, minutes from the
Canadian border; serves milk and
cookies each night; continental
breakfast. **$**

North Garden Inn Bed & Breakfast
1014 North Garden St, Bellingham,
WA
Tel: 360 671-7828 or 800
922-6414
www.nas.com/ngi/
Queen Anne Victorian house on
the National Historic Register with
relatively simple rooms and views
of gardens, Bellingham bay, Puget
Sound and the San Juan Islands.
It's also close to the Alaska Ferry
Terminal, the Cascade Amtrak
train station, whale-watching
excursions and skiing at Mount
Baker. **$-$$**

Bremerton/Puget Sound
Illahee Manor Bed & Breakfast
6680 Illahee Road NE, Bremerton
Tel: 360 698-7555 or 800
693-6680
Fax: 360 698-0688
www.illaheemanor.com
Well-decorated tranquil getaway on
a beautiful country property with
llamas and deer. Comfortable,
peaceful and private with Jacuzzi
tubs, water views, an a welcoming
and hospitable host. **$$-$$$**

Everett/Enumclaw/ Puget Sound
Howard Johnson Plaza Hotel
3105 Pine St, Everett
Tel: 360 339-3333 or 800 IGO-HOJO
Fax: 425 259-1547
Large hotel with 247 variously
styled but absolutely fine rooms;
restaurant and a fitness center .
This is a good place to stay if
you're going on the Boeing tour.
$-$$

Welcome Motor Inn
1205 Broadway, Everett
Tel; 425 252-8828 or 800
252-5512
Fax: 425 252-8880
Budget motel convenient to the
Boeing facility; cable TV. **$**

La Conner/Puget Sound
LaConner Channel Lodge
205 N. First St, La Conner
Tel: 360 466-1500 or 888
466-4113
Fax: 360 466-1525
www.laconnerlodging.com/
Clodge.html
Cedar lodge featuring waterfront
rooms with private balconies
usually good for watching passing
boats. Plus access to the famous
Tulip Festival or Deception
Pass and San Juan Islands to
view eagles, blue herons and loons.
$$
The Country Inn
107 S. Second St, LaConner
Tel: 360 466-3101 or 888
466-4113
Fax: 360 466-4113
www.laconnerlodging.com/Inn.html
Quaint and charming; includes a
library with fireplace and 28
bedooms, most with gas
fireplaces. Complimentary
continental breakfast plus notable
adjoining restaurant and pub.
$$

Mercer Island/Puget Sound
The Tree House Bed & Breakfast
Mercer Island
Tel: 206 230-8620
Fax 206 236-5274
www.treehousebedandbreakfast.com
Upper -floor rooms have phones,
down comforters, lovely linens,
fresh flowers, handmade soaps and
private decks. **$–$$**

Olympia/Puget Sound
Best Western Aladdin Motor Inn
900 Capitol Way S, Olympia 98501
Tel: 360 352-7200
Fax: 360 352-0846
www.bestwestern.com/
Functional comfortable motel within
walking distance of the Capitol
grounds and government offices,
restaurant. **$**

Harbinger Inn Bed & Breakfast
1136 E Bay Dr NE, Olympia
Tel: 360 754-0389
Fax: 360 754-7499
http://iyp.uswestdex.com/harbinge
rinn/Page1.html
Pillars and balconies grace a 1910
mansion with views of the bay and
mountains, no TVs. **$–$$**

Orcas Island /San Juan Islands
Deer Harbor Inn
Deer Harbor
Tel: 360 376-4110 or 877
377-4110
Fax: 360 376-2237
www.deerharborinn.com
Romantic, peaceful rooms with
down comforters, quilts and private
baths plus restaurant; also
cottages and spa. **$$–$$$**
**Doe Bay Village "Resort" and
Retreat**
107 Doe Bay Rd, Star Rt 86, Olga
Tel: 360 376-2291
www.davidgonzales.com/talesdoeba
y.html
Retreat for neo-hippies and
vegetarians who use the hot tub
clad only in a smile; clothing
optional; primitive cabins, yurts, a
hostel and campsites. **$**
Rosario Resort and Spa
1400 Rosario Road, East Sound
Tel: 360 376-2222 or 800
223-7637
www.rosario-resort.com
Nine buildings on large grounds,
guest rooms and suites with
fireplaces, Jacuzzi tubs and
private balconies, overlooking
Cascade Bay and the marina.
The historic parts of this
fabulous hotel have teak
parquet floors and a music
room with a Tiffany chandelier
and a working Aeolian organ.
$$$–$$$$
Spring Bay Inn on Orcas Island
Olga
Tel: 360 376-5531
Fax: 360 376-2193
www.springbayinn.com
Guest rooms feature waterfront
views, wood stoves, feather beds,
high ceilings, fresh flowers, and
private baths plus included kayak
tour and some meals. No smoking.
$$$$

*Paulsbo/Kitsap Peninsula/
Puget Sound*
Houseboats for Two
308913 Highway 101, Brinnon
Tel: 360 796-3440 or 800-
9ONLY42
www.houseboats4two.com
Unique getaway for weekend retreats
in a houseboat set up for two people.
At the marina are a small grocery
store, gift shop, laundry, a heated
pool (open April–October), boat and
airplane rides, and a deli with fresh-
baked pizza. **$$$$**
Manor Farm Inn
26069 Big Valley Rd NE, Poulsbo
Tel: 360 779-4628
Fax: 360 779-4876
www.manorfarminn.com
White farmhouse, full breakfast,
pine antiques, non-smoking, private
baths, restaurant. **$$**

Port Townsend
**FW Hastings House Old Consulate
Inn**
313 Walker St, Port Townsend
Tel: 360 385-6753 or 800
300-6753
Fax: 360 385-2097
www.oldconsulateinn.com/
A restored Queen Anne masterpiece
which is a National Historic
Landmark and State Landmark. This
"Painted Lady" is said to be the
most photographed Victorian
mansion in the Pacific Northwest;
rates are based on double
occupancy and include afternoon
tea, evening desserts, cordials and
a "Banquet Breakfast." **$$$–$$$$**
James House
1238 Washington St, Port
Townsend

Port Townsend B&Bs

The Victorian-era town of Port
Townsend is considered the Bed &
Breakfast capital of the
Northwest. From historic homes to
gracious modern lodgings, each
provides something unique,
usually with a warm and friendly
welcome. See the listings on this
page or check out this website:
www.ptguide.com/
accommodations

Tel: 360 385-1238 or 800 385-1238
Fax: 360 379-5551
www.jameshouse.com/
Eleven sweetly decorated rooms or two ground level garden suites. There's also the renovated Gardener's Cottage. Expansive water views and private baths, room rates include full breakfast. **$$–$$$**

San Juan Island
Argyle House
685 Argyle, Friday Harbor
Tel: 360 378-4084 or 800 624-3459
Email: info@argylehouse.net
www.argylehouse.net/
Craftsman-designed home located only 2 blocks from downtown Friday Harbor, with gardens and three upstairs guestrooms or cottage, each with private bath. **$$**
Bed and Breakfast Association of San Juan Island
Tel: 360 378-3030
www.san-juan-island.net
Various properties. **$–$$$**
Friday Harbor House
130 West Street, Friday Harbor
Tel: 360 378-8455
Fax: 360 378-8453
E-mail: fhhouse@rockisland.com
www.fridayharborhouse.com
Twenty elegant guestrooms with sitting areas and natural wood furnishings; all modern conveniences plus large windows with partial or full harbor views, whirl jetted tubs, and an elegant dining room serving good food.
$$$–$$$$
Roche Harbor Village & Hotel de Haro
248 Reuben Memorial Dr, Roche Harbor
Tel: 360 378-2155 or 800 451-8910
Fax: 360 378-6809
www.rocheharbor.com
Historical Hotel de Haro has been serving guests since 1886. It has four antique-filled suites with private bathrooms, plus 16 rooms with shared bathrooms overlooking beautiful formal gardens and a charming harbor. The hotel also has condominiums and town cottages.
$$–$$$$

Silverdale/Kitsap Peninsula/Puget Sound
WestCoast Silverdale Hotel
3073 NW Bucklin Hill Rd, Silverdale
Tel: 360 698-1000 or 800 544-9799
Fax: 360 692-0932 or Email: silverdalesales@westcoasthotels.com
www.westcoasthotels.com
Built in 1986, this is a great-value waterfront hotel. Guestrooms have private balconies and sweeping views of Dyes Inlet. There's also a fitness center and access to the Trident submarine base, specialty shops and antique stores. **$**

Whitbey Island/Puget Sound
Captain Whidbey Inn.
2072 West Captain Whidbey Inn Rd, Coupeville
Tel: 360 678-4097 or 800 366-4097
www.captainwhidbey.com
Built out of local madrone (tree) logs, the inn offers romantic rooms, cottages or chalets located in a forest, plus there's elegant dining on the wooded shore of Whidbey Island's Penn Cove. **$$**
Whitbey Island's Cliffhouse
727 Windmill Drive, Freeland
Tel: 360 331-1566
www.cliffhouse.net
Architectural spaces enhance romance by a crackling fireplace. Freshen up in a spa at this secluded luxury cottage with sunset views and miles of beach. **$$$**

COASTAL WASHINGTON

Aberdeen & Hoquiam
Hoquiam's Castle B&B
515 Chenault Ave, Hoquiam
Tel: 360 533-2005 or 877 542-2785
Fax: 360 533-2005
http://hoquiamcastle.com
Historical lumber baron's 3-story mansion recently converted into a fine B&B, with chandeliers, Tiffany-style lamps and a parlor. **$–$$**

Long Beach area
Lodging selections on Long Beach
www.discoverycoast.com/lodge_main.htm

The Breakers
Just north of Downtown Long Beach
Tel: 360 642-4414 or 800 219-9833
www.breakerslongbeach.com
Looking like a generic public housing project, rooms are plain but economical, next to the beach with view of ocean surf, some kitchenettes. **$**

Nahcotta
Moby Dick Hotel and Oyster Farm
Sandridge Road, Nahcotta
Tel: 360 665-4543
Fax: 360 665-6887
Old flat-roof US Coast Guard Horse Patrol Station converted into serviceable rooms, with a Japanese dry sauna, dining room and lounge area. Oysters are plentiful in season, but cost extra to eat. **$**

Neah Bay
Silver Salmon Motel
Neah Bay
Tel: 360 645-2388 or 888 713-6477
www.silversalmonresort.com
A basic motel across from the marina, no air conditioning. A plain motel in a plain Indian village, it's the only half-decent place to stay for many miles. **$**

Ocean Shores
Canterbury Inn
643 Ocean Shores Blvd
Ocean Shores
Tel: 360 289-3317 or 800 562-6678
www.canterburyinn.com

Each basic condominium in this long complex features a separate bedroom, a small living area and a full kitchen. Most have views of the ocean. On-site amenities include a pool and a hot tub, but the facility is a non smoking one. **$–$$**

Port Angeles
Domaine Madeleine B&B
146 Wildflower Lane, Port Angeles
Tel: 360 457-4174
Fax: 360 457-3037
www.domainemadeleine.com
Ten-acre wooded waterfront estate with views of the ocean and the towering mountains near Olympic National Park. There's private entrances and bathrooms, with great attention paid to detail. Delicious breakfast. **$$$**
Red Lion Hotel
221 North Lincoln, Port Angeles
Tel: 360 452-9215 or 800 RED-LION
Fax: 360 452-4734
www.redlion.com/properties/portan gel.html
A waterfront hotel with good, comfortable guestrooms, considered a well-located place to stay as it's only one block from the Black Ball Ferry to Victoria, BC. There's a seafood restaurant on the premises. **$–$$**

Seaview
Shelburn Country Inn
4415 Pacific Way, Seaview
Tel: 360 642-2442 or 800 INN-1896
Fax: 360 642-8904
www.theshelburne.com
Romantic Victorian-style home with stained glass and fireplace, antiques and flower gardens. No smoking. **$$**

Sequim
Dungeness Panorama Bed and Breakfast
630 Marine Drive, Sequim
Tel: 360 683-4503
www.awaterview.com
As the name implies, this is a fine ocean setting in the "sunbelt" of the Olympic Peninsula. Two suites, hand-painted furniture, French-style cuisine, adults only, but no smoking allowed. **$–$$**
Toad Hall Bed and Breakfast
12 Jerrlyn Lane, Sequim

Tel: 360 681-2534
www.toadhall.tv
Besides lavender plants and its *Wind in the Willows* theme, this "English-style" bed and breakfast inn has inspiring mountain views. No kids allowed. **$–$$**

Westport
Harbor Resort
Float 20, Westport
Tel: 360 268-0169
Fax: 360 268-0338
www.HarborResort.com
A choice of a second-story motel-type room, or cottages right next to the water. Some kitchenettes, many guests from Europe. **$**

WASHINGTON CASCADES

Cle Elum
Hidden Valley Guest Ranch
3942 Hidden Valley Rd, Cle Elum
Tel: 509 857-2344 or 800 5COWBOY
Fax 509 857-2130
www.ranchweb.com/hiddenvalley/
Rambling collection of cabins on an old ranch offers easy-going western vacation with outstanding scenery especially in springtime, hot tub, horseback riding (extra), meals included, minimum stay 2 nights, closed in winter. **$$$**

Leavenworth
Der Ritterhof Motor Inn
190 Hwy 2, Leavenworth
Tel 509 548-5845 or 800 255-5845
Fax: 509 548-4098
www.derritterhof.com
If you do not choose to stay in a B&B in this town, here are 51 standard hotel rooms in a park-like setting, seasonal pool, hot tub, kitchen units, and continental breakfast. **$**
Leavenworth Lodging Guide
Tel: 509 548-5807
Fax: 509 548-1014
Website:www.leavenworth.org/lodgi ng.html
A good selection of Leavenworth bed and breakfast inns, hotels, motels, pensions, rooms, out-of-area lodges, condominium and cabins. **$–$$$**

Snoqualmie Pass
Kimball Creek Inn Hotel
9050 384th Ave SE, Snoqualmie
Tel: 425 888-9399
Secluded in the meadows in a New England-style farmhouse, there are 10 well-cared-for rooms filled with antiques. Located near Snoqualmie Falls; no smoking. **$$**
The Thunder Mountain Lodge
38 & 40 Kendall Peak, Snoqualmie Pass
Tel: 425 434-7200 (no calls after 9pm please)
www.snoqualmiepass.com/Lodging. html
Big log cabin-style lodge nestled in the mountains. Perfect for enjoying ski activities or summer hiking, berry picking and, of course, the waterfalls. **$$**
Salish Lodge and Spa
6501 Railroad Ave, Snoqualmie
Tel: 425 888-2556 or 800 826-6124
Fax: 425 888-2533
www.salishlodge.com
Located on the crest of Snoqualmie Falls, this award-winning lodge offers picturesque surroundings, whirlpool tubs, and a tranquil spa. There's also luxury bedrooms, a dining room and a very good bar. **$$$$**

Vancouver, Washington
Heathman Lodge
7801 NE Greenwood Drive, Vancouver
Tel: 360 254-3100 or 888 475-3100
Fax: 360 254-6100
www.heathmanlodge.com
For anyone who does not wish to stay in one of the brand-name chain hotels in Vancouver, this alpine-style massive log cabin-style retreat is full of stone walls and timbers with Pendleton blanket bedspreads in the rooms, indoor pool, sauna and in-room hot tubs. It's also only one block from a convenient shopping mall. **$–$$$**

EAST OF THE CASCADES

Ellensburg
Campus View Inn B&B
706 N. Anderson St, Ellensburg
Tel: 509 933-2345 or 800
428-7270
Fax: 509 933-1775
www.virtualcities.com/ons/wa/c/w
acb901.htm
Built in 1910 and recently
refurbished, this residence near the
university features a wood foyer,
floors and curved staircase. There's
also a fine tiger-oak fireplace. Most
rooms feature queen-sized beds.
Check out the big breakfast in the
morning. **$–$$**

Grand Coulee Dam
Columbia River Inn
10 Lincoln Ave, Coulee Dam
Tel: 509 633-2100 or 800
633-6421
www.columbiariverinn.com
Good basic rooms with some in-
room Jacuzzi tubs; nestled along
the hillside at the southern
entrance to historic Coulee Dam.
Across the street from the Visitor
Center. **$–$$$**

Moses Lake
Shilo Inn Suites at Moses Lake
1819 E Kittleson, Moses Lake
Tel: 509 765-9317or 800
222-2244
Fax: 509 765-5058
Renovated comfortable large
rooms located near places to sail,
sand dunes and golf courses.
There's a guest laundromat;
indoor pool, spa, sauna, steam
room and fitness center, plus a
free local airport shuttle and
friendly staff. **$–$$**

Omak/Okanagan
The Cedars Inn Hotel
Junction Hwy 97 and Hwy 20,
Okanogan WA
Tel: 509 422-6431
Fax 509 422-4214
www.cedarshotels.com/CedarsInn-
Okanogan.html
Basic comforts in this hotel with
good access to Okanogan or Omak
and its famous Stampede and
Suicide Race. **$–$$**

The Palouse
American Travel Inn
515 S. Grand, Pullman
Tel: 509 334-3500
Fax: 509 334-0549
www.palouse.net/allamerican
Thirty-five standard (plain) motel
rooms, outdoor pool, restaurant
next door. **$**

Churchyard Inn B&B
206 Boniface Uniontown
Tel: 509 229-3200
www.moscowpullmanmeetings.com
/Accommodations/accom.htm
Registered as a National and State
historic site, this Flemish-style
parish house and former convent
features 7 rooms with private baths
and a Jacuzzi. It's across the drive
from historic and lovely Boniface
Church. **$–$$**

Hotel Prices

Prices are generally per room per
night in high to mid-season
(though in some cases they are
"per person" at the discretion of
the hotel). Low season rates may
be considerably reduced. In many
cases, these room prices include
a better-than-average continental
breakfast, and limitless coffee.

$$$$	over $200
$$$	$150–200
$$	$100–150
$	under $99

Republic
K-Diamond–K Guest Ranch
15661 Hwy 21 South, Republic
Tel: 888 345-5355
Fax 509 775-3536
www.kdiamondk.com
A huge 1,400-acre ranch located
125 miles north of Spokane in
Eastern Washington. There's a 3-
night minimum stay to enjoy ranch
life and ranch work. Take an
appetite and an open mind. **$$–$$$**

Soap Lake
Inn at Soap Lake
226 Main Ave E, Soap Lake
Tel: 509 246-1132
Fax: 509 246-1132
www.innsoaplake.com/
Odd stone building features cottages,

rooms, or "whirlpool suites" which
are designed to allow access to the
heavy-laden and heady smells of the
area's mineral waters. **$**

Spokane
Holiday Inn Express
North 801 Division, Spokane
Tel: 509 328-8505 or 800
465-4329
Fax: 509 325-9842
Located on top of a 40 ft rock bluff
in the heart of downtown Spokane
with views of the river. This Holiday
Inn is near shopping, fine dining,
entertainment, art galleries and
antique shops. There's also a hotel
fitness center. The standardized
rooms have balconies, king or
queen beds and refrigerators. **$–$$**

Westcoast Grand Hotel at the Park
W. 303 North River Dr, Spokane
Tel: 509 326-8000 or 800
325-4000
Fax: 509 325-7329
www.westcoasthotels.com
Located on the banks of the
cascading Spokane River just a
footbridge away from Riverfront Park
and a short stroll to the Spokane
Opera House and the shopping
district at River Park Square. There's
a sculpted swimming lagoon with
waterfall and waterslide; high-end
rooms with either queen or king
beds; and the Atrium Café in a
tropical garden of plants. **$$**

Tri-Cities: Richland, Pasco & Kennewick
Sleep Inn
9930 Bedford St, Pasco
Tel: 509 545-9554
Fax: 509 545-9554
Standard guest rooms plus an
indoor pool and hot tub. It's near
12 golf courses, 13 wineries, and
more than 10 miles of landscaped
parks with bicycle and walking
paths as well as Broadmoor Outlet
Mall. Be sure to see the sunset
over Rattlesnake Mountain. **$**

Walla Walla
Green Gables Inn B&B
922 Bonse Walla Walla
Tel: 509 525-5501 or 888
525-5501
www.greengablesinn.com

Five individual quarters with private bath inspired by the L.M. Montgomery book *Anne of Green Gables*. **$$**

Hawthorn Inn and Suites
520 N. Second, Walla Walla
Tel: 509 525-2522 or 800 527-1133
The Hawthorn has suites or double rooms with king, queen or double beds. There's also an indoor pool and a spa. **$–$$**

Marcus Whitman Hotel
6 W. Rose Street, Walla Walla
Tel: 509 525-2200 or 866 826-9422
www.marcuswhitmanhotel.com
Built in 1928, this historic building is slowly undergoing renovations. There are suites or nice rooms, fine dining in the restaurant and interesting winery tours offered by the hotel. **$$–$$$**

Mill Creek Inn
2014 Mill Creek Road, Walla Walla
Tel: 509 522-1234
www.millcreekbb.com
Four individual cottages well decorated with the warmth of home; there's a hearty breakfast to begin the day and a cozy communal parlor to end the evening. In addition, you'll find 22 acres of gardens, creeks and vineyards. There's a 2-night minimum stay and designated smoking areas. **$–$$**

Wenatchee Valley
Waterville Historic Hotel
Highway 2 102 East Park, Waterville
Tel: 509 745-8695 or 888 509-8180
Fax: 509 745-8180
www.watervillehotel.com
Listed on the National Register of Historic Places, this hotel is a trip back in time to 1903 with original fixtures and period décor plus old, high metal bed frames and claw foot tubs; no smoking. Semi-arid Waterville is centrally located for trips to Wenatchee, Chelan, Leavenworth, Grand Coulee, and sights in north-central Washington. **$–$$**

Winthrop
Sun Mountain Lodge
Near Winthrop

Hotel Prices

Prices are generally per room per night in high to mid-season (though in some cases they are "per person" at the discretion of the hotel). Low season rates may be considerably reduced. In many cases, these room prices include a better-than-average continental breakfast, and limitless coffee.

$$$$	over $200
$$$	$150–200
$$	$100–150
$	under $99

Tel: 509 996-2211 or 800 572-0493
Fax: 509 996-3133
www.bikesunmountain.com
Luxury lodge hotel and guest rooms or cabins with miles of trails for summer or winter activities; gourmet cuisine in dining room, spa program; especially noted for spring wildflowers. **$$–$$$**

The Virginian "Resort"
Highway 20, Winthrop
Tel: 509 996-2535 or 800 854-2834
www.methow.com/~virgnian/
Situated on the Methow River with direct access to the trail system and within walking distance of the "Wild West" downtown area. Choose from log cabins, deluxe or standard rooms. There's also a Jacuzzi and a swimming pool, and an onsite restaurant. **$–$$**

Yakima Valley
Birchfield Manor Country Inn
2018 Birchfield Rd, Yakima
Tel: 509 452-1960 or 800 375-3420
Fax: 509 452-2334
www.birchfieldmanor.com
Relaxing getaway cottage or guest quarters with dinners prepared by professional chef/owners knowledgeable about Washington wines. Served in the casual warm atmosphere of a gracious 1910 farmhouse. No smoking. **$$–$$$**

Sunnyside Inn Bed & Breakfast
804 E Edison Avenue, Sunnyside
Tel: 509 839-5557 or 800 221-4195
www.sunnysideinn.com

Located in the heart of Washington wine country with more than 20 wineries in the area. In-room Jacuzzi tubs in 8 of the 13 heavily decorated rooms. **$–$$**

NORTH CASCADES NATIONAL PARK

Lake Chelan
Campbells Resort
104 W Woodin Ave, Lake Chelan
Tel: 509 682-2561 or 800 553-8225
Fax: 509 682-2177
www.campbellsresort.com
There's a good chance of sunshine at this busy lakefront historic property. Choose between the terrace or the beach, the two-bedroom cottage or a room in the main lodge. Restaurant and swimming pools. **$$–$$$**

Mazama
The Freestone Inn
17798 Highway 20, Mazama
Tel: 509 996-3906 or 800 639-3809
Fax: 509 996-3907
www.freestoneinn.com
Surrounded by over 2.1 million acres of federal lands along beautiful North Cascades Scenic Highway, this tranquil resort in the style of early mountain lodges offers lakeside lodge rooms or refurbished cabins. Sweeping views of Freestone Lake and the North Cascade Mountains. **$$–$$$$**

Mt Baker
Mt Baker Bed and Breakfast
Glacier
Tel: 360 599-2299
http://members.tripod.com/~mtba kerbnb/
The closest B&B to the Mt Baker Recreation Area. Fine view of the mountain; full breakfasts. **$–$$**

Mt Baker Cabin Rentals
Tel: 360 599-2453
www.nas.com/baker/cabin.html
Various 1 to 3-bedroom cabins with kitchens in the Mt Baker Glacier area for skiing, hiking or relaxing. **$$–$$$**

Ovenells Heritage Inn
46276 Concrete Sauk Valley Rd,
Concrete
Tel: 360 853-8494
Fax: 360 853-8279
www.ovenells-inn.com
Cabins or rooms with shared or
private bathrooms situated near
(but not actually at) Mt Baker, in the
rugged foothills of the Cascade
Mountains. **$–$$**

North Cascades National Park
Strawberry Way B&B
61800 Highway 20
Marblemount
Tel: 360 873-4016
Victorian road house on 8 acres
of wilderness next to the Skagit
River just 4 miles west of the
park. The inn is decorated in
the style of old-gold miners
rooms; no phones, no TV, no
smoking. **$**

OLYMPIC NATIONAL PARK

Lake Quinault Lodge
345 South Shore Road, Quinault
Tel: 360 288-2900 or 800
562-6672
Fax: 360 288-2901
www.visitlakequinault.com
On the shores of a mountain
lake framed by Olympic National
Forest, Lake Quinault is a grand
old lodge with a large manicured
lawn. Full dining room, slow
service, but pleasant rooms in the
old lodge or in a newer addition.
$–$$

Kalaloch Lodge
157151 Hwy. 101 near Forks
Tel: 360 962-2271
Fax: 360 962-3391
www.visitkalaloch.com
The weather-beaten exterior
caused by constant onshore
winds in this hotel (pronounced
"Clay-lock") has the advantage
of being located on an ocean bluff
in Olympic National Park. Enjoy
ocean-overlook cabins or lodge-
rooms. The onsite restaurant
serves legendary salmon dishes.
$–$$

MOUNT RAINIER NATIONAL PARK

In the National Park
National Park Inn
6 miles from the SW entrance,
Longmire
Tel: 360 569-2275
Fax: 360 569-2270
www.americanparknetwork.com/par
kinfo/ra/lodging/
Nestled at an elevation of 2,700
feet, this inn has 25 basic rooms,
no TV or telephones, a restaurant,
and cozy lounge with oversize stone
fireplace. Open year round. **$$**

Paradise Inn
Longmire
Tel: 360 569-2275 or 360
569-2413
Fax: 360-569-2270
www.americanparknetwork.com/par
kinfo/ra/lodging/
Stunning setting at an elevation
of 5,400 feet, with exceptional
views of the glaciers, this is
the primary base camp for those
seeking to climb to the summit
of Mt Rainier. The 1917 historic
guest lodge has 125 basic rooms,
and no TV or telephones.
The Paradise Inn dining room
serves up a bountiful Sunday
brunch. **$$**

Near the National Park
**Accommodations near Mount
Ranier National Park**
www.mt-rainier.com/lodging.htm
Check out this site for a choice of
accommodations including cabins,
B&Bs, bunkhouses, lodges and
spas near the southwest corner of
Mount Rainier Park. **$–$$$**

**Cedar Creek Treehouse at Mount
Rainier**
Ashford
Tel: 360-569-2991
www.cedarcreektreehouse.com
Like having your own state park
for the weekend – except that your
cabin is 50 feet up in a giant
cedar tree with a view of Mount
Rainier from your bed. The 2-level
aerie is reached via a 77-step
staircase. No smoking; no
children. **$$$$**

MOUNT ST HELENS NATIONAL MONUMENT

Castle Rock near the National Monument
Blue Heron Inn
2846 Spirit Lake Hwy, Castle Rock
Tel: 360 274-9595 or 800
959-4049
www.blueheroninn.com
Looking out at St Helens, this inn
nestled in the forest makes sure
every room has a view. Nightly
dinner served to guests, along
with wine, dessert and a full
country breakfast the next day.
$$–$$$

To Smoke or Not

Whether or not to allow smoking
seems to be an individual
decision on the part of
Washington's hotel and
restaurant owners. If smoking is
a priority, always ask before
making a reservation.

**Stone's Throw Retreat Bed &
Breakfast**
200 Coyote Lane, Castle Rock
Tel: 360 274-2170
www.stonesthrowretreat.com
This retreat features two smallish
bedrooms, an outdoor hot tub,
forested paths, a stone labyrinth, a
bubbling creek, and Christian
hospitality. **$**
Timberland Inn & Suites
1271 Mt St Helens Way, Castle
Rock
Tel: 360 274-6002 or 888
900-6335
This is a regular motel a bit tattered
around the edges, but the basic
rooms are good enough for
overnight stays. **$**

Lakeview Cabin
240 Lakeview Dr, Silver Lake
Tel: 360 274-7482
www.toledotel.com/~leebo/
Rustic, crusty romantic getaway
for two, with log furniture, a
fireplace, and a kitchen with a
wildlife theme. A 2-night minimum
stay is in effect certain times of
the year. **$**

Where to Eat

SEATTLE

Anthony's at Pier 66
2201 Alaskan Way, Seattle
Tel: 206 448-6688
The place for lovers of fresh seafood. Panoramic Puget Sound view, well designed two level indoor or outdoor dining. Try "Northwest Duet" an apple wood char-grilled Chinook salmon. Business casual. **$$$**

Assaggio Ristorante
2010 4th Ave, Seattle
Tel: 206 441-1399
Feel the atmosphere of far-off Rome as Mauro Golmarvi greets diners with sincere friendliness. Northern Italian/Adriatic Coast cuisine. Try the house specilty, Assaggio di Carrello. Business casual to dressy. **$$$$**

Benihana Restaurant
1200 Fifth Ave, Seattle
Tel: 206 682-4686
Whirling and twirling knives yielded by chefs at every table that cleverly doubles as the grill. Community dining in this chain restaurant that is always good value. Try Japanese-style Teppanyaki and for dessert Azuki Red Bean ice cream. Business casual. **$$**

Chandler's Crabhouse & Fresh Fish Market
901 Fairview Ave, N, Seattle
Tel: 206 223-2722
Great views of Lake Union with seaplanes and boats coming and going, Northwest cuisine, noisy. Try Whisky Crab Soup or Dungeness crab and salmon. Reservations recommended. Casual. **$$$**

China Gate
516 7th Ave S, Seattle
Tel: 206 624-1730
One room with many tables; floral and jade décor and karaoke bar. *Dim sum* is served not only during the day, but also at night. Try steamed chicken with ginger-oil dipping sauce. Casual. **$**

Chinoise Cafe
12 Boston St, Seattle
Sushi, Thai, Vietnamese, Chinese and Korean cuisine, plain décor. Try General Cho's chicken. Casual. **$**

Cutters Bayhouse
2001 Western Ave, Seattle
Tel: 206 448-4884
Perched on Elliott Bay a block from Pike Place Market, this is a feel-good place serving good seafood. Try halibut cheeks with parmesan and asiago crust. Casual. **$$**

Dahlia Lounge
2001 Fourth Ave, Seattle
Tel: 206 682-4142
Try the "Best of Northwest" cuisine. Rich ambiance and regal pampering here. Nibble the tortellini, served with fresh goat's cheese and roasted asparagus. Casual to business casual. **$$$**

Fisherman's Restaurant
1301 Alaskan Way, Seattle
Tel: 206 623-3500
Heavy wood beams, indoor or outdoor dining, plus free live jazzy sounds. Chef Steve "Giaco" Giacomini brings King, Atlantic, White King, Coho and Wild Steelhead fish from Washington rivers. Great value. Casual. **$$**

Nikko Japanese Restaurant
1900 Fifth Ave, Seattle
Tel; 206 322-4641
Well-designed dining room, enormous sushi bar and teppan grill. Takeyuki Suetsugu holds a license as master chef. Try the ceremonial nine-course meal, the Kaiseki. Casual. **$$**

The Painted Table
92 Madison St, Seattle
Alexis Hotel's restaurant
Tel: 206 624-3646
Artsy, elegant and upscale, where the presentation is like sitting in a rotating art gallery. This is where food and art fuse. Northwest market fare, fresh veggies, lots of organics. Dressy. **$$**

Shiro's
2401 Second Ave, Seattle
Tel: 206 443-9844
Simple surroundings and crowded tables; chef Shiro Kashiba is a sushi magician. Try the oysters. Reservations suggested. Casual. **$**

Six Seven
2411 Alaskan Way, Seattle WA
Tel: 206 269-4575
Expansive view over Elliott Bay and of the Olympic mountains, with contemporary and Pacific Northwest decor. Pan-Asian and Pacific Rim cuisine. Business casual. **$$$**

SkyCity at the Needle
219 4th Ave N, Seattle
Tel: 206 443-2111
The Space Needle restaurant offers a revolving 360° view of Seattle, Olympic and Cascade ranges, Elliott Bay and Lake Union. After several disappointing years, attempts are being made to bring the food more in line with the view, ie, something outstanding. The jury is still out. Reservations compulsory. Casual to business casual. **$$$$**

Tai Tung Restaurant
659 S King St, Seattle
Tel: 206 622-7372
Practical and plain décor, live crab and lobster tank entertains folks waiting in line. Try Oyster sauce beef or Crab Meat foo yung. Parking lot available to patrons free of charge. Casual. **$**

Waterfront
2801 Alaskan Way, Seattle
Tel: 206 956-9171
Be pampered and entertained by the great views from the deck, the live nightly music, and the impressive wine list. Pan Asian seafood cuisine; try the yummy Thai seafood stew. Note: discounted prices during Happy Hour from 4–6pm Monday through Friday. Business casual. **$$**

Wild Ginger
1401 3rd Ave, Seattle
Tel: 206 623-4450
Bright, airy décor, in which the Wild Ginger serves Vietnamese, Thai and Korean dishes. Visitors love the atmosphere, but note the portions are small. Try the Bankok Boar Satay. Business casual. **$$**

Brewpubs and Sports Bars

FX McRory's
419 Occidental Ave S, Seattle
Tel: 206 623-4800
Meat lovers place this classic Seattle sports bar high on their list. It serves up premium grade, 21-day locker-aged meat, over 120 varieties of bourbon and 30 kinds of beer on tap. Go early before they run out of prime rib. Casual. **$$**

Gordon Biersch Brewery Restaurant
600 Pine Street, Suite 401, Seattle
Tel: 206 405-4205
Three house lagers are featured at all outlets of this brewpub chain: Pilsner, Maerzen, and Dunkles. There's an upscale menu with pretty good starters, several salads, pizzas, pastas and stir-frys. Casual. **$$**

McMenamins on Queen Anne
200 Roy Street, Suite 105, Seattle
Tel: 206 285-4722
Wildly popular with 17 beers on tap, of which eight are McMenamins house brews. Straightforward pub grub. Try Stormin' Norman sandwiches. Casual. **$$**

Pike Brewery and Pub
1415 1st Ave, Seattle WA
Tel: 206 622-6044
Assertive and distinctive beer is brewed here. The location, close by the Pike Place Market, can't hurt either; one lively, noisy room with an open atrium. Good selection of food from pizzas and salads to shellfish and salmon. Casual. **$$**

Price Guide

Prices are approximate for two people before taxes and tips, including house brand wine (where available).

$$$$	over $100
$$$	$60-$100
$$	$30-$60
$	under $30

Pyramid Brewery and Alehouse
91 S. Royal Brougham (at 1st Ave S), Seattle
Tel: 206 682-3377
Around 14 beers pour from the taps here. Good pub food, with both British and German influences. The decor is exposed brick, dark woods, and cement floor, and the big open kitchen bustles with activity. Crowding is inevitable during Major-League sports games. Casual. **$**

Ballard Area (near Seattle)
Madame K's
5327 Ballard Ave NW, Seattle
Tel 206 783-9710

Located in Old Ballard in what was once a brothel, the decor is hues of deep red and black with murals of ladies painted on the walls. Try the "kick ass" pizza. Casual. **$**

The People's Pub
5429 Ballard NW, Seattle
Tel 206 783-6521
Good for lunch, dinner, or a late night meal. This plain building is the place for Southwest German-style beer and food. Casual. **$**

Edmonds (near Seattle)
Windsor Garden Tea Room
110 4th Ave N, Edmonds
Tel: 425 712-1387
Old English tearoom serves tea sandwiches, scones, desserts, and both classic and exotic teas. Casual. **$**

Kent (near Seattle)
Hung's Chinese Cuisine and Lounge
24437 Russel Rd, Suite 120, Kent
Tel: 253 854-8907
A large selection of Chinese food at reasonable prices. Tables and chairs are set in one large room. Casual. **$**

Mirabella European Restaurant and Bakery
1819 W Meeker St, Kent
Tel: 253 854-0967
Unpretentious exterior belies Mirabella's commitment to fresh, delicious soups, sandwiches, pastas, calzones, and decadent desserts. Casual. **$**

Kirkland (near Seattle)
Bistro Provencal
212 Central Way, Kirkland
Tel: 425 827-3300
French cuisine and country-inn ambiance near the waterfront. Try the onion soup, duck or lamb. Business casual. **$$$**

Renton (near Seattle)
Spirit of Washington **Dinner Train**
625 South 4th St, Renton
Tel: 425 227-RAIL or 800-876-RAIL
Ride and dine in a vintage rail car traveling from Renton to Woodinville; the journey trundles along the shores of Lake Washington. Casual. **$$$**

Woodinville (near Seattle)
The Herbfarm
14590 N. 145th St, Woodinville
Tel: 206-784-2222
Each week, chefs choose the very best from farm, forest, and sea to create thematic nine-course dinners show casing the culinary glories of the Pacific Northwest. Rated among America's top 50 restaurants, this is romantic dining at its best. Reservations required. Dressy. **$$$$+**

TACOMA

CI Shenanigans Seafood and Chophouse
3017 N Ruston Way, Tacoma
Tel: 253 752-8811
Romantic waterside ambiance, premium seafood, steaks, pastas and salads in an atmosphere of casual elegance. The restaurant has the largest deck on Tacoma's Ruston Way, where every table has a view of Commencement Bay and the Olympic Mountains. Ram's Head/Big Horn microbrews are served under a spacious atrium. Casual. **$$$**

ER Rogers
1702 Commercial, Steilacoom
Tel: 206 582-0280
Ten miles south of Tacoma, American fine dining in an 1891 Queen Anne-style mansion with views of the Tacoma Narrows Bridge. Be sure to try the prime rib. Business casual. **$$$**

Katie Down's On the Water
3211 Ruston Way, Tacoma
Tel: 206 756-0771
American tavern famous for its Philly Deep Dish Pizza, steamer clams and microbrews. No children. Casual. **$$**

PUGET SOUND & THE SAN JUAN ISLANDS

Anacortes
Islands Inn and La Petite Restaurant
3401 Commercial Ave, Anacortes
Tel 360 293-4644
Enhanced by a view of Mt Baker and

Fidalgo Bay, the chef here combines European and Dutch influences in six different entrees. There's also a good wine list. Try the Tongfilet Met Krab Filet of Puget Sound Sole stuffed with Dungeness Crab and a slightly tart shellfish-based cream sauce. Business casual. **$$$**

Bellingham

While in Bellingham, be sure to travel scenic **Chuckanut Drive** to one of the restaurants overlooking Samish Bay and the San Juan Islands. This is where the very freshest of oysters are served. See website: www.chuckanutdrive.com/

Boundary Bay Brewery Bistro
107 Railroad Ave, Bellingham
Tel: 360 647-5593
Housed in an old brick building, on tap are smooth pale ales or Oatmeal Stout. The menu is pizza or chicken. Try the Yam-Alechiladas covered with *mole* (chocolate) sauce. Casual. **$**

Chuckanut Manor
302 Chuckanut Drive, Bellingham
Tel: 360 766-6191
This is a great place for Sunday brunch or dinner with its panoramic view from the glassed-in dining room. Steaks and seafood are on the menu, but oysters are the big draw. Reservations suggested. Casual. **$$**

Cliff House Restaurant
331 North State St, Bellingham
Tel 360 734-8660
Located in a residential district overlooking Bellingham Bay, the Cliff House dishes up seafood, angus steaks, or rich pastas. Try the terrific Whisky Crab Soup. Casual. **$$**

Oyster Bar
240 Chuckanut Drive, Bow
Tel: 360 766-6185
Romantic restaurant near Bellingham, in a house perched right by the side of the road. The menu features local fish, lobster, duck, steak, wild salmon and, of course, oysters on the halfshell, by the dozen, half dozen or singly. The 27-page long wine list is an enophile's dream. Casual. **$$$**

Bremerton

Boat Shed
101 Shore Dr, Bremerton
Tel: 360 377-2600
Watch the Washington State Ferriesply by from inside this building constructed on pilings, or weather permitting from the outdoor deck. As you might imagine, seafood specialties are the thing here. Try the Mixed Shellfish Sauté in Black Bean Sauce. Casual. **$$$**

Oyster Bay Inn Restaurant
4412 Kitsap Way, Bremeton
Tel: 360 377-5510
Prime rib, chicken or seafood served in an unpretentious building overlooking Oyster Bay. Try the Capellini with Tiger Prawns or Panko Pan Fried Oysters. Lunch or dinner only. Casual. **$$**

Chehalis

Mary McCranks Dinner House
2923 Jackson Highway
Tel: 360 748-3662
American country home-cookin' in a farmhouse restaurant, cozy with a touch of elegance. Try the chicken and dumplings, with great pie for dessert. Casual. **$$**

Price Guide

Prices are approximate for two people before taxes and tips, including house brand wine (where available).

$$$$	over $100
$$$	$60-$100
$$	$30-$60
$	under $30

Everett

Alligator Soul
2013 1/2 Hewitt Ave, Everett
Tel: 425 259-6311
Chef Hilary Craig blends Cajun, Creole and other Southern influences to deliver gumbos and catfish étouffee. Exposed brick wall décor. Try the bourbon bread pudding or pecan pie. Casual. **$$**

Anthony's Homeport or Anthony's Woodfire Grill
1725 or 1722 West Marine View Dr, Everett
Tel: 425 252-3333 or 425 258-4000
At the Marina Village, choose one of these two restaurants. Homeport has a view over Port Gardner Bay with indoor or patio dining, seafood, Dungeness crab and salmon. The nearby Grill restaurant specializes in prime rib, steaks and chicken. Great desserts in either or both places. Lunch and dinner, plus Sunday brunch. Casual. **$$$**

La Conner

Palmer's Restaurant and Pub
107 S. Second St, La Conner
Tel: 360 466-3101
Located inside the town's most charming hotel, Palmer's offers progressive cuisine focusing on Northwest and European styles. Palmer's Restaurant has a second location in Mount Vernon. Casual. **$$$**

Lopez Island

Bay Café
Entrance to Fisherman's Bay, Lopez Island
Tel: 360 468-3700
There's a white clapboard building, view of the sunset, plastic tablecloths, regional seafood and some meat dishes. Casual. **$**

Mercer Island

Thai On Mercer
7691 SE 27th St, Mercer Island
Tel: 206 236-9990
Sensual satays, curries and noodles served in a pleasant, plain-Jane atmosphere. Casual. **$**

Mount Vernon

Skagit River Brewing Co
404 S 3rd St, Mount Vernon
Tel: 360 336-2884
Former warehouse, now a microbrewery and pub, that serves up good American food. Try the barbecue fare or the wood-oven pizza. Casual. **$**

Olympia
Falls Terrace Restaurant
106 S Deschutes Way, Olympia
Tel: 360 943-7830
This multi-level family restaurant
has summer dining on the deck and
great views of Tumwater Falls.
Fancy steaks, seafood and
hamburgers. Casual. **$$**
Fish Bowl Brew Pub and Café
515 Jefferson St, Olympia
Tel: 360 943-3650
Good microbrews and Tex-Mex
accompaniments in a Downtown
fishy setting. Casual. **$**
La Petite Maison
101 Division NW, Olympia
Tel: 360 943-8812
This former farmhouse is
threatened by the city growing up all
around it. French inspired food
includes local oysters in season,
but leave room to sample the
desserts. No lunch, closed Sunday.
Reservations recommended.
Business casual. **$$$**

Orcas Island /San Juan Islands
Christina's
310 Main St, Orcas Island
Tel: 360 376-4904
Fresh flowers in this lovely
restaurant frame the ocean view
and there's open-air dining on the
rooftop, too. The chef specializes in
fresh seafood and meats, and the
ample wine list is to be savored. No
lunch. Casual to dressy casual. **$$$**
Doe Bay Café
At Doe Bay Resort and Retreat,
Olga
Tel: 360 376-2291
Above Otter Cove with panoramic
views, sit-down booths, and a
selection of vegetarian or seafood
dishes. Open seasonally, very
casual. **$**
Octavia's Bistro
At the Orcas Hotel, Orcas
Tel: 888 672-2792
View of English gardens and harbor,
delicious seafood, steaks and
spirits plusa fine and lively
atmosphere. Casual. **$$**

Port Ludlow
Harbormaster Restaurant
At Port Ludlow Resort, 200 Olympic
Pl, Port Ludlow

San Juan Island
Lovely San Juan Island has many
places to eat. Here are two that
we recommend:
Friday Harbor House
130 West Street, Friday Harbor,
WA
Tel: 360 378-8455
On a bluff with wonderful views
of the marina, ferry landing, San
Juan Channel and Mt
Constitution on Orcas Island.
Cedar shingles on the building
and fresh regional food on the
table. Reservations
recommended. **$$$**

Tel: 360 437-2222
High ceilings and a view over
Ludlow Bay, with a choice of dining
on the sundeck in the summertime.
Fresh seafood with the prerequisite
alternates of chicken and beef.
Casual. **$$**

Port Townsend
Ajax Café
271 Water St, Port Hadlock
Tel: 360 385-3450
Views of the harbor and kitchy
American décor are the backdrop
for a menu of wild salmon, fish,
seafood, pasta or steaks. No lunch.
Casual. **$$**
Lonny's Restaurant
2330 Washington St, Port
Townsend
Tel 360 385-0700
Down by the Boat Haven, Lonny's
has the best atmosphere in town.
Italian-Mediterranean dishes use
fresh Pacific Northwest ingredients.
Reservations suggested. Casual to
business casual. **$$**

Poulsbo
Benson's Restaurant
18820 Front St, Poulsbo
Tel: 360 697-3449
Located steps away from the
city docks, award-winning chef
Stephen Benson creates
sumptuous Northwest cuisine in
a décor of colorful floral artwork.
Try the blackened salmon.
Lunch, dinner or brunch. Casual.
$$$

Duck Soup Inn
Roche Harbor Road past Egg
Lake Road
50 Duck Soup Lane, Friday Harbor,
WA
Tel: 360 378-4878
Outside is a vine-covered, weather-
beaten exterior, inside critically
acclaimed French bistro food is
served. Try the island-made Quail
Croft goat cheese wrapped in
grape leaves. Yummy.
Reservations recommended; note
the restaurant is closed in the
winter. **$$–$$$**

Christopher's at the Inn
26069 Big Valley Road NE, Poulsbo
Tel: 360 779-4628
Dinner Wednesday through Sunday
evenings only in this bright white
restaurant, using ever-changing
Northwest ingredients. Try the Pacific
Salmon Dijonnaise. Reservations
suggested. Dressy casual. **$$$**
Molly Ward Gardens
27462 Big Valley Road, Poulsbo
Tel: 360 779-4471
The gardens supply fresh herbs,
vegetables, and fruit for the
restaurant and flowers for the
salads, the tables, and the dried
flower displays. As you might
imagine, this converted barn is
surrounded by lush gardens. Lunch,
dinner, or Sunday brunch. Try the
homemade desserts. Casual. **$$**
Poulsbohemian Coffeehouse
Egan Rank Building, 19003 Front
St, Poulsbo
Tel: 360 779-9199
Nerdy atmosphere of bookishness
where the coffee is only too strong
if you are too weak to take it.
Casual. **$**

Sekiu
Breakwater Restaurant
Hwy 112, Clallam Bay
Tel: 360 963-2428
Claiming to be the most northerly
eating establishment in the
continental US, Sekiu overlooks the
Strait of Juan de Fuca while serving
chicken, burgers or steaks. Casual.
$–$$

Sequim

Petals Garden Café
At Cedarbrook Herb Farm
1345 S Sequim Ave, Sequim
Tel: 360 683-4541
Enjoy "farmers market cuisine"
(ie, simple food, locally grown)
in a café setting in a fragrant
garden. Lunch or afternoon tea.
Casual. **$**

The 3 Crabs
11 Three Crabs Road, Sequim
Tel: 360 683-4264
Right on the beach, this tourist
favorite is the place for Dungeness
crab, crab cocktails, clam chowder
and oysters. Casual. **$**

Silverdale (near Bremerton)

Silver City Brewing Company
2799 NW Myhre, Silverdale
Tel: 360 698-3579
This fun brewhouse has seasonal
brews as well as year-round liquid
libations. Pub fare, plus
hamburgers, pizza, pasta and – on
the weekends – prime rib. Casual.
$–$$

Yacht Club Broiler
9226 Bay Shore Dr NW, Silverdale
Tel: (360) 698-1601
Upscale seafood dining and fine
wine on the shore of Dyes Inlet.
Business casual or "yacht-club"
attire. **$$$**

Tenino (near Olympia and Centralia)

Alice's Restaurant
At Johnson Creek Winery, 19248
Johnson Creek Rd. SE, Tenino
Tel: 360 264-2887
Five-course country-style dinners
are served in this charming
farmhouse tucked away in a lovely
vineyard which is just a few miles
south of the town of Tenino. Casual.
$$–$$$

Whitbey Island

Teddy's on Whitbey
1804 E Scott Rd, Freeland
Tel: 360 331-2882
Housed in a Victorian-style
mansion with deep comfortable
booths, Teddy's on Whitbey
serves from a menu offering
seafood, steak and pasta. Casual.
$

COASTAL WASHINGTON

Long Beach

Ark Restaurant and Bakery
273 St and 230 Sandbridge Rd,
Nahcotta
Tel: 360 665-4133
Considered a Northwest dining
adventure, the Ark is located in an
unassuming red wooden building
surrounded by mountains of oyster
shells, all testimonts to the
thousands of happy seafood diners
here, which includes at least one
American president. Feast on local
specialties like cranberries,
littleneck clams and Chinook
salmon, plus there's a well-
respected wine list. Reservations
recommended. Casual. **$$$**

My Mom's Pie and Chowder House
1113 Pacific Ave SW, Long Beach
Tel: 360 642-2342
Open May to October, this is a
small café famous for meatloaf
sandwiches, etc. Casual. **$**

The Sanctuary Restaurant
794 State Rt. 101, Chinook
Tel: 360 777-8380
Housed in a cozy and warm 1906
former Methodist Episcopal Church,
owners Joanna and Geno Leech
serve the freshest Northwest
cuisine done up with Scandinavian
touches. The Sanctuary is
deservedly acclaimed; try the
Chocolate Rum Cake. Reservations
recommended. Business casual.
$$$

Longview

The Masthead
1210 Ocean Beach Hwy Longview
Tel: 360 577-7972
The Longview serves Snoqualmie
beers, and has a good, low-key

menu of regular American staples.
Casual. **$**

Moclips (near Ocean Shores)

Restaurant at Ocean Crest Resort
4651 Hwy 109, Moclips
Tel: 360 276-4465 or
800 684-8439
Romantic dining with a view of trees
and the ocean, this is Northwest
cuisine with European flare, but can
be a bit amateur. Reservations
advised. Dressy casual. **$$$**

Ocean Shores

Alec's By the Sea
131 E Chance a la Mer Blvd, Ocean
Shores
Tel: 360 289-4026
Alec's is famous for razor clams,
complimented by American food in
generous portions. Casual. **$**

Port Angeles

Crab House
Next to Red Lion Hotel, 221
Lincoln, Port Angeles
Tel: 360 452-9215
The name seems to change
regularly, but this busy restaurant
overlooking the water serves up
very popular assortments of
seafood; try the Dungeness Crab
bisque. Also serves chicken, pasta
and fish. Casual and fun. **$$–$$$**

Landings & Dockside Lounge
115 E Railroad Ave, Port Angeles.
Tel: 360 457-6768
Voted best peninsula fish 'n' chips
and clam chowder. Casual. **$**

Seaview near Long Beach

42nd Street Cafe
4201 Pacific Way, Seaview
Tel: 360 642-2323
Cheri Walker and Co. turn out some
of the best comfort food on the
Long Beach Peninsula. Try the fried
razor clams. Casual. **$$**

Heron & Beaver Pub/Cafe
At the Shelburne Inn, 4503 Pacific
Highway, Seaview
Tel: 360 642-4142
The pub has an all-day menu of
light fare including Willapa Bay
Oyster Shooters, while the café
offers fine fresh food and a
great wine collection. Casual.
$–$$

The Shoalwater Restaurant

At the Shelburne Inn, 4503 Pacific
Highway, Seaview
Tel: 360 642-4142
The Shoalwater serves the freshest
of regional cuisine with over 500
wines on the wine list. Try the
Northwest Bouillabaisse, then
admire the 100-year old Art
Nouveau stained-glass window.
Dressy casual.
$$$

WASHINGTON CASCADES

Leavenworth
Andreas Keller
829 Front St (downstairs)
Leavenworth
Tel: 509 548-6000
Bavarian-style dining in a rustic
gasthaus setting specializing in
rotisserie pork hocks, chicken,
schnitzels, *spätzle* and sausages.
Live music; German spoken.
Casual. $$

King Ludwig's
921 Front St, Leavenworth
Tel: 509 548-6625
Music and dancing; outdoor dining
in summer. Try the *Schweinshax'n*
and other Bavarian specialties.
Casual. $$

Restaurant Oesterreich
Tyrolean Ritz Hotel, 633 Front St,
Leavenworth
Tel: 509 548-4031
Austrian décor and occasional
accordion player; open-air dining in
summer. Menu changes daily;
closed Mon–Tues. Good strudels
and dumplings. Reservations.
Casual. $$$

Vancouver
Bell Tower Restaurant and
Brewhouse
707 SE 164th Ave,
Vancouver
Tel: 360 944-7800
Located in an old church with
cathedral ceilings, the Bell
Tower serves American-style
steaks, burgers, ribs and fish plus
its own microbrews. Outdoor
patios in summer and Tuesday is
the night for prime rib. Casual.
$–$$

Vancouver's Chart House
101 E. Columbia Way, Vancouver
Tel: 360 693-9211
Views of the water and seafood
specialties, outdoors dining in
summer. Reservations essential on
weekends. Casual to business
casual. $$$

EAST OF THE CASCADES

Coulee Dam
Coulee Dam Casino Deli
515 Birch St Coulee Dam
Tel: 509 633-0766
Regular deli fare only a few steps
away from slot machines, blackjack
tables and video poker. Casual. $

Hollywood Steakhouse
Hwy 155, mile post 25.6, 512 River
Drive, Coulee Dam
Tel: 509 633-1151
Photographs of old-time stars, and
serving American dishes, burgers,
fries, tacos, and appetizers, plus a
few Filipino dishes. Very casual. $

Moses Lake
Michael's on the Lake
910 West Broadway, Moses Lake
Tel: 509 765-1611
American food seems to taste best
at sunset as warm light floods this
lakeside restaurant. Soup and
sandwiches or prime rib. Casual. $$

Omak
Waconda Café, General Store and
Post Office
2432 Route 20 Wauconda
Tel: 509 486-4010
Straight out of the Old West, this is
a store-café with simple food and
good hamburgers. Closed Sundays.
Casual. $

Tri-Cities: Richland, Pasco
& Kennewick
The Blue Moon
20 N Auburn, Kennewick
Tel: 509 582-6598
Stone fireplace, fresh flowers and a
fine menu starring chef Dale
Shepard's lamb creations. Try the
sautéed ostrich with wild
mushrooms. Reservations
essential. Business casual to
dressy. $$$

Spokane
Cucina! Cucina! Italian Cafe
707 W Main Avenue, Suite A-1
Spokane
Tel: 509 838-3388
Great traditional and/or cutting-
edge Italian food served in a
fun-filled environment. Casual. $$

Cyrus O'Learys
516 West Main St, Spokane
Tel: 509 624-900
A quaint building set against
Spokane's tall buildings. The
waitresses dress up in masks,
while the cook – or even the busboy
– serves dinner. Pleasant family
restaurant, big menu. Casual. $$

Walla Walla
Paisanos
26 E Main St, Walla Walla
Tel: 509 527-3511
Surrounded by Historic District
buildings and serving Italian-style
pastas, seafood or steaks. Try the
smoked duck capellini. Casual. $$

Winthrop
Virginian Resort Restaurant
808 North Cascades Hwy, Wintrop
Tel: 509 996-2535
Western singers occasionally strum
guitars here, with "Yahoo"as the
byword. Seating indoors or out, and
a menu of burgers, steak or pasta.
Closed Oct to April. $

Yakima
Birchfield Manor
2018 Birchfield Rd, Yakima
Tel: 509 452-1960
Located in a 1910 valley
farmhouse, this elegant dining room
has a great wine list, and gourmet
seafood, veal, lamb and beef.
Business casual. $$$

NORTH CASCADES
NATIONAL PARK

Buffalo Run Restaurant
60084 State Rte 20, Marblemount
Tel: 360 873-2461
Buffalo heads and Old West
memorabilia are the background for
meats such as ostrich, buffalo,
venison and elk. There's also a
patio garden. Casual. $$

OLYMPIC NATIONAL PARK

Forks
Smoke House Restaurant
193161 Highway 101, Forks
Tel: 360 374-6258
Rustic décor and hearty good
eating. Try the custom-smoked
salmon or steak. Casual. **$–$$**

Lake Quinalt
Lake Quinalt Lodge Restaurant
S Shore Road, Lake Quinalt
Tel: 360 288-2900
Rainforest setting with an
old-fashioned feel. Go for the
baked salmon. Casual. **$$**

Olympic National Park
Lake Cresent Lodge
416 Lake Crescent Rd, Port Angeles
Tel: 360 928-3211
21 miles west of Port Angeles, and
surrounded by the rainforest.
There's a huge stone fireplace; the
dining room overlooks the lake.
American dishes. Closed mid-Oct to
mid-April. Casual. **$$$**

MOUNT RAINIER NATIONAL PARK

Paradise Inn
19 miles inside the National Park
Tel: 360 569-2275
Great fireplaces and park-style
décor, the busy lobby is a prelude
to the first-come-first-served high-
ceiling dining room. Mostly
hamburgers and pasta, but justly
famous for Sunday brunch in
summer. Closed Oct–mid-May.
Casual. **$$**

MOUNT ST HELENS NATIONAL MONUMENT

Hoffstadt Bluffs Visitor Center
Hwy 504, Mount St Helens
Tel: 360 274-7750
Panoramic views of the Toutle
Valley surround this, the only
full service restaurant along Hwy
504. American favorites –
hamburger, chicken, sandwiches.
Casual. **$**

Shopping

SHOPPING MALLS

Centralia Factory Outlets
1342 Lum Road, Off I-5 at Exit 82,
Centralia
Tel: 360 736-3327
www.centraliafactoryoutlet.com
Major factory outlet center.

Sea-Tac Mall
1928 S Sea-Tac Mall, Federal Way,
Seattle
Hwy 99 & 320th St
Tel: 253 839-6151
www.seatacmall.com

Southcenter Mall
633 Southcenter Mall/Junction of
I-5 & I-405, Seattle
Tel: 206 246-7400
www.shopyourmall.com

SuperMall
1101 SuperMall Way, Auburn
Tel: 253 833-9500
www.supermall.com

ARTS AND CRAFTS MARKETS

**Country Crafts Home and Gift
Shows**
www.country-craft.com/
A collections of gift shows in
Washington state.
**Upcoming Washington Arts and
Crafts Shows, Festivals, and Street
Fairs**
www.craftmasternews.com/shows_
washington.asp
Click for details on shows
throughout Washington state.

FARMERS' MARKETS

Washington Farmers' Markets
www.ams.usda.gov/farmersmarkets
/states/washingt.htm
Check on dates and locations for
the freshest produce and baked
goods.
Pike Place Market
85 Pike Street,
Seattle
Tel: 206 682-7453
www.pikeplacemarket.org/
One of America's favorite and
oldest open-air markets.

ANTIQUES

Seattle Antique Market
1400 Alaskan Way, Seattle
Tel: 206 623-6115
Part of a neighborhood full of
antique shops.
Seattle Antique Stores
www.antiqueinfo.com/states/washi
ngton/seattle.htm
Complete listing of all city antique
stores.

Annual Events

**Washington Festivals & Events
Association**
115 E Railroad Ave, Suite 302, Port
Angeles
Tel: 360 452-7019
www.wfea.org/regionfind.cfm?regio
n=NorthCascades
Consult for local events throughout
the state of Washington.

**Seattle and Tacoma
Events, Film Festivals and Music
Concerts in Seattle**
www.halcyon.com/tmend/seattle1

January
New Year's Eve celebrations at
restaurants, hotels and clubs
throughout the state.
Chinese New Year, based on the
lunar calendar, sometime in Jan or
Feb: International District, Seattle.

February
Mardi Gras: Pioneer Sq, Seattle.
Wintergrass: world's largest indoor
bluegrass festival: Tacoma

April
Cherry Blossom & Japanese
Cultural Festival: Seattle Center.
Daffodil Festival Grand Floral
Parade: Tacoma.
Puyallup Spring Fair: livestock &
agricultural exhibits: Puyallup.

May
Seattle International Children's
Festival: Seattle Center.
Northwest Folklife Festival & Ethnic
Traditions: Seattle Center.

June
Seattle Pride Day: Seattle.

July

Emerald Queen Taste of Tacoma: Chefs and restaurants: Tacoma.
Seattle Chamber Music Society Summer Festival: Seattle.
Bite of Seattle: 35 food product companies & 4 beer gardens: Seattle Center.
Caribbean Festival; music and cuisine: Seattle.
Ethnic Fest: Annual celebration of cultures: Tacoma.

July–August

Seafair – largest festival in the Northwest; includes US West Air Show and Hydroplane Races: Seattle.

August

Seattle Music Fest – Alternative Rock Festival: Seattle.
Fort Nisqually Brigade Encampment – life in 1855: Tacoma.

August–September

Bumbershoot – Seattle's largest arts festival: Seattle.

September

Western Washington Fair – largest fair in Washington state; headliner entertainment rodeo and carnival: Puyallup.
Commencement Bay Maritime Fest – port tours & cruises: Port of Tacoma.

October

Earshot Jazz Festival – jazz players from around the world: Seattle.
Candlelight tours of Fort Nisqually – dress re-enactment: Tacoma.
Holiday Food & Gift Festival: Tacoma.

November–December

Zoo Lights – 500,000 holiday lights in animal shapes: Tacoma.
Victorian Country Christmas: Tacoma.

December

Community Hanukkah Celebration: Seattle.
The Nutcracker – Pacific Northwest Ballet: Seattle.

Oregon

Where to Stay

PORTLAND

Portland Airport

Holiday Inn Express Airport
11938 NE Airport Way, Portland
Tel: 503 251-9991 or 800-HOLIDAY
Fax: 503 251-9992
Reliable and comfortable rooms, located 3 miles east of the Portland International Airport. Easy access to highways. **$–$$**

Portland

Embassy Suites Portland Downtown
319 SW Pine Street, Portland
Tel: 503 279-9000
Fax: 503 497-9051
www.embassysuites.citysearch.com
In its previous incarnation as the Multnomah Hotel, the "Grand Lady of Fourth Avenue" welcomed American presidents, Joan Crawford and Elvis Presley. As well as the usual classy amenities (valet parking, free use of fitness center, a day spa, video checkout) included in the price is a full, cooked-to-order breakfast. **$$–$$$**

The Governor
611 SW 10 Ave, Portland,
Tel: 503 224-3400 or 800 554-3456
Fax: 503 241-2122
www.govhotel.com
Expensive historical hotel with mahogany walls and a club-type lobby. 1920s arts-and-crafts style, large windows in guest rooms, many services, including health club. **$$$**

The Heathman Hotel
1001 SW Broadway at Salmon, Portland
Tel: 503 241-4100 or 800 551-0011

Fax: 503 790-7110
www.heathmanhotel.com
Superior service, central Downtown location, swanky public areas in this pricey hotel that exudes refinement. **$$$–$$$$**

Hilton Portland & Executive Tower
921 SW 6th Ave, Portland
Tel: 503 226-1611
Fax: 503 220-2293
www.portlandhilton.com
Located within walking distance of Pioneer Courthouse Square and MAX light rail, panoramic views, more than 60 restaurants in a 3-block radius. Large hotel with great fitness amenities and surprisingly well priced. The Executive Tower, with over 300 guestrooms, is a newer addition. **$–$$**

MacMaster House
1041 SW Vista, Portland
Tel: 503 223-7362 or 800 774-9523
www.macmaster.com
Sanctuary nestled on King's Hill adjacent to Washington Park, home of the famous Japanese and Rose gardens; City Center is minutes away by front-door bus service. Good 23rd Street boutiques, restaurants and art galleries are an easy stroll on foot. 2-night minimum on weekends. **$$**

Mallory Hotel
SW 15th Avenue at Yamhill St, Portland
Tel: 503 223-6311
Fax: 503 223-0522
www.malloryhotel.com
Well-priced rooms in a vintage 1920s hotel 8 blocks from the downtown core. Fresh paint and refurbished rooms are still nicely old-fashioned. Free parking garage; dining room; near MAX light rail. **$–$$**

The Mark Spencer Hotel
409 SW 11th Ave, Portland
Tel: 503 224-3293 or 800 548-3934
Fax: 503 223-7848
www.markspencer.com
One of the best values in town, artsy, clean and comfortable; near MAX light rail, Powell's City of Books and gay bar district; rooftop garden, continental breakfast included. **$–$$**

COLUMBIA GORGE & MOUNT HOOD

Gorge Central Vacation Rentals
Tel: 541 386-6109 or 877 386-6109
www.gorgeres.com
A selection of vacation rental homes, condos or apartments for multi-day stays in and around the Columbia River Gorge Area. **$–$$$**

The Dalles
Lone Pine Village
I-84 at Hwy 197, 351 Lone Pine Dr, The Dalles
Tel: 541 298-2800
Fax: 541 298-8282
Economical rooms, some with kitchenettes, many with river views. A favorite with windsurfers. **$**

Hood River
Columbia Gorge Hotel
4000 Westcliff Dr, Hood River
Tel: 541 386-5566 or 800 345-1921
Fax: 541 386-9141
www.columbiagorgehotel.com
A restored 1920s hotel with gardens; each room is distinct. Views of the Columbia River Gorge and nearby windsurfing facilities. Excellent dining room. **$$$**
Hood River Hotel
102 Oak Ave, Hood River
Tel: 541 386-1900 or 800 386-1859
Fax: 541 386-6090
www.hoodriverhotel.com
On the National Register of Historic Places. Jacuzzi and spa, romantic guestrooms have wood floors and four-poster beds. Access to Mount Hood Railroad excursion. **$$**

Mount Hood
Falcon's Crest Inn
PO Box 185, Government Camp
Tel: 503 272-3403 or 800 624-7384
Fax: 503 272-3454
www.falconscrest.com
Only 54 miles east of Portland, on the southern slope of Mount Hood, this is an elegant and intimate mountain lodge. Run with a personal touch by two ex-townies who are living out their mountain

dream. A mountain breakfast is included in the price. **$$**
Timberline Lodge
On Mount Hood
Tel: 503 272-3311 or 800 547-1406
Fax: 503 272-3710
www.timberlinelodge.com
A National Historic Landmark paying tribute to the rugged spirit of the Pacific Northwest. Spectacularly located and always busy, but considered a masterpiece among the mountain lodges. Hiking or skiing in season, on-site restaurants. **$$–$$$**

Hotel Prices

Prices are generally per room per night in high to mid-season (though in some cases they are "per person" at the discretion of the hotel). Low season rates may be considerably reduced. In many cases, these room prices include a better-than-average continental breakfast, and limitless coffee.

$$$$	over $200
$$$	$150–200
$$	$100–150
$	under $99

Welches
The Resort at the Mountain
68010 E Fairway Ave, Welches
Tel: 503 622-3101 or 800-669-ROOM (7666)
www.theresort.com
Northwest golf-and-ski resort at the western base of Mt Hood. There are two restaurants, 27 holes of golf, croquet courts and lawn bowling greens, 4 tennis courts, an outdoor pool and Jacuzzi, as well as access to wildlife, hiking, mountain biking and fly fishing. **$$–$$$$**

White Salmon Washington
Inn of the White Salmon,
172 West Jewett Blvd, White Salmon
Tel: 509 493-2335 Reservations: 800 972-5226
www.innofthewhitesalmon.com
On the Washington side, near the Columbia Gorge. 1937 inn with antiques, and providing an excellent breakfast. **$–$$**

WILLAMETTE RIVER VALLEY

Corvallis
Harrison House B&B
2310 NW Harrison Blvd, Corvallis
Tel: 541 752-6248 or 800 233-6248
Fax: 541 754-1353
www.corvallis-lodging.com
Located 3 blocks from the Oregon State University campus, Dutch-Colonial style home constructed in 1939. Has comfortable guest rooms and memorable breakfast. Within minutes of Oregon wine country, about an hour from the Oregon coast, and two hours from uncrowded Oregon ski slopes. **$–$$**

Cottage Grove
Apple Inn B&B
30697 Kenady Lane, Cottage Grove, Or
Tel: 541 942-2393 or 800 942-2393
www.moriah.com/appleinn
Forested setting with mountain view near six restored covered bridges, antique shops and galleries. **$**

Eugene
Campbell House, A City Inn
252 Pearl Street, Eugene
Tel: 541 343-1119 or 800 264-2519
Fax: 541 343-2258
www.campbellhouse.com
Large, historic Victorian-style inn located within walking distance of Downtown, restaurants, galleries, Hult Center Performing Arts Theater, Cuthbert Amphitheater, U of O Autzen football stadium, rock climbing on Skinner's Butte, McKenzie River and riverside bike paths. Private bathrooms, complimentary wine in the evening, four-poster beds. **$–$$$$**

McKenzie Bridge Area
Osprey Inn
6532 North Bank Road, McKenzie Bridge
Tel: 541 822-8186
www.innsnorthamerica.com/or/Osprey.htm
On banks of the McKenzie River, private bathrooms, sitting area, new

furnishings. Near hiking, biking, and white-water rafting. **$$**

McMinnville
Youngberg Hill Vineyards & Inn
10660 SW Youngberg Hill Rd, McMinnville
Tel: 503 472-2727 or 888 657-8668
Fax: 503 472-1313
www.youngberghill.com
Four lovely rooms and three expansive suites in a hilltop farmhouse. Overlooking the Willamette Valley, Cascades and Coast Range. Private bath, gardens, sitting rooms, located in Oregon wine country. **$$**

Newburg
Springbrook Hazelnut Farm
30295 N Highway 99w Newberg
Tel: 503 538-4606 or 800 793-8528
Fax: 503 537-4004
www.nutfarm.com
On the wine route, a 70-acre nut farm on the National Register of Historic Places. There's a tennis court, pool, pond and gardens surrounded by orchards and vineyards. A private carriage house and a romantic cottage are available. **$$**

Salem
A Creekside Inn, the Marquee House
333 Wyatt Court NE, Salem
Tel: 503 391-0837 or 800 949-0837
Fax: 503 391-1713
www.open.org/~rickiemh
Colonial house overlooking Mill Creek 6 blocks from the Capitol. Delicious breakfasts. **$**
Phoenix Inn Suites South Salem
4370 Commercial St, Salem
Tel: 503 588-9220 or 800 445-4498
Fax: 503 585-3616
www.phoenixinn10.citysearch.com
Quiet, good value all-suites hotel, continental breakfast included, five minutes from downtown Salem. **$**
Red Lion Hotel
3301 Market Street NE, Salem
Tel: 503 370-7888
Fax: 503 370-6305
www.redlion.com

About five minutes from the Capitol, this clean functional hotel has laundry facilities, free parking and the usual amenities. **$**

Silverton
Egg Cup Inn B&B
11920 Sioux Rd NE, Silverton
Tel: 503 873-5497 or 877 417-1461
www.moriah.com/eggcup
A cute little house in a rural area near Gallon House covered bridge. Features include a wood stove from a bygone era and an egg-cup collection. Private bathrooms, and near Silverfalls Park, Cooley Iris Gardens, Mt Angel Abbey and the Oregon Gardens. No smoking. **$**

Yamhill
Flying M Ranch
23029 NW Flying M Rd, Yamhill
Tel: 503 662-3222
Fax: 503 662-3202
www.flying-m-ranch.com
Fly-in or drive-in ranch with austere cabins or riverside hotel units. The log lodge is eclectic. Offers a dining room and a heated indoor pool. Serves home-style meals. Horseback riding and good, old country-style fun. **$–$$**

COASTAL OREGON

Astoria
Benjamin Young Inn
3652 Duane St, Astoria
Tel: 503 325-6172 or 800 201-1286
www.benjaminyounginn.com
Listed on the National Register of Historic Places, ideal for groups, families, and romantic getaways. Five rooms with private baths; each room with a view of the crystal waters of the Columbia River. **$$–$$$**
Franklin Street Station
1140 Franklin Street, Astoria
Tel: 503 325-4314 or 800 448-1098
Fax: 801 681-5641
www.franklin-st-station-bb.com
A relaxed atmosphere in a 1910 Victorian home. Delicious breakfast, glorious views. **$–$$**

Cannon Beach
Cannon Beach Hotel Lodgings
1116 S Hemlock, Cannon Beach
Tel: 503 436-1392 or (800) 800-8000
Fax: 503 436-1396
www.cannonbeachhotel.com
Comfortable accommodations at reasonable prices. Not on the ocean, but only half a block from the beach and about 8 blocks south of Downtown. The hotel is actually three European-style properties put together; various types of rooms available. Continental breakfast included. Good restaurant. **$–$$**
Stephanie Inn
2740 S Pacific St, Canon Beach
Tel: 503 436-2221 or 800 633-3466
www.stephanie-inn.com
Located 8 miles from Cannon Beach, this luxurious waterfront facility has full services, dining room, special events and is a great place to watch ocean storms. **$$$**

Coos Bay
Coos Bay Manor
955 S. 5th Street, Coos Bay
Tel: 541 269-1224 or 800 269-1224
Fax: 541 269-1224
www.virtualcities.com/ons/or/c/orc 36010.htm
Colonial-style home on the National Register of Historic Places, detailed woodwork, lake-, ocean-, and river-fishing. Tide pools, whale watching, seal rookery, crabbing, clamming, and Esturine Park are all nearby. Five large bedrooms; three rooms with private baths, and two with shared bath. **$**

Depoe Bay
Channel House
35 Ellingson St, Depoe Bay
Tel: 541 765-2140 or 800 447-2140
Fax: 541 765-2191
www.channelhouse.com
Small, exceptionally romantic country inn in magnificent coastal scenery, whirlpool tubs offering panoramic views, and whales to be watched just a stone's throw away – if your timing is right. **$$$–$$$$**

Florence
Driftwood Shores Resort
88416 First Ave, Florence
Tel: 541 997-8263 or 800
422-5091
Fax: 541 997-5857
www.driftwoodshores.com
The location above long, sandy
Hecata Beach is great. Standard
rooms with views, suites have
fireplaces, some kitchenettes. Golf
packages. **$–$$$**

Lincoln City
Guide to Lincoln City B&Bs
www.nwcoast.com/city/bb.asp?linc
olncity
Numerous facilities are available
from this popular gateway city for
exploring the wild Northern Oregon
Coast.
Rodeway Inn on the Bay
861 SW 51st St, Lincoln City
Tel: 541 996-3996 or 800
843-4940
Fax: 541 994-7554
Some suites offer Jacuzzis, and
some have ocean and bay views.
Continental breakfast is included.
Across from Mo's Restaurant and
the beach. Within walking distance
to shops, but note there's no air
conditioning. Often has good
special-rate offers. **$–$$**
**Westin Salishan Lodge and Golf
Resort**
Gleneden Beach
Tel: 541 764-2371 or 888 SALISHAN
www.salishan.com
This is a self-contained resort with
restaurants, lounges, a renowned
wine cellar, luxury amenities and
award-winning landscape
architecture. The lodge has been

voted one of the best places to
stay anywhere in the world.
$$$–$$$$

Newport
Newport Sylvia Beach Hotel
267 NW Cliff St, Newport
Tel: 541 265-5428 or 888
795-8422.
www.sylviabeachhotel.com
This is a place for book lovers, storm
watchers and nature lovers. No
televisions, no radios, and no
phones. Meals are shared as guests
eat together "family style." The hotel
was built around 1913, and has
books in all the rooms. Characterful,
or maybe oddball, depending on your
perspective. Coastal panorama
includes Yaquina Head Lighthouse.
$–$$
Nye Beach Hotel
219 NW Cliff St, Nye Beach
Tel: 541 265-3334
Fax: 541 265-3622
www.nyebeach.com
Seems centuries old in
appearance, but was actually built
in 1922. A characterful hotel
perched on a cliff above a
generally uncrowded beach.
Balconies, restaurant and live
macaws on the premises. **$–$$**
Ocean House
4920 NW Woody Way, Newport
Tel: 541 265-6158 or 800 56-BANDB
www.oceanhouse.com
An oceanfront inn for adult
travelers. All rooms have
fireplaces and private baths, some
have luxury/spa baths. Most have
views of the incomparable Oregon
coast. Cottages also available.
$–$$$

Tyee Lodge Oceanfront B&B
4925 NW Woody Way, Newport, Or
Tel: 541 265-8953 or 888 553-8933
www.tyeelodge.com
Oceanfront B&B in a 1940s home
on Agate Beach with dramatic
ocean views. Convenient for
Bayfront, Hatfield Marine Science
Center, Oregon Coast Aquarium,
Nye Beach historic oceanfront
village. No kids. **$$**

Pacific City
Inn at Cape Kiwanda
33105 Cape Kiwanda Drive, Pacific
City
Tel: 503 965-7001 or 888
965-7001
Fax: 503 965-7002
www.innatcapekiwanda.com
All rooms have a fireplace and a
view of the ocean. Some Jacuzzi
rooms, two-person tub and queen-
size beds, exercise room, located
on the Scenic Loop. **$–$$$**
**Seaside Sand Dollar Bed &
Breakfast**
606 N Holladay Dr, Pacific City
Tel: 503 738-3491 or 800
738-3491
Members of the Oregon Bed and
Breakfast Guide. A basic, well rated
B&B. **$**

Reedsport
Best Western Salbasgeon Inn
1400 Highway Ave, Reedsport
Tel: 541 271-4831
Fax: 541 271-4832
Easy access to the dunes and
immaculately kept rooms in this
chain-motel property. Offers views
of the river and a complimentary
breakfast. **$**

Shakespeare Slept Here

**Ashland's Bed and Breakfast
Network** is a cooperative
organization of 31 inns, rooms,
suites, cottages and carriage
houses to introduce visitors to
Ashland's lodgings. All
accommodations are handy for the
hugely popular Oregon
Shakespeare Festival, so be sure
to book early. Tel: 800 944-0329
or visit the site www.abbnet.com

Other Ashland opportunities:
Mt Ashland Inn
550 Mt. Ashland Rd, Ashland
Tel: 541 482-8707 or 800 830-
8707 www.mtashlandinn.com
This two-story, romantic lodge has
extremely comfortable suites with
large Jacuzzi tubs, gas fireplaces,
handmade quilts and Turkish
robes. For the morning, there's
delicious breakfasts. **$$–$$$**

Best Western Bard's Inn
132 N Main St Ashland
Tel: 541 482-0049
Fax: 541 488-3259
www.bardinn.com
Most of the Bard's standard but
comfortable rooms and suites
have wonderful views of the
surrounding mountains. Prices are
as reasonable as you would expect
to find in a chain motel. **$–$$**

Seaside
Best Western Oceanview Resort
414 North Prom, Seaside
Tel: 503 738-3334 or 800
234-8439
Fax: 503 738-326
Ideal central location within walking
distance of shops, eateries and
arcades. Family-style rooms
featuring a kitchenette or fireplace.
Oceanfront balcony or romantic
beachfront rooms with an ocean
view, Jacuzzi, fireplace, and balcony.
Restaurant. **$–$$$**

Sand Dollar Bed & Breakfast
606 N Holladay Dr, Seaside
Tel: 503 738-3491 or 800
738-3491
www.ohwy.com/or/s/sanddobb.htm
A seashell-pink 1920s craftsman-
style home. Rooms are decorated
with bright quilts, wicker and
stained glasswork. There's also a
cottage perched on the banks of
the Necanicum River. Close to the
beach, shopping, restaurants and
the convention center. **$–$$**

Yachats
Shamrock Lodgettes
105 Hwy 101 S, Yachats
Tel: 541 547-3312 or 800
845-5028
Fax: 541 547-3843
www.beachesbeaches.com/shamro
ck.html
Situated in the park, located near
the ocean and Yachats River,
minimum 2-night stay on weekends.
Cozy rooms in rustic log cabins,
some kitchenettes. Nude beaches,
massage therapists. **$–$$**

Yachats Serenity Bed & Breakfast
5985 Yachats River Rd, Yachats
Tel: 541-547-3813
www.casco.net/~serenitybnb/seren
ity.htm
King-size beds, a whirlpool tub and
some Bavarian touches, located in
a peaceful area near river. Deer
congregate on the grounds. **$–$$**

ROGUE RIVER COUNTRY

Brookings
The Chetco River Inn
21202 High Prairie Rd, Brookings
Tel: 541 670-1645

www.chetcoriverinn.com
Eighteen miles inland from the
coast, set on a river. Swim, fish and
hike. Library, no smoking. **$$**

Spindrift Motor Inn
1215 Chetco Ave, Brookings
Tel: 541 469-5345
Fax: 541 469-5213
Highway 101 on the north side of
town, the Spindrift has 35 basic
rooms with traditional-style
furnishings. There is a restaurant
nearby, and the Pacific Ocean in the
distance. **$**

Hotel Prices

Prices are generally per room per
night in high to mid-season
(though in some cases they are
"per person" at the discretion of
the hotel). Low season rates may
be considerably reduced. In many
cases, these room prices include
a better-than-average continental
breakfast, and limitless coffee.

$$$$	over $200
$$$	$150–200
$$	$100–150
$	under $99

Gold Beach
Ireland's Rustic Lodges
29330 S Ellensburg, Gold Beach
Tel: 541 247-7718
Fax: 541 247-0225
Forty basic and rough-hewn rooms
on the ocean side of Highway 101.
Free cable, TV movies. **$**

Tu Tu'Tun Lodge
96550 North Bank Rogue Gold
Beach
Tel: 541 247-6664 or 800
864-6357
Fax 541 247-0672
www.tututun.com
Seven miles up the north side of
Rogue River, the Tu Tu'tun Lodge
has the feel of a hideaway. Fishing,
white-water boat trips, private decks
overlooking the river, and a
restaurant. Closed Nov-April. **$–$$**

Grants Pass
Doubletree Ranch
6000 Abegg Rd, Merlin
Tel: 541 476-0120
www.doubletree-ranch.com

Twenty minutes from Grants Pass, a
secluded 160-acre ranch with
cabins (housekeeping provided) on
a private Rogue River frontage.
Offers miles of trails, and within
driving distance of Crater Lake,
Ashland Shakespeare Festival,
Oregon Caves National Monument
and Jacksonville. Open
June–September. **$–$$**

Hawthorne Inn & Suites
243 N.E. Morgan Lane, Grants Pass
Tel: 541 472-1808 or 541
476-6873
Three-story hotel with standard
rooms and complimentary
breakfast. Some rooms have
kitchenettes. **$**

Riverside Inn Resort
971 SE Sixth St., Grants Pass, Or
Tel: 541 476-68731 or 800
334-4567
www.riverside-inn.com
Near the docks for the Hellgate
Jetboat Excursions, this 3-block
hotel has been a landmark on the
banks of the Rogue River for over
40 years. Many amenities. **$–$$**

Wolf Creek Inn
Exit 76, Interstate 5, near Grants
Pass
Tel: 541 866-2474
www.rogueweb.com/wolfcreekinn/
This tavern, inn and hotel complex,
20 miles north of Grants Pass, is
on the National Register of Historic
Places. Formerly an old stagecoach
stop, rooms preserve a 1890s
character. Famous folks are known
to frequent, some for the far-famed
Oktoberfest. **$–$$**

Jacksonville
B&Bs in Historic Jacksonville
www.bbonline.com/or/jacksonville.h
tml
Select from a smorgesbord of bed
and breakfasts and country inns,
convenient for Ashland's
Shakespeare Festival. **$$–$$$**

The Jacksonville Inn
175 E. California St, Jacksonville
Tel: 541 899-1900 or 800
321-9344
www.ibbp.com/or/jacksonville.html
A historic landmark with eight
elegant hotel rooms furnished with
western Gold-Rush era antiques.
Extensive wine shop, outdoor patio

and distinctive cuisine in the restaurant. Also has three honeymoon cottages. **$$–$$$**

Medford
Under the Greenwood Tree B&B
3045 Bellinger Lane, Medford, Or
Tel: 541 776-0000 or 800
766-8099
www.greenwoodtree.com
Romantic setting in 10 acres of gardens. Full breakfast and complimentary afternoon tea. This picturesque hotel has featured in several movies – you'll have to ask them which ones. **$$–$$$**

Roseberg
Steamboat Inn
42705 North Umpqua Hwy,
Steamboat
Tel: 541 498-2230 or 800
840-8825
Fax: 541 498-2411
www.thesteamboatinn.com
A famous 1930s fishing lodge 38 miles east of Roseburg, author Zane Grey's territory. Riverside cabins, some with Japanese soaking tubs, fish guide services. No television, renowned restaurant with a 20-ft long table. Closed Jan–Feb. **$$$–$$$$**
Windmill Inn
1450 NW Mulholland Dr, Roseburg
Tel: 541 673-0901 or 800
547-4747
Fax 541 673-0901
www.windmillinns.com/ie30nscp/ro
s/ros.htm
Spacious accommodations, a lounge and a restaurant adjacent. Complimentary continental breakfast is offered. Discount packages to Wildlife Safari. **$**

OREGON CASCADES

Crescent Lake
Crescent Lake Lodge & "Resort"
Crescent Lake
Tel: 541 433-2505
Located on Deschutes National Forest Land, under permit to the US Forest Service. Rustic, well used cabins offer living rooms, equipped kitchens with utensils, dishes and linens supplied. A cozy spot in summer or winter. **$–$$**

Detroit
Breitenbush Hot Springs Retreat
Detroit
Tel: 503 854-3314
www.breitenbush.com/
Place of personal retreat, or New Age workshops and conferences, basic accommodations. **$–$$**

Diamond Lake
Diamond Lake Resort
Diamond Lake
Tel: 541 793-3333 or 800 733-7593
Fax: 541 793-3309
www.ohwy.com/or/d/dilakere.htm
Boat or horseback riding, bike riding, only a few miles from Crater Lake National Park. Motel units or basic guest cabins. **$–$$**

Sisters
Black Butte Ranch
13653 Hawks Beard Rd, Black Butte Ranch
Tel: 800 452-7455
www.blackbutteranch.com/
Eight miles west of Sisters, expensive golf resort and overall recreation center. Vacation home rentals, minimum bookings are for two nights. **$$$–$$$$**
Conklin's Guest House
69013 Camp Polk Road, Sisters
Tel: 541 549-0123 or 800
549-4262
Fax: 541 549-4481
www.conklinsguesthouse.com/
Rooms with private baths include a full country breakfast and refreshments in the evening. There is a swimming pool and trout ponds. Spectacular surroundings. **$$**

Metolius River Resort
25551 SW FS Rd 1419, Camp Sherman
Tel: 541 595-6281 or 800 81 TROUT (818-7688)
Fax: 541 595-6281
www.metolius-river-resort.com
Fourteen miles from Sisters, Metolius offers 11 quality crafted and well appointed cabins on the riverside. Miles of streamside and forest trails, fly-fishing, two-night minimum. **$$$**
Rags to Walkers Guest Ranch B&B
17045 Farthing Lane, Sisters
Tel: 541 548-7000 or 800
488-5622
www.ragstowalkers.com
Unique guest ranch with spectacular mountain views offers bed and breakfast, and 3 vacation rental homes. Horseback riding, fishing, in-line skating and biking (bikes are provided). Work out, or walk miles of paved paths. **$–$$$**

Warm Springs
Kah-Nee-Tah
Warm Springs
Tel: 541 553-1112 or 800 554-4SUN (4786)
www.kah-nee-taresort.com/
Warm Springs is in a remote desert location on an Indian reservation. Lodge-style large facility hotel caters to customers of the casino, and has Spa Wanapine with massages etc. Central fireplace and dining room. **$$**

EAST OF THE CASCADES

Bend and Sun River
Bend Vacation Rentals
Tel: 541 385-9492
www.bendvacationrentals.com
Select a vacation rental home – cabin, condo or inn in price ranges from economy to deluxe. Many homes and condos are within walking distance of downtown Bend. **$$–$$$**
Inn of the Seventh Mountain
18575 SW Century Dr, Bend
Tel: 541 382-8711 or 800
452-6810
Fax: 541 382-3517
www.7thmtn.com

This destination resort is situated in Deschutes National Forest, minutes from Mt Bachelor or downtown Bend. Facilities include jogging and hiking trails, a tennis court, swimming pools, whitewater rafting, canoe trips, guided horseback rides or golfing. Bedrooms or suites. **$$–$$$$**

Shilo Inn Suites Hotel
3105 O.B. Riley Rd, Bend
Tel: 541 389-9600 or 800 222-2244
Fax: 541 382-4310
www.shiloinns.com/Oregon/bend.html
On the Dechutes River, this very pleasant remodeled facility offers comfortable rooms, laundry facilities, an airport shuttle, and a swimming pool. Bend is the headquarters for accessing Newberry National Monument. **$$**

Sunriver Resort
1 Center Dr, Sunriver
Tel: 541 593-1000 or 800 801-8765
Fax: 541 593-5458
http://sunriver-resort.com
Located on the dry side of the Cascade Mountain range, golf and outdoor activities are provided. Wide range of accommodations includes village rooms and suites, river lodge guest rooms, as well as over 250 fully furnished private homes or condominiums. There are three restaurants. Minimum stay rules apply. Access to Newberry National Volcanic Monument and the High Desert Museum.
$$–$$$$

Klamath Falls
Holiday Inn Express Hotel and Suites
2500 South 6th St, Klamath Falls Or 97601
Tel: 541 884-9999
Fax: 541 882-4020
Standard chain-hotel rooms in a good location not that far from the falls. **$–$$**

Lake of the Woods Mountain Lodge & Resort
950 Harriman Route, near Klamath Falls
Tel: 541 949-8300
Fax: 541 949-8229

www.lakowoods.com
Cute furnished cabins with cast iron stoves and knotty pine walls, set among majestic firs and lofty pines. Boat and bike rentals available. Two-night minimum stay on weekends and holidays. **$$–$$$**

Maverick Motel
1220 Main St, Klamath Falls
Tel: 541 882-6688 or 800 404-6690
Fax: 541 885-4095
Friendly, quiet, clean and very cheap. **$**

Nature Lovers Retreat and Tree Houses
Chiloquin
Tel: 541 783-2697
www.retreatfornaturelovers.com
This rustic spot is approximately 30 miles north of Klamath Falls. Offering simple cabins or tree houses, this is a great place to sleep in a tree. Bring your own bed linens. Conveniently located for Crater Lake National Park, Wetlands & National Wildlife Refuges, which have the largest population of bald eagles in mainland USA. **$–$$**

Running Y Ranch Resort
5391 Running Y Rd, near Klamath Falls
Tel: 541 850-5500 or 888 850-0275
Fax: 541 885-3194
www.runningy.com
With an Arnold Palmer-designed golf course, exercise facilities, two restaurants, comfortable rooms, suites or townhouses, this is the only destination resort in Southern Oregon. Lots of birds. **$$–$$$$**

Shaniko
Historic Shaniko Hotel
4th & "E" St, Shaniko
Tel: 541 489-3441 or 800 483-3441
Fax: 541 489-3441
www.virtualguidebooks.com/Oregon/EasternOregon/Deschutes/ShanikoHotel.html
Currently run as a bed and breakfast, this old western hotel is located in a revived ghost town and offers a unique experience. Plain rooms with 1890s decor. The Old West at an Economical price. **$**

NORTHEAST OREGON

Baker City
Always Welcome Inn
175 E. Campbell St, Baker City
Tel: 541 523-3431 or 800 307-5206
www.easy-finder.com/exit/or/welcomeinn.htm
Hillside inn with clean, comfortable standard rooms. Views of Elkhorn Mountains. Continental breakfast. **$**

Geiser Grand Hotel
1996 Main St, Baker City
Tel: 541 523-1889 or 888 434-7374
Fax: 541 523-1800
www.oregonattractions.com/2001/2001/eastern/GeiserGrand.htm
Built in the 1880s with Gold Rush money, Italian Renaissance Revival architecture and more than 100 Viennese crystal chandeliers. The original saloon and Palm Court Dining Room have period furnishings. Mountain views, access to the Oregon Trail Center and Regional Museum. **$–$$$**

Enterprise
Wilderness Inn
301 W North St, Enterprise
Tel: 541 426-4535 or 800 965-1205
Fax: 541 426-0128
Despite its name, the property is located in town within walking distance of restaurants. Standard basic rooms, some offer views of Wallowa mountains. **$**

Joseph and Wallowa Lake
Eagle Cap Chalets
59879 Wallowa Lake Hwy, Joseph
Tel: 541 432-4704
Fax: 541 432-3010
www.eaglecapchalets.com
Chalet rooms, cabins and condos; an indoor pool and spa. Located in a village next to a Wallowa glacial lake. Fishing, gondola and Tramway rides are available close by. **$–$$**

Indian Lodge Motel
Main & Third, Joseph
Tel: 541 432-2651
Fax: 541 432-4949
Cozy and comfortable rooms, this property once belonged to actor Walter Brennan, who lived here in

the 1950s. The lake is just one mile away. **$**

Matterhorn Swiss Village,
950 Wallowa Lake Hwy, Joseph
Tel: 541 432-4071
www.wallowalake.net/MatterhornSwissVillage.html
Located next to the Wallowa Lake tram, and offering furnished, "Swiss" style cottages, nestled in the pines. **$–$$**

Wallowa Lake Lodge
60060 Wallowa Lake Hwy Joseph
Tel: 541 432-9821
Fax: 541 432-4885
www.wallowalakelodge.com/
Historic, 1920s rustic wooden lodge, offering views of the lake and mountains, with a dining room for group meals. 22 rooms and eight cabins. Hiking and horseback riding are available. No smoking. **$–$$$**

La Grande

Best Western Rama Inn and Suites
1711 21st Street, La Grande
Tel: 541 963-3100 or 888 726-2466
Fax: 541 963-8621
On the way to the town of Joseph, these standard chain-motel rooms are located near to the large and convenient Grande Ronde Shopping Center. **$**

Stang Manor B&B
1612 Walnut Street, La Grande
Tel: 541 963-2400 or 888-2UNWIND (888-286-9463)
Fax: 541 963-2400 (same number)
www.stangmanor.com/
Built by a timber baron, this Georgian revival mansion has been tastefully decorated and boasts a stone fireplace. Lavish breakfasts are served in a formal dining room. There are restaurants within easy walking distance. No smoking. Good value. **$**

JOHN DAY FOSSIL BEDS NATIONAL MONUMENT

Accommodation, food, fuel and public telephone services are available in nearby communities, but not within John Day National Monument itself. Travelers to Oregon can access the park from the towns of **Warm Springs**, **Bend**, **John Day**, **Kimberly**, **Madras**, **Prineville** or **Redmond**.

Hotel Prices

Prices are generally per room per night in high to mid-season (though in some cases they are "per person" at the discretion of the hotel). Low season rates may be considerably reduced. In many cases, these room prices include a better-than-average continental breakfast, and limitless coffee.

$$$$	over $200
$$$	$150–200
$$	$100–150
$	under $99

John Day (the town)

Dreamers Lodge
144 N Canyon Blvd, John Day
Tel: 541 575-0526
Fax: 541 575-2753
www.grantcounty.cc/business.php/61
Twenty-five standard, but perfectly comfortable rooms right in the center of town. Free cable TV movies, some kitchenettes, and the nearest access to the John Day Fossil Beds. **$**

Kimberly

Holmes River Ranch Inn
Remote location, near Kimberly
Tel: 541 934-2276
www.holmesriverranchinn.com/
Comfortable, simple ranch-theme rooms and down-home Western hospitality, overlooking the north fork of the John Day River. The ranch offers access to National Monument sites. **$**

Madras

Hoffy's Motel
600 N Highway 26, Madras
Tel: 541 475-4633 or 800 227-6865
Fax: 541 475-7872
Located near good eatin' restaurant, these standard rooms occupy five buildings set on prettily landscaped lawns. For truly outdoor-types there is also a teepee for rent, but you need to provide your own bedding for this. Laundry facilities and a putting green are also available. **$**

Prineville

Elliott Marion Reed House B&B
305 W 1st Prineville
Tel: 541 416-0423
Fax: 541 416-9368
www.empnet.com/elliotthouse/
Featured in the National Register of Historic Places, this 1908 Queen Anne House is in an undistinguished neighborhood. Antiques, down comforters and a wraparound porch. No children, no smoking. **$**

Rustlers (Roost) Motel
960 NW 3rd St, Hwy 26, Prineville
Tel: 541 447-4185
Fax: 541 447-4185
With its western look and an eclectic mix of furnishings, this is a fun place to stay. A Mexican restaurant is conveniently nearby. **$**

Redmond

Eagle Crest Resort
1522 Cline Falls Rd, Redmond
Tel: 541 923-2453 or 800 845-8491
Fax: 541 923-1720
www.eagle-crest.com/main.html
Located on 1,700 acres of grounds, Eagle Crest offers golf courses, bike trails and is near to Mount Bachelor for skiing. The resort offers a selection of rooms, suites and town houses. **$$–$$$$**

Redmond Inn
1545 Hwy 97 S, Redmond
Tel: 541 548-1091
Fax: 541 548-0415
Conveniently located for horseback riding, fishing, skiing and rock climbing at Smith Rock State Park. 3 blocks from the town center. Complimentary breakfast. **$**

NEWBERRY NATIONAL VOLCANIC MONUMENT

Lodging, food, fuel and public telephone services are available in the nearby communities of **Bend** or **Sunriver**. Within the National Volcanic Monument itself are rustic facilities at Paulina and East Lakes.

Paulina and East Lakes
Paulina Lake Lodge
Near Paulina Lake at La Pine
Tel: 541 536-2240
Located on National Forest Land and operating under a special use permit from the Deschutes National Forest. There is a primitive general store, restaurant, cabins, boat rentals, gas and oil. Open mid-Dec to mid-March and May to October. **$**
East Lake Resort
Near East Lake at La Pine
Tel: 541 536-2230
www.eastlakeresort.com
Located on National Forest Land and operating under a special use permit from the Deschutes National Forest, rustic with rather basic facilities; a general store, coffee shop, cabins, a boat house, boat rentals, gas and oil, fishing tackle, some swimming, and hiking. Hot springs are primitive, algae-filed and muddy. June–September only. **$**

CRATER LAKE NATIONAL PARK

Lodging, food, fuel, and public telephone services are available only in the two places listed here. The national park is open year round. However, due to heavy snowfall, the park lodgings and services close by them are often closed as specified. Additional lodging and facilities are available at **Chiloquin**, 35 miles south. The North Entrance to Crater Lake National Park is open mid-June to mid-October and **Diamond Lake** is 20 miles north of this entrance. Diamond Lake is located 45 miles from **Rim Village** via Hwy 62 and Hwy 230.

In the National Park
Crater Lake Lodge
565 Rim Village Dr, Crater Lake
Tel: 541 830-8700
Fax: 541 594-2622
www.crater-lake.com
An authorized concessionaire of the National Park Service operates this historic 1915 lodge. Recently remodeled, on the rim of the caldera with excellent views of the lake, it has wood floors, stone fireplace and a dining room. No air conditioning, room phones or TV, small rooms. Available only mid-May through late October. Best to reserve. **$$–$$$**
Mazama Village Motor Inn
Highway 62, Mazama Village
Tel: 541 830-8700
www.crater-lake.com
There are 40 basic motel rooms nestled in the woods in this convenient location, seven miles south of the lake. A convenience and gift store, gas station, and showers are close by. There is also a campground. Reservations required. Open May through October. **$$**

Near the National Park
Crater Lake Resort
Fort Creek Campground, Fort Klamath
Tel: 541 381-2349
Fax: 541 381-2343
www.craterlakeresort.com
Eight cabins with kitchenettes, located just seven miles south of Crater Lake National Park at MP 92 on Hwy 62, open April to Oct. These rustic accommodations tend to book up early, and so, therefore, should you. **$$**

OREGON CAVES NATIONAL MONUMENT

In the Monument
Oregon Caves Lodge
2000 Caves Highway, Oregon Caves
Tel: 541 592-3400
Fax: 541 592-6654
www.oregoncaves.com/oclodge.htm
Built in 1934, this rustic lodge has a number of small rooms, with no TV or telephone in the rooms. Remodeled, fireplace in the lobby. Dining room. Reservations required. No smoking. Closed November to April. **$$**

Cave Junction
Out N' About Treesort
300 Page Creek Rd, Cave Junction
Tel: 541 592-2208 or 800 200-5484
www.treehouses.com
The word "Treesort" describes a number of roosts *up in the trees*, all with fridges, some with baths, some connected by suspension bridges. Breakfast included. Two-night minimum stay. This is a community as much as a hotel, with its own school high in the trees. Horses, dogs, cats and chickens. **$–$$**
Junction Inn
406 Redwood Hwy, Cave Junction
Tel: 541 592-3106
www.cavejunction.com/cgi-bin/axs/ax.pl?http://home1.gte.net/louiegf/homepage/ji.htm
Standard guestrooms are furnished with either a king bed or two double beds. Within walking distance of shopping and services. There is a restaurant on site, one hour from Oregon Caves. **$–$$**

Native Americans and Working Girls

Wildhorse Resort & Casino
72777 Hwy 331, Pendleton
Tel: 541 278-2274 or 800-654-WILD (9453); Fax: 541 276-0297
www.wildhorseresort.com/wild.html
Owned and operated by the Confederated Tribes of the Umatilla Indian Reservation, this modest hotel has suites, views, an indoor pool, a simple breakfast, golf and a casino. **$**

Working Girls Hotel & Condo
17 SW Emigrant Ave, Pendleton
Tel: 541 276-0730 or 800 226-6398
Fax: 541 276-0665
www.pendletonundergroundtours.com Once a bordello, now on the National Register of Historic Places, this hotel has refurbished turn-of-the-19th century suites and is associated with Pendleton Underground Tours. **$**

Where To Eat

PORTLAND

Alameda Cafe
4641 NE Fremont St, Portland
Tel: 503 284-5314
Airy, mellow, French-influenced
eclectic restaurant, considered the
best for breakfast but also offers
excellent burgers and Caesar salad.
Be sure to save room for the
peanut butter pie. Casual. **$**

Assaggio
7742 SE 13th Ave, Portland
Tel: 503 232-6151
Coved ceilings, earth-colored walls,
a copper-topped bar and a long wait
on weekends but three forks up for
the nightly trio of pastas. For
dessert try the tiramisu. Dressy
casual. **$$**

Cafe des Amis
1987 NW Kearney St, Portland
Tel: 503 295-6487
Vine-clad brick to the lace curtains,
antiques and spacious, linen-topped
tables. No privacy but good value.
No fads, no frills French-inspired
food. Try the chicken with 40
cloves. Extensive wine list. Casual.
$$

Campbell's Bar-B-Q
8701 SE Powell Blvd, Portland
Tel: 503 777-9795
Feeling like a little slice of Texas?
This barbecue, southern and soul
restaurant feels just right. Sauces
are slathered over gigantic portions
of meat, and for dessert:
marionberry cobbler topped with
vanilla ice cream. Casual. **$**

Cassidy's Restaurant and Bar
1331 SW Washington St, Portland
Tel: 503 223-0054
For the atmosphere of an after-work
bar and eatery, check the vintage,
dark-wood and leaded glass in this
bar. Known for late-night madness,
Cassidy's, is home to the last of
the last calls. Try the steamed
mussels in chipotle, coconut milk
and vegetable broth. Casual. **$$**

Chez Grill
2229 SE Hawthorne Blvd, Portland
Tel: 503 239-4002
Tex-Mex without yuppie pretensions.
California-airy with outside tables in
summer. Try the rough-cut

guacamole, served chunky with
cilantro, onion, tomato and warm,
hand-made tortillas or fish tacos.
Fruit Margarita heaven! Casual. **$$**

Compass World Bistro
4741 SE Hawthorne Blvd, Portland
Tel: 503 231-4840
Romantic rendezvous by night,
brunch-lovers' bistro by day.
American comfort favorites like
banana coffeecake, corn pudding,
roasted potatoes and marinated
lamb with yogurt sauce. Casual. **$$**

Dan and Louis Oyster Bar
208 SW Ankeny Street, Portland
Tel: 503 227-5906
A Portland institution, the plain
décor is rememiscent of dining in
the Army mess hall, but oysters and
fresh shellfish are the name of the
game here. Maritime memorabilia
deck the walls, with a huge ship's
wheel gracing the entrance.
Sublime. Casual. **$–$$**

Price Guide

Prices are approximate for two
people before taxes and tips,
including house brand wine
(where available).

$$$$	over $100
$$$	$60–$100
$$	$30–$60
$	under $30

Dragonfish Asian Cafe
Paramount Hotel Restaurant, 909
SW Park Ave, Portland
Tel: 503 243-5991
The sushi bar is the place to get
personal with the chef. Pan-Asian
and Pacific Rim cuisine and
windows for people-watching. Try
the clam lo mein, made with Manilla
clams. Food portion sharing is
encouraged. Suggestion: buy your
tickets early for a movie at the Fox
Towers and head to Dragonfish for
Happy-Hour specials. Casual. **$$**

El Gaucho
319 SW Broadway, Portland
Tel: 503 227-8794
Real American men like to eat
prime rib beef, washed down with
wine and served with pomp in dark
caverns. Why? Who knows? Here's

the best place to experience it. Try
the tableside Caesar salad, and
Bananas Foster for dessert to make
the waiter work for his money. Also
has a cigar lounge. Casual. **$$$**

Flying Pie Pizzeria.
7804 SE Stark St, Portland
Tel: 503 254-2016
Voted among the best, decorated by
your crazy aunt and uncle; there's
no host or hostess, so get in line,
grab a booth, pick up your pizza and
utensils, and dig in. Food heavy on
the toppings, they're not flying
anywhere. The Vegetarian Presto
has pesto, spinach, artichoke
hearts, olives, roasted red peppers
and feta cheese. Casual. **$**

The Heathman Restaurant & Bar
Hotel, 1001 SW Broadway, Portland
Tel: 503 790-7752
A charming wood-paneled lounge
near a marble fireplace. Heathman
is an American regional and French
restaurant. Northwestern
Specialties from the classically
trained French chef are generally
excellent as are such favorites as
crab cakes and venison. Live jazz
Tuesday through Saturday.
Business casual. **$$$**

Ivy House Restaurant
1605 SE Bybee Blvd, Portland
Tel: 503 231-9528
Family restaurant set in an old
home, with wood floors and white
linens. Try the butternut-squash
risotto. Kid friendly. Casual. **$$**

La Calaca Comelona
1408 SE 12th Ave, Portland
Tel: 503 239-9675
If this pastel- walled place had a
motto, it would be "No burritos,
amigo." Try the *choriqueso*,
Mexican sausage with melted
cheese, or *pastor* – marinated pork
with pineapple. Prices and portions
are modest. Casual. **$**

McCall's Waterfront Cafe
1020 SW Front Ave, Portland
Tel: 503 248-9710
Food is so-so but the splendid
location next to Salmon Street
Springs and on the Willamette River
offers diners on the patio an
exceptional view. Easterly views of
the river are there for indoor diners.
Lunch and dinner menus are served
all day. Appetizers, soups and

salads, fish and chips, burgers, steaks, pastas, and sandwiches. Casual. **$–$$**

Mother's Bistro & Bar.
409 SW 2nd Ave, Portland
Tel: 503 464-1122
All-American comfort food like Mom used to make. After good beef rolls with mushroom sauce, especially fork-worthy is the molten-chocolate cake. Comfy eating so good you won't notice the tables are close together. Brunch too. Casual. **$**

The Old Spaghetti Factory
0715 SW Bancroft Street, Portland
Tel: 503 225-0433
Cheap and classy, most tourists love these places. Magnet for kids. Mostly pasta. Casual. **$**

Oritalia
750 SW Alder St, Portland
Tel: 503 295-0680
Asian, Pan-Asian and Pacific Rim fusion cuisine and chandeliers with low-light ambiance at this East-meets-West eatery. Booths are the best places to sit. Try the smooth-as-butter tuna tartare mixed with shiso (Japanese basil) and crisp Asian pears. Business casual. **$$$**

Pazzo Ristorante
621 SW Washington St, Portland
Tel: 503 228-1515
Roaring '20s clubby comfort and busy Italian-style cuisine with Los Angeles swagger. Try the wood-fired Piedmontese beef burger and cannelloni di carne, roasted in its own terracotta dish. Chef Nathan Logan cooked his way across Italy earning his tall hat. Casual. **$$**

Ringside Steakhouse
2165 W Burnside St, Portland
Tel: 503 223-1513
Dark, cavernous and comfortable with upholstered booths. Steakhouse with one hell of a punch offering a large menu of chicken and seafood. Try the popular, well-marbled New York or rib-eye cuts or the bacon-wrapped tenderloin steaks with sweet Walla Walla onions coated in a melt-in-your-mouth batter. Casual. **$$–$$$**

Saucebox
214 SW Broadway, Portland
Tel: 503 241-3393
A sushi restaurant in a two-tiered space. Sit outside in the summer.

Dress Code

"**Casual**" means good-looking leisureware, not battered old jeans. "**Business casual**" is an upscale version of the same, but with a jacket or jewelry to make the look more formal. "**Dressy**" is all-out glamor, but go easy on the frills and fancy fabrics.

Try the *Zefiro ahi* and avocado, or the Korean baby-back ribs, a gift to your soul. Casual. **$$**

Sungari Restaurant
735 SW 1st Ave, Portland
Tel: 503 224-0800
Stellar Szechuan under low lighting with arched windows. Probably the finest Chinese food Portland has to offer. Try the potstickers, the light, crisp eggrolls, or the "Sea Scallops in Spicy Tangy Sauce". Casual. **$$**

Thai Orchid
2231 W Burnside St, Portland
Tel: 503 226-4542
Among the top Thai places in town. Try the *Miang kum* – a tasty do-it-yourself appetizer of spinach leaves and a host of salty, bitter, spicy and sweet fillings. Specify the degree of hotness. Casual. **$$**

Tuscany Grill
811 NW 21st Avenue, Portland
Tel: 503 243-2757
Tiny dining room with great sidewalk tables. The Italian dishes are short on eye appeal, long on flavor. Try the Tagliatelle al Sugo – wide noodles with a sauce of braised veal. Waiting too long for a table? There's an Italian restaurant on either side, and they're both good too. Casual. **$$**

Wildwood Restaurant and Bar
1221 NW 21st Ave, Portland
Tel; 503 248-9663
Chef Corey Schreiber is constantly promoting his American cuisine restaurant; the bar was repainted in black and taupe to better complement Schreiber's cookbook. Accolades are deserved. Try the beet and citrus salad with fried artichokes and saffron aioli. Business casual. **$$$**

Brewpubs and Sports Bars
Bridge Port Ale House
3632 SE Hawthorne Blvd, Portland
Tel: 503 233-6540
This rustic-warehouse pub thrives among the storefronts of Hawthorne Boulevard. Try the hot, bubbly ramekin of crab and artichoke dip, served with crisp triangles of pizza dough. One of the best brewpubs in Portland. Casual. **$–$$**

Widmer Brothers Brewing Company
929 N Russell St, Portland, Or
Tel: 503 281-2437
Great *gasthaus* ambiance and delicious pub grub; many microbrews. Variations on German styling. Casual. **$–$$**

COLUMBIA GORGE & MOUNT HOOD

The Dalles
Bailey's Place
515 Liberty St, The Dalles
Tel: 541 296-6708
On the National Register of Historic Places, this 1865 House has period chandeliers. Try the Chicken Ole in brandy, cream and mushrooms or the prime rib – a specialty here. Business casual. **$$–$$$**

Hood River
Full Sail Brewing Tasting Room and Pub
506 Columbia St, Hood River, Or
Tel: 541 386-2281
In the former cannery building, Full Sail overlooks the Columbia River. Award-winning brews plus nachos, sausages and pubfood. In summer there's a grill menu. Casual. **$–$$**

Mount Hood
Cascade Dining Room, Timberline Lodge
Timberline Road, Mount Hood National Forest
Tel: 503 272-3311
This National Historic Landmark is one of several restaurants in this high mountain location. Chefs prepare "Best of Oregon" products. Try the rack of lamb or the marion-berry cobbler. Good wine list. Business casual. **$$$**

WILLAMETTE RIVER VALLEY

Albany
Novak's Hungarian Paprikas
2835 Santaim Hwy, Albany
Tel: 541 967-9488
Simple décor, serves *kolbasa* and beef *szelet* along with other Hungarian favorites. Casual. **$$**

Corvallis
Bombs Away Cafe
2527 NW Monroe, Corvallis
Tel: 541 757-7221
First surprise upon walking in – it doesn't look like a pub, but there are 24 taps pouring at least 20 craft brews, three imports and a cask-conditioned beer. All this plus great aromas and Mexican eats, including *rellenos*, burritos, tamales, tacos, *quesadillas*, *chimichangas*, and dinner specials. Casual. **$–$$**

Michael's Landing
603 NW 2nd St, Corvallis
Tel: 541 754-6141
In this former railroad depot overlooking the Williamette River is an extensive menu of steak, seafood or chicken. Try the Northwest salmon in wine-butter. Casual. **$$–$$$**

Cottage Grove
Stacy's Covered Bridge Restaurant
401 E Main St, Cottage Grove
Tel: 541 767-0291
A 1906 bank building transformed into this white-linen restaurant with a changing menu. Serves seafood, chicken steaks or pasta and, on the weekend, prime rib. Try the Chicken Taylor. Near to one of Oregon's famous covered bridges. Good wine selection. Casual. **$$–$$$**

Eugene
Café Zenon
898 Pearl St, Eugene
Tel: 541 343-3005
Ever-changing menu of fresh foods and international styles. 20 to 30 desserts daily. Open-air dining in summer. Sunday brunch, too. Casual to business casual. **$$$**

High Street Brewery and Café
1243 High St, Eugene
Tel: 541 345-4905
Voted the best brewpub in town, best French fries and the best finger foods. Housed in a renovated 1900s residence, original artwork. Backyard beer garden under branches of apple, fir, ash, hawthorne and tulip trees in the summer, yard enclosed for winter. Regular menu and daily specials. Casual. **$**

Price Guide

Prices are approximate for two people before taxes and tips, including house brand wine (where available).

$$$$	over $100
$$$	$60–$100
$$	$30–$60
$	under $30

Poppi's Anatolia
992 Willamette St, Eugene
Tel: 541 343-9661
Wooden beams and a friendly kitchen at Poppi's, offering home-style Greek food and a few East Indian curries. No lunch on Sunday. Casual. **$–$$**

McKenzie Bridge
Log Cabin Inn
56483 McKenzie Hwy, McKenzie Bridge
Tel: 541 822-3432
The saloon has log walls in this 1906 stagecoach stop. Outdoor deck in summer, views of the river. Try the Mesquite prime rib and salmon. Sunday brunch too. Casual. **$$–$$$**

McMinnville
Nick's Italian Café
521 East 3rd St, McMinnville
Tel: 541 434-4471
In these modest surroundings the chef presents northern Italian specialties. An extensive wine list. Five course prix-fixe meals. Casual. **$$$**

Oregon City (south of Portland)
McMenamin's Pub
102 9th St, Oregon City
Tel: 503 655-8032
Aa American as it gets; this busy place serves its own ales and pub grub. Try the Communication Breakdown Burger. Casual. **$**

Salem
Gerry Frank's Konditorei
310 Kearney St SE, Salem
Tel: 503 585-7070
Gourmet cake shop that serves meals all day as well as over 30 varieties of cake, many of the chocolate variety, and assorted cheesecakes. Black-and-white harlequin floors and shiny clean tables and chairs. Casual. **$**

The Joel Palmer House Restaurant
600 Ferry St, Dayton
Tel: 503 864-2995
Try the Wild Oregon Salmon with Curried Cous Cous, Porcini Duxelles, and Dill Chimichurri in this colonnaded mansion near Salem. Chef Jack Czarnecki's specialty is mushrooms. Business casual. **$$$**

Mt Angel Brewing Company
210 Monroe St, Mt Angel
Tel: 503 845-9624
Bavarian and barbecue theme restaurant and microbrewery located near Salem serves barbecued meats and smoked salmon, pastas, pizza and appetizers cooked in Traeger Grills and smokers. Oktoberfest. Casual. **$**

COASTAL OREGON

Astoria
Pier 11 Feed Store Restaurant
77 Eleventh St, Astoria
Tel: 503 325-0279
Overlooking the Columbia River, with a rustic décor. Specializes in American steaks and seafood. Casual. **$$**

Ship Inn
1 Second Street, Astoria
Tel: 503 325-0033
A favorite with tourists, try the fish & chips or other tasty seafood offerings. Casual. **$–$$**

Bandon (near Coos Bay)
Bandon Boatworks
275 Lincoln Ave, Bandon
Tel: 541 347-2111
Romantic jetty-side restaurant
serves steak and seafood.Try the
New Orleans Bayou steamers in
gumbo broth. Summer patio.
Casual. **$$**

Brookings
Wharfside Seafood Restaurant
16362 Lower Harbor Rd, Brookings
Tel: 541 469-7316
Here is the best in casual dining.
Known to many as Oregon's
"banana belt" because the average
temperatures are the warmest on
the Oregon coast. Fresh seafood.
Casual. **$$**

Cannon Beach
The Bistro
263 N Hemlock St, Cannon Beach
Tel: 503 436-2661
Chef Bill Pappa's small restaurant
serves imaginative three-course
prix–fixe dinners, often of lamb,
prawns or oysters. Try the Black
Forest salad and salmon cordon
bleu. Reservations recommended.
Closed Tues from Nov to Jan. No
lunch. Dressy casual. **$$$**
Dooger's Seafood and Grill
1371 S. Hemlock St, Cannon Beach
Tel: 503 436-2225
Great seafood and hamburgers
served in a modern setting. Try the
clam chowder or steamer clams.
Closed in January. Casual. **$$**

Coos Bay
Blue Heron Bistro
1000 West Commercial, Coos Bay
Tel: 541 267-3933
Busy sky-lit and tiled-floor
restaurant with well-prepared sea
food, chicken or pasta, soups and
desserts. Many microbrew choices.
Patio in summer. Casual. **$$**

Depoe Bay
Tidal Rave
279 NW Highway 101, Depoe Bay
Tel: 541 765-2995
Ocean view enhances the grilled
seafood offerings. Try the Crab
Casserole. Reservations
recommended. Business casual. **$$**

Sea Hag Restaurant & Lounge
53 Hwy 101, Depoe Bay
Tel: 541 765-2760
Popular seafood restaurant and
lounge features a Friday-night
seafood buffet and lavish salad bar,
plus prime rib with Yorkshire pudding
on Saturday night. Casual. **$$**

Florence
Mo's
1436 Bay St, Florence
Tel: 541 997-2185
These well-known chain-style family
restaurants, six of them along the
Oregon coast, are an Oregon
institution. This restaurant is right
over the water. Often called "little
joints on the waterfront," they are
unique to each other and to other
seafood restaurants. Try the clam
chowder. Casual. **$**

Gleneden Beach (near Lincoln City)
Chez Jeanette
7150 Old US Hwy 101, Gleneden
Beach
Tel: 541 764-3825
Country-cottage styling, the chef
puts a French accent on local
favorites. Try the Carpetbagger
Steak with local oysters wrapped in
bacon. No lunch. **$$$**

Gold Beach
Nor'wester Seafood
22971 Harbor Way, Gold Beach
Tel: 541 247-2333
The Nor'wester overlooks the boats
in the harbor and the Rogue River,
and serves seafood, steak and
pasta. Wine list. No lunch. Casual.
$$

Lincoln City
Fathom's Restaurant and Bar
4009 SW Highway 101, Lincoln City
Tel: 541 996-2161
Airy setting upstairs at the Inn at
Spanish Head with a great view of
the ocean. Try the fish & chips.
Breakfast, lunch, dinner and
Sunday brunch. Casual. **$$–$$$**
**McMenamin's Lighthouse Brew
Pub**
4157 Highway 101, Lincoln City
Tel: 541 994-7238
Always busy and serving fresh local
ales with pub grub of burgers or
sandwiches. Fish & chips and
psychedelic art. Casual. **$**

Newport
Nye Beach Café
219 NW Cliff, Newport
Tel: 541 265-3334
A contemporary café with a grand
piano, and a view across the beach.
Try the Seafood Cioppino or one of
the fish stews, and sample the
home -made desserts. **$$**

Pacific City (near Lincoln City)
Pelican Pub and Brewery
33180 Cape Kitwanda Dr, Pacific
City
Tel: 503 965-7007
Breakfast, lunch or dinner with
views of the capes. An outdoor
patio in summer. Steaks, fish and
seafood as well its own
microbrews. Casual. **$–$$**

Seaside
Breakers Restaurant
At Best Western, 414 N.
Promenade, Seaside
Tel: 503 738-3334

Say Cheese

Roseanna's Café
1490 Pacific Ave, Oceanside
Tel: 503 842-7351 A few miles
west of the "Cheese Town" of
Tillamook, this rustic beach-type
place is across from Three Arch
Rock. As well as treats from the
local creameries, try the
Gorgonzola seafood pasta, Copper
River salmon and the terrific
oysters. Casual. **$$$**

**Blue Heron French Cheese
Company**
2001 Blue Heron Dr, Tillamook
Tel: 503 842-8281 Located in a
1927 barn, enjoy lunch in the
delicatessen where hot bread,
homemade soups and salads and
specialty sandwiches are prepared
every day to show off the French
brie and homemade mustards,
jams and dips. Casual. **$**

All types of reliable food; steaks, pasta or seafood served with freshly cut French fried potatoes. Casual. **$**

Yachats
La Serre Restaurant
160 Beach St, Yachats
Tel: 541 547-3801
In this skylit fern-filled restaurant, Lambert family chefs show their skills with fresh local seafood, grilled steaks and roasted free-range chicken, as well as mouthwatering desserts. Try the Dungeness crab cakes. Closed Tuesdays. Closed January. No lunch. Casual. **$**

ROGUE RIVER COUNTRY

Ashland
Chata
1212 Pacific Hwy, Ashland
Tel: 541 535-8949
Very small roadside cottage located 4 miles north of Ashland on Hwy 99. Serves Polish dishes and fusions of the freshest seasonal ingredients. Cozy, informal atmosphere, patio dining, excellent wine list, full bar. Casual. **$$**

Chateaulin Restaurant Francais & Wine Shop
50 E Main St, Ashland
Tel: 541 482-2264
Romantic ivy covered storefront look. Chef/co-owner David Taub and maitre d'/co-owner Michael Donovan serve French specialties. Prix-fixe menu. Business casual. **$$$**

Peerless Hotel Restaurant
265 Fourth St, Ashland
Tel: 541 488-6067
On the National Register of Historic Places, executive chef Stu Stein presents signature seasonal dishes. Try the wild mushroom crusted Alaskan halibut. Award-winning wine list with microbrews too. Business casual. **$$$**

Grants Pass
Hamilton House Restaurant
344 Terry Lane, Grants Pass
Tel: 541 479-3938
A long-time favorite of valley residents, the rooms at Hamilton

House have garden views. Select local seafood from the "fresh sheet." There's also good steaks, fresh pasta, wines and cocktails. Casual. **$**

Yankee Pot Roast
720 NW 6th St, Grants Pass
Tel: 541 476-0551
Set in a 1905 farmhouse, an American favorite of biscuits and potroast. Also serves fish, chicken and meatloaf. Closed Tuesdays. No lunch. Casual. **$$**

Price Guide

Prices are approximate for two people before taxes and tips, including house brand wine (where available).

$$$$	over $100
$$$	$60–$100
$$	$30–$60
$	under $30

Jacksonville
Bella Union Restaurant and Saloon
170 West California St, Jacksonville
Tel: 541 899-1770
The casual, fun atmosphere in this 1870s saloon is unpretentious, but manages to serve up to 20 daily specials, great seafood and pasta. Comfortable lounge with live entertainment. Patio in summer. Try the pizza. Casual. **$–$$**

Medford
Samovar Restaurant
101 East Main St, Medford
Tel: 541 733-4967
Candlelit Russian atmosphere, serves namesake specialties. Try the borscht. Closed Sunday and Monday. Casual. **$$**

Roseburg
Galleria Internationale
809 SE Main Street, Roseburg
Tel: 541 677-9032
Listed on the National Historic Register, this former Gothic-revival style Methodist church features original Povey Brothers stained glass windows, and offers international cuisine. Business casual. **$$$**

Gourmet Kitchen at La Garza Cellars
491 Winery Lane, Roseburg
Tel: 541 679-9654
Fine food and quality wines, all served in a lovely vineyard setting. with its own pond. South of Roseburg, located beyond I-5's exit 119. Chef Donna Souza-Postles prepares dishes to match local wines. Casual and fun, good for the afternoon or early evening. **$$–$$$**

Steamboat Inn
42705 N. Umpqua Hwy, Steamboat
Tel: 541 498-2230
Located 38 miles east of Roseburg, and with great views of the towering fir trees of a national forest. The Steamboat Inn specializes in "honest home cooking" like yummy soup, meat dishes, and pies. Closed January and February. Casual. **$$**

Village Bistro and Bakery
500 SE Cass St, Suite 120, Roseburg
Tel: 541 677-3450
High ceilings and an abundance of windows, but casual setting. Good dining at an attractive price. Try the chicken vindaloo with bow-tie pasta. Good wine list. Closed Sunday. Casual. **$$**

OREGON CASCADES

Sisters
Hotel Sisters Restaurant
190 West Cascade St, Sisters
Tel: 541 549-7427
Old-style hotel and Billy Bronco saloon. Tex-Mex menu serves nachos, chili, seafood, chicken and locally raised "Corriente Beef." Casual. **$–$$**

Warm Springs
Kah-Nee-Tah Juniper Dining Room
100 Main Street, Warm Springs
Tel: 541 553-1112
Offering specialties such as buffalo steak, venison and bird-in-clay with fruit stuffing. The windows and candlelight offer a sanctuary from the gambling, which is nearby and can be noisy. Casual to dressy. **$$–$$$**

EAST OF THE CASCADES

Bend
Dechutes Brewery & Public House
1044 NW Bond, Bend
Tel: 541 382-9242
Upscale brewpub serves its own brands, plus excellent large-portion burgers and sandwiches. Daily dinner and Monday night specials too. Casual. **$**

Guiseppe's Ristorante
932 NW Bond, Bend
Tel: 541 389-8899
Acclaimed Italian dishes, pasta, chicken seafood. Try the veal *piccata*. Closed Mon. No lunch. Casual. **$$**

Pine Tavern
Foot of NW Oregon St, Bend
Tel: 541 382-5581
Inside the dining room grow 200-year-old Ponderosa pines, hence the name. The tavern serves seafood and steak, with fine views the Dechutes River. Try the Cherry Pork Madeira. Patio seating in summer. No lunch on Sundays. Casual. **$$**

Klamath Falls
Mia Pia's Pizzaria and Brewhouse
13788 Matney Rd, Klmath Falls
Tel: 541 884-4880
Huge dining room with popular summer patio seating. House brews and a large menu serving pizza, hamburger and chicken dishes. Casual. **$**

NORTHEAST OREGON

Baker City
Geiser Grand Hotel
1996 Main St, Baker City
Tel: 541 523-1889
Of the few interesting places to eat in Baker City The Palm Court dining room with its stained-glass ceiling is the place for steaks and hickory- smoked prime ribs. Casual. **$$–$$$**

La Grande
Mamacita's
110 Depot St, La Grande
Tel: 541 963-6223
Specials of Mexican favorites

including *fajitas*, tacos, tostados or salads; closed Mondays. No lunch. Cash only. Casual. **$**

Joseph
Wallawa Lake Lodge
60060 Wallawa Lake Hwy, near Joseph
Tel: 541 432-9821
Rustic wood lodge with fine views of the lake and the mountains. Serves mainly fairly simple salmon and chicken dishes. Open Memorial Day to Labor Day only. No lunch. Casual. **$$–$$$**

Pendleton
Cimmiyotti's
137 Main St, Pendleton
Tel: 541 276-4314
There's something about this place that makes visitors want a good steak (except for vegetarians, of course). Take Exit 210, US 395, Hwy 37 as this may be the best place in the area for satisfying that craving. American steaks and burgers or pasta for the non-meat eaters. Casual. **$**

Raphael's
233 SE 4th St, Pendleton
Tel: 541 276-8500
A 1878 Queen Anne House containing three dining rooms. For the adventurous, the chef creates dishes from venison, elk and rattlesnake along with more traditional fare. Outdoor garden dining in summer. Closed Sunday and Monday. No lunch. Business casual. **$$$**

JOHN DAY FOSSIL BEDS NATIONAL MONUMENT

Prineville
Crooked River Company Dinner Train
4075 O'Neill Rd, Redmond, Or
Tel: 541 548-8630
Western-theme train and dinner theater operates all year round. It features the Western Murder Theater on Saturday nights or the Sunday Supper Ride – watch your pockets in the Jesse James Train Robbery. Casual, theatrical and fun. **$$$**

CRATER LAKE NATIONAL PARK

Dining Room at Crater Lake Lodge
565 Village Rim Dr, Crater Lake
Tel: 541 594-2255
Historic 1915 lodge has views of the famous cobalt-blue lake, stone fireplaces; and fare such as steak Oscar or northwest seafood. Good wine list. Reservations essential. Closed mid-Oct to mid-May. Casual. **$$$**

OREGON CAVES NATIONAL MONUMENT

Cave Junction-Illinois Valley
Wild River Pizza Co & Brewery
249 Redwood Hwy, Cave Junction
Tel: 541 592-3556
Redwood picnic tables are shared with other patrons here, pizza is the centerpiece but they also serve chicken and sandwiches. Wild River Ales are brewed on premises. **$**

Shopping

SHOPPING MALLS

Lloyd Center
2201 Lloyd Center, Portland
Tel: 503 282-2511
www.lloydcentermall.com/
One of the original enclosed shopping malls.

Oregon Shopping Centers and Malls
www.ohwy.com/or/s/shopctr.htm
Overview of several malls.

Pioneer Place
888 SW 5th Ave #410, Portland
Tel: 503 228-5800
www.therousecompany.com/operation/mixed/pioneerplace.html
Bright and airy renovated Downtown mall.

Washington Square Shopping Center
9585 SW Washington Square Rd, Portland
Tel: 503 639-8860
Five major department stores and more than 140 specialty shops keep them flocking in.

ARTS AND CRAFTS MARKETS

Portland Saturday Market
108 W Burnside St, Portland
Tel: 503 222-6072
Local sellers of arts and crafts and some produce.
Saturday Markets in Oregon
www.eugenesaturdaymarket.org/links.html
Check on dates and locations for arts and crafts and some fresh produce; so-called "Saturday Markets" often sell far more arts and crafts than produce.

FARMERS' MARKETS

Oregon Farmers' Markets
Oregon Dept of Agriculture
121 Southwest Salmon, Suite 240
Portland
Tel: 503 229-6734
www.ams.usda.gov/farmersmarkets/states/oregon.htm
Check here for the freshest produce and baked goods.

ANTIQUES

Antiques and Arts along the Oregon Coast
www.doormat.com/antiques.htm
A favorite hunting ground to find interesting antiques, almost-antiques and reproductions.
Classic Antique (Warehouse)
1805 SE Martin Luther King Blvd, Portland
Tel: 503 231-8689
www.classicantique.com/
Antiques, antique reproductions and Amish furniture.
Oregon Multidealer Antique Shops and mini-Malls
http://ourworld.compuserve.com/homepages/herbbreese/oregon.htm
Listings for antique shoppers throughout the state of Oregon.
Portland Antique Company
2929 SE Powell Blvd Portland
Tel: 503 232-4001
Fancy antiques, large scale with a huge selection of furniture from all over the world.

Annual Events

Oregon Festivals and Events
www.ohs.org/exhibitions/celebrate.htm
A sampling of what Oregonians celebrate each year.

Oregon Coast Festivals & Events
www.pacific101.com/oregon/entertainment/festivals.htm Also
www.traveloregon.com/
Check out the Calendar of Events; the list is dynamic and constantly being updated.

February
Portland International Film Festival: Portland.

April
Vancouver Discovery Walk Festival: Vancouver.

May
Indian Art Northwest – traditional and contemporary arts: Portland.
Cinco de Mayo Mexican fiesta: Portland.

June
Portland Arts Festival : Portland.
Portland Rose Festival – month-long festival with parades: Portland.

July
Waterfront Blues Festival: Portland.
Oregon Brewers Festival – one of the best craft beer events: Portland.
Blueberry Tasting Festival: Vancouver.

September
Autumn Brewmasters' Festival: Vancouver.
Portland Creative Conference: film, TV, & new media: Portland.

September/October
North by Northwest: 300 bands perform: Portland.

Further Reading

History & Culture

First Fish, First People: Salmon Tales of the North Pacific Rim
by Judith Roche (editor),
Meg McHutchison (editor)
University of Washington Press
ISBN: 0295977396
Thirteen writers from cultures profoundly connected to salmon were asked to write about "the fish of the gods", from both a historical and a contemporary perspective. This collection of poems, stories, narratives, folktales, oral histories and essays aptly portrays the vital importance of salmon to the Native peoples of the northern Pacific Rim - not just as a food resource, but as a basis for culture and identity

One Woman's West: Recollections of the Oregon Trail and Settling of the Northwest Country
by Martha Gay Masterson,
Lois Barton
Spencer Butte Press
ISBN: 0960942025
The real-life West from the Oregon Trail to World War I. The story of a woman who came to Oregon in a covered wagon in 1851 and lived long enough to observe enormous changes, like automobiles passing by her home.

Outlaws of the Pacific Northwest
by Bill Gulick
Caxton Press
ISBN: 087004396
Gulick believes the outlaws of the Northwest have never received the recognition of their counterparts in other parts of the Wild West, in spite of their exploits often exceeding those of their better-known kinsmen.

Pacific Destiny: The Three Century Journey to the Oregon Country
by Dale L. Walker
Forge: ISBN: 0312869339

Traces the history of the Oregon Territory through tales of mountain men, pioneers and emigrants in the vast wilderness. Walker has a keen sense of the times.

Salmon Without Rivers: A History of the Pacific Salmon Crisis
by Jim Lichatowich
Island Press
ISBN: 1559633603
A well-researched book presents the impassioned history of the Northwest salmon: reasons for their decline, why billions of tax dollars have had paltry returns, and insights into where to go from here.

That All People May Be One People, Send Rain to Wash the Face of the Earth
by Chief Joseph
Mountain Meadow Press
ISBN: 094551915
A reprint of Chief Joseph's account of the Nez Perces' dealings with their white brothers and the Nez Perce War of 1877. The final portion of the book is Joseph's plea that all people treat each other with respect and human decency.

Sources of the River
by Jack Nisbet
Sasquatch Books
ISBN: 1570610207
This book follows the early 1800s diaries and journeys of fur trader David Thompson around the Native populations of the Pacific Northwest, in his quest for the mouth of the Columbia River. Truthful recounting of Native American life that puts into perspective today's political correctness.

Wet and Wired: A Pop Culture Encyclopedia of the Pacific Northwest
by Randy Hodgins, Steve McLellan
Taylor Publications
ISBN: 0878331697
Humor and insight as well as a stroll down memory lane from Jimi Hendrix to Pamela Anderson, plus most of the famous people who have made the Pacific Northwest such a strange place to come from.

Natural History

100 Hikes in Northwest Oregon (Second Edition)
by William L. Sullivan
Navillus
ISBN: 0961815280
This up-to-date guide covers Oregon's most popular hiking region – the trails within a two-hour drive of the Portland area. This edition features a dozen new or dramatically changed paths in the Columbia Gorge, Mount Hood and Mount St Helens areas. It also includes tips for mountain bikers and equestrians.

The Pacific Northwest Trail Guide: The Official Guidebook for Long Distance & Day Hikers
by Ron Strickland
Sasquatch Books
ISBN: 1570611777
As the title says, the official guide to the spectacular and challenging long-distance trail that stretches 1,200 miles from Glacier National Park in Montana to Washington's Olympic National Park.

River-Walking Songbirds & Singing Coyotes: An Uncommon Field Guide to Northwest Mountains
by Patricia K. Lichen, Linda M. Feltner (Illustrator)
Sasquatch Books
ISBN: 1570612218
Lichen combines standard field-guide information with delightful and engaging descriptions of the little-known facts, surprising details, and amusing – even bizarre – tidbits rarely found in ordinary field guides.

Sea Kayaker's Deep Trouble: True Stories and Their Lessons from Sea Kayaker Magazine
by Matt Broze (contributor), George Gronseth, Christopher Cunningham (editor)
McGraw-Hill Professional Publishing
ISBN: 0070084998
Twenty harrowing, real-life tales of sea kayaking accidents and near accidents that not only keep readers on the edge of their seats, but also instruct them in potentially life-saving lessons.

A Waterfall Lover's Guide to the Pacific Northwest: Where to Find Hundreds of Spectacular Waterfalls in Washington, Oregon and Idaho
by Gregory Alan Plumb
Mountaineers Books
ISBN: 089886593X
Detailed guide directs backpackers, dayhikers, and car travelers to hundreds of spectacular waterfalls. Each waterfall is rated for ease and aesthetic value.

Cuisine

Heaven on the Half Shell: The Story of the Northwest's Love Affair With the Oyster
by David G. Gordon, Nancy E. Blanton, Terry Y. Nosho, Kenneth K. Chew
Graphic Arts Center Pub Co
ISBN: 1558685502
Photos about the pioneering aquaculturists, scientists, and oyster connoisseurs who have shaped this industry over the last 150 years. Eighteen oyster recipes round out this lively portrait of the bivalve that has influenced the economy and the culture of the Pacific Northwest.

Inside the Pike Place Market: Exploring America's Favorite Farmers' Market
by Braiden Rex-Johnson, Paul Souders (Photographer)
Sasquatch Books
ISBN: 1570611769
As fresh and vibrant as the Seattle marketplace itself, the country's oldest continuously operating farmer's market is captured in two ways: by its nooks and thoroughfares and by its personalities. Also features 20 market recipes, photographs, and behind-the-scenes tales of fish buyers, musicians, organic farmers, herbalists and tattoo artists.

The Northwest Best Places Cookbook: Recipes from the Outstanding Restaurants and Inns of Washington, Oregon, and British Columbia
by Lori McKean
Sasquatch Books
ISBN: 1570610754
As Northwest cuisine takes the US by storm, the author heads into the kitchen with a collection of 125 recipes from star-rated establishments. Great chefs share their favorite adaptations of local Northwest ingredients.

The Way We Ate: Pacific Northwest Cooking, 1843-1900
by Jacqueline B. Williams, Ruth Kirk
Washington State Univ. Press
ISBN: 0874221374
Moving from early kitchens to the perils of pickling, Jackie Williams paints an engaging picture of the improvisational skills of early settlers and their appreciation for the bounty of the land – when it came their way.

Fiction

The Coast of Good Intentions: Stories
by Michael Byers
Mariner Books
ISBN: 0395891701
Short stories that reflect the region's cloudy and overcast landscape. Byers gives each location the particularity of a fingerprint as he explores how the landscape shapes his characters, many of whom seem alternately depressed and comforted by the sight of clouds "piling themselves against the Olympics, like gray balloons against a ceiling."

Dream Keeper: Myth and Destiny in the Pacific Northwest
by Morrie Ruvinsky
Sasquatch Books
ISBN: 1570611167
This novel is rich in Pacific Northwest Indian lore. Dream Keeper invokes the spirits of the First Peoples, weaving the legacy of the pioneers and the trials of love and family into an imaginative tale.

Snow Falling on Cedars
by David Guterson
Harcourt Brace
ISBN: 0151004439
Set on an island in the straits north of Washington's Puget Sound, the story is nominally about a murder trial. But since it is set in the 1950s, lingering memories of World War II, internment camps and racism help fuel suspicion of a Japanese-American fisherman, a lifelong resident of the islands. Evocative and well written.

Winds of Allegiance
by Linda L. Chaikin
Bethany House
ISBN: 155661442
In the rugged Northwest, the strong and the powerful battle to conquer uncharted places. Savana Rezanov Mackenzie is a young Russian-English woman loyal to her British heritage. Caught up in the British-American fight for power in the Pacific Northwest, Savana becomes a spy.

Winterkill
by Craig Lesley
Picador USA
ISBN: 0312152442
Lesley weaves an engrossing story of a contemporary Native American family, in the process relaying a great deal about Native culture. The culture in question is the Nez Perce of eastern Oregon,. This story shows how history weighs on its descendents.

Other Insight Guides, Pocket Guides and Fleximaps which highlight destinations in this region include:

Insight Guide: Seattle. This beautiful, vibrant city is explored by a team of resident writers and photographers.

Insight Pocket Guide: Seattle. A local Seattleite leads the reader through the sites and sounds of Seattle.

Insight Fleximap: Seattle and *Insight Fleximap: Vancouver* are easy to use, contain lots of information and have a laminated, wipe-clean finish.

ART & PHOTO CREDITS

INSIGHT GUIDE
The PACIFIC NORTHWEST

Cartographic Editor **Zoë Goodwin**
Production **Linton Donaldson**
Art Direction
Klaus Geisler, Derrick Lim
Picture Research
Hilary Genin, Britta Jaschinski

Index

Numbers in italics refer to photographs